OXFORD STUDIES IN AFRICAN AFFAIRS

General Editors
JOHN D. HARGREAVES *and* GEORGE SHEPPERSON

THE EMIN PASHA
RELIEF EXPEDITION
1886–1890

I. EMIN PASHA

THE EMIN PASHA
RELIEF
EXPEDITION,
1886–1890

BY

IAIN R. SMITH

OXFORD
AT THE CLARENDON PRESS
1972

Oxford University Press, Ely House, London W. 1

GLASGOW NEW YORK TORONTO MELBOURNE WELLINGTON
CAPE TOWN IBADAN NAIROBI DAR ES SALAAM LUSAKA ADDIS ABABA
DELHI BOMBAY CALCUTTA MADRAS KARACHI LAHORE DACCA
KUALA LUMPUR SINGAPORE HONG KONG TOKYO

Printed in Great Britain
at the University Press, Oxford
by Vivian Ridler
Printer to the University

TO THE MEMORY OF
THE LATE
SIR JOHN GRAY
AND
H. B. THOMAS

PREFACE

THE fall of Khartoum to the Mahdist forces in January 1885 marks
the final collapse of the Egyptian administration of the Sudan. Slatin
Bey, Governor of Darfur, had surrendered his province to the Mahdists in December 1883. The Bahr al-Ghazal, under Lupton Bey, had
been conquered in April 1884. Only the southernmost province of
Equatoria, under Emin Pasha, remained.

After mounting a desultory attack on Equatoria, the Mahdist
forces withdrew. Abandoned by the Egyptian Government, forgotten
in Europe, Emin moved his headquarters to Wadelai, close to Lake
Albert, in 1885. There he waited for news, orders, and relief from
Egypt. By 1886 Emin had succeeded through Mackay, the leader of
the C.M.S. missionaries in Buganda, in opening up a new route of
communication between Equatoria and the East African coast at
Zanzibar. It was by this route that eventually, in February 1886,
Emin received letters from the Egyptian Government notifying him
that Equatoria was to be abandoned and encouraging him to with-
draw. By this time, however, Mackay had encouraged Emin to believe
that the growing British interest in East Africa might create the
possibility of re-establishing Equatoria as part of the British Empire.
In July 1886 Emin wrote letters via Mackay to the British Consul-
General at Zanzibar inviting the British Government to annex
Equatoria.

In 1886 the British Government showed no interest in becoming
involved in such a scheme. News of Emin's position, cut off in the
heart of Africa, had, however, become widely known. The situation
was an immensely appealing one to the British public, coming so soon
after the failure of the expedition to relieve General Gordon at
Khartoum. Emin was seen as 'a second Gordon' in need of relief
which it was the responsibility of Britain to bring. In the absence of
an initiative by the Government, a Scottish businessman and philanthropist, William Mackinnon, organized an expedition led by H. M.
Stanley. He was joined in the venture by his long-standing and more
hard-headed collaborator, J. F. Hutton, a Manchester businessman
with already established African interests. Since Stanley had a personal ambition to lead the expedition to Equatoria via the Congo and

since this coincided with the wishes of King Leopold II of the Belgians, in whose employment Stanley was at this time, the expedition was compelled to adopt the Congo route. The Egyptian Government supported the expedition and contributed a total of £14,000 towards it in the hope of using it to bring Egyptian responsibility for Equatoria to an end. The British Government acquiesced in the dispatch of the expedition in order to achieve the objectives of the Egyptian Government and assuage public opinion through the auspices of someone else's expedition. King Leopold encouraged it in the hope that it would open up a route between the Congo and the Nile and enable him to enrol Emin and his soldiers in the service of the Congo State. Mackinnon and his associates financed and organized it partly for philanthropic reasons, but also to utilize it for the extension of British claims in the East African interior and in the hope that Emin and his soldiers would serve with the East African Company which Mackinnon hoped to charter. Amidst many illusions, mixed motives, and intrigues, the expedition set out for Equatoria at the beginning of 1887. After surmounting great obstacles and successive set-backs, the expedition emerged at Bagamoyo in December 1889, bringing with it Emin Pasha and a number of followers from Equatoria.

*   *   *

The Emin Pasha Relief Expedition is probably the best-documented expedition that ever went through Africa in the nineteenth century. It also took place during a period long recognized by historians as of crucial importance in the partition of East Africa. During the course of its progress this expedition came to be regarded with mounting interest by colonial strategists and schemers in Europe. Reference to it has since been made in every serious work on the partition of Africa. Its importance has long been accepted, though this importance does not necessarily lie in what it achieved. It is therefore surprising that no full and serious study of this expedition has previously been written. Langer, the mentor of so many who have written about the partition of Africa, declared that he found it 'impossible to unravel the tangled and diverse motives that lay behind Stanley's last great exploit'.[1]

Whilst motives are perennially the concern of historians, this expedition is also of great interest because of the extent of its

[1] William L. Langer, *The Diplomacy of Imperialism* (New York, 1951), 2nd edn., p. 113.

documentation. For most of the expeditions led by Europeans in Africa, including the earlier expeditions of H. M. Stanley, the historian is virtually dependent on the accounts given by the men who led them. Often this is the only source which exists. Such a complete dependence on what is in many cases only one source usually makes bad history; it also makes for a record of African expeditions based entirely on the leaders' point of view.

The Emin Pasha Relief Expedition is a quite exceptional case. Eleven Europeans went on this expedition and all of them have left us accounts, in the form of diaries and many letters, of their experiences. Many of these were later published, in edited form, as books or in the newspapers. Others have only come to light in manuscript form very recently.

This expedition is also an exception in the wealth of material concerning the interested parties who sent it. The important papers of King Leopold II of the Belgians in the Palace Archives, Brussels, and elsewhere, have only recently become available. It was the discovery of the complete papers of the Emin Pasha Relief Committee amongst the Mackinnon Papers in London which first started me on the subject of this book. These papers give a comprehensive coverage of the expedition from the point of view of those who sent it. In addition, there is a great deal of material concerning the role of the British Government in the whole affair in the Public Record Office.

From these sources alone it would have been possible to write an account of the expedition which would probably have been better documented than that of any other expedition in Africa. But such an account would have suffered in at least one respect from the same limitation as other accounts of European-led expeditions in Africa and elsewhere. It would have been an account of the activities of Europeans encapsulated, as it were, by their own evidence.

It was at this point that it became clear that this expedition was exceptional in yet another respect. Not only was there abundant evidence concerning the Europeans who went on it, and those who sent it, but the material concerning those in Africa who were affected by it also proved to be remarkably extensive. Some of these people were also Europeans. Of their testimonies, the diary and the many letters of Emin Pasha, the man for whose 'relief' the expedition was sent, form a historical source which is of quite outstanding value. But the evidence also extends beyond the limits necessarily set by literate Europeans for an African subject. The autobiography and letters of

Tippu Tip, the several statements later recorded by Emin's own soldiers and clerks, the letters to and from the Mahdists, comprise a considerable amount of material concerning the effect of the expedition on diverse groups of the indigenous population and on their reactions to and accounts of its progress.

The written evidence is, however, limited and at no point have I attempted to go beyond its limitations. This is not because I do not acknowledge the value and the viability of other forms of historical evidence. Rather it is because at no point did I find myself without written sources which appeared to me to be more reliable and informative than any other sources which were available. A recent attempt by Emin Pasha's great-nephew to discover and utilize oral sources for a reconstruction of events in Africa which took place less than a hundred years ago cannot be said to indicate that a rich untapped source for the history of Equatoria lies in this direction.[1]

It is the first objective of this book to give an account 'in the round', as it were, of an expedition organized and led by Europeans through Africa in the nineteenth century. I have utilized for this purpose the varied and extensive documentary evidence which exists and which approaches the expedition from many different points of view.

My second objective is to make a modest contribution to the history of Equatoria in the period 1876–89. Like most colonial creations in Africa, Equatoria began as a quite arbitrary unit. Whereas the expedition is a unit of study clearly defined in time and scope, Equatoria is not. It was first defined as a province of the exiguous Egyptian administration of the southern Sudan. Its history has hitherto been approached primarily through the abundant records of its three most notable governors, Baker, Gordon, and Emin Pasha. This approach has of necessity been continued here, despite its obvious limitations. For although more has been known for longer about the peoples of the southern Sudan than about almost any other area in Africa—thanks to the exhaustive researches of two generations of outstanding anthropologists—this abundant material has so far proved of only limited value for the historian. My aim in this book has been the very modest one of making fuller use of Emin Pasha's remarkable diary and letters than has been made hitherto.

A third and lesser objective lies in the sphere of European diplomatic history. In an account of an expedition which came to occupy

[1] E. W. Schnitzer, 'On the Trail of Emin Pasha', *Uganda Journal*, xxxi, no. 1 (1967).

a notable place in Anglo-German rivalry over East Africa, it may be wondered why the German factor in this expedition, and the sequence of events in Germany which led to the dispatch of a German Emin Pasha relief expedition under Carl Peters, have been relegated to a place of such minor importance. The reason is that in the context of the actual organization and progress of this expedition these events were of minor importance. German interest in the position of Emin Pasha only became translated into effective action in 1888, long after Stanley's expedition had been dispatched. Carl Peters's expedition only succeeded in setting off for the interior in 1889, as Stanley and Emin Pasha were approaching the coast. German activity with regard to Emin Pasha therefore really belongs beyond the scope of this book, and it has been succinctly treated in the work of F. F. Müller.[1] In this book, my contribution to the well-covered subject of the colonial rivalry between the European powers is at most a very minor one. I have attempted to give a full account of the negotiations involved in the sending of the Emin Pasha Relief Expedition. In this I hope I may have made a few significant additions to the work of my distinguished predecessors in this field, Professor G. N. Sanderson, Dr. R. Gray, Father Ceulemans, and Professor R. T. Anstey.

[1] F. F. Müller, *Deutschland—Zanzibar—Ostafrika 1884–1890* (East Berlin, 1959).

ACKNOWLEDGEMENTS

THIS book was first written as a thesis, at a time when its author was in the position of an apprentice amongst historians. I was working in a number of libraries and archives for the first time and I was therefore especially dependent on the information, assistance, and advice of other people.

This was also a period when I learnt a great deal from several masters in the historian's craft. Foremost amongst these was my supervisor, Professor J. A. Gallagher. He tempered my enthusiasm with a certain scepticism and managed to combine this with constant encouragement. Professor G. N. Sanderson, Professor Jean Stengers, Professor R. T. Anstey, John Rowe, and Alison Smith were also both helpful and encouraging. I owe a special debt to Professor George Shepperson, who first aroused my academic interest in East Africa and who first put me on the track of the Mackinnon Papers.

In the course of my work I gained a great deal from the knowledge of the late H. B. Thomas and D. Simpson about Emin Pasha and East Africa. In London I was assisted by Mr. Blomfield of the School of Oriental and African Studies Library; in Brussels by M. Vandewoude, of the Palace Archives, and by Madame van Grieken-Taverniers; in Khartoum by Mr. Muhammad Malik. Throughout my work I enjoyed the constant co-operation of Mrs. D. Middleton, of the Royal Geographical Society, who first located and then edited the diary of A. J. Mounteney-Jephson for the Hakluyt Society.

During my work on the thesis I was in the privileged position of being supported financially by the Department of Education and Science, the Beit Fund, and St. Antony's College, Oxford. Their generous support made the thesis possible. To the members of St. Antony's College I also owe a great deal for providing such a stimulating and congenial context for my work.

Finally, in preparing the thesis for publication, I am grateful to the following for giving me copyright permission: the Marquess of Salisbury, for the Salisbury Papers; Sir Brian de Barttelot, for the Barttelot Papers; Commander Maurice Jephson, for the Jephson Papers; Mr. Valentine Baker, for the Valentine Baker Papers; the Church Missionary Society; the Royal Geographical Society; the School of

Oriental and African Studies, for the Mackinnon Papers; and the Cambridge University Press and the Hakluyt Society for permission to quote from the published version of the diary of A. J. Mounteney-Jephson.

IAIN R. SMITH

Oxford
April 1971

CONTENTS

LIST OF PLATES

LIST OF MAPS

ABBREVIATIONS

A.S.S.   Anti-Slavery Society Papers, in Rhodes House Library, Oxford.

B.P.   Barttelot Papers, in the possession of the Barttelot family, Keepers Stopham, Sussex.

C.M.S.   Church Missionary Society. The archives are at the Society's headquarters, which are now in the Waterloo Road, London.

E.P. in C.A. *Emin Pasha in Central Africa*, the collection of the letters and articles of Emin Pasha translated into English and published by G. Schweinfurth, F. Ratzel, R. W. Felkin, and G. Hartlaub (eds.), London, 1888.

Extracts   The Diaries of Emin Pasha, Extracts I–XIV, translated by the late Sir John Gray and published in *The Uganda Journal*, 1961–8.

F.O.   Foreign Office files at the Public Record Office, Chancery Lane, London.

F.O.C.P.   Foreign Office Confidential Print, also at the Public Record Office.

IDA   *In Darkest Africa*, the account of the Emin Pasha Relief Expedition written by H. M. Stanley and published in London in 1890.

I.R.C.B.   Institut Royal Colonial Belge.

J.A.H.   *Journal of African History.*

M.P.   Mackinnon Papers, School of Oriental and African Studies Library, London.

P.R.G.S.   *Proceedings of the Royal Geographical Society.*

Schweitzer   Schweitzer, G., *Emin Pasha: his life and work*, 2 vols. (London, 1898).

S.N.R.   *Sudan Notes and Records.*

Tagebücher Stuhlmann, Dr. Franz (ed.), *Die Tagebücher von Dr. Emin Pascha*, 5 vols. (Braunschweig, Berlin, Hamburg, 1917–27).

NOTE ON TRANSLATIONS

THROUGHOUT this book quotations given in the text from sources in French and German have been translated into English. Where good translations already exist, these have been used and acknowledged; in other cases, the translations are my own.

I have used extensively the series of extracts from Emin's *Tagebücher* translated into English and published by the late Sir John Gray in successive issues of the *Uganda Journal*, 1961–8. I am grateful to Mrs. Jutta Jacobmeyer for checking these and other translations from the German original with me.

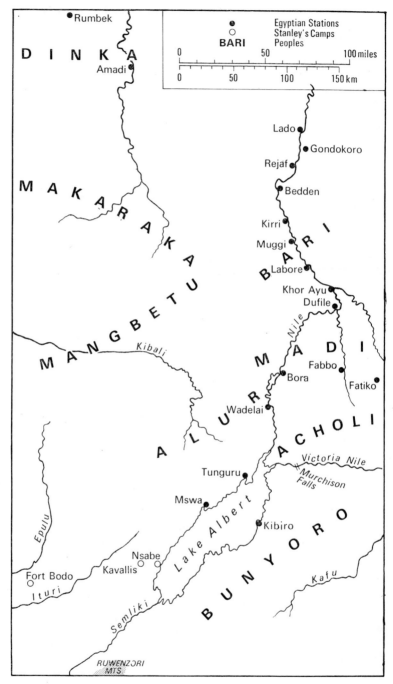

Fig. 1. Equatoria during the last years of Egyptian rule.

CHAPTER I

An African Province in the Nineteenth Century: Equatoria under Egyptian Rule

ON the morning of Saturday 14 April 1883 the steamer *Telhawin* set out from Lado, headquarters of the Egyptian province of Equatoria, on the voyage 1,000 miles down the Nile to Khartoum. Amongst those watching the departure of the steamer were two Europeans: Emin Bey,[1] the Governor of the province, and Gaetano Casati, an Italian traveller.[2] The *Telhawin* had been the first steamer from Khartoum to visit the Equatorial province since August of the previous year and it had arrived with very few of the supplies which Emin had urgently requested his Government to send him. It had, however, brought news of the important events which had recently occurred in Egypt. Writing later in the day to his friend, Wilhelm Junker, who was at this time travelling and collecting botanical specimens in the Zande country, Emin related the news he had received of the defeat of the 'Urābist rebellion, the bombardment of Alexandria, and the subsequent British occupation of Egypt during 1882.[3] In the Sudan all was in turmoil. From origins not dissimilar to those of earlier reformist movements in the Muslim world, the Mahdist revolt in the Sudan was, by 1883, in a position to present a very real threat to the Government in Khartoum.[4] Emin already knew of the annihilation of the army under Yūsuf Pasha Hasan al-Shallālī which had occurred in

---

[1] Emin Pasha was born a German, Eduard Schnitzer, but lived most of his life away from Germany. On arriving at Khartoum in 1875 he took the Muslim name Mehemet Emin (Turkish)—Muhammad al-Amīn (Arabic)—but it was simply as Dr. Emin that he was chiefly known until 1878 when, as Governor of Equatoria, he was promoted to the rank of Bey. In 1886 he was made a Pasha by the Khedive of Egypt. It is as Emin Pasha that he is best known and is referred to in this book. Emin preferred to sign himself simply 'Dr. Emin' or 'Emin Bey'.

[2] *Tagebücher*, ii. 408; G. Casati, *Ten Years in Equatoria* (London, 1891) (Colonial edition), p. 185.

[3] Emin to Junker, 14 Apr. 1883, printed in Schweitzer, i. 142–4.

[4] The best study of the Mahdist revolt is P. M. Holt, *The Mahdist State in the Sudan* (Oxford, 1958).

B

May 1882. As a result of this third major defeat of Government troops, the originally meagre resources of the Mahdist forces had again been swollen with large quantities of modern arms and booty, and a mortal blow had been struck at the prestige of the Egyptian army and administration in the Sudan.[1] Emin now reported to Junker news of fighting in Kordofan and Sennar, panic in Khartoum, rumours that General Gordon was to return to the Sudan, and the absence of any news from the neighbouring province of the Bahr al-Ghazal.[2]

The implications for the future of his own province of these major events in Egypt and the northern Sudan did not occupy a great deal of Emin's attention. What did disturb him was the lack of news from the Bahr al-Ghazal. This neighbouring province shared with Equatoria the distinction of being in the south. This meant that neither of these provinces had ever possessed more than the most tenuous links with Khartoum, and the interest shown by the Government in their affairs had always been slight. Orders passed from Khartoum to the south very infrequently; requests from the south to Khartoum much more often. Both were usually ignored. The important thing was the channel of communication itself. So long as it existed, successive Governors of these two provinces built upon its precarious foundations a world of possibilities for the future.

*   *   *

Situated in the extreme south of the Sudan, astride the river Nile as it emerges from Lake Albert, the area known as Equatoria had been established as a province of Egypt by Sir Samuel Baker during the years 1870–3. Long before the European powers interested themselves in creating colonial empires in Africa, Muhammad 'Alī and the Khedive Ismā'īl had acquired a large African empire for Egypt.[3] In the years after 1820 the forces of Muhammad 'Alī had succeeded in conquering most of what is now the northern Sudan. After the consolidation of the Egyptian position at Khartoum, numerous expeditions were dispatched during the 1840s and 1850s to open up a route

---

[1] P. M. Holt, *The Mahdist State in the Sudan*, p. 50.
[2] Schweitzer, loc. cit.
[3] Still the best study is the monumental work by G. Douin, *Histoire du règne du Khédive Ismaïl* (Cairo, 1936–41), 7 vols. See esp. vol. iii, *L'Empire Africain*, Parts 1, 2, 3A, and 3B. See also R. L. Hill, *Egypt in the Sudan 1820–1881* (London, 1959).

to the south. The Nile was navigated as far as the rapids south of Gondokoro, and the area was revealed as rich in ivory.[1]

The ivory of Equatoria aroused an enduring interest for the rest of the century. Partly this reflects the poverty in other resources of the area; partly it is an expression of the rapidly increasing value of ivory in Europe during the nineteenth century. Between the 1840s and the 1870s both the price of ivory on the London market and the quantity imported more than doubled. Africa was by far the most important source of ivory, and the most valuable kind—soft, opaque, and easily worked—came from a relatively small area in the interior of East Africa.[2] Until the opening of the Congo route in the 1880s this area could be tapped only from Zanzibar and from the Nile. The middle-class Victorian taste for ivory knife-handles, combs, billiard balls, and piano keys was accompanied by two other developments in Europe which combined to work for the more effective extraction of the one commodity readily obtainable in Africa. The first of these was the availability of cheap, manufactured guns. These began to be available in large numbers after the Napoleonic wars, and the market in firearms subsequently received massive supplies of obsolete weapons as the armies of Europe were equipped first with breech-loading, later with repeating rifles, in place of the traditional muskets.[3] The second development was the production of cheap manufactured goods, especially cloth, as a result of the Industrial Revolution.[4]

The first expeditions sent to exploit the ivory of Equatoria were organized by traders based in Khartoum. Initially, many of these traders were Europeans. Some of them had first come to the Sudan in the employment of Muhammad 'Alī, but after the Government monopoly on trade with the south was ended in 1851 (chiefly through the pressure of European consuls), many stayed on to open businesses on their own account. The real profits of the ivory trade, however, went to the middlemen who controlled the markets, extended credit, and exerted political influence in Cairo and Khartoum. These were Ottoman subjects. By the end of the 1850s the

---

[1] In the following section, as throughout this chapter, I am much indebted to the work of R. Gray, *A History of the Southern Sudan, 1839–1889* (London, 1961).

[2] R. Beachey, 'The East African Ivory Trade in the 19th century', *J.A.H.*, viii, no. 2 (1967).

[3] See R. Beachey, 'The Arms Trade in East Africa in the late 19th century', *J.A.H.*, iii, no. 3 (1962).

[4] This important combination was first suggested to me by D. A. Low, 'The British and Uganda, 1862–1900', D.Phil. thesis (Oxford, 1957), p. 12.

White Nile trade was firmly in the grasp of Egyptians, Copts, Syrians, and northern Sudanese. These men, and those they employed on their expeditions, came to be known as 'Khartoumers'.[1] Equipped with cloth, beads, and firearms, and accompanied by numerous followers recruited chiefly from the Danāqla and Shāīqīya in the north, the expeditions organized by the 'Khartoumers' set out for the south.

The area into which they penetrated forms a wide, shallow basin, every part of which drains into the Nile. Here the rainfall, though variable, is considerably above the marginal level so prevalent in most of the Sudan, but the pattern is one of heavy rains during part of the year (April–August) and drought for the remainder. In the northern part of the region, around Lake No, this pattern of rainfall, in con- junction with the flatness of the land, leads to extensive seasonal flooding. Further south, towards Lake Albert, the land rises gradually and is broken up by ridges and hills, some of which reach altitudes of over 6,000 feet. Flooding is less extensive in the south, and the country has a wooded parkland aspect which favours a settled form of agriculture.

The peoples of the southern Sudan have usually been classified by anthropologists according to language.[2] The resulting groups often appear to reflect the abstractions of outsiders rather than the effective units recognized by the peoples themselves. Throughout the southern Sudan in the nineteenth century the effective groups in terms of which various aspects of life were organized and expressed were very small. This was an area of Africa where there were no states or kingdoms, in the sense of highly centralized political or administrative struc- tures, even within one linguistic unit. The size and basis on which communities were organized depended a great deal on regional ecology. In the south, where seasonal flooding was not such an important factor, the settled village, surrounded by small plots of millet, sorghum, maize, and groundnuts, predominated. The home- steads could be concentrated as among the Acholi,[3] or scattered over a large area, as in the case of the Bari.[4] Several villages might form

---

[1] P. M. Holt, *A Modern History of the Sudan* (London, 1965), pp. 61–2.

[2] See esp. C. G. and B. Z. Seligman, *Pagan Tribes of the Nilotic Sudan* (London, 1932); L. F. Nalder, *A Tribal Survey of Mongalla Province* (London, 1937); A. Butt, *The Nilotes of the Anglo-Egyptian Sudan* (Part 4 of *Ethnographic Survey of Africa*, ed. Daryll Forde) (London, 1952); G. W. B. Huntingford, *The Northern Nilo-Hamites* (Part 6, ibid.) (London, 1953).

[3] F. K. Girling, *The Acholi of Uganda* (London, 1960), pp. 55–6.

[4] G. W. B. Huntingford, op. cit., p. 40.

a larger regional unit in which common ritual specialists were recognized (in an area of unreliable rainfall, these specialists were often concerned with rain-making). In most cases, further divisions in terms of kinship and age-sets cut across the territorial units of the villages, though these divisions were of widely varying extent and importance.

Transcending divisions of linguistic classification and social organization, the peoples of the southern Sudan exhibit some notable cultural similarities. Prominent amongst these is an intense interest in cattle. The preoccupation of the Nuer and the Dinka with cattle, like that of the Hima, Tutsi, and Masai further south, is exceptional in its single-mindedness. Other peoples of the southern Sudan cultivate the ground reluctantly, as do the Nuer and the Dinka. Some, such as the Alur, Bari, Madi, and Acholi, cultivate diligently and with considerable skill. Most also have sheep and goats. But all who have cattle regard them as a major interest. In the nineteenth century the technology of these societies was extremely simple. The natural resources of their areas were meagre. Their material needs were few. Trade was local and direct. It took the form of exchange between neighbours rather than that of an elaborate complex involving intermediaries and long-distance trade routes which is to be found elsewhere in Africa in the nineteenth century, and notably in the areas to the north and south of the southern Sudan.

The absence of suitable trading patterns and middlemen among the peoples living along the Nile in the south meant that in their pursuit of ivory the 'Khartoumers' rapidly became involved in direct expeditions into the interior. Here they established settlements under a permanent agent (*wakīl*), accompanied by large numbers of armed followers, usually from the northern Sudan (Danāqla), surrounded by palisades or thorn fences (*zarības*).[1] Cattle were indispensable for food and for bartering with the local people for ivory and grain. Slaves were needed as concubines and porters, and also as a form of payment. Cattle and slaves could be obtained in sufficient numbers only by raiding. Armed with guns, the 'Khartoumers' showed a readiness to resort to violence, often in alliance with one local leader against another, which characterizes the dealings with the local inhabitants of the successive regimes in the south. Trade in slaves developed as a consequence of the trade in ivory and it steadily increased as the *zarības* of the ivory-traders became the bases from

[1] P. M. Holt, *A Modern History of the Sudan*, p. 61.

which the professional slave-traders from Kordofan and Darfur penetrated the south.[1] None the less, it was the Bahr al-Ghazal, not Equatoria, which provided the richest field for the slave-traders, and it was the overland route via Kordofan and Darfur, not the Nile, which carried the major part of the trade to the markets of the north.[2]

With the accession of the Khedive Ismāʿīl (1862–81), a new attempt was made to establish Egyptian dominion over the Upper Nile. Where previous invaders had been content with informal, mainly commercial relations, Ismāʿīl now attempted to establish an administration. His efforts received considerable support from those bodies in Britain who were convinced that the slave-trade and the oppression of the 'Khartoumers' would melt away before the combined onslaught of 'legitimate commerce', Christian missions, and the presence of an 'organized force' in the country.[3] For this enterprise Ismāʿīl recruited a collection of the most extraordinary, cosmopolitan, and determined Europeans ever to work in Africa. Foremost amongst them were Sir Samuel Baker and General Charles Gordon.

The appointment of first Baker then Gordon as Governor of Equatoria aroused considerable resentment in Egyptian circles. Quite apart from suspicions that they would further British rather than Egyptian interests, there was the fact of a Muslim ruler appointing avowed Christians to suppress the slave-trade. Slavery was permitted by Islam and it occupied an important place in both Sudanese and Egyptian society in the nineteenth century.[4] The attempts of a modernizing ruler to use foreign employees to suppress the slave-trade therefore aroused widespread opposition. Both Baker and Gordon were also obsessed by this aspect of their mission. The objectives of the Khedive Ismāʿīl in Equatoria, however, were much more extensive, and are clearly outlined in the instructions with which Baker set out in 1870. They were

to subdue to our [the Khedive's] authority the countries situated to the south of Gondokoro; to suppress the slave-trade; to introduce a system of regular commerce; to open to navigation the great lakes of the Equator; and to establish a chain of military stations and commercial depots, distant

[1] P. M. Holt, *The Mahdist State in the Sudan*, p. 11.
[2] R. Gray, *A History of the Southern Sudan*, p. 68.
[3] See Douin, *Histoire du règne du Khédive Ismaïl*, iii, Part 1, 477.
[4] See, most recently, G. Baer, 'Slavery in 19th-century Egypt', *J.A.H.*, viii, no. 3 (1967).

at intervals of three days' march, throughout Central Africa, accepting Gondokoro as the base of operations.[1]

Between 1870 and 1876 Baker and Gordon established the province of Equatoria which Emin was to inherit. Both men set out with the highest hopes. Both felt themselves to be working virtually single-handed in Equatoria amidst conditions which reduced them to despair. Both left the province profoundly disillusioned. The truth is that Baker and Gordon, like other Europeans in Africa, but with fewer resources, wanted to create in the Sudan a model province with an administration run on European lines. They found themselves defeated by the conditions of the area, the poor communications, the hostility of the local people, the half-hearted efforts of their garrisons 'whose utter dishonesty and tricks', declared Gordon, 'keep me in a continual rage'.[2]

Both Baker and Gordon attempted to establish an administration and to crush the ivory- and slave-traders in Equatoria by a series of coercive measures. This policy might have had some success had their presence and that of their garrisons seemed likely to continue into the future, and their superiority in terms of force and numbers been established. In fact the garrisons introduced into Equatoria by Baker and Gordon soon took on the attributes of the *zarⁱbas* already established in the area by the 'Khartoumers'. In many cases these *zarⁱbas* simply continued as Government stations, most of their inhabitants remaining under the new regime as irregular soldiers under the nominal control of new *mudⁱrs*, many of whom were selected from the colourful body of men, aptly known as 'The Forty Thieves', which Baker had brought with him to the south.[3] These garrisons eked out a precarious existence as intruders by their armed intervention in local disputes and by the seizure of cattle, slaves, and grain. Gordon found on his arrival in 1874 that the main garrison of the province at Gondokoro 'did not dare to venture a hundred yards from their station except when in bands and well-armed on

---

[1] The original document of these instructions is in the Valentine Baker Papers, File 17. The version in the Abdin Palace Archives is printed in M. F. Shukry, *The Khedive Ismā'īl and Slavery in the Sudan* (Cairo, 1937), Appendix A. Baker gives an English translation in S. W. Baker, *Ismailia*, 2 vols. (London, 1874), i. 7.

[2] Gordon to Stanley, 17 May 1876, 'Unpublished Correspondence of C. G. Gordon', *S.N.R.*, x (1927), 40.

[3] Baker, op. cit. i. 16; ii. 4–5. Also H. B. Thomas, 'A Note on the Sudanese Corps in Mexico (1863–1867)', *Uganda Journal*, viii, no. 1 (1940).

account of the enmity of the natives'.[1] This hostility of the local people to the Egyptian stations established in their midst remained endemic throughout this period, although it became blunted as semi-arabized communities, chiefly of dependants and menials, grew up around the stations. The people living in the southern Sudan, however, recognized few differences between the predatory habits of the representatives of the successive regimes who lived in the stations. Whether 'Khartoumers', employees of the Egyptian Government, or Mahdists, they were all known as *al-Turk* (the Turks) and their regimes collectively as *al-Turkiyya*.[2]

It is only in a limited sense that the Egyptian presence established in Equatoria under Baker, Gordon, and Emin can be said to have been an administration. In the course of his expedition, Baker established two stations and transported to Equatoria the bulk of the stores and equipment and the parts of the two future steamers *Khedive* and *Nyanza* which Gordon and Emin were to utilize. On his arrival in Equatoria in 1874, Gordon declared:

> The only possessions Egypt has in my provinces are two forts, one at Gondokoro and the other at Fatiko. There are 300 men in one, and 200 in the other. As for paying taxes or any government existing outside the forts it is all nonsense. You cannot go out in any safety half-a-mile—all because they have been fighting the poor natives and taking their cattle.[3]

During the next two years Gordon's achievements in Equatoria were impressive. He moved the headquarters of the province from Gondokoro to the better site at Lado; he dispatched expeditions to the Bahr al-Ghazal, the Makaraka area, and south to Bunyoro and Buganda; he surveyed, mapped, and developed a route of communications of enduring importance along the Nile—despite the discovery of a series of cataracts—between Lado and Lake Albert; he established a chain of eleven stations along this route and several other outposts away from the Nile to the east and west; he assembled and launched the two steamers, *Nyanza* and *Khedive*, which were henceforth to ply between the stations on the navigable stretches of the Nile. But it can hardly be said that Gordon created an administration.

[1] Gordon to Khairy Pasha, 7 Feb. 1875, printed in M. F. Shukry, *Equatoria under Egyptian Rule* (Cairo, 1953), p. 39.
[2] P. M. Holt, *A Modern History of the Sudan*, p. 37. Initially based on the fact that some of the Egyptians spoke the Turkish language, this term came to be applied to all members of alien ruling élites.
[3] G. B. Hill, *Colonel Gordon in Central Africa* (London, 1885), p. 15.

The garrisons he had established administered themselves; they did not administer the local people. They continued to raid and oppress them, they succeeded in extracting levies of grain and services of wood-cutting and porterage from some of them; to a limited extent they traded with them.[1] But they also felt constantly threatened by them and interfered with the internal affairs of the local people as little as possible. Both Gordon and Emin were rarely appealed to as arbitrators; they established no system of justice; their preoccupation was with the administration of their own stations. The Egyptian presence in Equatoria is perhaps best considered in terms of a half-hearted military occupation of limited extent and duration. At no point did the regular garrisons in the province exceed a total of 1,500 men, though the irregular soldiers recruited from the settlements of the 'Khartoumers' and from the local population probably amounted to at least an equal number.[2] In the 1880s the proportion of locally recruited southern Sudanese soldiers in the Government stations greatly increased. Having moved away from their traditional societies, these men became good soldiers, fond of their uniforms and military drill, loyal to the Khedive of Egypt (whom they had never seen), and remarkably unresponsive to Mahdist propaganda. They were despised and treated as inferiors by the officers, clerks, and officials in the stations, who were predominantly Egyptians and northern Sudanese, and hated them in turn.[3] A significant number of the Egyptian and northern Sudanese elements in the stations was made up of convicts, criminals, and men who were deported to Equatoria from Egypt after participating in Arabi's rebellion. As Emin observed, 'the Equatorial Province has always been considered a sort of Egyptian Siberia by the authorities at Cairo'.[4] It was this group, which probably never consisted of more than 100 people, that was to cause Emin so much trouble in the future.[5]

[1] Junker estimated that less than 10 per cent of the goods arriving in Equatoria from Khartoum ever reached the local people through trade—the rest were absorbed by the station communities: W. Junker, *Travels in Africa*, 3 vols. (London, 1892), ii. 28.

[2] Emin to Hansal, 28 Nov. 1880, printed in *E.P. in C.A.*, pp. 258–9; Junker, op. cit., ii. 395; R. W. Felkin, 'The Position of Dr. Emin Bey', *Scottish Geographical Magazine*, Dec. 1886; H. M. Stanley to the Emin Pasha Relief Committee, 28 Aug. 1888, printed in *The Times*, 3 Apr. 1889.

[3] See esp. Junker, op. cit. iii. 440.

[4] T. Stevens, 'Conversations with Emin Pasha', [1889], in *Scouting for Stanley in East Africa* (London, 1890), p. 280.

[5] In 1874 Gordon stated 'there are not more than 50 Arab soldiers and 6 Arab officers in the Province, all the rest are Blacks', Gordon to Stanton,

The stations showed a marked tendency to increase greatly in size, owing to the acquisition by the soldiers of large numbers of dependants. Gordon found that 'for every 100 soldiers there are 120 women and children, boys etc.: so, 500 soldiers are equal to 1,100 souls'.[1] The number of stations also proliferated. At its furthest extent, in 1881–3, the province of Equatoria consisted of some fifty stations divided into ten districts.[2] But it is doubtful whether many of these stations were ever effectively under the authority of either the Governor or the Government. There is a contrast between the riverain stations, strung out along the backbone of the province between Lado and Lake Albert, and the zarības in the vast hinterland to the east and west.

In the former, the stations consisted of rows of neatly built houses separated by broad avenues and surrounded by an earthen wall, a moat, or a palisade. By 1881 Lado had developed into a settlement of several hundred buildings, and Emin had founded a mosque, a Koranic school, and a hospital, which he ran with the assistance of a Tunisian chemist, called Vita Hassan.[3] The garrison cultivated extensive fruit and vegetable gardens, grew cotton and wove it into cloth, and established links through concubinage and trade with the local population. Around this and the other riverain stations a new way of life was slowly emerging in which Middle Eastern traits of manners, material objects, religious observance, and the Arabic language were being assimilated by sub-Saharan African cultures.[4] But most of the population of Equatoria did not live in the immediate vicinity of Government stations and for them life continued largely unaffected by the Egyptian incursion.

In the outlying stations the situation was rather different. Here, the buildings were constructed not of sun-dried bricks with walls and moats, but of less permanent materials surrounded by thorn fences. Some of these zarības, established by the 'Khartoumers', had existed for over twenty years, and the original pattern of violence and slave-

---

21 Dec. 1874, printed in S.N.R., x (1927), 13. Although further recruits arrived in Equatoria from the north during the following years, many quickly fell ill, and either returned home or died.

[1] G. B. Hill, Colonel Gordon in Central Africa, p. 128.

[2] A full list is given in Junker, op. cit. iii. 366–7.

[3] R. Gray, A History of the Southern Sudan, pp. 140–1, citing Vita Hassan, Die Wahrheit über Emin Pascha, 2 vols. (Berlin, 1893), i. 13. Vita Hassan estimates a total of 2,000 huts at Lado, but this, like much else in his book, is probably an exaggeration.   [4] R. Gray, op. cit., pp. 143–4.

trading had continued. The relations between these garrisons and the Government consisted largely of obtaining trade goods, guns, and ammunition from Khartoum, and sending ivory and slaves in return. Some of these stations were visited by Gordon or Emin perhaps once in five years, and their attempts to reform the situation they encountered in them lasted no longer than their presence there. Many of the stations situated far away from the Nile were never visited at all.

In this situation the impact of men like Gordon and Emin was slight. Both appear in the extraneous role of 'technical experts', representing the alien, but respected, authority of Khartoum and Cairo; standing, as Europeans, above the local situation; attempting to limit and control the predatory existence of the garrisons; discountenancing robbery, corruption, and the slave-trade.[1]

The administration and development of Equatoria were greatly hampered by the extremely poor communications of the province. The problem of establishing more elaborate systems of communications existed in many parts of Africa in the nineteenth century; in the southern Sudan it was never effectively mastered. Throughout the area roads were non-existent. Streams were liable to rise in a few hours and become raging torrents which it was impossible to cross for days or even weeks.[2] Camels, donkeys, and elephants imported by Gordon from India sickened and died, and Emin's carrier pigeons were devoured by birds of prey. Porters remained the sole means of transport overland. Communications between Equatoria and Khartoum were no more reliable than those within the province itself. Lado was more than 1,000 miles up the Nile from Khartoum and separated from it by an obstacle to navigation almost as great as the cataracts which separated Khartoum from Cairo. This was the *sudd*. Between Lado and its confluence with the Sobat river the Nile enters a region of immense flats and papyrus marshes through which the river winds in numerous, constantly changing channels for several hundred miles. Known as the *sudd* (Arabic: *sadd*, 'barrier') because of the obstruction caused by floating islands of vegetation, this area has played a critical part in the successive attempts of northern regimes to establish effective communications with the south.

The obstructions to navigation caused by the *sudd* were constantly changing in both location and extent throughout the nineteenth century. For a short period in the mid 1870s, the river was clear and the journey by steamer from Khartoum to Gondokoro was done by

Gordon in twenty-five days in March 1874.[1] In 1876, Gordon did the downstream journey in only thirteen and a half days.[2] This was exceptional. The endless delays experienced by Baker were more common. In 1878 a party of C.M.S. missionaries bound for Buganda took over two months to travel from Khartoum to Lado.[3] The *sudd* completely closed the river behind them and so, between 1878 and 1880, no other steamer reached Equatoria from Khartoum.

The development of Equatoria as a province of Egypt was in any case prevented by the declining interest and resources of the Government. In the 1870s a disastrous war with Ethiopia and a public debt which grew at an average rate of £7,000,000 per year brought to an end the era of Egyptian expansion. The Sudan railway was abandoned, and Gordon, after serving on a Commission of Inquiry into the financial situation in Egypt in 1878, became convinced that large areas of the Sudan would have to be evacuated.[4]

After Gordon's departure from Equatoria, in 1876, to become Governor-General of the Sudan, a good deal of what he had managed to establish lapsed under the rapid succession of two Americans, Prout and Mason, and then an Egyptian, Ibrāhīm Fawzī, as Governors. When Emin Bey was appointed by Gordon as Governor of Equatoria in 1878, he inherited 'a disordered province of declining importance'.[5] The Egyptian thrust into Equatoria had lost its force and all that remained of it was a tenuous straggle of isolated stations presided over by a Governor whose position was precarious and restricted. He possessed the limited authority and prestige of a European who had been appointed by the Khedive, spoke Arabic, and possessed a remarkable ability to adapt himself to circumstances. Small, slim, and bespectacled, Emin was not at all imposing in appearance. By training a doctor, by inclination a naturalist, he was by his nature and by his past experience well suited to the modest role that lay before him.

*   *   *

Emin Pasha was born as Eduard Carl Oscar Theodor Schnitzer on 28 March 1840 at Oppeln, in the Prussian province of Silesia.[6] His

[1] B. M. Allen, *Gordon and the Sudan* (London, 1931), p. 17.
[2] G. B. Hill, *Colonel Gordon in Central Africa*, pp. 196–7.
[3] C. T. Wilson and R. W. Felkin, *Uganda and the Egyptian Sudan*, 2 vols. (London, 1882), i. 289–99.   [4] R. Gray, op. cit., pp. 120, 136–7.
[5] The phrase is Richard Gray's, see R. Gray, op. cit., p. 138.
[6] For this brief account of Emin's early life I have drawn heavily on the work of his cousin and biographer, George Schweitzer, *Emin Pasha: His Life and Work*, 2 vols. (London, 1898), esp. i. 1–30.

father, Ludwig Schnitzer, was a merchant, and Emin's upbringing was that of a gifted child in a typical middle-class German family.[1] When he was two, the family moved to Neisse and it was here that Emin had all his schooling. At eighteen, he went to the university of Breslau and then to the universities of Königsberg and Berlin, where he qualified as a doctor in 1864. Disqualified from practising in Germany on a mere technicality, Emin left Germany abruptly. After travelling via Vienna and Trieste, Emin set out for Constantinople, where he hoped to enrol in the Turkish service. He arrived at Antivari in Albania (then a Turkish province) at the end of December 1864. Here he was warmly received by the cosmopolitan European community and was soon in practice as a doctor. He already spoke French, English, and Italian as well as German, and he soon learnt Turkish, Albanian, and modern Greek. Emin's remarkable linguistic abilities later enabled him to become fluent in Arabic and conversant in several African languages. He also exhibited a notable cultural adaptability. In 1865 he wrote to his sister, describing his life in Antivari:

> I have turned so brown that I no longer look at all like a European, and the fez and clothing of course add to my foreign appearance . . . In the five months I have been here I have so completely familiarised myself with the customs and habits, the language and the people, that everyone expresses his surprise; and I believe myself that it would be somewhat hard for me to return to Germany for good and reaccustom myself to its stiff and ceremonious conventionalities.[2]

Until 1870 Emin remained at Antivari as quarantine officer of the port and medical officer for the district. At the end of 1870 he joined the staff of Ismā'īl Hakki Pasha, Governor of northern Albania, in whose service he remained until the latter's death in 1873. About these years of Emin's life we know rather little, but he travelled a good deal all over the Ottoman empire and became involved in various political intrigues and insurrections. He also formed a close friendship with Hakki Pasha's Transylvanian wife, and after her husband's death, she and her children accompanied Emin on a visit to Germany, where Emin passed her off as his own wife. It is very

---

[1] The family may have been Jewish in origin but Emin was baptized in a Protestant church at the age at six and there is no evidence that he ever considered himself as Jewish. The assertion that Emin was a Jew was made most vociferously by Englishmen after 1890 when Emin took service with the Germans in Africa. In the context of the 1890s it served as a common and useful term of abuse.   [2] Schweitzer, i. 11–12.

doubtful whether in fact Emin ever married her. After establishing her and her children with his family in Neisse in September 1875, Emin suddenly disappeared. He never again returned to Germany and he had no contact with his family for the next fourteen years.

A month after he had left Germany so unexpectedly, Emin appeared in Cairo. He set out almost at once for Khartoum, where he arrived in December 1875. Here he was soon established in medical practice and became well known in the European community. He was regarded as talented and intelligent and he was noted for the great meticulousness he exhibited in everything he did, not least in his dress and personal habits and in his handwriting—which has a quality of exquisite neatness and astonishing minuteness. Emin also began at this time to express his lifelong interest in all branches of botany and zoology by assembling collections of plants, animals, and birds (which he skinned and stuffed himself) and which he dispatched from time to time to the museums of England and Germany. Hearing of Emin's presence in Khartoum, Gordon—who was at this time still in Equatoria—asked him to come as chief medical officer to the province. In May 1876 Emin arrived in Equatoria.

Gordon, who had emphatic and distinctly idiosyncratic views about what he expected from other Europeans in Africa in terms of national identity and religious convictions, at first had little respect for this German 'who, now professing the Musulman religion, pretends to me that he is an Arab by birth and religion'.[1] None the less, Gordon at once made use of Emin by sending him on what was to be the first of a series of missions to Buganda and Bunyoro.

The rulers of these two African kingdoms to the south of Equatoria had already had extensive contacts with the 'Turks' to the north, and had good reason to be suspicious and fearful of their intentions. In 1869 some of the 'Khartoumers' had intervened in a dispute over the succession to the throne of Bunyoro. Three years later Baker had attempted to annex the kingdom to Egypt, but he had been forced by its ruler, Kabarega, to beat a hasty and fighting retreat. In 1876 the

---

[1] G. B. Hill, *Colonel Gordon in Central Africa*, p. 187. The question of Emin's religious convictions has always been something of an enigma. Gordon despised him as a Muslim, but neither the Mahdists nor Emin's own soldiers ever regarded him as such. Kabaka Mutesa of Buganda set out to respect him as a Christian—but was soon dissuaded from doing so by Emin himself. H. M. Stanley thought that Emin was a Materialist. R. W. Felkin records that Emin told him that the god he worshipped was simply that of 'science and humanity' (Felkin to Wright, 17 Oct. 1878, C.M.S. Archives, CA6/010).

Kabaka of Buganda, Mutesa, had every reason to suspect that Gordon had similar designs on his kingdom. The previous emissaries sent by Gordon, Chaillé-Long and Linant de Bellefonds, had both acted in a domineering manner and had not made nearly so favourable an impression as the more co-operative H. M. Stanley, who had arrived from a quite different direction so dramatically five days after Linant de Bellefonds in April 1875.[1] Whereas Stanley's arrival from the East African coast represented new possibilities of interest and value to Mutesa in the sphere of Buganda's foreign policy, any emissaries from the 'Turks' to the north represented a threat. In January 1876 Gordon had dispatched Nuer Agha with a force of 160 men to Buganda in an attempt to obtain Mutesa's consent to the erection of two Egyptian stations on the Victoria Nile close to Lake Victoria. In a fascinating series of letters to Gordon (written by Dallington, a boy who had attended Bishop Steere's mission school at the coast and had been left in Buganda by Stanley), Mutesa adopted diversionary tactics and suggested an alliance between Buganda and Equatoria to partition Buganda's great rival, Bunyoro. But by 1876 Gordon was in no position to embark on such a design, and, much as Mutesa might fear him, Gordon's chief desire was simply to launch a steamer on Lake Victoria. Having accomplished this gesture in the direction of the earlier ambitions of Baker, the Khedive, and himself, Gordon wished to withdraw from Equatoria and a position which he found exasperating and uncongenial as soon as possible.[2] Mutesa, however, prevaricated and in the meantime Nuer Agha and his men had been persuaded to remain under Mutesa's close surveillance near to his capital. It was to negotiate the return of these men that Gordon now sent Emin to Buganda.

Little as Gordon may have appreciated the fact, he could scarcely have chosen a better man to accomplish what was a rather delicate task. Emin stands in sharp contrast to the previous emissaries who had come to Buganda from the north. Modest and self-effacing, he was soon conversant in Luganda and exhibited little of that arrogance and ethnocentrism so prevalent among European visitors to African states in the nineteenth century. He brought about the withdrawal of Nuer Agha and his men from Buganda successfully and established

---

[1] See H. M. Stanley, *Through the Dark Continent*, 2 vols. (London, 1879), i, ch. ix.

[2] See esp. Gordon to Stanton, 16 July and 1 Aug. 1876, *S.N.R.*, x (1927), 49 et seq.

himself so favourably in Mutesa's eyes that when he left Buganda to
return to Equatoria, Mutesa wrote to Gordon begging him to send
'Hakim' (the doctor) to stay with him permanently.[1]

After Gordon's departure from Equatoria, Emin visited Buganda
again. He also visited Kabarega of Bunyoro.[2] Amongst the many
Europeans who met one or both of these African rulers it is hard to
find anyone with a record of such close and successful personal
relations with them as Emin Pasha. The reality of an Egyptian threat
to Buganda came to an end with the departure of Gordon and the
increasing preoccupation of the Egyptian Government with events
elsewhere. But the fear of a potential threat from the armed garrisons
of Equatoria continues as a constant theme in the history of Buganda,
Bunyoro, and the Mahdist state in the Sudan until the end of the
century. 'The Turks', declared Mutesa, three years after Gordon's
departure, 'have been gnawing at my country like rats.'[3]

During the years after 1876, from a base at Lado, Emin travelled
a good deal. Quite apart from his visits to Buganda and Bunyoro, he
went on expeditions to the Makaraka and Mangbetu areas and to the
borders of the Bahr al-Ghazal; he also went by steamer to Lake
Albert. Emin wrote vivid accounts of these journeys, and his detailed
descriptions of the life and customs of the peoples among whom he
moved would be a credit to any twentieth-century field-researcher's
notebook.[4] Emin's own life at Lado, after his appointment as Governor of Equatoria in 1878, is well described by several of the people
who visited him during this time. Junker and Casati stayed with him
in between their travels to the south-west. In the latter part of 1878
the C.M.S. missionaries Litchfield, Pearson, and R. W. Felkin stayed
at Lado, where they were considerably impressed by Emin's talents
and achievements, on their way to Buganda.[5] Both Gordon and Emin

[1] Kabaka Mutesa to Gordon, 31 Aug. 1876, printed in M. F. Shukry, *Equatoria under Egyptian Rule*, p. 359.

[2] Emin has left extensive accounts of these visits in the *Tagebücher*, and these
have been translated into English and edited by Sir John Gray. See 'The Diaries
of Emin Pasha', Extracts I, II, and III, published in the *Uganda Journal*, xxv,
nos. 1 and 2 (1961) and xxvi, no. 1 (1962).

[3] Reported in Mackay to Wright, 14 July 1879, C.M.S. Archives, CA 6/016.

[4] From his extensive notes in the *Tagebücher*, Emin later wrote articles, several
of which are printed in *E.P. in C.A.*

[5] See R. W. Felkin and C. T. Wilson, *Uganda and the Egyptian Sudan*, 2 vols.
(London, 1882). A new edition of this work, with an Introduction by the
present author, is to be published by Frank Cass & Co., London, in 1972. Felkin's
original diary is in the C.M.S. Archives, CA 6/010, as are the letters written by
the other missionaries during their stay at Lado.

were very sceptical about the plan to establish a C.M.S. mission in Buganda, and tried to redirect the attention of the missionaries to the western shore of Lake Albert.[1] When this failed, Emin tried to arouse the interest of Roman Catholics in the area. But this also met with no response, and the idea of a mission station on Lake Albert operating along the lines so successfully achieved by Dr. Robert Laws on Lake Nyasa was never realized.[2] In place of this, Emin began to outline schemes for a secular, colonial venture, involving the establishment of stations from Lake Albert westwards to Nyangwe, in the Congo State, or south to Lake Tanganyika, possibly in co-operation with King Leopold II of the Belgians.[3] Behind both of these schemes lay Emin's growing conviction that much the richest and potentially the most promising area of the province lay in the south. But Emin despaired of the development of any part of the southern Sudan until the two provinces of Equatoria and Bahr al-Ghazal were united into one 'separate, self-governing province under an efficient administrator, independent of Khartoum and subject only to the ministry at Cairo'.[4] Emin encountered little response to this suggestion, indeed little interest in Equatoria at all, during his two brief visits to Khartoum during these years. On his last visit to Khartoum in the middle of 1882 Emin found the Government wavering in the face of 'tidings of revolution in Alexandria' and preoccupied with the gathering momentum of the movement under the Mahdi in the Sudan.[5] It was an unhappy and frustrating time for Emin and it was with a great sense of relief that he arrived back in Equatoria in August.

Almost at once, however, the situation in the frontier area between Equatoria and the Bahr al-Ghazal began to cause Emin serious concern. The Dinka in the Rohl district rose in revolt, sacked the station of Rumbek, and annihilated the garrison. Emin feared that the revolt would spread amongst the neighbouring peoples in Equatoria. He

[1] 'To my mind, Mtesa will further the mission till he finds he cannot get what he wants, and then he will throw them over, it may take 2 years, but come this will. I cannot myself understand why the Church Missionary Society, neglecting Kings, do not establish themselves on Lake Albert, not in our territory but beyond it . . .', Gordon to Sir Samuel Baker, 26 May 1878. Papers in the possession of Mr. Valentine Baker, Salisbury.
[2] For Dr. Robert Laws's venture on Lake Nyasa, see W. P. Livingstone, *Laws of Livingstonia* (London, 1928).
[3] See Emin to Schweinfurth, 3–18 Mar. 1883, *E.P. in C.A.*, p. 427, and Felkin to Wright, 17 Oct. 1878, C.M.S. Archives, CA 6/o10, reporting a conversation with Emin.
[4] Schweitzer, i. 143.
[5] Ibid. i. 121–2.

wrote at once to his friends Junker and Casati, who were both in the western districts, urging them to come to Lado. Casati arrived in April 1883; Junker did not come until the following January.

It was amidst this disturbed situation that the steamer *Telhawin* arrived from Khartoum in March 1883, bringing ominous news from the north. Emin feared that the Government in Khartoum had allowed the Mahdist revolt to get beyond control, that Darfur was probably already lost, and that Lupton in the Bahr al-Ghazal was unable to rely on the support of his own garrisons.[1] Emin also felt that his own position in Equatoria had become

not an enviable one . . . for our province has received absolutely no support . . . Hitherto, my personal influence has kept things in order, and made the Negroes my allies, but I begin to be tired of it, for I see that the Government does not understand us, and never will; and if I retire, things will fall to pieces here in a very short time . . .[2]

So preoccupied was the Government with events elsewhere that Emin feared 'they may quietly draw their pens through the names of our provinces in a couple of years'.[3]

In April 1883 Emin had been in Equatoria for nearly seven years, during the previous six of which only nine steamers had come from Khartoum.[4] Yet the lessons of experience were always lost amidst the hopes which were raised by the arrival and departure of a steamer. As Emin and Casati watched the departure of the *Telhawin* from Lado on 14 April they looked to its prompt return by August—this time with the supplies which Emin had repeatedly requested, and very much needed. Emin and Casati were to remain in Equatoria for a further six years. But there were to be no further steamers from Khartoum.

[1] Emin to Schweinfurth, 3–18 Mar. 1883, *E.P. in C.A.*, p. 430.
[2] Ibid. 426.   [3] Ibid. 425.   [4] Schweitzer, i. 141–2.

CHAPTER II

Equatoria 1883–1886

A t the time of the departure of the last steamer from Lado to Khartoum in 1883, Emin still regarded the situation in Equatoria itself with a certain optimism. In 1882 the province had yielded a surplus revenue (in the form of ivory) which Emin estimated at £8,000.[1] For the current year a surplus of £12,000 was anticipated.[2] None the less, Emin was only too aware that even if conditions in the rest of the Sudan improved, the huge distance and the poor communications with the south, quite apart from the Government's lack of interest, made it 'easy to understand how very small is the prospect of developing our provinces, and it is far more than questionable whether anyone else will ever be found willing under similar circumstances to drag out existence here like an outcast from civilisation'.[3]

In May 1883 Emin was so little alarmed at the prospect of any immediate threat to Equatoria that he set out on a journey with Casati to the Mangbetu area, in the south-west corner of the province. Rich in ivory, this fertile country had been brought to Emin's attention by Schweinfurth and Junker, whose travels in the region of the Kibali and Uele rivers had convinced Emin of the possibility of developing a route of communications via this area with the Congo. By 1883 Emin was aware of H. M. Stanley's activities on the Congo and of the approach towards the Mangbetu area of the eastern frontier of King Leopold's Congo State. On his journey in 1883, Emin had the quite specific objective of establishing further Egyptian stations in the area. 'I should not care to be troubled in the immediate future by Mr. Stanley,' he observed, 'so we must try to forestall him.'[4] Emin's ambitions in 1883 for this area represent an early counterpart to those of King Leopold. Five years later Leopold was to become only too aware of Emin's interest in the Mangbetu country, and in a

[1] Emin to R. W. Felkin, 22 Mar. 1883, M.P., F. 7. See also R. W. Felkin, 'The Egyptian Sudan', *Scottish Geographical Magazine*, i (1885).
[2] Emin to Schweinfurth, 19 Oct. 1883, *E.P. in C.A.*, p. 456.
[3] Schweitzer, i. 142.
[4] Emin to Junker, May 1883, printed in Schweitzer, i. 145.

correspondence with Mackinnon, Leopold was emphatically to deny any claims by Emin to an area which might become an important geographical obstacle to the realization of Leopold's Nile dream.[1] Emin's ambitions, however, unlike those of King Leopold, disappeared in the face of hostile circumstances. Emin had only just arrived in Mangbetu when, in July, he heard of the renewed uprising of the Dinka in the Bahr al-Ghazal.

The revolt of the Dinka, in co-operation with certain sections of the Nuer, in 1883–4, was similar in character to their revolts both before and since. Essentially, it was a revolt against alien government as such, and in particular a response to the oppression and extensive cattle-raiding of the soldiers in the Egyptian stations. The Governor of the Bahr al-Ghazal at this time was the young and inexperienced Englishman, Lupton.[2] Lupton's position was a difficult one since he felt unable to rely on the loyalty of his own soldiers and feared that they would defect in large numbers to the Mahdists in Kordofan. Lupton's fears proved well founded. When, at the end of January 1884, he had succeeded temporarily in quelling the Dinka revolt, the news arrived of the complete annihilation of the expedition sent by the Government under General Hicks against the Mahdists the previous November. This sensational Mahdist victory finally convinced waverers all over the Sudan that Egyptian rule was doomed.[3] Slatin surrendered Darfur to the Mahdists in December. The Mahdi then set out to besiege Khartoum itself. He also appointed Karam Allāh Muhammad Kurqusāwī as *amīr* of the Bahr al-Ghazal and sent him south at the head of an army consisting of several thousand men to take possession of Lupton's province and of Equatoria.[4] On the march south Karam Allāh's army attracted wholesale desertions from Lupton's garrisons and support from the Dinka against whom Lupton had recently been fighting. By April 1884 Karam Allāh's army was before Lupton's headquarters at Daym al-Zubayr. In the first of three last dramatic letters to Emin, Lupton informed him of Karam Allāh's arrival and ultimatum ordering him to surrender the province. 'I will fight to the last', Lupton declared.[5] But Lupton's

[1] The important letter on this subject is Leopold to Mackinnon, 9 May 1888, Palace Archives, Brussels, Dossier 82, no. 74.
[2] See E. Macro, 'Frank Miller Lupton', *S.N.R.*, xxviii (1947).
[3] P. M. Holt, *A Modern History of the Sudan*, p. 85.
[4] P. M. Holt, *The Mahdist State in the Sudan*, p. 71.
[5] Lupton to Emin, 12 Apr. 1884. Copies of Lupton's last three letters to Emin are in the Khartoum Archives, Cairint, 1/5/30. The letters are also printed in

troops refused to fight and Lupton capitulated. In a last letter to Emin on 26 April he announced 'It is all up with me here, every one has joined the Mahdi, and his army takes charge of the Mudireh [province] the day after tomorrow . . . Look out you; some 8,000 to 10,000 men are coming to you well armed.'[1] Lupton was sent north to join Slatin in the Mahdists' capital at Omdurman. Here he dragged out a miserable existence until his death in May 1888.

Lupton's last letters reached Emin on 23 May at Lado, whither he had hurriedly returned, and four days later they were followed by letters from Karam Allāh himself. Emin was informed of the fall of the Bahr al-Ghazal, the Mahdist victories throughout the Sudan, and the siege of Khartoum—facts confirmed by Lupton in a postscript.[2] Emin was ordered to surrender the Equatorial province and to come with his chief officers to submit to Karam Allāh.[3]

The evidence is conclusive that Emin's initial inclination was to follow the example of Slatin and Lupton and to capitulate.[4] The Mahdist threat to Equatoria came at a time when Emin was feeling profoundly discouraged. He felt that if Hicks's well-equipped army had been so easily defeated, and the provinces of Kordofan, Darfur, and the Bahr al-Ghazal had succumbed, there appeared little chance that Equatoria would be able to put up much resistance. Emin also anticipated that there would be extensive defections to the Mahdists amongst the Danāqla in his own province. Emin therefore concluded that 'it would be folly to fight, without rifles, without ammunition, without men that I can depend on, with Danāqla before and behind me'.[5]

Defections to the Mahdists were to occur in Equatoria but the potentially pro-Mahdist elements in the stations, as among the population generally, were never so extensive as in the Bahr al-Ghazal. Like Lupton, Emin was to be faced with external attacks on the province by Mahdist forces and internal revolts by the local negro

A. J. Mounteney-Jephson, *Emin Pasha and the Rebellion at the Equator* (London, 1890), pp. 359–60.
[1] Ibid. [2] *Tagebücher*, 27 May 1884, iii. 16.
[3] Karam Allāh's letters, originally in Arabic, are printed in English translation in Junker, *Travels in Africa*, iii. 382–9.
[4] See esp. Emin to Schweinfurth, 27 May 1884, *E.P. in C.A.*, p. 462; Emin to E. Harders, 28 May 1884, printed in Schweitzer, i. 159; Emin to Casati, 28 May 1884, printed in Casati, *Ten Years in Equatoria*, pp. 195–6. Emin later attempted to explain his conduct as a ruse to gain time. See Emin to Charles Allen, 30 Dec. 1885, A.S.S. C. 155/136.
[5] Emin to Schweinfurth, 27 May 1884, cited above.

population against the depredations of the garrisons. But the Bahr al-Ghazal fell because Lupton's own soldiers were pro-Mahdist and refused to fight. In Equatoria such defections to the Mahdists as did take place only reinforced the belief amongst the southern Sudanese soldiers in the stations, who by 1884 were considerably in the majority, that in fighting against the Mahdists they were fighting for themselves.[1]

Emin soon encountered resistance to the idea of submission to Karam Allāh amongst the garrison at Lado, and this resistance increased as news arrived of the massacre and enslavement of negroes in the Bahr al-Ghazal under the Mahdists. In a petition to Emin, his southern Sudanese soldiers declared 'We are the children of Effendina [the Khedive] and we will die in his service.'[2] Emin, together with Junker and Vita Hassan, had also come to the conclusion that 'at the slow rate at which the history of these countries is made, months might elapse ere the rebels [i.e. the Mahdists] really made their appearance before Lado'.[3] The objectives of Karam Allāh appeared to be limited and specific: he wished to increase his own prestige by a victory, and his own strength by acquiring the arms and ammunition present in Equatoria. By a 'surrender' of Equatoria, he appeared to wish to procure a written declaration of submission which he could send to the Mahdi. Above all, it was a clear priority of the Mahdists, both in 1884 and again in 1888, to secure as prisoners the higher officials of the Egyptian stations in Equatoria and in particular Emin himself.[4] It was therefore decided at Lado that 'a written declaration of the surrender of the province would be quite enough for the present' and that it did not need Emin himself to take it to Karam Allāh.[5] Accordingly, a delegation led by 'Uthmān Hajj Hāmid, the Qāḍī [judge] of the province, left Lado for the Bahr al-Ghazal on 3 June with a letter from Emin indicating his readiness to submit. In the train of this delegation went many of the Mahdist sympathizers, whom Emin encouraged to leave.[6] None of the party ever returned to

[1] R. O. Collins, *The Southern Sudan, 1883-1898: a Struggle for Control* (New Haven and London, 1962), p. 51. I am considerably indebted to this work during the rest of this Chapter.
[2] Statement of Basili Boktor, Cairo, 1890, Khartoum Archives, Cairint, 1/11/56.
[3] Junker, *Travels in Africa*, iii. 395.
[4] See Ch. IX, p. 236 below. The most important letter in this context is 'Umar Sālih to the Khalifa, 2 Shawal 1305, (13 June 1888), Khartoum Archives, Mahdiya, 1/33/5.   [5] Junker, op. cit. iii. 392.
[6] *Tagebücher*, 3 June 1884, iii. 17. Statement of 'Uthmān Latīf, Cairo, 9 July 1890, Khartoum Archives, Cairint, 3/14/237.

Equatoria. 'Uthmān Hajj Hāmid later gave a colourful account of its progress, and of his own experiences as a 'prisoner' of the Mahdists in the Bahr al-Ghazal and at Omdurman before he escaped to Cairo.[1] Emin was probably closer to the truth when he concluded that the entire delegation had defected.[2]

Throughout the rest of 1884, a Mahdist attack on Equatoria was expected. But until the very end of the year the gradual dissolution of the province which took place stemmed chiefly from internal reasons only remotely connected with the Mahdist presence in the neighbouring Bahr al-Ghazal. Many of the outlying stations in the province, away from the Nile, were simply abandoned at this time. Casati, who passed through the south-western districts on his way back to Lado (where he arrived in January 1885), has left a vivid account of the mounting violence and disorder which he encountered in the stations in that area.[3] The Makaraka region, long established as an important source for the supplies of grain on which Lado and the other northern riverain stations depended, also passed out of Emin's control. Even in the heartland of the province, along the Nile, the stations were attacked by the local population. Such attacks occurred constantly throughout the period of the *Turkiyya* in Equatoria, but from 1884 onwards they increased in both scale and frequency. Few of these attacks had much to do with the proximity of the Mahdists. Rather, as Emin observed, it was simply the growing weakness of the 'Turks' which invited attack.[4]

So long as Khartoum had not fallen to the Mahdists, the hope that a steamer would come from the north continued in the south. This hope played an important part in maintaining morale amongst the riverain garrisons in Equatoria throughout 1884. As late as January 1885, Junker states, 'we all of us dreamed of nothing but the steamer from Khartoum'.[5] These hopes were founded on two illusions. First, the only news reaching Equatoria of events in the rest of the Sudan at this time came from Mahdist sources, and Emin and Junker continued to hope that Karam Allāh's assertions that 'the whole Sudan is lost, Khartoum besieged' were, like other Mahdist claims, inflated

[1] Statement of 'Uthmān Hajj Hāmid, Cairo, 12 Nov. 1891, Khartoum Archives, Cairint, 3/14/237.
[2] Emin to Schweinfurth, 2 Jan. 1885, *E.P. in C.A.*, p. 475.
[3] Casati, *Ten Years in Equatoria*, pp. 195–205.
[4] Emin to Schweinfurth, 14 Aug. 1884, *E.P. in C.A.*, pp. 462–9.
[5] Junker, *Travels in Africa*, iii. 445.

rumours rather than actual achievements.[1] Second, as Junker records,
Emin and Junker, like many in Europe,

went on the assumption that after the Hicks disaster, which our calculations fixed as having occurred in the autumn, say October or November last
year [1883], neither Egypt nor Europe would leave the Soudan to its fate;
but that as soon as the catastrophe was made known, a mixed relief force
would be despatched from the north. This, however, would mean, even
assuming that a temporary railway was laid from Suakin to Berber, that
we could not expect help for at least a year, that is not before October or
November [1884].[2]

Emin thought in June 1884 that Turkish troops would be sent from
Constantinople if necessary, if Khartoum really were besieged.[3] But
by October, Emin was more pessimistic; a further letter had come
from Karam Allāh declaring that Khartoum was besieged by the
Mahdi himself and Emin reflected gloomily that it had 'probably
capitulated by this time'.[4]

During the last months of 1884 Emin became preoccupied with
the fate of Amadi. This station in the north-west of the province lay
on the direct route from the Bahr al-Ghazal to Lado in a region
where the Danāqla traders, who had always been the most effective
power in the area, were openly pro-Mahdist. In November a mixed
force of Danāqla and Karam Allāh's troops launched an assault on
the station. When this was repulsed, they established a siege and
awaited reinforcements from the Bahr al-Ghazal. Emin at once
attempted to strengthen the garrison at Amadi, but his orders were
disregarded and his men either refused to rally to the defence of the
besieged station or drifted off independently while *en route* to its
relief. The fate of Amadi was settled by the arrival of Karam Allāh
himself before the station in February 1885 at the head of a large
army. While the northern Sudanese commander and officers of the
station made ready to hand it over to the Mahdists, the southern
Sudanese soldiers broke out of the station and some of them successfully evaded the besieging forces and reached Bedden, a station on
the Nile. By the end of March, Amadi was in Mahdist hands. On
3 April 1885 Emin received an ultimatum: either he appeared at Amadi
to make his submission, or Karam Allāh would march on Lado.[5]

[1] Emin to Schweinfurth, 27 May 1884, *E.P. in C.A.*, p. 462.
[2] Junker, op. cit. iii. 418.
[3] Emin to Junker, 12 June 1884, printed in Schweitzer, i. 169.
[4] Emin to Schweinfurth, 22 Oct. 1884, *E.P. in C.A.*, p. 472.
[5] Emin to Schweinfurth, 1 Dec. 1885, *E.P. in C.A.*, pp. 480-1.

The situation which Emin had long feared had now come about. Totally dependent on his own impoverished resources, and unsure of the extent of his authority, he faced the prospect of a Mahdist attack on his headquarters. This time Emin did not even contemplate capitulation. Instead, he decided to withdraw to the south.

*   *   *

The idea of withdrawing to the south of the province had been in Emin's mind for a considerable time. It had been discussed by Emin and Junker in May 1884 at the time of the fall of the Bahr al-Ghazal. It had also come increasingly to occupy Emin's attention as his contacts with the African rulers immediately to the south of Equatoria had increased during 1884-5.

Between 1879 and 1884 relations between Emin and the rulers of Buganda and Bunyoro had lapsed. So little news reached Emin at Lado of events in the south that in 1884 he did not know whether the C.M.S. mission station in Buganda still existed; nor did he know that Kabaka Mutesa had died in October 1884 and had been succeeded by Mwanga.[1]

In November 1884, however, envoys arrived at Lado from Anfina, the African ruler of a small area along the Victoria Nile on the northern periphery of Bunyoro, urging Emin to set up a new station in the south at Magungo.[2] Emin took advantage of their visit to send the first of many letters to be dispatched by this route to the East African coast at Zanzibar. In these letters, which Emin hoped would be forwarded by the C.M.S. missionaries who, he learnt, were still in Buganda, Emin requested the British Consul-General at Zanzibar to inform the Egyptian Government of his presence in Equatoria, along with Junker and Casati, and of his need of assistance.[3] It is clear that in 1884 Emin still regarded himself as a representative of the Egyptian Government and it is exclusively to this body that his appeal for help was directed.

It was only at the time of the Mahdist attack on Amadi that Emin became convinced that 'if this affair turns out badly, nothing will be

---

[1] Junker, *Travels in Africa*, iii. 399-400. Until the second part of John A. Rowe's eagerly awaited study of Buganda 1856-1900 becomes available, there is no really satisfactory account of Buganda for the period 1884-1900, though many useful ones.

[2] *Tagebücher*, 14 Nov. 1884, iii. 59.

[3] *Tagebücher*, 17 Nov. 1884, iii. 60 (Extracts, V, p. 4).

left for us but a retreat to the south'.[1] By a retreat to the south Emin envisaged merely the removal of his headquarters to Dufile or Wadelai; Lado was to be retained, but purely as a military garrison.[2] Such a move had much to recommend it. Relations with Bunyoro and Buganda could be developed more easily from the south and in this way further letters might be sent to Zanzibar. At Dufile there were the two steamers *Khedive* and *Nyanza*, and south of Dufile the Nile was navigable all the way to Lake Albert—and the countryside was rich in grain. Should a Mahdist attack be launched on the province, the headquarters would be far more secure in the south, since Emin was convinced that even if Lado were to fall, the Mahdists would be unlikely to penetrate much further south into an area where the Mahdist ideology, the Islamic religion, and the Arabic language were all quite alien. Even if the Mahdists did advance, Emin could withdraw still further to Bunyoro, Buganda, or the region of Lake Victoria. 'There, the great chiefs Anfina, Kabrega and Mtesa will readily receive me, and from there communication with Egypt by Zanzibar might be possible.'[3] Emin did not envisage such a withdrawal as anything but a temporary possibility. Once communications were established with Egypt he expected to be reinforced, and eventually, when the reconquest of the Sudan took place, to be able to re-establish himself in Equatoria.

When the news arrived of the fall of Amadi in March 1885, therefore, Emin decided to bring his plan of a withdrawal to the south into the open. When he did so, he encountered the open opposition of his garrisons. Despite the arrival of Karam Allāh's ultimatum, Emin's soldiers refused to move. This first open expression of opposition to the idea of a retreat to the south by Emin's men contains all the elements which were to occur again later. In addition to a natural reluctance to move with their numerous dependants, and a distrust of 'foreign lands', Emin's garrisons regarded the whole idea of a new route of communication with Cairo via Zanzibar with the greatest suspicion. To them the only route to Cairo lay to the north, via Khartoum. And it was from this direction that any steamer, any relief, any authentic instructions, were expected to come. The intensity and persistence with which the garrisons in Equatoria clung to the belief that the Khedive's government continued in Khartoum,

---

[1] Emin to Schweinfurth, 6 Jan. 1885, *E.P. in C.A.*, pp. 475–6.
[2] Junker, op. cit. iii. 396.
[3] Emin to Schweinfurth, 6 Jan. 1885, cited above.

and that it would not abandon them, is one of the most remarkable and important features of the situation in Equatoria during the next few years.

But the Khedive's government in fact no longer existed in Khartoum. Emin first heard of the fall of Khartoum and the death of General Gordon through a letter from Karam Allāh which arrived at Lado on 18 April.[1] With this letter Emin received a copy of a letter from the Mahdi himself. Dated Khartoum, 28 January 1885, this letter convinced Emin that the fall of Khartoum was no longer a rumour.[2] Believed by Emin, the fall of Khartoum was disbelieved by almost everyone else. Emin's garrison refused to move and Emin was forced to give way. Anxious and despondent, he noted:

> There can be no longer any question of my going to the south, for on my leaving Lado, the whole card-house would fall together, and I should in all probability be held fast by my men. There have been voices here heard to say that we intend to lead the soldiers to the south and sell them to the great chiefs there to save ourselves . . . the road to the south is rejected on all hands.[3]

None the less, Emin continued to work to bring about a withdrawal from Lado. Certain local factors were in his favour. The loss of the Makaraka area (rich in grain) and the arrival of hundreds of refugees at Lado from Amadi and the area bordering on the Bahr al-Ghazal created the immediate prospect of famine. By the end of April it had become imperative to disperse the large numbers of people at Lado elsewhere. On 24 April Emin called a meeting of his officers and officials to discuss 'the measures to be adopted to save us from famine, and to guard against unnecessary exposure to danger'.[4] The meeting, during which Emin withdrew in order that the decision might be 'impartial', concluded by adopting a resolution which shows every sign of having been drawn up beforehand by Emin himself. It was decided that Emin and the other officials, together with the large numbers of women and children, should leave for the south, while the soldiers remained at Lado, as they later put it, 'to defend the honour of the Khedive'.[5] There seems little doubt that Emin's plan of a

[1] *Tagebücher*, 18 Apr. 1885, iii. 90.

[2] A copy of this letter translated into English is printed in F.O.C.P. 5433, 'Correspondence respecting the relief of Emin Pasha at Uganda', May 1887, p. 37.

[3] Emin to Junker, 1 Apr. 1885, printed in Junker, *Travels in Africa*, iii. 491–2.

[4] Emin to Schweinfurth, 1 Dec. 1885, *E.P. in C.A.*, p. 482.

[5] Report of the Officers, Soldiers, and Officials stationed in the Equatorial Province, 1890, Khartoum Archives, Cairint, 1/11/56.

withdrawal to the south was reluctantly agreed to for primarily local reasons and that the majority of the officers and soldiers in Emin's northern garrisons had no intention of applying its provisions to themselves. It is also clear that Emin's own withdrawal from Lado brought about the collapse of his authority in the north—the soldiers concluding that he had deserted them.[1] Emin himself foresaw this; why, therefore, did he persist in his determination to withdraw from Lado? It might appear that his action was a direct response to the fear of an imminent Mahdist attack. Certainly, this was an important factor. But there is also, I think, about Emin's withdrawal an element of a personal retreat from a situation which was rapidly becoming beyond his control. He was weary of coaxing the soldiers at Lado into some sort of order; their unreliability and oppression of the local population exasperated him, as they had done his predecessors. It is significant that Emin established his new headquarters not at Dufile —the largest and most obvious station in the south, but also the place where conditions most closely resembled those at Lado—but at Wadelai. Wadelai was not only the southernmost station, it was also at this time small and insignificant. Thus, it presented Emin with an opportunity to get away from the factions and intrigues of the larger stations and to establish a new headquarters amidst conditions which were largely unformed. At Wadelai Emin was also well placed not only to develop communications with Bunyoro and Buganda, but also to pursue his great interest as a naturalist and ethnologist in an area which had always been of greater fascination to him than almost anywhere else in Equatoria.

The fear of a Mahdist attack on Lado, in any case, soon receded. In June, on his way to the south, Emin heard that Karam Allāh and his forces were in full retreat back to the Bahr al-Ghazal, where a mutiny had broken out. Later, after the death of the Mahdi, Karam Allāh left for the north, followed by his straggling army. Thus, the expected attack by the Mahdists on Lado in 1884-5 never took place; and by the end of 1885 the Mahdists had also disappeared from the Bahr al-Ghazal.[2]

On 10 July 1885 Emin arrived at Wadelai, the place which was henceforth to serve as his headquarters. The station, situated on the west bank of the Nile about thirty-five miles north of Lake Albert,

---

[1] Statement of 'Uthmān Latīf, 1890, Khartoum Archives, Cairint, 3/14/237. Statement of Basili Boktor, 1890, ibid., Cairint, 1/11/56.

[2] R. O. Collins, *The Southern Sudan*, p. 50.

had first been established by Emin in 1879. It occupied the best riverain site south of Dufile; it was situated in the Alur country, an area rich in grain; most important of all, it provided the best position from which Emin could develop communications with Bunyoro and Buganda and, via the C.M.S. missionaries in Buganda, with Zanzibar and Egypt.

The establishment of these communications now became Emin's primary concern. A frequent exchange of letters and envoys developed between Emin, Kabarega, and the missionaries in Buganda. Kabarega showed a shrewd ability to turn Emin's position to his own advantage; the missionaries exhibited a constant fear of arousing the hostility of the Kabaka; and Mwanga remained as suspicious as Mutesa had been of the manœuvres of the 'Turks' to the north. The situation was greatly complicated by the recurrent wars and skirmishes between Bunyoro and Buganda. By the beginning of 1886, Emin had established a modest trade in goods between Equatoria, Bunyoro, and Buganda, and a channel of communication by which letters could be sent to and received from Zanzibar, Egypt, and Europe.

Communication with Zanzibar lay through the eager hands of Alexander Mackay, the leading C.M.S. missionary in Buganda. This irascible and determined Scot had studied engineering at Edinburgh University before joining the Church Missionary Society. After his arrival in Buganda in 1878, successive Kabakas appear to have found his engineering abilities, and especially his usefulness as a gunsmith, at least as interesting as his missionary zeal. Outwitting and outlasting a series of lesser companions, Mackay defied repeated orders to return home, and periodic disputes with Buganda's rulers, to play a major role in the establishment of the Anglican Church in Buganda. An imperialist of the most 'forward' school, Mackay showed no hesitation when it came to politics. His influence on Emin Pasha was considerable, and his importance in the sequence of events which resulted in the British involvement in the interior of East Africa up to his death in 1890 has perhaps been underrated.

Emin at first cast Mackay in the role of a useful postman and entrepreneur, but after the beginning of 1886 Emin relied more and more on Mackay for information and advice and Mackay came to occupy a central role in the sending of news, goods, and relief to Emin in Equatoria.

In January 1886 Junker at last decided to leave Equatoria and attempt to reach Zanzibar via Bunyoro and Buganda. While he was in Bunyoro in February, Junker received a letter from Mackay brought by Emin's most useful messenger throughout this period, Muhammad Biri.[1] In this letter Mackay reported news of the events in the Sudan down to the previous November, the fall of Khartoum, the death of Gordon, and the abandonment of the Sudan by Egypt. Before setting out for Buganda on what was to be a successful journey to the coast, Junker forwarded Mackay's letter to Emin, along with others from Sir John Kirk (the British Consul-General at Zanzibar), and Nubar Pasha (the Egyptian Prime Minister in Cairo). These, the first letters to reach Emin since April 1883, arrived at Wadelai on 26 February 1886. 'The Egyptian despatch', Emin noted,

informs me that the Government is unable to assist us for the Sudan is to be given up, gives me *carte blanche* to take any measures I please, should I decide to leave the country, and, further, authorises me to draw on the English Consul-General at Zanzibar. It is a cool business despatch, in the fullest sense of the word, not acknowledging by a single word the cares I have borne for three years . . . nor giving me a word of encouragement in the superhuman task of leading home the soldiers, which now lies before me . . . In Egypt and elsewhere they have certainly no notion of the diffi- culties of my situation. They simply suggest to me the way to Zanzibar, just as they would a walk to Shubra.[2]

After three years of uncertainty, Emin now had confirmation from a European source of events in the Sudan, and a clear indication of the attitude of the Egyptian Government to Equatoria. Nubar Pasha's letter made it clear that Emin could hope for nothing in the way of relief or assistance from Egypt. The suggestion was that Emin and his garrisons should withdraw. Emin, however, did not 'see the slightest ground for believing that our Soudanese officers and troops, except in a few rare cases, will consent to go to Egypt'.[2] In a letter to Dr. Schweinfurth on 3 March, Emin assessed the situation with remarkable candour:

The greater part of our soldiers, coming, as they do, from our own districts (Makaraka, Dinka, etc.) and having never seen Egypt, naturally prefer to remain here . . . while the Negro soldier, sent hither from Egypt . . . has forgotten in the lapse of years what strict discipline means, and, further, has adapted himself to the country to such a degree that it has quite taken the place of his native land. Each has his family, often a very large one, if all its dependants be counted, and each has his couple of goats

---

[1] Junker, *Travels in Africa*, iii. 532. See also H. B. Thomas, 'Muhammad Biri', *Uganda Journal*, xxiv, no. 1 (1960).

[2] Emin to Schweinfurth, 3 Mar. 1886, *E.P. in C.A.*, pp. 495–7.

or cows. Everyone knows that the journey is long and the toils great, that many days of hunger and hardship lie before him, and that when he arrives in Egypt the loose bonds of discipline will be tightened again . . . Then consider how little attention has been shown to our soldiers from Khartoum, how they have been left without supplies, without clothing, without pay—but enough, you can now understand why the men do not wish to move. Besides, it is quite impossible to make a Sudanese understand why the Government has given up the Sudan, and he refuses in so many words to believe that a horde of Danāqla [Mahdists] is able to crush a well-trained army. Even now, it is believed here, that the news of General Hicks's defeat in Kordofan is a fiction . . . Now, if I send copies of the letter from Egypt, written in French too (an error much to be regretted—it should have been written in Arabic), it will at least be considered a fabrication, that is, a device of my own, and will not be obeyed . . . Of course it would be best to expedite our retreat, but how am I to set about it?[1]

At first Emin drew up plans for a withdrawal from the province, but these were soon abandoned in the face of the opposition of his garrisons.[2] When Nubar Pasha's letter was read at Lado and Dufile it was disbelieved, as Emin had predicted, and the garrison at Lado sent word that they would never come to the south to be sold as slaves to Kabarega and that they would oppose anyone who tried to make them. Emin feared that if he persisted with his plans for withdrawal 'discipline would soon entirely disappear'.[3] He therefore decided to withdraw from further communication with the northern garrisons and disband them. In fact the garrisons soon disbanded themselves. When grain supplies began to run out at Lado, 250 of the soldiers decamped to the Makaraka area, and in the next dry season fire almost entirely destroyed the station. The remaining soldiers moved to Rejaf and by the beginning of 1887 Lado was deserted.[4] The situation amongst the southern garrisons was scarcely more encouraging and everywhere Emin observed that 'the disintegrating process is gradually taking its course, and the province [is] falling to pieces'.[5] Weary, dejected, and in poor health, Emin wrote to his friend, R. W. Felkin, of his own reluctance to leave Equatoria and return to Egypt:

. . . That I personally am in no hurry to return to Egypt you will no doubt easily understand; the work to which I have devoted my efforts and hopes

[1] Emin to Schweinfurth, 3 Mar. 1886, *E.P. in C.A.*, pp. 497–8.
[2] See Emin to Sir John Kirk, 27 Feb. 1886, enclosed in Holmwood to Iddesleigh, 23 Sept. 1886, F.O. 84/1775.
[3] Emin to Junker, 29 June 1886, printed in Schweitzer, i. 205.
[4] Emin to Junker, 15 Apr. 1887, ibid. i. 217.
[5] Emin to Junker, 27 June 1886, ibid. i. 204.

during the last ten years, for the sake of which I have suffered gladly difficulties and hardships, is now broken down and so all that I have accomplished and all my struggles have been in vain. The knowledge of a wasted life, of a useless work, hangs like a veil over the future and robs me of all joy in life and of all courage for further efforts. Shall I go to Egypt and be laughed at? Or, at the best, after a few cool words of thanks see myself dismissed? . . . It is quite clear to me that there would be no calling or position for me in Egypt after the loss of the Soudan, and I should therefore be more of a burden than of use to the great lords there. I must therefore be thankful to the soldiers that they will not let me go and must accommodate myself to my fate.[1]

*   *   *

Events took a new turning with the arrival at Wadelai on 2 July 1886 of an important letter from Mackay. In this letter Mackay urged Emin not to withdraw from Equatoria but to remain where he was. Egypt may have abandoned the Sudan, and Britain may have failed to relieve General Gordon, but, observed Mackay, 'there is a great interest in the affairs of East Africa in these times. Germany today wants many colonies and in the neighbourhood of Zanzibar Bismarck has already . . . seized two or three districts. England will also do something in East Africa, she only wants a good opportunity . . .'[2] In Emin's situation in Equatoria Mackay had come to see precisely that opportunity. In letters to the C.M.S. headquarters in London Mackay had elaborated on his ideas for a British Consular presence in Buganda, or, even better, for 'the establishment of a Free State, as on the Congo, to include the whole of East Africa from the Tanganyika [Lake] to the coast, and Equator to the Zambezi'.[3] Such vague and Utopian schemes were soon abandoned as the national rivalry of the European powers over the partition of East Africa increased. In a series of letters to the British Consul-General at Zanzibar Mackay outlined the great opportunities he saw for Britain in the East African interior. 'The future of the Victoria Lake', he declared, 'will depend very much upon the relations between this country [Buganda] and England . . . You say truly "Better the Germans

---

[1] Emin to R. W. Felkin, 5 May 1886, copy in M.P., F.7.
[2] Mackay to Emin (in German), 2 June 1886, *Tagebücher*, 4 July 1886, iii. 239–40 (Extracts, vi, pp. 158–9).
[3] Mackay to Hutchinson, 2 May 1886, printed in F.O.C.P. 5433, 'Correspondence respecting the relief of Emin Pasha at Uganda', pp. 93–4. See also Mackay to the C.M.S. Committee, 22 Aug. 1886, ibid., pp. 94–100.

than the French". But better the English than either.'[1] Mackay was determined that Emin in Equatoria must receive outside support, but he was decidedly nervous when a German, Dr. Fischer, set out to bring it. 'Who can tell what plans may be conceived by Fischer and Emin when they think of Berlin?', he commented darkly.[2] Britain could afford to let the Germans steam into the swamps of the Makata valley. The miserable wastes of the northern Sudan might well be left to the Mahdi,

but there is no Mahdism in the whole vast region south of the Bahr al-Ghazal . . . Between here [Buganda] and the Ghazal are the finest provinces in all Africa, in fact, the only part of East Africa worth much. You have, besides, in Emin's peculiar position there a rare combination of circumstances which I cannot believe you will fail to take advantage of.[3]

This championing of Emin's cause by Mackay was by no means disinterested. Mackay believed that in Emin's presence in Equatoria lay 'the nucleus of a more civilised power' which, if strengthened and brought under British control, would serve as 'a lever . . . for holding in check the pretensions' of the Kabaka of Buganda.[4]

To Emin himself, Mackay now expanded on the possibilities of his position:

The old government at Khartoum no longer exists, but you can deliver over a large territory into English hands, if you wish to do so. Remain there, dear Sir . . . a good governor such as you are, should take over the whole territory of the Nile sources. I know quite well that you could bring all this about if you took it in hand. You must, however, be supported and England will without doubt help you if you say so.[5]

Mackay's encouragement, and the grand prospect which he outlined for the future, made a profound impression on Emin. After ten years of neglect in the Egyptian service, Emin had come

[1] Mackay to Sir John Kirk, 8 and 22 Dec. 1885, enclosed in Kirk to F.O., 12 Mar. 1886, F.O. 84/1773. See also R. Oliver, *The Missionary Factor in East Africa*, pp. 130-1.
[2] Mackay to Kirk, 14 May 1886, enclosed in Holmwood to F.O., 23 Sept. 1886, F.O. 84/1775.
[3] Mackay to Kirk, 24 Aug. 1886, enclosed in Holmwood to Iddesleigh, 18 Oct. 1886, F.O. 84/1775.
[4] Mackay to Kirk, 26 Dec. 1886, enclosed in Holmwood to Salisbury, 9 Apr. 1887, F.O. 84/1852.
[5] Mackay to Emin (in German), 2 June 1886, *Tagebücher*, 4 July 1886, iii. 239-40 (Extracts, VI, pp. 158-9).

to the conviction that the time had come 'to break loose from the old regime' which had, in any case, abandoned both him and Equatoria. Emin also feared that even if the Sudan were reconquered, it would come directly under Ottoman control and he would be relieved of 'Egyptian mismanagement only to be handed over to a still worse plight as a Turkish dependant and menial'.[1] The prospect of establishing Equatoria as a British protectorate was infinitely more attractive. On 6 July 1886, four days after receiving Mackay's letter, Emin replied:

To your question, am I prepared to aid in the annexation of this country by England, I answer frankly 'Yes'. If England intends to occupy these lands and to civilise them, I am ready to hand over the government into the hands of England, and I believe that thereby I should be doing a service to mankind and lending an advance to civilisation . . .[2]

In accompanying letters to the British Consul-General at Zanzibar, to R. W. Felkin, and to Charles Allen (the Secretary of the Anti-Slavery Society in London), Emin made clear his hope that 'at the present time, when the European Powers are racing neck and neck to gain possession of districts in Africa', England would 'take advantage of the position in which we find ourselves . . . to occupy the whole of our province'.[3]

It was Mackay, therefore, who first suggested to Emin that in England lay the future source of outside support for Equatoria, and it was to England—'the champion of humanity and justice'[4]—that Emin henceforth looked in preference to all other European powers. When Junker wrote that he was urging, in letters to Europe, the incorporation of Equatoria in King Leopold's Congo State, Emin at once feared 'that Stanley and others will not be slow to profit of the occasion and push ahead as quickly as they can'. 'Personally', Emin commented, 'I do not like at all the perspective

---

[1] Emin to R. W. Felkin, 22 July 1886, M.P., F.7. An edited version of this letter is printed in Felkin's Introduction to Schweitzer, i. xxix–xxx.

[2] Emin to Mackay, 6 July 1886, enclosed in Mackay to Kirk, 24 Aug. 1886, enclosed in Holmwood to Iddesleigh, 18 Oct. 1886, F.O. 84/1775.

[3] Emin to R. W. Felkin, 7 July 1886, printed in R. W. Felkin, 'The Position of Dr. Emin Bey', *Scottish Geographical Magazine*, Dec. 1886, p. 715; Emin to Charles Allen, 22 July 1886 (a tantalizing fragment of a copy), A.S.S. 155/137; Emin to Sir John Kirk, 7 July 1886, enclosed in Holmwood to Iddesleigh, 18 Oct. 1886, F.O. 84/1775.

[4] The phrase used by Emin in his letter to Mackay, 6 July 1886, cited above.

Junker opens me. I think that later or sooner, the whole Congo scheme must explode; a neutral state seems as Utopian a being as a neutral man.'[1] Mackay feared that the British Government would be so slow to act over Emin's position that Emin would turn to the Germans. Mackay even suggested to Emin that he should 'take advantage of Germany's desires before they cool down, either to turn them directly to your benefit, or indirectly, by expressing your readiness to do so should England fail you. In diplomacy it is well to have a reserve, and to take advantage of the jealousies of nations.'[2] Emin, however, showed no great readiness to turn to Germany. He regarded the recent German incursion into East Africa with great scepticism and thought the Germans quite untried in colonial matters. In his reply to Mackay's suggestion, Emin concluded, 'You will therefore not blame me if I abstain from your advice . . . viz. to secure assistance from the quarter most likely to afford it. I appealed through your kind interposition to England, and I shall abide to this appeal without addressing whomsoever.'[3]

The establishment of Equatoria as part of the British Empire was therefore Emin's long-term hope. The acquisition of arms, ammunition, and supplies to enable him to maintain his position at Wadelai was, however, the immediate necessity. In a letter to Mackay in October 1886, Emin outlined his proposal as to how both these objectives might be achieved:

I never had the pretension of a great military expedition being sent to relieve us. All that I request is that some paltry caravans of ammunition and arms be started from Mombasa to Mount Masaba [Mt. Elgon] . . . from whence I am able to fetch it; that some intelligent officers be sent out with whom I may confer, or to whom, eventually, I would hand over the government of the country if my services be not requested. Once strengthened in this manner, the organisation of the British Protectorate as a *fait accompli* is very easily done . . . Your Consul-General in Egypt informs our Government that some small caravans are to be started for supplying us with arms and other things, and all is said.[4]

The one thing on which Emin became increasingly set was that he

[1] Emin to Mackay, 1 Oct. 1886, enclosed in Holmwood to Salisbury, 9 Apr. 1887, F.O. 84/1852.
[2] Mackay to Emin, 15 Nov. 1886, *Tagebücher*, 17–23 Jan. 1887, iii. 307–11.
[3] Emin to Mackay, 7 Feb. 1887, enclosed in Macdonald to Salisbury, 27 Aug. 1887, F.O. 84/1853.
[4] Emin to Mackay, 1 Oct. 1886, enclosed in Holmwood to Salisbury, 9 Apr. 1887, F.O. 84/1852.

himself would not abandon Equatoria. Writing to his friend, R. W. Felkin, Emin declared:

I remain here the last and only representative of Gordon's staff. It therefore falls to me, and is my bounden duty, to follow up the road he showed us. Sooner or later a bright future must dawn for these countries; sooner or later these people will be drawn into the circle of the ever-advancing civilised world. For twelve long years I have striven and toiled, and sown the seeds for future harvest . . . Shall I now give up the work because a way may soon open to the coast? Never!

If England wishes really to help us she must try, in the first place, to conclude some treaty with Uganda and Unyoro . . . A safe road to the coast must be opened up, and one which shall not be at the mercy of the moods of childish kings or disreputable Arabs. This is all we want, and it is the only thing necessary to permit of the steady development of these countries . . . Evacuate our territory? Certainly not![1]

[1] Emin to R. W. Felkin, 17 Apr. 1887, *E.P. in C.A.*, pp. 508-11.

CHAPTER III

The Sending of the Expedition

IN the summer of 1886 the British Foreign Office was far more concerned with events in Bulgaria than with the situation of an obscure German doctor in an obscure province of the Sudan. Emin was almost unknown in Europe at this time outside scientific circles. Those who did know of him had hoped that after the fall of Khartoum in January 1885 he, together with Junker and Casati, who were believed to be with him, would retreat south either to Buganda or to one of the recently established stations on the Upper Congo. When they failed to appear, Junker's brother commissioned a German, Dr. Fischer, to lead an expedition to Equatoria from the East African coast. At about the same time another expedition led by an Austrian, Oscar Lenz, set out to reach Equatoria via the Congo river. Both attempts were failures. While Emin hopefully awaited their arrival in Equatoria, neither expedition succeeded in getting anywhere near the province. Fischer's caravan was forced to turn back on the outskirts of Buganda owing to the hostility of the Kabaka. When it arrived back in Zanzibar in June 1886, seventy men had either been killed or had died of famine and Kirk described it as 'a total failure'.[1] The experience of Fischer's expedition reinforced the view that the route recently opened to the interior through the Masailand by Joseph Thomson presented enormous difficulties. Meanwhile, the latest news of Oscar Lenz was that he was still at Stanley Falls with diminishing prospects of advancing into the as yet unexplored area of the eastern Congo, let alone reaching Wadelai.[2]

From Emin himself nothing had been heard since November 1884. Nubar Pasha's letter to Emin of May 1885, informing him that the Egyptian Government had abandoned Equatoria, was written from a position of admitted ignorance concerning 'the exact circumstances in which you and your garrisons at present may be'.[3]

---

[1] Kirk to F.O., 25 June 1886, F.O. 84/1774.
[2] *Le Mouvement géographique* (Brussels), 21 Nov. and 5 Dec. 1886.
[3] Nubar to Emin, 27 May 1885 (in French), *Tagebücher*, 26 Feb. 1886 iii. 170-1. (An English translation is given in Schweitzer, i. 192-3.)

The letter, therefore, had been sent not to give instructions but 'to leave you unlimited freedom of action . . . to do the best for yourself and the garrisons'.[1] Whether or not Emin and his garrisons withdrew from Equatoria was at this time regarded as less important than that the Egyptian Government should serve notice that it had abandoned the territory. This, it would seem, was the essential purpose of the letter which Nubar had written to Emin at the instigation of Sir Evelyn Baring, the British Consul-General in Cairo.

As early as November 1883, when discussing the possibility of a total evacuation of the Sudan, Baring had decided that although Egypt might some day return to the northern Sudan, there could 'be no question of the Egyptian Government reconquering any of the provinces south of Khartoum'.[2] Baring never changed this opinion. The frontier of Egypt to be held against the Mahdists might ebb and flow with the fortunes of the Government in Cairo and the state of Egyptian finances. But about the abandonment of the southern Sudan, Baring remained adamant. Even in 1898 he was quite prepared to give away the area to anyone who would take it—to King Leopold, to the Negus Menelik, even to the French, if they would stop their 'constant heckling' in Egypt.[3]

Baring considered the southern Sudan to be the least profitable part of an unprofitable region which 'hung like a dead-weight round the necks of Egyptian reformers' such as himself.[4] In 1884-5, when the Egyptian withdrawal from the area south of Wadi Halfa had created a major political crisis in Egypt, the evacuation of the southern garrisons had been scarcely contemplated. The area was regarded as certainly beyond British and, it was hoped, beyond Egyptian responsibilities. When General Gordon, on his last mission to Khartoum, had put forward a plan to send five steamers to the south to evacuate the Equatorial garrisons, the Khedive had refused to sanction such a scheme.[5] In 1884 Baring wrote:

I do not see how we are to get away the distant garrisons in Bahr al-

[1] Schweitzer, i. 193.
[2] Baring to Granville, 22 Nov. 1883, F.O. 633/6/14.
[3] G. N. Sanderson, *England, Europe and the Upper Nile* (Edinburgh, 1965), p. 19, citing Cromer to Salisbury, 15 Nov. 1898, F.O. 1/35.
[4] Cromer, *Modern Egypt*, 2 vols. (London, 1908), i. 392.
[5] Gordon to Baring, 28 Jan. 1884, F.O. 633/7/266. Khedive to Gordon, 21 Sept. 1884 (received at Khartoum 25 Nov. 1884 via the steamer *Bordein*), F.O. 78/3679. *Report on the Siege of Khartoum*, by Mohammed Nushi Pasha and others, ii. 191 (b), Khartoum Archives. See also B. M. Allen, *Gordon and the Sudan* (London, 1931), p. 351.

Ghazal and the Equatorial Province, but they are in no danger, I fancy, so long as they stop quiet; and as most of the men have what is called 'formed relations in the country'—that is to say, that they have each some half-a-dozen to a dozen wives—I expect they are pretty happy where they are.[1]

Subsequently, Baring stated, there was some 'vague talk' of Emin's relief, but the hope was that after receiving Nubar's letter, Emin would withdraw with his garrisons from Equatoria on his own account, and that Sir John Kirk, the British Consul-General at Zanzibar, might be able to assist with arrangements along the route to the East African coast.[2]

In 1886 Sir John Kirk was preoccupied with events in Buganda. The arrival of successive European-led expeditions on the borders of Buganda had increased the suspicions of Kabaka Mwanga that the ultimate intention of the Europeans was 'to eat the country'. Mwanga became increasingly hostile towards European influence and an outburst of anti-Christian activity began in Buganda which included the murder of Bishop Hannington and the persecution of Christians at the Kabaka's court.[3] The position of the C.M.S. missionaries in Buganda, led by Mackay, appeared to be extremely precarious and formed the main subject of Sir John Kirk's dispatches about the area at this time. The position of Emin warranted no more than the occasional footnote. In January 1886 there was still no news of him.[4] In March Emin was believed to be safe and in communication with Kabarega of Bunyoro.[5] With the outbreak of war between Buganda and Bunyoro the fate of Emin once more became an open question. In June letters arrived from Emin himself, dated 16 November 1884, and letters of a much more recent date came from Mackay in Buganda.[6] From these it was clear that Emin was still at Wadelai, having so far withstood any Mahdist attacks on Equatoria, and that with him were both Junker and Casati. As further letters from Emin were believed to be on the way, it appeared

[1] Baring to Granville, 14 Jan. 1884, F.O. 633/6/21.
[2] Baring to Kirk, 30 May 1885, Zanzibar Secretariat Archives, E. 84, cited in D. A. Low, 'The British and Uganda 1862–1900', D.Phil. thesis (Oxford, 1957), p. 91.
[3] Mackay to Kirk, 28 June 1886, enclosed in Holmwood to Iddesleigh, 23 Sept. 1886, F.O. 84/1775. See also J. A. Rowe, 'The Purge of Christians at Mwanga's Court', *J.A.H.*, v, no. 1 (1964).
[4] Kirk to F.O., 5 Jan. 1886, F.O. 84/1777.
[5] Kirk to F.O., 12 Mar. 1886, F.O. 84/1777.
[6] Emin to Kirk, 16 Nov. 1884, and Emin to Mackay, 16 Nov. 1884, both enclosed in Holmwood to Iddesleigh, 23 Sept. 1886, F.O. 84/1775. Kirk to F.O., 25 June 1886, F.O. 84/1774.

best to defer any consideration of possible action until they arrived. Kirk was in any case due to leave Zanzibar a week later on leave, and, as it turned out, not to return. The summer months—rarely the most active of times in the Foreign Office—brought no new developments other than the approval in July of Frederick Holmwood as Acting British Consul-General at Zanzibar.

*   *   *

The event which awakened an interest in Europe in the situation in the southern Sudan was the emergence of Junker from Equatoria in the summer of 1886. Having left Emin at Wadelai in January, Junker had been delayed for some time in Bunyoro. In June he was in Buganda. By August he was on his way to the coast, bringing with him Emin's letters to numerous correspondents in Britain and Germany and the first authentic news of the province since 1884.[1]

Like most European travellers in Africa in the late nineteenth century, Junker did not describe his experiences in particularly moderate language. To his friend Dr. Schweinfurth, Junker wrote from Msalala, the C.M.S. station at the south of Lake Victoria, in August:

Dear Friend,
    Escaped at last from the clutches of Mwanga at Uganda, I find myself here this morning, and make use of the last courier that departs from the station for the coast to send two lines to you . . .
    Must we believe that nothing will ever be done for these unhappy Equatorial Provinces?
    Write, write on, dear friend! Send forth words of thunder that will open the eyes of all the world! I am most urgent that all that is possible may be done. It is absolutely necessary that Emin Bey should receive help without delay . . . It is with this hope alone that I essay to return to Europe.[2]

Junker's sense of the dramatic was not without its effect on Holmwood, who was already exhibiting that proneness to enthusiasm which the Foreign Office in London found so tiresome and which

---

[1] For Junker's journey after leaving Wadelai, see W. Junker, *Travels in Africa*, iii, ch. xiii.

[2] Junker to Schweinfurth, 16 Aug. 1886, published in *The Times*, 27 Nov. 1886. The full version of this letter, with enthusiastic comments by its recipient, was published in French in *Le Mouvement géographique* (Brussels), 21 Nov. 1886.

was later to contribute to his removal from his post.[1] On receiving Junker's news, Holmwood cabled to London at once:

> News from Uganda, 12 July. Junker left for Zanzibar. Terrible persecution broken out, all native Christians being put to death. Missionaries in extreme danger; urgently requests our demanding from King their being allowed to withdraw. Emin at Wadelai holds province, but urgently needs ammunition and stores. Objects, if he can avoid it, deserting the 4,000 loyal Egyptian subjects there. No time to be lost if assistance decided on.[2]

This telegram caused some perplexity at the Foreign Office. Sir Percy Anderson, the head of the African section, confessed that on the few occasions when events in the southern Sudan had been discussed since the death of General Gordon, the position of Emin had been lost sight of altogether, and the news that he was still holding out had been received with considerable surprise.[3] Junker's news that Emin was still in Equatoria and in need of relief was at first interpreted as a request for a caravan of supplies and ammunition to be sent from the East African coast. The matter was referred to the War Office for detailed consideration, where Brackenbury remarked that plans for such an expedition were not kept in stock at his department: 'our interests there are not so great that we have ever made this a special subject of study.'[4]

Meanwhile, Holmwood was instructed to write to the Kabaka of Buganda and, with the help of the Sultan of Zanzibar, to endeavour to persuade Mwanga to allow the C.M.S. missionaries to withdraw.[5] Holmwood interpreted this as permission to write to Mwanga in the peremptory manner which Mackay had long advocated. He accordingly did so, entrusting the delivery of the letter to the doubtful care of Suliman bin Zuheir, considered by Mackay as 'the ringleader and acknowledged chief' of the Arab party in

---

[1] The circumstances leading to the transfer of Holmwood from Zanzibar are related in Lady Gwendolen Cecil, *Life of Salisbury*, vol. iv (London, 1932), 42-3. See also, E. de Groot, 'Great Britain and Germany in Zanzibar: Consul Holmwood's Papers, 1886-1887', *Journal of Modern History*, vol. xxv, no. 2, June 1953.

[2] Holmwood to Iddesleigh, telegram, 23 Sept. 1886, F.O. 84/1775.

[3] Minute by Sir Percy Anderson, 18 Oct. 1886, on Holmwood to Iddesleigh, cited above.

[4] Brackenbury to Wolseley, 29 Sept. 1886, F.O. 84/1775. R. Gray, op. cit., p. 197. G. N. Sanderson, op. cit., p. 29. (To both of these works I owe a great deal throughout this Chapter.)

[5] Iddesleigh to Holmwood, 25 Sept. 1886, F.O.C.P. 5433, no. 3.

Buganda.[1] Holmwood's blunder was not without its effects on the
situation in Buganda, but eventually, in July 1887, Mackay was
allowed to withdraw to the southern end of Lake Victoria.

The incident reflects the general British policy towards the interior
of East Africa at this time. Such interests as Britain had in East
Africa were centred on Zanzibar and the coast, as they had been for
half a century. As far as the interior was concerned, the British
Government was no more prepared to back up the missionaries in
Buganda in 1886 than it was to support the missionaries in the
Lake Nyasa region two years later.[2] Buganda was regarded with a
certain caution and respect, although the numbers of men and arms
its Kabaka was believed to be able to put in the field were probably
exaggerated.[3] The interior of East Africa presented a sphere for
diplomacy and if necessary for a policy of withdrawal. It was
emphatically not an area for a new imperial advance.

Yet this was precisely what Mackay and Holmwood had in mind.
In May Mackay had declared that

it is no solution of the difficulty of Emin's position to try to remove him
from his post, just as it is no solution of the difficulty of our position merely
to desert our work. Dr. Emin needs only to have his position strengthened
by securing the protection of the one Power which is able to protect the
cause of liberty and good government. Besides, had Emin been anxious to
leave, he could with a few hundred of his soldiers have easily made a dash
for the coast, either through the Masailand or this way [Buganda], asking
no permission from Mwanga or any one else.[4]

Holmwood's ideas concerning British policy towards East Africa
were similar to those of Mackay and differed markedly from those of
the Foreign Office. Holmwood believed that England should abandon
her traditional priority of supremacy on the coast, and concentrate
on the Lake Victoria region and the Upper Nile. Whilst pressing for 'a
new and comprehensive Egyptian policy', Holmwood's real concern

[1] Mackay to Holmwood, 10 Aug. 1887, F.O. 84/1854. R. Oliver, *The Missionary Factor in East Africa* (London, 1965), 2nd edn., pp. 106-8.

[2] R. Robinson and J. A. Gallagher with Alice Denny, *Africa and the Victorians* (London, 1961), pp. 199, 124.

[3] The War Office reported in Oct. 1886 that 'the King of Uganda is said to have 40,000 or 50,000 fighting men'. Memorandum by Brackenbury, 1 Oct. 1886, F.O. 84/1775. Emin Pasha, who twice visited Buganda, estimated in 1876 that the Buganda army consisted of 2–3,000 men. *Tagebücher*, 31 July 1876, i. 139.

[4] Mackay to Kirk, 14 May 1886, enclosed in Holmwood to Iddesleigh, 23 Sept. 1886, F.O. 84/1775.

was that Britain should secure the short line of communication from the East African coast to the Sudan, 'the back door to Egypt'. Once this was done he had no doubts that 'immense strides towards the real opening up of the interior will rapidly follow'.[1] Whilst the Foreign Office in London insisted on dealing with the problems of Equatoria and Buganda separately, Mackay and Holmwood urged their simultaneous solution. Acting under the misapprehension that any expedition organized to relieve Emin Pasha would be sent under the auspices of the Egyptian Government, Holmwood wrote to Sir Evelyn Baring in Cairo on 25 September:

> Both Dr. Junker and Mr. Mackay strongly urge the necessity of the immediate relief of Wadelai, if it is not to be abandoned to the same fate as that which overtook Khartoum . . . I would, however, suggest that, should it be decided to relieve Emin, this would be a good opportunity for dealing at the same time with Uganda, the infamous conduct of whose King has for many years been prejudicial to the development of the interior . . . Were Uganda freed from this tyrant, the Equatorial Province . . . would be within eight weeks' post of Zanzibar, and a safe depot on the Albert Nyanza would provide a base from which any further operations that might be decided upon for the retention of the Upper Nile could be undertaken effectively and without anxiety.[2]

Holmwood went on to outline plans not merely for a trading caravan but for a military expedition consisting of at least 1,200 porters under a body of 500 'seasoned Nubian or Egyptian troops under experienced leaders'. The Sultan of Zanzibar might be induced to send 'a few companies of his well-armed native force under Brigadier Mathews'. Once united with Emin's own soldiers, this would provide 'an overwhelming force' capable of 'dealing with Uganda'.[2]

Holmwood's grand vistas of imperial expansion eight hundred miles in the interior of East Africa came in for some caustic comments at the War Office, to which the whole subject had been referred. All the authorities were in agreement. To embark upon an armed expedition into the little-known regions of Uganda would be the height of folly.[3] To send even a small expedition inland from Mombasa would be at best 'a perilous undertaking'. If the King of Buganda

---

[1] Holmwood to Sir Percy Anderson, 23 Nov. 1886, F.O. 84/1776.

[2] Holmwood to Baring, 25 Sept. 1886, enclosed in Portal to Iddesleigh, 19 Oct. 1886, F.O. 78/3930.

[3] Memorandum by Wolseley, 2 Oct. 1886, enclosed in Thompson to Currie, 2 Oct. 1886, F.O.C.P. 5433, no. 8.

were hostile 'it would be almost madness to do so'.[1] The most that could be recommended was that a small caravan of supplies might be sent to the southern end of Lake Victoria to await Emin and his people if they cared to get themselves out of Equatoria and withdraw to the south. As Wolseley remarked: 'if Emin Bey, with 4,000 Egyptian troops, and his knowledge of the country . . . is unable to reach Lake Victoria Nyanza, it is useless to talk of our sending a column to his relief of "500 seasoned Egyptian troops".'[2] Since the whole matter revolved around the action of the King of Buganda, Wolseley concluded that 'the question should, I think, be regarded as one for diplomacy, and not a military one'. Wolseley suggested that perhaps a small diplomatic mission might be sent to Buganda to bribe the Kabaka to release the missionaries and open the way for Emin to withdraw. Lord Salisbury thought this last suggestion might be a possibility, particularly if such a mission could come 'within the very narrow surplus at the command of the Egyptian Treasury'. Concerning any such schemes as Holmwood's, Salisbury was quite emphatic: 'An armed expedition is quite out of the question. It simply means war with Uganda conducted out of British resources . . . If a fierce persecution is going on at Uganda at this moment, it may not be prudent to send any servant of the Crown there. We might have to rescue or avenge him.' Salisbury's lack of interest in a British advance towards the Upper Nile at this time, and his pre-occupation with pushing through the Anglo-German Agreement, are reflected in his often-quoted conclusion: 'I think the Germans should be placed in possession of our information. It is really their business if Emin is a German.'[3]

[1] Memorandum by Leverson, 1 Oct. 1886, enclosed in above.
[2] Memorandum by Wolseley, cited above.
[3] Minute by Salisbury, n.d. (19?) Oct. 1886, from Balmoral, on Holmwood to Iddesleigh, 23 Sept. 1886, F.O. 84/1775. The idea of referring the matter to Germany had originated with Anderson and been approved by Iddesleigh. Memo. by Anderson, 15 Oct. 1886, F.O. 84/1775. Note by Iddesleigh on Pauncefote to Iddesleigh, 18 Oct. 1886, F.O. 84/1775. G. N. Sanderson (*England, Europe and the Upper Nile*, p. 30) implies that Emin's offer of his province to Britain was known to Salisbury before this first minute on the subject of an expedition. This is open to doubt because Salisbury's minute is not dated. Sanderson suggests 19 Oct. I would agree. Emin's offer first reached the F.O. in Holmwood's telegram to Iddlesleigh of 17 Oct. (F.O. 84/1775). In the memorandum by Anderson of 18 Oct., summarizing all the papers on the matter laid before Salisbury at Balmoral, there is no mention of Emin's offer (Memorandum by Anderson, 18 Oct. 1886, F.O. 84/1775). Nor does Salisbury refer to this aspect of the case. And Sir John Kirk, on 19 Oct., specifically states that 'Emin's letter of November 1884

Emin's position was, however, beginning to attract popular attention in England and Anderson observed that 'there may be a strong feeling in favour of saving this able and gallant man and the last of the Egyptian garrisons'.[1] On 29 October Charles Allen, the Secretary of the Anti-Slavery Society, published in *The Times* the letter which he had received from Emin the previous day.[2] The situation which Emin described in this letter was an immensely appealing one to the Victorian public. Only the previous year failure to act promptly had resulted in the death of Gordon at Khartoum. Emin now appeared as 'a second Gordon' in danger of being left to the same fate.[3] 'Having betrayed the master', declared one correspondent, 'we might well exert ourselves a little to deliver his man.'[4]

On 6 November R. W. Felkin published a further letter from Emin and letters and leading articles now appeared in the newspapers urging that a relief expedition should be sent at once to Emin's assistance.[5] Emin's past might be 'mysterious' and his personality 'enigmatic', but the 'true heroism' of this 'noblest . . . of Gordon's lieutenants' was now acclaimed.[6] Armchair explorers vied with each other in the columns of *The Times* and *The Fortnightly Review* to plot the most practical route by which Emin could quickly be reached.[7] That some sort of an expedition should be organized was scarcely questioned, and that it should be of a 'pacific' nature was widely agreed. 'So wild an enterprise as a *military* expedition for the relief of Emin Bey is scarcely to be dreamed of', declared *The Scotsman* soberly.[8]

At first the dispatch of a relief expedition was widely considered as a rescue mission: 'another errand of mercy and of peril—to rescue

is still the latest we have from him, although others of recent date have since reached Zanzibar' (Kirk to Anderson, 19 Oct. 1886, F.O. 84/1775). In the volume F.O. 84/1775, as in the Confidential Print F.O.C.P. 5433, the telegram of 17 Oct. from Holmwood is placed *after* Salisbury's minute. This seems to me to reflect the actual sequence of events.

[1] Memorandum by Anderson, 18 Oct. 1886, F.O. 84/1775.
[2] *The Times*, 29 Oct. 1886.   [3] Ibid., 15 Dec. 1886.
[4] Ibid., 1 Nov. 1886, letter to the editor from P. L. Sclater.
[5] Ibid., 6 Nov. 1886. *The Scotsman*, 6 Nov. 1886. See also *The Times*, 24 Nov. and 2, 9, 11, 18 Dec. 1886; *The Scotsman*, 24 Nov. and 1, 15 Dec. 1886.
[6] 'The Rescue of Emin Pasha', *The Times*, 15 Dec. 1886.
[7] J. T. Wills in *The Times*, 2, 15, 18 Dec. 1886. Edward Hutchinson in *The Scotsman*, 1 Dec. 1886. Joseph Thomson in *The Times*, 24 Nov. 1886. R. W. Felkin in *The Times*, 9 Dec. 1886. *The Scottish Geographical Magazine*, Dec. 1886. J. T. Wills in *The Fortnightly Review*, Dec. 1886.
[8] *The Scotsman*, Leading Article, 25 Nov. 1886.

Emin Pasha (a gallant lieutenant of the lamented General Gordon) who is surrounded by savage and hostile tribes and cut off from the reach and resources of civilisation'.[1] Emin needed to be 'rescued' from the forces of 'fanaticism' and an expedition would enable him and his men to withdraw. With the publication of more recent letters from Emin, however, it became clear that Emin himself did not wish to be 'rescued' but hoped to be maintained in Equatoria;[2] had he wished to leave Equatoria, it was pointed out, 'he could have done so, as Junker has done'.[3]

A relief expedition now came to be conceived in terms of dispatching a caravan of supplies and ammunition which would enable Emin to remain where he was. 'With a little outside help', wrote one correspondent with an interest in the area, Emin's province 'might be made to yield a large annual surplus'.[3] To remove Emin 'would be to deliver over his province once more to barbarism and the slaver; to maintain him where he is, and give him adequate support, would be to plant a broad area of civilisation in the very heart of Africa that might ultimately spread to leaven the whole mass'.[3]

The public interest in Emin's position in the autumn of 1886 was carefully fostered by Emin's friends and correspondents in England, Charles Allen of the Anti-Slavery Society, and R. W. Felkin, now a doctor in Edinburgh.

On 8 November Allen forwarded to the Foreign Secretary, Lord Iddesleigh, a resolution from the Anti-Slavery Society which stated that 'the position of Dr. Emin Bey presents a very strong claim upon Her Majesty's Government' which should 'be sparing of neither exertion nor expense in order to rescue him . . . or to enable him to hold a friendly position amongst the natives of his province'.[4] In adopting this resolution, Allen confided to Felkin, 'our Committee purposely avoided committing themselves to any opinion as to how Emin Bey was to be reached. We wish to throw the onus of relieving him on the Government.'[5]

---

[1] *The Times*, 14 Jan. 1887.

[2] Felkin published an edited version of Emin's important letter of 7 July 1886 in *The Times*, 9 Dec. 1886.

[3] 'The Rescue of Emin Pasha' by a correspondent (internal evidence suggests that the author was J. T. Wills), *The Times*, 15 Dec. 1886.

[4] Allen to Iddesleigh, 8 Nov. 1886, F.O. 84/1793. R. Gray, *A History of the Southern Sudan*, p. 198.

[5] Allen to Felkin, 19 Nov. 1886, Anti-Slavery Society Papers (A.S.S.), Letter-book, E. 3/4.

In Edinburgh, R. W. Felkin was writing letters to *The Scotsman* and mobilizing the Scottish Geographical Society. As he wrote to Allen, 'We too are going to try and get up a petition to the Government . . . In order to get the Scotch to stir I must have a good humanitarian, utilitarian and several other "arian" objects in my paper. Can you help me ? Do try—think of all poor Emin has tried to do and really has done, of his long weary holding out.'[1] Felkin later reported that he had asked Joseph Thomson, the explorer, to write to *The Times*, as he had private information that unless the papers and the public took the matter up it would fall through. 'I understand the Royal Geographical Society petitioned last week. Could you not get Wylde or Horace Waller to write to the *Standard* or *Daily Telegraph*? . . . Burleigh of the *D.T.* said he would write a leader on the subject if he had one or two strong letters to go on.'[2]

On 23 November Felkin called a special meeting of the Scottish Geographical Society and on the basis of a statement by him a resolution was passed urging the British Government to send 'a *pacific* relief expedition' under the leadership of Joseph Thomson.[3] When it appeared unlikely that a Government expedition would be sent, the Society, at Felkin's prompting, offered to organize an expedition itself, possibly in conjunction with the Italian Società d'Esplorazione Commerciale in Africa which had recently received letters requesting help from Casati.[4]

Felkin was emphatically against any idea that Emin should withdraw. He believed that if a regular line of communications could be opened up and Emin supplied with stores, Emin could hold the province indefinitely. In this Felkin was following Emin's own wishes. The letters which Emin had written to him on 7 and 22 July 1886 made clear Emin's desire to remain in Equatoria and his hope that 'as Egypt is incapable of supporting us, England may perhaps one of these days come to the determination to occupy these countries'.[5] But the British Government showed no such determination and

[1] Felkin to Allen, 17 Nov. 1886, A.S.S. MSS. C. 57/58. R. Gray, op. cit., p. 198.
[2] Felkin to Allen, 20 Nov. 1886, A.S.S. MSS. C.57/59. R. Gray, op. cit.
[3] A. Silva-White (Secretary to the Scottish Geographical Society) to Iddesleigh, 23 Nov. 1886, F.O. 84/1794.
[4] Scottish Geographical Society Minute Book, 16 Dec. 1886, pp. 27–8. A. Silva-White to Iddlesleigh, 3 Dec. 1886, enclosing Cesari Rossi to Scottish Geographical Society, 29 Nov. 1886, F.O. 84/1794.
[5] Emin to Felkin, 7 and 22 July 1886, printed in the Introduction by Felkin to Schweitzer, i. xxix–xxx.

Felkin observed to Allen, 'I should not be at all surprised if the German Government do not act before ours, their fingers are itching to extend their territory and this gives them a splendid opportunity.'[1]

Others, whose concern for Emin was by no means so personal or paramount as Felkin's, also had schemes for Equatoria.[2] Francis Fox (a Quaker businessman and a prominent member of the Aborigines Protection Society), who was interested in the Sudan, came to see Felkin to discuss a scheme which he and J. T. Wills had for an expedition to reach Equatoria via the Congo.[3] Their main object was 'to get a station in the Nyam-Nyam country which they would take care not to give up'. They were not discouraged when Felkin pointed out that Dr. Oscar Lenz had already been unsuccessful by this route, and a few days later Wills submitted a scheme to Lord Iddesleigh whereby the services of Junker would be secured to lead an expedition via the Congo and Uele rivers to Wadelai. Then 'with Government assistance of a certain amount' a private company would be formed for the 'permanent maintenance of Emin Bey's province'. This would 'secure the back entrance of the Egyptian Sudan and a most valuable ivory trade to English enterprise'.[4] When the Government showed no interest, Wills appealed to a wider audience: in a lecture to the Royal Geographical Society he later declared, 'turn away the ivory from Khartoum to the Congo and the great incentive to the slave-trade is gone; philanthropy is cheap, for the profits will be enormous. Ivory is now worth 20–25 times the cost of transport from Stanley Pool and the remaining £900 a ton will pay for the steamers, stations, and the rest.'[5]

Such schemes received short shrift from Lord Salisbury. At a time when he was hoping, through the second Drummond–Wolff mission, to make the British occupation of Egypt the temporary affair it had set out to be, he was strongly opposed to getting Britain bogged down in territorial acquisitions in the Sudan.[6] In 1886 Salisbury was as unimpressed as he was to be in 1888 by the wild schemes of 'the

---

[1] Felkin to Allen, 20 Nov. 1886, A.S.S. MSS. C57/59.

[2] R. Gray, *A History of the Southern Sudan*, p. 199.

[3] Felkin to Allen, 20 Nov. 1886, A.S.S. MSS. C57/59.

[4] J. T. Wills to Iddesleigh, 25 Nov. 1886, F.O. 84/1794.

[5] *P.R.G.S.*, (1887). R. Gray, op. cit., p. 200.

[6] Salisbury's position on Egypt and the Sudan in Nov. 1886 is presented with particular clarity in a conversation he had with Waddington, the French Ambassador, at this time. See Waddington to Freycinet, 3 Nov. 1886, printed in *Documents diplomatiques français (1871–1914)*, 1ʳᵉ Série, vol. vi, Section iii, no. 342. See also Robinson and Gallagher, op. cit., pp. 260–4.

curious collection of fanatics who believe that by some magic wave
of the diplomatic wand the Soudan can be turned into a second
India'.[1] After the disaster of the expedition to the Sudan to relieve
General Gordon the previous year, Salisbury had expressed his
determined hope 'that there may be no more "expeditions".'[2]
He was now decidedly against exposing his Government to responsibilities such as those which had so shaken Gladstone. To Lord
Salisbury, in 1886, Equatoria was devoid of any economic or strategic
importance. The well-meaning efforts of those who had responded
to the news of Emin's plight appeared to stem more from Victorian
charity than from unscrupulous designs of empire.[3] The more hard-
headed proposals of men like Fox and Wills seemed quite impractical.
When one of Emin's correspondents wrote to Salisbury declaring
that 'nothing is required but supplies of merchandise which can
be sent from Zanzibar', Salisbury was extremely sceptical. 'A military
expedition through Uganda would at least very probably be required',
he answered, and this would be 'very far in excess of what we could
undertake'.[4]

A much more important approach, however, was being made on
the matter by Mr. William Mackinnon. He had a long-standing
interest in East Africa and was well known at the Foreign Office;
and his intervention was eventually to prove decisive.

A Scottish businessman and philanthropist, Mackinnon's initial
interests had been in India where, together with a school friend, he
founded the British India Steamship Company.[5] In 1871 Mackinnon
extended his Company's steamship services to Zanzibar and from
this time can be dated his interest in East Africa. In 1877–8 Mackinnon
made an abortive attempt to obtain a concession from the Sultan
of Zanzibar for the establishment of a British chartered company
on the mainland of East Africa; the object was not just a trading
concern but an administrative company on the lines of the British
East India Company. After the German *Schützbrief* over East

Africa in March 1885, Mackinnon, together with J. F. Hutton (a Manchester businessman), had attempted to revive the concession scheme. Although encouraged by Holmwood, the project had again met with failure since the British Government refused to give the extravagant guarantees which Mackinnon demanded. Originally Mackinnon's interest had centred on the coast, but in 1885 first Holmwood, and later Sir Percy Anderson, had pointed to the even 'greater openings for trade' in the East African interior.[1] It was at this point that the possibility of building an East African railway was first discussed. In October 1885 Anderson—who was concerned about the inroads being made on British influence in East Africa by the Germans—urged Mackinnon and Hutton to take up the concessions recently obtained by H. H. Johnston in the Kilimanjaro area.[2] Hutton was enthusiastic, but without Government backing Mackinnon 'refused to have any faith in East Africa'.[3] An agent was sent to the Taveta district but he achieved little and was recalled the following year. In the meantime, Mackinnon and the German, Carl Peters, engaged in fruitless negotiations concerning British and German 'spheres of interest' in East Africa which were an embarrassment to both their Governments.[4]

Mackinnon's real interest in the period 1880–6 was not in East Africa at all, but in the Congo.[5] He had attended the Brussels Conference of 1876 and was one of the earliest subscribers to the International Association; thus he had been involved with Leopold II's Congo venture from the beginning. Mackinnon and Leopold were personal friends and regular correspondents. Leopold appreciated Mackinnon's many connections with people in influential circles and more than once made use of them.[6]

During the years 1880–6 Mackinnon, J. F. Hutton, H. M. Stanley, Sir Francis de Winton, and other members of what Stanley described as 'the Mackinnon Clan' had endeavoured to create a British

---

[1] Holmwood to J. F. Hutton, 10 Apr. 1885, enclosed in Aberdare to Granville, 22 Apr. 1885, F.O. 84/1737. Memorandum by Anderson, 2 July 1885, F.O. 84/1740, cited in D. A. Low, 'The British and Uganda 1862–1900', D.Phil. thesis (Oxford, 1957), p. 88.

[2] de Kiewiet, op. cit., pp. 70–1.

[3] H. H. Johnston, *The Story of my Life* (London, 1923), p. 149.

[4] de Kiewiet, op. cit., p. 72.

[5] For Mackinnon's activity with regard to the Congo, see R. T. Anstey, *Britain and the Congo in the 19th Century* (Oxford, 1962).

[6] Mackinnon's attempts to recruit General Gordon on behalf of King Leopold are documented in the Palace Archives, Brussels, Dossier 82.

economic presence in the Congo.[1] Until 1885, when he was succeeded by Sir Francis de Winton, Stanley himself was employed by Leopold in the Congo, where he laid the foundations for the future administration of the vast area below Stanley Falls.[2] On his return to Europe, Stanley led the members of the Mackinnon Clan in an attempt to form a syndicate in Britain for the building of a Congo railway. The attempt failed in the summer of 1886. In July Leopold had already decided that the contract for the construction of the railway should go into Belgian hands.[3] As Stanley wrote sadly to Mackinnon in September, 'I can see that every day the King is closing the Congo against the English and seems resolved to make it more and more Belgian.'[4] The failure to obtain the contract for the Congo railway became final in September.[5] Mackinnon was disappointed but his devotion to Leopold remained unimpaired.[6] He remained in frequent personal contact with the King and went on to invest large sums of money in the *Compagnie du Chemin de Fer du Congo* and the *Compagnie du Katanga*.[7] None the less, September 1886 marks an important watershed in the careers of both Mackinnon and Stanley.[8] After this date, they both turn away from the Congo and their real interest is in East Africa. The names of those other members of the 'Mackinnon Clan' which feature so prominently in connection with Leopold's Congo State up to 1886 figure conspicuously thereafter in Mackinnon's last two African ventures: the sending of the Emin Pasha relief expedition and the formation of the Imperial British East Africa Company.

These two projects developed together during November–December 1886.[9] Amongst Mackinnon's circle of influential friends were Sir Percy Anderson and Sir John Kirk. During October both

[1] See R. Anstey, op. cit., esp. chs. iv and viii.

[2] See H. M. Stanley, *The Congo and the Founding of its Free State*, 2 vols. (London, 1885). M. Luwel, *Sir Francis de Winton: Administrateur-Général du Congo 1884–1886* (Tervuren, 1964).

[3] Leopold to Strauch, 15 July 1886, Strauch Papers (1), Archives du Ministère des Affaires Étrangères, Brussels, AF I–XIII, no. 616.

[4] Stanley to Mackinnon, 18 Sept. 1886, Mackinnon Papers (M.P.). R. Anstey, op. cit., p. 207.

[5] Hutton to Mackinnon, 14 Sept. 1886, M.P., 68.

[6] See the two letters which Mackinnon wrote to Henry Sanford at this time. Mackinnon to Sanford, 5 June and 29 Sept. 1886, Sanford Papers, Box 127.

[7] R. Anstey, op. cit., pp. 208–9.   [8] Ibid. 207.

[9] This is not the view of Miss de Kiewiet (op. cit., p. 83) who asserts that the organization of the Emin Pasha relief expedition and the formation of the I.B.E.A. Company developed separately, the latter not before Feb. 1887.

these men were closely involved in the discussions with Dr. Krauel, of the German Foreign Office, which took place in London and resulted in the Anglo-German Agreement over East Africa which was concluded by an exchange of Notes on 29 October and 1 November; indeed, the negotiations on the British side were led by Anderson.[1] The progress of these negotiations was passed on to Mackinnon in a series of letters by Sir John Kirk.[2]

Both Kirk and Anderson were dismayed at the failure of the British Government to back up British interests and influence in East Africa in the face of the increasing German activity in the area. Both had strongly encouraged Mackinnon's interest in East Africa in the past, but whereas Anderson had been exasperated at Mackinnon's lack of initiative, Kirk appreciated Mackinnon's reluctance to act in the absence of any security. 'I quite understand your unwillingness to embark in our East African concerns', he wrote to Mackinnon on the eve of the Anglo-German negotiations; 'there is little to encourage you.'[3] By the end of October, Kirk's attitude had changed. The details of the Anglo-German Agreement over East Africa had been settled, and in communicating these to Mackinnon Kirk concludes with a certain optimism:

> Thus we have Mombasa under the Sultan and a free run inland to the Lake [Victoria] etc. but not Kilimanjaro. We have the best of any line for a rail if ever one is made. We also have the Equatorial Province now held by the brave Emin Bey, well-governed and quiet to this day. Germany will rent Dar Salaam from the Sultan, which arrangement we may make at Mombasa. This is the outline of the scheme and you will see we have an opening as good as any.[4]

A week later Kirk is even more enthusiastic: 'Our hands are free and we hold the situation if we act at once . . .'[5]

In fact Kirk's letters to Mackinnon convey an inflated idea of what the Anglo-German Agreement of 1886 secured for the British

---

[1] See Hertslet, *The Map of Africa by Treaty* (London, 1894), ii. 615–21. Pauncefote and Anderson handled the negotiations on the British side. Austin Lee told Mackinnon that: 'The former [Pauncefote] has not the knowledge or the time to study the question and the decision practically rests with the latter [Anderson] whose views you know as well as I do.' Austin Lee to Mackinnon, 21 Oct. 1886, M.P., 109.

[2] Kirk to Mackinnon, 5, 6, 11, 22, 30 Oct. and 6 Nov. 1886, M.P., 94.

[3] Kirk to Mackinnon, 11 Oct. 1886, M.P., 94.

[4] Kirk to Mackinnon, 30 Oct. 1886, M.P., 94.

[5] Kirk to Mackinnon, 6 Nov. 1886, M.P., 94. R. Anstey, op. cit., pp. 214–15.

'sphere' in East Africa. The Agreement was essentially concerned with the coast. For the interior, especially the far interior of Buganda and the Equatorial province, it offered very little security indeed— as events during the next few years were to prove. But the very enactment of the Anglo-German Agreement created an atmosphere of confidence with regard to the future of the area which had not existed before. The manner of Kirk's portrayal of the Agreement was probably not without some influence on Mackinnon.[1] And the reference to Emin's position in Equatoria came the day after Emin's situation had become widely known through the newspapers. Together, these two events appear to have reawakened Mackinnon's interest in East Africa. The Anglo-German Agreement seemed to provide the security for a commercial and administrative concession on the East African mainland which Mackinnon had long been seeking. And the news of Emin's position, as it was dramatically envisaged in Europe, provided a new dynamic to the situation.

The situation of Emin in Equatoria also provided a new opportunity. Until 1886 such interest in the East African interior as existed in Europe was focused chiefly on Buganda. Stanley's 'pearl of Africa' appeared to be the centre from which the whole of the Lake region might eventually be controlled.[2] Since 1885, however, the murder of Bishop Hannington, the persecution of Christians at the Kabaka's court, and Mwanga's increasing hostility towards Europeans had discouraged hopes of further European intervention in Buganda. In the autumn of 1886 the situation of Emin in Equatoria suddenly appeared as an alternative. The position of Equatoria as an abandoned province of Egypt, astride the Nile, made it the most annexable part of the interior. Emin's isolation, his immediate need, and his offer of his province presented an opportunity to enlist Emin himself and to annex his province. Through Emin in Equatoria the whole Lake region might be controlled and its resources exploited and Buganda, at least for the present, could be ignored. Thus, between 1886 and 1889 Equatoria came to occupy in the minds of schemers and strategists in Europe the place in East African affairs which Buganda was again to occupy thereafter.

By the beginning of November it was apparent that the Government was itself very unlikely to dispatch an expedition to relieve Emin Pasha. Mackinnon therefore began to sound his friends about

[1] R. Anstey, op. cit., pp. 214–15.
[2] de Kiewiet, op. cit., p. 88.

the possibility of organizing a 'private' expedition, though it appears to have been Mackinnon's initial hope that Government funds would be forthcoming.[1] On the advice of Kirk,[2] Mackinnon approached Stanley, who at once declared his readiness to put himself 'at a moment's notice' under Mackinnon's orders to lead an expedition 'without hope of fee or reward'.[3]

The Emin Pasha relief expedition, as originally envisaged by Mackinnon and Stanley, would appear to have been a very modest affair, costing no more than £20,000 and taking only a year to eighteen months to complete its object.[4] This was to convey the ammunition and supplies to Emin which he obviously needed and to open a way for him to withdraw to the East African coast should he wish to do so. Mackinnon soon approached J. F. Hutton, the Manchester businessman who had been closely involved with Mackinnon's attempts to obtain an East African concession in the past.[5] Hutton was not enthusiastic about the proposal for an expedition to relieve Emin Pasha and doubted whether many of his business friends would 'go in for it'. 'You cannot give any hopes of a return', he wrote to Mackinnon, and 'there are so few men here of public spirit sufficient to give on that prospect'.[6] He himself

did not feel at all inclined to undertake what the Government is morally bound to do . . . If the whole matter goes through I will put my name down for £1,000—but am not going to contribute this to a mere relief fund which is the duty of the Government. If they do nothing, appeal to the public and money will soon come forth.[7]

Hutton was much more interested in the opportunity provided by the arrival of Emin's offer of his province to England and the enactment of the Anglo-German Agreement for a revival of the scheme for an East African concession. On 27 November Hutton sent to Mackinnon a document outlining his proposals for the formation of a 'Syndicate for establishing British commerce and influence in

---

[1] Hutton to Mackinnon, 27 Nov. 1886, M.P., 68.
[2] Kirk to Mackinnon, 6 Nov. 1886, M.P., 94.
[3] Stanley to Mackinnon, 15 Nov. 1886, enclosed in Mackinnon to Fergusson, 15 Nov. 1886, F.O. 84/1793.
[4] Ibid. Also Mackinnon to Iddesleigh, 27 Nov. 1886, F.O. 84/1794.
[5] Hutton was also closely involved at this time in the Royal Niger Company. See J. Flint, *Sir George Goldie and the making of Nigeria* (London, 1960).
[6] Hutton to Mackinnon, 26 Nov. 1886, M.P., 68.
[7] Hutton to Mackinnon, 27 Nov. 1886, M.P., 68.

East Africa and for relieving Emin Bey'.[1] The object of these proposals was 'to open a direct route to Victoria Nyanza and the Sudan
and thereby establish stations and commerce in the interior of East
Africa'. The sanction of the Government was to be sought for the
concession of further territories in East Africa 'outside the territories
already under the protection or jurisdiction of other European
states'. These, it was hoped, would eventually be governed by a
'Company under Charter on terms similar to that of the Royal
Niger Company'. A 'primary part' of these proposals was to be the
dispatch of an expedition under H. M. Stanley 'to carry relief to
Emin Bey'. On his way to Equatoria, Stanley was to follow the example which Carl Peters had set in 1884 in what was now the German
'sphere'. Treaties and concessions were to be made with the 'rulers
and chiefs' of the districts between Mombasa and Wadelai during
the course of the expedition and these, together with 'any other
advantages obtained through this expedition', were to be retained
for the benefit of the Syndicate.

As in 1885, it was Hutton who pressed the matter and Mackinnon
who hesitated. While Hutton clarified and improved the proposals
'in accordance with Sir Percy Anderson's suggestions',[2] Mackinnon
demurred. Hutton was so discouraged by Mackinnon's reluctance
to make the relief expedition a part of these more extensive proposals
that in December he wrote to Mackinnon declaring that it was
impossible for him to take part in 'the mere relief fund' and that
without Mackinnon he had given up 'all thoughts of going on with
the Syndicate'.[2] Eventually, it appears, Mackinnon was convinced
that if Stanley led an expedition to assist Emin in Equatoria, 'the
opportunity which his going there offers of extending British influence
from the coast up to Wadelai is one which if . . . not taken advantage
of now, will be lost for ever'.[3]

It was these wider aspects of the scheme, with their implications
for the development of the British 'sphere' in East Africa against
German encroachment, rather than a concern for Emin, which
attracted the support of Kirk and prompted Anderson and Sir
James Fergusson at the Foreign Office to press for the dispatch of

[1] This document, together with a final version dated 21 Dec. 1886, is in the
Mackinnon Papers (uncatalogued).
[2] Hutton to Mackinnon, 21 Dec. 1886, M.P., 68.
[3] Mackinnon to Henry M. Sanford, 29 Sept. 1887, Sanford Papers. I owe this
reference to Professor J. Stengers.

Mackinnon's expedition in the face of steady discouragement by Salisbury, Iddesleigh, and the Cabinet.[1] Even before Mackinnon's intervention, Anderson had been in favour of sending an expedition to relieve Emin Pasha.[2] Together with Sir John Kirk, he had urged the dispatch of a strongly armed trading caravan with supplies and ammunition from the East African coast. The expedition should avoid Buganda altogether and bring Emin out by the southern route.[3] In October, Sir John Kirk had been quite clear that as he understood it 'the only question is how to communicate with Emin Bey and enable him to retire; the question of holding the Equatorial province is now not under consideration'.[3] Initially, therefore, Anderson and Kirk were in favour of sending an expedition whose objective was to enable Emin to withdraw. But after the conclusion of the Anglo-German Agreement and the arrival of Emin's letters offering his province to Britain, their objectives change. Emin's position was revealed as rather different from that which had been imagined—on the basis of very little evidence—in September and October. As Anderson commented, after reading these letters, 'I rather gather that he [Emin] would hold on if he could get ammunition.'[4] By December Kirk was openly pressing for the dispatch of an expedition whose object, as he informed Emin, was 'to secure you not help to come away, but support to enable you to remain'.[5]

On 12 November Anderson minuted: 'Mr. Mackinnon will shortly submit a proposal under which Stanley may be employed for communicating between Her Majesty's Government and Emin.'[6] During the following week Anderson saw a good deal of Mackinnon, and Sir James Fergusson, who was a business associate of Mackinnon, saw both Hutton and Mackinnon 'separately and several times'. The object of their proposal for an expedition was, Fergusson observed, 'political as well as philanthropic. Mr. Mackinnon offers to find £10,000 for the establishment of trading posts *en route*, and Mr. Hutton says that others, including himself, will also subscribe,

[1] G. N. Sanderson, *England, Europe and the Upper Nile*, p. 33.
[2] Memorandum by Anderson, 15 and 18 Oct. 1886, F.O. 84/1775.
[3] Memorandum by Kirk, 13 Oct. 1886, F.O. 84/1775.
[4] Minute by Anderson, 22/23 Nov. 1886, on Holmwood to Iddesleigh, 23 Sept. 1886, F.O. 84/1775.
[5] Kirk to Emin Pasha, 1 Dec. 1886, printed in the *Tagebücher* under 27 June 1887, iii. 356. See also Ch. VII, p. 144 below.
[6] Memorandum by Anderson, 12 Nov. 1886, F.O. 84/1793.

their object being to form a large trading colony from the Mombasa base.'[1] It later emerged that according to this scheme it was hoped that Wadelai might become the last of a chain of stations from the coast to the interior and that Emin and his soldiers would be employed to garrison the interior stations under the Company which Mackinnon and his associates hoped to charter.[2]

On 15 November, in a letter to Fergusson, Mackinnon formally outlined his proposals for an expedition 'to open communication with Emin Bey' which Stanley would lead 'without demanding any official recognition for his mission from Her Majesty's Government' and which would thus 'relieve them of all responsibility for his personal safety'.[3] This proposal was now actively promoted by Anderson and Fergusson. The 'private' nature of such an expedition involving 'no responsibility on the part of Government' was stressed by Fergusson in his memorandum for the Cabinet, while Anderson declared: 'I think there is little doubt that, if we decide to do anything, Stanley is our man.'[4] The ghost of General Gordon was, however, already beginning to haunt the proceedings. On 23 November the Cabinet declined to consider the Mackinnon–Stanley proposal 'as it would involve Government in responsibilities similar to those in General Gordon's case' with their 'risks of future entanglements in case of disaster'.[5]

A new development now took place with the intervention of Sir Evelyn Baring, the British Consul-General in Cairo. When the news had arrived in September that the last of Gordon's Governors persisted in holding on in the Equatorial province, the Egyptian Government was no longer able to avoid the problem inherent in Emin's situation. The Equatorial province may have been abandoned, but the Egyptian Government would still be held responsible for the fate of Emin and his garrisons. Baring's response to the situation was clear and consistent with his policy hitherto. He wanted to remove the last representatives of the Egyptian Government from a position which others might seek to utilize for further Egyptian embroilments in the Sudan. This was *all* Baring wanted. As he pointed out to Lord Iddesleigh, the objectives of Holmwood,

---

[1] Memorandum by Fergusson, 20 Nov. 1886, F.O. 84/1790.
[2] See Ch. VII, pp. 160–1 below.
[3] Mackinnon to Fergusson, 15 Nov. 1886, F.O. 84/1793.
[4] Memorandum by Fergusson, 20 Nov. 1886, F.O. 84/1794. Memorandum by Anderson, 16 Nov. 1886, F.O. 84/1794.
[5] Minutes by Pauncefote and Fergusson, 23 Nov. 1886, F.O. 84/1794.

Mackay, Junker, and Dr. Schweinfurth (the correspondent of Emin and Junker who was at this time in Cairo) were

not altogether identical with those of the Egyptian Government. The former want, besides relieving Emin, to avenge the murder of the Christians in Uganda, to set up a new Government there, and to keep the Equatorial Provinces for Egypt with a view possibly to an ultimate extension of Egyptian territory. The latter wants to abandon the Equatorial Provinces and to merely bring Emin and such of the Egyptians as wish to leave. The Black [i.e. Sudanese] soldiers mostly wish to stay, hence considerable caution is necessary in dealing with the question.[1]

Baring was in favour of sending an expedition to bring Emin and the remaining soldiers out of Equatoria but, as he soon informed the Foreign Office, the Egyptian Government itself was not in a position to send an expedition.[2] Mackinnon's proposal to organize an expedition under Stanley presented a solution. But this proposal had been made 'on the condition that Her Majesty's Government will supply the necessary funds' and the Government had decided that 'this is a responsibility which they cannot undertake'.[3] On 20 November Fergusson had suggested that the British Government might escape responsibility for the expedition 'if the Egyptian Government can, in the first place, be the paymasters, seeing that they are chiefly interested in the rescue'.[4] On 23 November Baring reported that Schweinfurth had approached him in Cairo with the suggestion that Junker should organize an expedition and that the Egyptian Government should contribute £10,000 towards the cost. In reporting this proposal to the Foreign Office, Baring declared that 'the Egyptian Government would not be unwilling to contribute £10,000'.[5]

The question which the Cabinet decision seemed to have closed was once more reopened. Fergusson pointed out that the Egyptian offer opened 'fresh possibilities': 'it is very possible that Messrs. Mackinnon and Hutton may supplement the Egyptian undertaking if it is sanctioned'.[6] Anderson urged that Baring's offer should be accepted. But Junker and Schweinfurth were known to favour a

[1] Baring to Iddesleigh, 25 Nov. 1886, F.O. 84/1777.
[2] Baring to Iddesleigh, 16 Nov. 1886, F.O. 84/1770.
[3] Iddesleigh to Baring, 25 Nov. 1886, F.O. 84/1794.
[4] Memorandum by Fergusson, 20 Nov. 1886, F.O. 84/1794.
[5] Baring to Iddesleigh, 23 Nov. 1886, F.O. 84/1770.
[6] Minute by Fergusson on Baring to Iddesleigh, 23 Nov. 1886, F.O. 84/1794, and Anderson's comment on this minute.

German expedition to relieve Emin,[1] and Mackinnon, who had been informed of Baring's offer, declared himself 'not indisposed' to provide the remaining expenses for an expedition but insisted that 'the employment of an Anglo-Saxon . . . was a *sine qua non*'.[2] After consultation with Kirk and Mackinnon, Anderson was convinced that 'we can have nothing to do with Schweinfurth and Junker', and so Baring and Holmwood were informed accordingly.[3]

On 25 November the Cabinet were still 'of opinion that they could not take part in sending out an expedition, even of a peaceful character, to rescue Emin Bey, without exposing the country to the risk of having to rescue the rescuers'.[4] But they were no longer as implacable as they seemed. In a letter to Hutton the following day, Salisbury explained that the British Government was under no responsibility for Emin Pasha 'as he was appointed to his present post under Ismail Pasha, and he is not a British subject'. No renunciation on Stanley's part could absolve the British Government from the responsibility of rescuing Stanley if he got into difficulties 'if he goes at the cost and under the auspices of H.M.G.'. While the Government were therefore 'willing to give all the facilities in their power, they cannot take any action which would make the expedition other than a private effort'.[5]

The way was open, in other words, for a 'private' expedition financed and organized by Hutton and Mackinnon, although it seems doubtful whether the Government could have avoided incurring 'responsibilities similar to those in General Gordon's case' had Stanley met with disaster.[6] Sir James Fergusson wrote confidentially to Hutton informing him that the Egyptian Government would provide £10,000.[7] Lord Iddesleigh discussed the proposed expedition with Mackinnon privately in London.[8] On 27 November Mackinnon formally submitted through Iddesleigh his proposal to form a small committee 'to organise and send out a private expedition to open

[1] Junker's hopes for an initiative by the German Government are outlined in Holmwood to Iddesleigh, 23 Sept. 1886, F.O. 84/1775.
[2] Minute by Anderson, 24 Nov. 1886, F.O. 84/1794. R. Gray, *A History of the Southern Sudan*, p. 201.
[3] Pauncefote to Baring, 25 Nov. 1886, F.O. 84/1770. Pauncefote to Holmwood, 25 Nov. 1886, F.O. 84/1771.
[4] Memorandum by Iddesleigh, 25 Nov. 1886, F.O. 84/1794.
[5] Salisbury to Hutton, 26 Nov. 1886, Salisbury Papers, C/6, no. 279.
[6] G. N. Sanderson, op. cit., p. 33.
[7] This is stated in Hutton to Mackinnon, 27 Nov. 1886, M.P., 68.
[8] Mackinnon to Iddesleigh, 27 Nov. 1886, F.O. 84/1794.

communications with, and carry relief to, Emin Bey . . . and to assist the withdrawal to the coast of the Egyptian garrison'.[1] Mackinnon and his friends would provide £10,000 towards the cost of the expedition, it being understood that a similar amount would be contributed by the Egyptian Government. The Government was also to supply the expedition with arms and ammunition and also to instruct 'its Agents and naval officers to render every assistance and exert themselves in its favour'. Joseph Thomson, in a letter to *The Times* on 24 November, had drawn attention, for the first time, to the considerable stores of ivory that Emin was believed to possess. Mackinnon was careful to lay claim to 'a just proportion' of this ivory, should any be found, to offset the costs of the expedition.[2]

Mackinnon's proposals seemed to contain something for everybody, as Sir Percy Anderson pointed out in a memorandum for the Cabinet on 30 November:

Stanley would go as a private agent of a private Company, who send him at their, and his, own risk . . . If he fails, the Egyptian Government lose their money, otherwise are no worse off than they were before. If he succeeds, they rescue their last Soudan garrison, or at least so many of them as wish to retire, and thenceforth wash their hands of the Equatorial Provinces . . . the risk could not be compared to that of the Soudan expedition . . . if he [Stanley] lost his life there would be no more obligation on the British Government to avenge him than there is to avenge Bishop Hannington.[3]

The stakes did not seem high; and the odds did seem rather promising. It was someone else's money that was being risked, and under someone else's responsibility. The Egyptian Government was prepared to support the scheme. The British Government saw in Mackinnon's proposal a way to assuage public opinion and to get themselves off the hook. On 3 December 1886 Iddesleigh telegraphed to Baring: 'Her Majesty's Government approve the proposal, and the persons by whom the offer is made have been informed that it is understood by us that the agreement of the Egyptian Government is assured.'[4]

*   *   *

It is not easy to say exactly what had been approved. The ambiguous concept of 'relief' covered two quite different interpretations

---

[1] Mackinnon to Iddesleigh, 27 Nov. 1886, F.O. 84/1794, and memorandum enclosed therein.

[2] Mackinnon to Iddesleigh, 27 Nov. 1886, F.O. 84/1794.

[3] Memorandum by Anderson, 30 Nov. 1886, F.O. 84/1794.

[4] Iddesleigh to Baring, 3 Dec. 1886, F.O. 84/1770.

of the expedition's objective.[1] Initially it had been assumed by the Foreign Office and by the public that the purpose of a 'relief' expedition was to enable Emin and his men to withdraw. This continued to be the objective of the Egyptian Government. On 28 November, before Mackinnon's expedition had been authorized by the Cabinet, Sir Evelyn Baring, acting on behalf of Nubar Pasha, had sent a letter to Emin, via Holmwood, informing him that he had been promoted by the Khedive to the rank of Pasha and instructing him 'to retire . . . to the best position for ultimate withdrawal via Zanzibar when circumstances allow'.[2]

The arrival of Emin's letters during November,[3] proclaiming his intention to remain in Equatoria and offering the province to England, had introduced quite new possibilities into the situation. It was then that a 'relief' expedition came to be conceived in terms of carrying ammunition and supplies to Emin to maintain him where he was. It was to lead an expedition for 'conveying relief to Emin with a view to enable him to hold his own' that Stanley later stated he was first approached by Mackinnon and Hutton.[4] On 15 November, however, Stanley had declared his readiness to lead an expedition 'by which Emin Bey could be relieved and extricated from his dangerous position'.[5] And by the scheme which Mackinnon formally submitted on 27 November, Stanley was 'to convey any communications with which he might be entrusted by Her Majesty's Government or by the Egyptian Government, and to assist the withdrawal to the coast of the Egyptian garrisons'.[6] Whether Emin himself was to withdraw or stay was left an open question. Emin's own inclination was obviously to stay, and, after reading Emin's latest letters, Anderson observed on 30 November that it now appeared 'that a considerable proportion of the Egyptian troops would be willing to settle in the Equatorial provinces, and that the

[1] G. N. Sanderson, op. cit., p. 33.

[2] Nubar to Emin, 28 Nov. 1886, enclosed in Baring to Iddesleigh, 28 Nov. 1886, F.O. 84/1770. The original draft of this letter is in the Khartoum Archives, Cairint, 1/11/56.

[3] The substance of Emin's letters was telegraphed to the F.O. on 17 Oct. 1886. The letters themselves arrived on 22 and 29 Nov.

[4] H. M. Stanley, In Darkest Africa, 2 vols. (London, 1890), i. 31. (This work is henceforth referred to throughout this book as IDA.)

[5] Stanley to Mackinnon, 15 Nov. 1886, enclosed in Mackinnon to Fergusson, 15 Nov. 1886, F.O. 84/1793.

[6] Memorandum on the Relief of Emin Bey, enclosed in Mackinnon to Iddesleigh, 27 Nov. 1886, F.O. 84/1794.

proportion that would come away with the civilian officials would not be very large'.[1] Stanley still undertook 'to take communications from the Egyptian Government to their Governor [Emin] and to help the latter in withdrawal if that Government orders him to withdraw'.[1]

Stanley's first task, therefore, was to deliver to Emin the instructions of the Egyptian Government, and these were likely to urge withdrawal. If, however, the Egyptian Government supported an expedition which would enable those of its employees who wished to leave Equatoria to do so, then it could renounce all responsibility for the province thereafter, and for those who remained. The way would then be open for those who stayed in Equatoria, including Emin himself, to be employed by some other agency with a more active interest in the area. The instructions which Stanley eventually carried from the Egyptian Government provided for precisely this possibility. In this way the different objectives of the Egyptian Government and Mackinnon and his associates were reconciled. Among the deliberate omissions, the veiled references, and the false trails which Stanley made about this expedition when it was all over —and most obviously and assiduously in his book about it—one can occasionally perceive the glint of truth. In a speech at a banquet in Cairo in January 1890 there is a relevant passage which supports the interpretation given above. 'Please consider what kind of a relief this was', urged Stanley. 'My English friends told me that they should like Emin to stay in Africa and not abandon his province. Everyone indeed expressed the same feeling ... The Egyptian Government ... would much prefer that Emin would abandon his province and come home. Nevertheless, Emin alone was to decide which course he preferred.'[2] But what if Emin decided to remain in Equatoria: what had Stanley to offer him then?

It is clear that Mackinnon and Hutton hoped to utilize the expedition to obtain treaties and extend 'British influence from the coast up to Wadelai'; further, that the origins of the future Imperial British East Africa Company (I.B.E.A. Co.) lay in the 'large trading colony' which they hoped to establish 'from the Mombasa base'. It would seem that the employment of Emin and his soldiers under this Company was discussed only in general terms by Mackinnon and Stanley before the expedition set out—Stanley talks of his

[1] Memorandum by Anderson, 30 Nov. 1886, F.O. 84/1794.
[2] Stanley's address was published in *Le Journal officiel*, Cairo, 25 Jan. 1890. A copy of this was enclosed in Baring to F.O., 25 Jan. 1890, F.O. 84/2057.

'verbal bond' with the Committee.[1] The East Africa Company which Mackinnon and Hutton hoped to charter was not yet formed, and so little was known of Emin's circumstances that a great deal was left to Stanley's own judgement of the situation *in situ*. The proposal which Stanley eventually put to Emin in 1888, by which Emin and those who remained with him would be employed by Mackinnon's company, owed a good deal to Stanley's own initiative.[2] None the less, Stanley exercised this initiative within a general framework which had been discussed by himself and Mackinnon before the expedition left England.

Lord Salisbury's role in the sending of the Emin Pasha relief expedition is also of some interest. His consistent opposition to the project has often been noted.[3] G. N. Sanderson draws attention to the fact of Salisbury's ultimate concurrence.[4] The point is of some relevance to the whole question of the development of Salisbury's African policy, in his interpretation of which Sanderson perhaps gives an exaggerated importance to the Emin Pasha relief expedition:

Salisbury's approval of the expedition may well represent his first step towards a policy which he was gradually to develop in the course of 1887 and 1888—that of encouraging private enterprise to peg out claims in regions of East Africa where the Germans were sooner or later likely to be active. He may even have already been insuring, at what doubtless seemed a very low premium, against the still remote possibility of German penetration towards the Upper Nile.[4]

The latter part of this interpretation is surely questionable. As Sanderson later observes, Salisbury's approval of the Emin Pasha relief expedition was followed almost immediately by a determined attempt to shake off the burden of Egypt.[5] And so long as Salisbury hoped to bring to a timely end the British occupation of Egypt, he showed remarkably little interest in the Upper Nile. Salisbury still sustained these hopes in 1886 and, despite the impressive amount of literature accumulating on the subject, there is no evidence to suggest that he abandoned them before the end of 1887.

Salisbury's acquiescence in the dispatch of the Emin expedition would seem to reflect, as Sanderson suggests, a policy 'of encouraging

---

[1] Stanley to de Winton, 31 Aug. 1889, M.P. This letter was also printed in *The Standard*, 31 Dec. 1889.
[2] See Ch. VII, p. 161 below.
[3] See, e.g., R. Robinson and J. A. Gallagher, *Africa and the Victorians*, p. 199.
[4] G. N. Sanderson, *England, Europe and the Upper Nile*, pp. 33-4.
[5] Ibid., p. 41.

private enterprise to peg out claims in regions of East Africa where the Germans were sooner or later likely to be active'. It would not, however, appear to be 'a first step' towards this policy. Salisbury's action in 1886 with regard to the Emin Pasha relief expedition in fact follows a similar pattern to that which he had already taken in 1885–6. When Salisbury had become Prime Minister and Foreign Secretary in June 1885, he had brought a more resolute attitude to the conduct of foreign affairs. German claims in East Africa had been met with counter-claims based on the treaties which H. H. Johnston had made in the Taveta district, as well as on the usual grounds of the territorial rights of the Sultan of Zanzibar on the mainland. In October 1885 Anderson, acting in his 'private capacity', but with Salisbury's approval, had urged Hutton to take up the treaties obtained by H. H. Johnston in 1884 in the Kilimanjaro and Taveta districts. Anderson had suggested to Mackinnon and Hutton that they should send an expedition to the area to establish British claims there. They should then inform Kitchener—who was at this time serving on the Anglo-German Delimitation Commission in Zanzibar—that a British Company would be formed to administer the area.[1] With Foreign Office sanction, an expedition had duly been sent, although Mackinnon's interest in the matter had been half-hearted.[2] As with the Emin Pasha relief expedition, this reflected a policy of 'pegging out claims' through the encouragement of individual enterprise. There had been no occasion for such a policy in 1877–8 when Salisbury had vetoed Mackinnon's earlier attempt to obtain an East African concession. After the German Schützbrief of March 1885, however, this comes to be standard British policy with regard to East Africa. It achieves its clearest expression in the establishment of the I.B.E.A. Company in 1887–8. This, like the Royal Niger Company, emerges from a situation in which British commercial and strategic interests were being threatened by foreign competition at a time when the British Government was not itself prepared to assume the responsibilities of administration.

In the autumn of 1886 Anglo-German rivalry in East Africa appeared to have been stabilized by the Anglo-German Agreement. The Emin Pasha relief expedition was dispatched without a thought

[1] Anderson to Hutton, 3 Oct. 1885, F.O. 84/1774. Johnston to Hutton, 31 Oct. 1885, M. P. de Kiewiet, op. cit., pp. 70–1. See also H. H. Johnston, The Story of my Life, p. 124.
[2] F.O. to Mackinnon, 27 Mar. 1886, F.O. 84/1783. de Kiewiet, loc. cit.

for the protection, by British possession, of the waters of the Upper Nile. In agreeing to the sending of this expedition, Salisbury had little reason to expect that this British initiative would stimulate the competition of other Powers and that this expedition would come to occupy an initiatory role in the scramble for the interior.[1]

[1] G. N. Sanderson, op. cit., p. 26.

CHAPTER IV

The Leader Takes Over

THE leader of this expedition was at this time in the United States, where he had gone on 18 November for a lecturing tour. Before leaving England, Stanley had made plans for his recall. Only a telegram from Mackinnon was needed. It reached him at St. Johnsbury, Vermont, on 11 December: 'Your plan and offer accepted. Authorities approve. Funds provided. Business urgent. Come promptly.'[1] Stanley rose as usual to the call of duty. 'My agent was in despair—the audiences were so kind—the receptions were ovations, but arguments and entreaties were of no avail.'[2] The rest of his lecture tour was cancelled—which he estimated involved him in a personal loss of $40,000[3]—and Stanley sailed at once for England. He arrived on Christmas Eve 1886, and immediately set about organizing the Emin Pasha relief expedition.

To say that Stanley took charge of the organization of the expedition is perhaps to underestimate the way in which his strong personality dominated the entire proceedings. The Emin Pasha Relief Committee which Mackinnon had formed was in any case a rather insubstantial body. Its members were drawn chiefly from among Mackinnon's own friends, who had been prevailed upon to subscribe to the 'relief' fund; most of the Committee meetings were attended by a minority of the members.[4] Many of the most important decisions were made at hurriedly convened meetings of two or three men. Having made their donations, men like Sir Lewis Pelly, Colonel J. A. Grant, Lord Kinnaird, the Honourable Guy Dawnay, and the Revd. Horace Waller appear to have been content to follow the lead given less by Mackinnon himself than by the secretary,

---

[1] Mackinnon to Stanley, 11 Dec. 1886, M.P.

[2] *IDA* i. 34.

[3] *The Scotsman*, 28 Dec. 1886. Stanley had also tentatively planned a lecture tour in Australia which would have earned him a similar amount.

[4] Minute Book of the Emin Pasha Relief Committee, M.P. For a full list of the members of the Committee see Appendix 1.

Sir Francis de Winton and, before the expedition set out, by Stanley. At its very first meeting on 29 December, the Committee placed the fullest powers in Stanley's hands:

> The Committee, having approved the appointment of Mr. H. M. Stanley to the leadership of the expedition, decided that, having the fullest confidence in his experience and abilities, the interests of the expedition would be best promoted by giving Mr. Stanley full discretion as to its organization and equipment, the choice of the route to be adopted, and the selection and appointment of his officers. Mr. Stanley accepted the charge on these terms, and proceeded to the work of organization and equipment. Henceforward, therefore, the Committee ceased to control the arrangements or interfere with the direction of the expedition, the only office remaining to them being that of providing the ways and means considered necessary by Mr. Stanley to the success of the enterprise.[1]

The means were never in doubt. The cost of the expedition had originally been estimated by Stanley at £20,000 and Mackinnon had undertaken to raise half of this himself and from his friends, on the understanding that the Egyptian Government would contribute £10,000.[2] This first subscription, which eventually amounted to £20,906, covered the costs from January 1887 to December 1888. The delay and difficulties encountered by the expedition then necessitated a second subscription. Of the total raised through the two subscriptions, the Egyptian Government contributed £14,000 and Mackinnon £3,000. The Royal Geographical Society contributed £1,000, as did Messrs. Gray, Dawes & Co., who equipped the expedition. Various individuals, including most of the Committee members, gave rather less, and the records suggest that Hutton contributed only £250.[3] The total of private subscriptions was £15,945 and a further £2,200 was realized through the publication of some of Stanley's letters in the press during the course of the expedition. At the conclusion of the whole venture the accounts balanced at just over £32,000. At no point did Mackinnon follow Hutton's advice and appeal to the general public.

The means being assured and the organization of the expedition having been placed firmly in Stanley's hands, great debate now

---

[1] Report of the Emin Pasha Relief Committee (confidential), n.d. (1891), M.P., pp. 10–11. See also the letter Mackinnon later wrote to *The Times*, 5 Nov. 1888.

[2] Mackinnon to Iddesleigh, 27 Nov. 1886, F.O. 84/1794.

[3] For the accounts of the expedition see Appendix 2.

ensued about the route it should take. As early as the middle of
November, Stanley had been 'industriously sketching out the routes
with the various costs attending each route'.[1] The suggestion of a
Mr. H. F. Harrison Smith (who had recently been on a mission to
Menelik) that Wadelai should be approached through Ethiopia,
and the proposal by the African Lakes Company that the expedition
should go via the Zambezi and Shiré rivers to Lake Tanganyika,
were never seriously considered.[2] Four other routes had, however,
been widely canvassed, and three of these were variations on the
route inland from the East African coast opposite Zanzibar to the
Lake Victoria region.[3]

There were several serious objections to the adoption of the direct
route to Wadelai via Buganda and Bunyoro, the most serious of
which was the hostility of the Kabaka. The Church Missionary
Society and the French Government also expressed their fears to
the Foreign Office that Mwanga might react to the presence near
Buganda of Stanley's large expedition by murdering the English
and French missionaries.[4]

Joseph Thomson had urged a second, more northerly route
through the Masailand, which he himself had taken in 1883.[5] By
this route Buganda could be avoided altogether and Stanley would
be able to make the treaties in the Masai area which Mackinnon
wanted. But General Brackenbury at the War Office pointed out that
the country between the north-east corner of Lake Victoria and
Wadelai was 'unexplored and probably swampy', and it was believed
in some quarters that Emin had already lost many troops in attempting to open up a way in this direction.[6] In any case, supplies of food
and water were known to be scanty and inadequate for a large
expedition, and Stanley was convinced that he would not get through
the Masai area 'without fighting'.[7]

[1] Stanley to Mackinnon, 15 Nov. 1886, enclosed in Mackinnon to Fergusson,
15 Nov. 1886, F.O. 84/1793.
[2] H. F. Harrison Smith to Sanderson, 22 Nov. 1886, and H. F. Harrison
Smith to Pauncefote, 11 Dec. 1886, nos. 29, 59, in F.O.C.P. 5433. African
Lakes Co. to F.O., 30 Dec. 1886, F.O.C.P. 5617, no. 2. See also Ch. VII, p. 151
below.   [3] See map, pp. 90–1.
[4] Minute by Pauncefote, 28 Dec. 1886. Pauncefote to Mackinnon, 29 Dec.
1886, F.O. 84/1796.
[5] Joseph Thomson, letter to The Times, 24 Nov. 1886.
[6] Memorandum by Brackenbury, enclosed in War Office to T.V. Lister, 4 Dec.
1886, F.O.C.P. 5433, p. 103.
[7] Anderson to Pauncefote, 24 Dec. 1886, F.O. 84/1795.

The third East African possibility was the long-established southern caravan route inland from Bagamayo via Msalala to the southern end of Lake Victoria. This route was advocated by R. W. Felkin and many others.[1] By it both Karagwe and Buganda could be avoided and Stanley would make his way up the western side of Lake Victoria to Lake Albert. This route lay largely through the recently demarcated German sphere and it was feared that the adoption of a route through German territory might arouse German suspicions that behind the expedition to 'relieve' Emin Pasha lay projects for the annexation of further territory by Britain behind the German sphere.[2] Such suspicions were not unfounded, as Stanley's treaty-making activities on this route during the return journey were to prove. Against all three of these East African routes Stanley urged the likelihood of widespread desertion amongst his porters recruited in Zanzibar.[3] For a man of Stanley's pioneering inclinations there was the additional disadvantage that they had all been opened up before.[4]

All of these objections would be removed if a route inland from the West African coast were adopted. From the very beginning Stanley had been in favour of leading the Emin Pasha relief expedition to Equatoria via the Congo.[5] He had brought forward many arguments in support of this rather unexpected scheme. By utilizing the river Congo, and its tributary the Aruwimi, great stretches of navigable waterway could be used for conveying the expedition into the heart of Africa, although Stanley admitted that carrying the boats around the series of rapids on the lower Congo would be 'a heavy labour'.[6] Stanley himself had opened up the Congo as a waterway into the African interior during the years 1879–84 when he had been working for King Leopold II's Congo State, and in 1883 he had ventured up the Aruwimi as far as the falls below Yambuya.[7] This was therefore the route best known to him. If the expedition went by the Congo route the overland march from the

---

[1] R. W. Felkin, 'The Position of Emin Bey', *The Scottish Geographical Magazine*, Dec. 1886, pp. 712–14.

[2] Memorandum by Anderson, 5 Jan. 1887, F.O.C.P. 5617, p. 4. D. Stanley, *Autobiography of H. M. Stanley* (London, 1909), p. 355.

[3] H. M. Stanley, *IDA* i. 32.

[4] I owe this point to Mrs. D. Middleton, who has recently edited the Diary of A. J. Mounteney-Jephson for the Hakluyt Society.

[5] H. M. Stanley; speech reported in *The Times*, 3 May 1890.

[6] *IDA* i. 33.

[7] H. M. Stanley, *The Congo and the Founding of its Free State*, ii. 120–30.

furthest point of navigation on the Aruwimi to Lake Albert would
be much shorter in distance than by any of the East African routes—
only 322 miles, Stanley estimated—and the likelihood of desertions
would be removed.[1] Although this march through the eastern Congo
to Lake Albert would be through completely unexplored territory,
food and water were expected to be adequate and Stanley anticipated
that Emin could be reached in four months.[2]

As soon as he arrived back in England from the United States,
Stanley went to see Sir Percy Anderson and told him of his preference
for the Congo route 'as the quickest, easiest and safest'. He also
indicated his intention, if this route were approved, to establish a
base camp on the Aruwimi and to evacuate those who wished to
leave Equatoria via this camp down the Congo to the sea. Anderson
reported that Stanley was most anxious 'that his Congo idea should
be a secret for the present, even from Holmwood, as he may have to
alter it'.[2] From the point of view of the Foreign Office, there were
three main obstacles to the Congo route: the difficulty of obtaining
a ship to transport the expedition to the Congo round the Cape
and the considerable extra expense this would involve; the reluctance
of the Sultan of Zanzibar to allow Zanzibari porters to go to the
Congo; and the fact that the scheme would depend on the assent,
indeed the active support, of King Leopold. Otherwise it appeared
to have much to recommend it, at least in political terms. As
Anderson saw it, 'we should escape German jealousy, quiet the fears
of the French and our Missionary Societies about the safety of the
missionaries in Uganda, and avert the dangers feared by General
Brackenbury'.[2]

The Emin Pasha Relief Committee were by no means so enthusiastic and adhered strongly to their conviction 'that it would be best
to adopt the Eastern route'.[3] Stanley appeared to submit to the
Committee's wishes and initial arrangements were made for the
expedition to go via Msalala and the southern end of Lake Victoria
to Lake Albert. But Stanley had other plans. Immediately after the
first meeting of the Committee on 29 December, and armed with the

---

[1] *IDA* i. 34–5. Stanley's estimate of the distance between Yambuya and Lake
Albert was wildly wrong; he later admitted that it was over twice as far, i.e.
about 650 miles. *IDA* i. 391.

[2] Anderson to Pauncefote, 24 Dec. 1886, F.O. 84/1795, reporting a conversation with Stanley.

[3] *IDA* i. 35. See also Report of the Emin Pasha Relief Committee, 1891,
M.P., pp. 13–14.

carte blanche he had received there, Stanley caught the boat train to Brussels.

*   *   *

Technically, Stanley was still at this time in the employment of King Leopold II of the Belgians. During the two years since Stanley had returned from the Congo, however, Leopold's failure to make use of his services and the King's persistent evasion and prevarication about his plans for Stanley's future had led to a feeling of intense frustration on Stanley's part and to a deterioration in the relations between the two men.[1] As early as 1882 Stanley had advocated that Leopold's Congo State should be divided into two administrative departments: one for the Upper Congo and one for the Lower Congo. It was as Administrator-General of the Upper Congo that Stanley had been hoping to return to Africa since 1884. Failing this, he thought that Leopold might utilize his services on 'an exploring mission' in the north-eastern regions of the Congo: 'It is a great region', Stanley declared, 'and . . . it might contain great natural wealth of some kind or better facilities for navigation than we can at present anticipate'.[2] In the Congo itself, it was expected in some quarters that if Stanley returned to the Congo it would be in no less a position than that of Governor-General.[3] But the period 1885–6 was a difficult one for Leopold's Congo State.[4] Financially the situation was precarious, and administratively it was a period of recession, when several of the stations which had been established by Stanley on the Upper Congo were abandoned. In addition, Leopold had to reckon with the fact that to send Stanley back to the Congo would be interpreted in France as an unfriendly act.[5] During the year 1885–6, therefore, Leopold had procrastinated over the problem of Stanley's

---

[1] F. Hird, *H. M. Stanley: the Authorised Life* (London, 1935), pp. 204–15.

[2] Stanley to Henry M. Sanford, 20 Aug. 1886, Sanford Papers, printed in Bontinck, *Aux origines de l'état indépendant du Congo* (Louvain, 1966), pp. 358–60.

[3] Van de Velde to Stanley, 11 Sept. 1885, cited in P. Ceulemans, *La Question arabe et le Congo* (Brussels, 1959), p. 174. (I am much indebted to this work in the following section.)

[4] 'The King is always in his Congo business up to his very nose. Succeeding in nothing and yet not discouraged. The famous Austrian loan is a failure. The French lottery is a failure, and the railway seems to be very nearly the same. There are heavy difficulties with France about the delimitation of frontiers, our purse here is *bleeding* constantly and getting awfully light. In fact everything goes wrong, and yet His Majesty is full of go.' Devaux to Mackinnon, 9 Apr. 1886, M.P., 7.   [5] Hird, op. cit., p. 210.

future. He had no particular task for him in Africa and during the discussions concerning the building of the Congo railway, Leopold had felt that Stanley could be much more useful in Europe.[1] In any event Leopold did not wish to lose his claim on Stanley's services. As the King observed to his *chef du Cabinet*, Strauch, 'The Congo State may need to have someone in Africa and we have no-one but Stanley. I wish to keep him at my disposal in case anything happens.'[2]

By the autumn of 1886, Stanley was exasperated at the way the King 'has kept me on the quiver of expectation, month after month, making it impossible for me to enjoy anything'.[3] But when Mackinnon had asked him to lead an expedition to the relief of Emin Pasha, Stanley had at once realized that he would first have to obtain the permission of King Leopold.[4] The whole scheme was so uncertain before he left for the United States that Stanley had delayed approaching the King about the matter. On his return to England in December Stanley wrote to Leopold explaining the situation and asking his permission to lead the expedition; he also inquired whether his contract with the King 'will continue or cease with the acceptance of this present mission'.[5] Leopold's reply was to summon Stanley to Brussels.[6] On the morning of 30 December the two men met at the palace, and Stanley returned to London the same night.

At this important meeting—which Stanley completely omits from his book—Leopold did not explain his reasons for the persistent prevarication over his plans for Stanley's future. The King merely stated: 'Circumstances were such that I could not employ you as I intended. *Haute politique*, you know, to which we must all bend. It was no fault of yours or mine.'[7] Stanley was under the impression that this 'referred to some threat made by the French Government, who did not desire my presence on the Congo. However, the King was wonderfully benevolent, almost paternally so, and my hot anger at the "tricks" I had conceived he had been playing me cooled.'[8] The two men then proceeded to discuss the Emin Pasha relief expedition.

The idea of sending an expedition to Equatoria via the Congo and

[1] Count Lalaing to Mackinnon, 5 July 1885, M.P., 105.
[2] Leopold to Strauch, 18 Dec. 1886, Strauch Papers (2), Archives du musée de la dynastie, Brussels, No. 8695.
[3] Stanley to Mackinnon, 18 Sept. 1886, M.P., 218.   [4] *IDA* i. 33.
[5] Stanley to Leopold, 27 Dec. 1886, Van Eetvelde Papers, Brussels, 63, no. 1.
[6] Leopold to Stanley, 28 Dec. 1886, ibid. 63, no. 2.
[7] Hird, op. cit., p. 222.   [8] Ibid. 223.

Aruwimi rivers was by no means a new one to Leopold of the Belgians; indeed by December 1886 it already had a considerable history. The idea had first been suggested to Leopold in 1884 by General Gordon, the man whom Leopold himself later acknowledged as having been the first to draw his attention to the possible value of the southern Sudan.[1] In January 1884 Leopold had been attempting, for the third time, to obtain the services of Gordon to succeed Stanley on the Congo—a task in which, as in the past, the King was assisted by Mackinnon and Sir John Kirk. Gordon had visited the King in Brussels and it was then that he had put forward the revolutionary proposal of an approach to the southern Sudan via the Congo. The defeat of Hicks Pasha's army by the Mahdi in November 1883 had made it clear that as far as Egypt was concerned the provinces of Equatoria and the Bahr al-Ghazal would have to be abandoned. Gordon reported that 'H.M. [Leopold] told me that he would take those two provinces if he could get them, when I was in Brussels, also that he would take over the troops in them.'[2] Gordon—who had a rather naïve view of Leopold's purposes in the Congo State[3]— was convinced that the slave-trade in the southern Sudan would be suppressed only when these areas were annexed and administered by a European Power, preferably one not embroiled with Egypt. He therefore proposed to Leopold that he should lead an expedition up the Congo and Aruwimi rivers and then strike overland to Emin's province and the Bahr al-Ghazal. Once established there, Gordon hoped to be able 'to take every province back' while the Egyptian forces in the north kept the Mahdi fully occupied.[4] The British War Office, however, stepped in and claimed Gordon's services for the evacuation of Khartoum. From Korosko, on his way to Khartoum, Gordon wrote to Leopold offering, after completing his Khartoum mission, to go to the south and to take over the provinces of Equatoria and the Bahr al-Ghazal for the Congo State and to administer them as Leopold's agent.[5] Gordon coolly estimated that

[1] R. Gray, *A History of the Southern Sudan*, pp. 191–2, citing Plunkett to Kimberley, 29 Apr. 1894, F.O. 10/614, and Plunkett to Kimberley, 23 June 1894, F.O. 10/616.
[2] Gordon to Sir Evelyn Baring, 1 Feb. 1884, printed in B. M. Allen, *Gordon and the Sudan* (London, 1931), p. 446.
[3] See, for example, the letter which Gordon wrote to Stanley at this time (6 Jan. 1884) printed in *Biographie Coloniale Belge*, iv. 350.
[4] R. Gray, op. cit., p. 191, citing Gordon to Allen, 5 Jan. 1884, British Museum, Add. MSS. 47609.
[5] Gordon to Leopold, 1 Feb. 1884, printed in B. M. Allen, op. cit., pp. 446–9.

the administration of these two provinces might cost Leopold
£50,000 a year at first, but suggested that this could be met by econo-
mizing elsewhere, e.g. by 'giving up to France those stations Y.M.
now holds on north of Congo river . . . Y.M. may also hope to see
the object of your vast expenditure fulfilled within a few years, and
with it the cutting off of the slave-trade in a way nothing else can
do'.[1] In 1884, Leopold had neither the financial nor the administrative resources to extend the frontiers of his Congo State to the Nile,
but this remained an objective, indeed an obsession, which the King
pursued with remarkable tenacity throughout the next two decades.[2]

Stanley had lightly dismissed Gordon's scheme when he heard of
it at Vivi in April 1884,[3] but a few months later he himself suggested
that an expedition manned by 600 Zanzibaris should be sent by the
same route to 'relieve' Lupton Bey in the Bahr al-Ghazal. Once
'relieved', the services of Lupton and his soldiers could be utilized
by Leopold for his Congo administration. A further objective of
the expedition would be 'to further and extend the influence' of the
International Association over the north-eastern portions of the
territory recently marked out by Stanley for the Congo State; this
should be done by annexing by treaty all lands up to the Nile-Congo
watershed. The permission of the British Government would be
needed and they might also be asked to assist in persuading the
Sultan of Zanzibar to allow the recruitment of the 600 Zanzibaris
and in chartering a steamer (at an estimated cost of £5,000) to bring
the expedition round from Zanzibar to the Congo. If the British
Government asked Leopold what reasons he could put forward why
they should help in these ways, Stanley suggested 'Why not say to
distract the Mahdi's attention from Gordon?'. As Stanley pointed
out, Leopold had nothing to lose by sending such an expedition.
'Lupton Bey has £100,000 worth of ivory and rubber. If we can
carry it, such a sum will more than twice pay you for your munificent
offer.'[4] Here in prototype are all the elements which reappear two
years later in the Emin Pasha relief expedition. In 1884 Strauch
found Stanley's plan 'seductive like a mirage', and recoiled before

[1] Gordon to Leopold, 1 Feb. 1884, printed in B. M. Allen, op. cit., pp. 446-9.
[2] The most recent work on Leopold's Nile policy is R. O. Collins, *King Leopold,
England and the Upper Nile 1899–1909* (Yale, 1968).
[3] Stanley to the International Association, 23 Apr. 1884, printed in H. M.
Stanley, *The Congo and the Founding of its Free State*, ii. 226-7.
[4] Stanley to Leopold, 3 Sept. 1884, Palace Archives, Brussels, Dossier 102,
no. 2.

the difficulties it might involve.[1] Stanley was not deterred. He later told Leopold that ever since he had met Linant de Bellefonds (one of Gordon's assistants in the Sudan) at the court of the Kabaka of Buganda in 1876, the Sudan had been 'an irresistibly fascinating subject of study to me'.[2] Until 1884 Stanley was occupied in opening up the Congo—the unfinished task of his great predecessor and mentor, David Livingstone. Thereafter it became Stanley's determined ambition to pioneer the exploration of one of the major remaining stretches of unknown territory in Africa—the area between the Congo and the Nile. Stanley's scheme for the relief of Lupton Bey in 1884 was the first of several occasions on which he was to urge the organization of an expedition which, whilst having an immediate objective in the Equatorial provinces, would also enable him to fulfil this personal ambition.

A second opportunity had arisen in 1885, soon after Stanley had returned to England from the Congo. At the time of the discussion about the construction of a Suakin-Berber railway, Stanley had led the humanitarians—including Allen and Felkin—in urging 'all who lament the death of Gordon' to unite their forces and form a Gordon Association for the Nile on the model of the Congo International Association.[3] Stanley proposed that an expedition should be organized which would reach Equatoria via the Congo and Aruwimi and unite the peoples of the Equatorial region into 'a confederacy for their own self-preservation' on the lines previously suggested by Gordon himself. Stanley's appeal was warmly supported by Hutton, and Schweinfurth welcomed the 'great conception of reconquering the area of the Upper Nile . . . approaching from the south'.[4] But the public response was slight and Stanley's plans once more remained in abeyance.

In March 1886 Stanley again approached Leopold with a suggestion for an expedition from the Congo to the southern Sudan. This time his proposal undoubtedly owed much to Gordon's scheme two years previously.[5] Stanley pointed out that since the outbreak

[1] Strauch to Leopold, 4 Sept. 1884, Strauch Papers (3), Archives du Ministère des Colonies, Brussels, I.R.C.B. 505. Ceulemans, op. cit., p. 89.
[2] Stanley to Leopold, 18 Mar. 1886, Palace Archives, Brussels, Dossier 102.
[3] This account of this episode is based on R. Gray, A History of the Southern Sudan, pp. 193-4.
[4] Schweinfurth to Allen, 17 Aug. 1885, cited in R. Gray, op. cit., p. 194.
[5] Stanley to Leopold, 18 Mar. 1886, Palace Archives, Brussels, Dossier 102. Stanley also published an article on the Congo-Aruwimi route in Le Mouvement géographique, 24 Jan. 1886, p. 7.

of the Mahdist rebellion in the Sudan, the provinces of Equatoria and the Bahr al-Ghazal had been beyond the concern of the Egyptian Government and the Mahdists alike. The opportunity was wide open for these two provinces to be 're-organised . . . by way of the Congo' since 'the Equatorial Soudan is as near to Europe by way of the Congo as it is via the Nile'. While the Nile route was blocked by both the *sudd* and the Mahdists, the Congo route was not, and the Equatorial provinces were 'but a step, as it were, from the depots and steamers of the Congo State. . . . They are as easy of access from the Upper Congo flotilla as Stanley Pool is from the sea-coast, the mileage intervening being the same.' Stanley's suggestion was that Leopold should offer, in return for a subsidy from Egypt, to order his troops on the Congo 'to cross the frontier and commence the re-establishment of order in the Equatorial Provinces in the name of Egypt'. Stanley considered that such a task would be 'merely an extension' of Leopold's present administration and that the remaining Egyptian soldiers in the provinces could be recruited for the Congo State. With a subsidy of £200,000 a year from Egypt, Stanley estimated that 'the remittance would greatly exceed the expenditure'. Stanley's scheme was wildly out of touch with the realities of the situation in Egypt, where there was not the slightest chance that Baring would be prepared to devote £200,000 out of an unbalanced budget to enable Leopold to occupy the southern Sudan. Leopold, however, appears to have been impressed by what Stanley had said with regard to the ease of reaching the southern Sudan by the Congo. In April the King wrote to Gladstone tentatively inquiring whether the Congo State might be of some service to Egypt in the Bahr al-Ghazal.[1] Gladstone's reply was merely to the effect that the British Government did not contemplate 'any renewal of operations in the Soudan on our own account'.[2] During the next few months Leopold was preoccupied with the financial difficulties of the Congo State. The matter of a possible expedition to the southern Sudan was set aside and there is no evidence that it was even mentioned when Stanley and Leopold met in Brussels in September.[3]

The whole matter was revived when it became known that Mackinnon, with the assistance of the British Government, was

---

[1] Leopold to Gladstone, 2 Apr. 1886, Palace Archives, Brussels, Dossier 170, no. 2.

[2] Gladstone to Leopold, 10 Apr. 1886, ibid., Dossier 170, no. 3.

[3] Bontinck, *Aux origines de l'état indépendant du Congo*, p. 361.

organizing an expedition to relieve Emin Pasha and that Stanley was to lead it. The Belgian journal *Le Mouvement géographique* (which the British Minister in Brussels described as 'the mouthpiece of the Congo Government'[1]) pointed to the advantages of the Congo-Aruwimi route for such an expedition in its issue of 5 December 1886.[2] On 19 December, the same journal emphasized the fact that Stanley was still in the service of King Leopold and again stressed the advantages of the Congo route.[3] Meanwhile, in a letter of 8 December, Strauch had suggested to the King that an offer should be made to the British Government whereby an expedition, led by Stanley, would be organized under the auspices of the Congo State; Emin would be evacuated and repatriated to Egypt in return for a subsidy from the British Government of £60,000.[4] Leopold was of the opinion that nothing should be done until an approach was made on the matter to Brussels.[5] In New York and London it was widely believed that it was Leopold, not Mackinnon, who had summoned Stanley back from the United States, but Leopold denied this.[6]

By the middle of December, Leopold was expecting that Stanley would soon approach him with the request that he be released from his contract with the King in order to lead the Emin Pasha expedition. This would place the King in a difficult position. Stanley's knowledge of the Congo was unsurpassed and he remained the most distinguished employee of the Congo State. Leopold was therefore anxious to retain his services. In addition, there was a particular reason why Leopold wished to keep Stanley at hand. At the end of August 1886 the station of Stanley Falls had been attacked and destroyed by the Arabs in the eastern Congo, whose headquarters were at Nyangwe. Leopold wanted Stanley to be available 'in case I am in a position to send him to recapture the Falls and to march on Nyangwe'.[7] Strauch, however, felt that 'the most propitious time to begin a campaign against the Arabs has not yet arrived', and that since there was no other immediate task for Stanley it would be

[1] Gosselin to Iddesleigh, 19 Dec. 1886, F.O.C.P. 5433, no. 64.

[2] *Le Mouvement géographique*, 5 Dec. 1886. The article was written by the editor, A. J. Wauters. See A. J. Wauters, *Stanley's Emin Pasha Expedition* (London, 1890), p. 131.   [3] *Le Mouvement géographique*, 19 Dec. 1886.

[4] Strauch to Leopold, 8 Dec. 1886, Strauch Papers (3), no. 505.

[5] Leopold's comment on Strauch to Leopold, 8 Dec. 1886, cited above.

[6] Leopold to Baron Lambermont, 15 Dec. 1886, Lambermont Papers, no. 240, Archives du Ministère des Affaires Étrangères, Brussels. Ceulemans, op. cit., p. 93.

[7] Leopold to Strauch, 17 Dec. 1886, Strauch Papers (2), no. 8694.

difficult and impolitic to refuse him permission to lead the Emin Pasha expedition.[1] On the eve of Stanley's arrival in Brussels, Leopold reaffirmed his determination not to deprive himself of Stanley's services and his intention to put Stanley in charge of a military expedition against the Arabs in the immediate future. In the meantime, the King decided to tell Stanley that he would be required for an undefined but most important mission within the next two months.[2]

When Leopold and Stanley began to discuss the matter of the Emin Pasha relief expedition on 30 December, the King found himself in a position of unexpected strength. Stanley's services were requested to lead an expedition to Equatoria which was financed and organized by someone else. And Stanley himself was determined to lead it by the Congo-Aruwimi route which he had twice previously recommended to the King. Stanley's ambition, and his genuine conviction that this route possessed considerable advantages over all others, were in close accord with Leopold's own desire to open up a route of communication between his Congo State and the Nile. The interests both of the Congo State and of Stanley's own ambition would therefore be served if the expedition adopted the Congo route. Mackinnon and the Emin Pasha Relief Committee, however, wanted the expedition to take the east-coast route so that Stanley could make treaties in the interior which could then be used in support of the claims for the East African Company which Mackinnon hoped to charter. This part of Mackinnon's objective was almost certainly made clear to Leopold by Stanley. The King, however, insisted that the Congo route must be taken. Stanley reported that Leopold declared:

If the Committee will not agree to this, I do not see how I can lend your services, which are, as you know, pledged to me, for this expedition. I shall want you myself in a few weeks from now on a far more important work than relieving Emin. It is a mission of which you will be proud. But if the Committee will let you go via the Congo I can postpone the mission for another eighteen months.[3]

Stanley pointed out that the Committee would almost certainly object to the change of route because of the extra expense which would be involved in transporting the expedition from Zanzibar to the Congo. The King was 'obstinate and said it must be so, or the

---

[1] Strauch to Leopold, 18 Dec. 1886, Strauch Papers (3), no. 505.
[2] Leopold to Strauch, 29 Dec. 1886, Strauch Papers (2), no. 86102.
[3] F. Hird, *H. M. Stanley: the Authorised Life*, p. 223. The 'mission' would be that referred to in Leopold's letter to Strauch of 29 Dec. See above.

Committee must choose another leader'.[1] Immediately after the meeting, Leopold wrote a letter to Mackinnon in which he gently pressed the point.[2] Mackinnon and the Committee in effect had no choice but to act according to Leopold's wishes.[3] Leopold offered to put the flotilla of steamers belonging to the Congo State at the disposal of the expedition for the transport up the Congo. This offer was gratefully accepted by the Emin Pasha Relief Committee. The problem of transporting the expedition from Zanzibar to the Congo remained, and Stanley refused to commit himself completely to the Congo route until this was solved. Leopold hoped that Mackinnon's British India Steamship Company would lend a steamer.[4] When this was finally arranged, Leopold asked Strauch to instruct the Congo State authorities that every assistance was to be given to the expedition not only in the provision of transport but in the preparation of camps along the route and in the cutting of wood for the steamers in advance.[5] Thus, the decision to adopt the Congo route was made in principle at Brussels at the end of December and not, as Stanley claims in his book, as a result of the letter received from the Comte de Borchgrave in January.[6]

There was one obvious solution by which the interests of Leopold, Mackinnon, and Stanley himself concerning the route of the expedition could all be combined. This was if the expedition went out by the Congo and returned overland through the East African interior to Zanzibar. This was almost certainly the plan on which Stanley had already decided. Shortly after his return to London he informed Sir Percy Anderson that although any refugees from Equatoria would be evacuated by the Congo, he himself would not return via the Congo but 'would make his way to the [East African] coast on his return by whatever route he fancied on his own account'.[7] By the time the expedition set out this was accepted on all sides.[8]

[1] F. Hird, *H. M. Stanley: the Authorised Life*, p. 223.
[2] Leopold to Mackinnon, 30 Dec. 1886, copy in the Van Eetvelde Papers, 63, no. 6, Archives du Royaume, Brussels.
[3] Mackinnon to Stanley, 4 Jan. 1887, printed in *IDA* i. 44.
[4] Leopold to Lambermont, 15 Jan. 1887, Palace Archives, Brussels, 72, no. 14.
[5] Leopold to Strauch, 20 Jan. 1887, Strauch Papers (1), AF. 1-13, no. 635. (A copy of the Memorandum enclosed with this letter is in the Mackinnon Papers.)   [6] *IDA* i. 43-4.
[7] Memorandum by Anderson, 5 Jan. 1887, F.O.C.P. 5617, p. 4.
[8] See Mackinnon to Sultan of Zanzibar, 28 Jan. 1887, printed in *IDA* i. 61-2. Salisbury to Baring, 20 Jan. 1887, F.O. 84/1878. de Winton to F.O., 25 Mar. 1887, F.O. 84/1860.

Leopold's interest in the Emin Pasha relief expedition was by no means limited to the question of the route it was to take. As has been shown, Leopold had for some years been interested in, even covetous of, the territories towards which the expedition was directed. The proposals of Gordon and Stanley had been for expeditions whose objective was to acquire these territories and to enlist their remaining administrators and soldiers in the service of Leopold's Congo State. The proposal which Leopold now put forward to Stanley, should Emin wish to remain in Equatoria, resembled very closely the suggestion which Stanley himself had previously made to the King with regard to Lupton Bey. When Stanley reached Equatoria he was to offer Emin employment under the Congo State as Governor of Equatoria, at a salary of £1,500 per year and with the rank of General. In addition, Leopold offered to find £10,000 to £12,000 per year for the administration of the province, provided that it could 'yield a reasonable revenue' in ivory and other produce. Emin's duties would be to continue with the government of the province and to 'keep open the communications between the Nile and the Congo' which Stanley's expedition would hopefully have developed.[1] The significance of this proposal can easily be exaggerated. At no time was the employment in Equatoria of Emin and his garrisons by the Congo State considered by Leopold as the foundation for a future Nile policy. Rather, the proposal has about it the character of an idea of the moment, a passing inspiration of Leopold himself. Leopold's correspondence is littered with the record of such flashes of inspiration—ideas and proposals hurriedly scribbled in almost illegible handwriting on envelopes or round the edges of other people's letters. These jottings have about them a visionary quality which is also to be found in the papers and sketch-maps of Cecil Rhodes. Most of the proposals recorded by Leopold in this way came to nothing; many were soon forgotten by the King himself. The proposal to employ Emin and his garrisons would seem to belong to this category. Leopold, in fact, gave only a passing attention to the Emin Pasha relief expedition. In this his role is markedly different from that of Mackinnon and those who sent it. In the initial stages

---

[1] *IDA* i. 387. Stanley's version of these instructions must be read in conjunction with that later recorded by Emin Pasha in a long interview with Euan-Smith, the British Consul-General at Zanzibar. See Euan-Smith to Salisbury, 14 Mar. 1890, F.O. 84/2060. A copy of this important dispatch is also in the Mackinnon Papers.

the King was concerned to obtain some return, in the form of services for his Congo State, out of the fact that Stanley was to lead this expedition. Leopold considered his loan of Stanley's services to Mackinnon as a real sacrifice. None the less, Leopold's action in the matter was not disinterested. In the assessment of the King, the fact that Stanley was to lead the expedition by the Congo route would safeguard the interests of the Congo State and would provide the best guarantee for a share in the results if the expedition were successful.[1] Leopold himself showed no lasting expectation that his offer of employment to Emin and his garrisons would be accepted. Indeed, by the time that Stanley was in a position to pass on this proposal to Emin, Leopold would appear to have resigned himself to the likelihood that if Emin was to be employed by anybody, it would be by Mackinnon's I.B.E.A. Company.[2]

None the less, it has never been clear quite how this proposal from Leopold was to be reconciled with that which Stanley had discussed with Mackinnon. The point is of some interest since it raises issues in the context of this early stage of Leopold's drive to the Nile and the delimitation of British East Africa which were to continue through the Mackinnon Treaty of 1890, the Anglo-Congolese Agreement of 1894, and Leopold's final acquisition of the Lado Enclave. To what extent can it be said that the collaboration which characterizes the relationship between Leopold and Mackinnon in the period 1876–86 is continued in the Emin Pasha relief expedition? In writing to Mackinnon about the expedition, Leopold expressed the hope that, as in the past, 'you will be able to see this time also how to combine all those interests [of the Congo State] with the accomplishments of your own project, and we may both agree that no-one fitter than Mr. Stanley could be found for this'.[3] But how much did Leopold know about Mackinnon's 'project', and in whose camp was Stanley?

Whether Stanley ever told Leopold before the expedition set out of Mackinnon's tentative proposal regarding the employment of Emin and his men is not clear—but all the evidence suggests that he did not; and Mackinnon's actions suggest that he in turn was not

---

[1] Ceulemans, op. cit., p. 95.
[2] See Leopold to Strauch, 6 Jan. 1888, Strauch Papers (2), Brussels, no. 8802. Also Resumé du Dossier 'British East Africa Company', Feb.–Sept. 1888, Van Eetvelde Papers, Archives du Royaume, Dossier 117.
[3] Leopold to Mackinnon, 30 Dec. 1886, Van Eetvelde Papers, 63, no. 6, Archives du Royaume, Brussels.

aware of Leopold's proposal until much later.[1] Mackinnon's proposal
was in any case a good deal less concrete than that of Leopold. So far
as can be judged from limited evidence, at the time of the organization of the Emin Pasha relief expedition Mackinnon appears to have
been interested less in annexing the Equatorial province as such than
in enlisting Emin and his men for employment in his projected East
Africa Company.[2] Certainly, the annexation of Equatoria was not
Mackinnon's immediate objective at this stage, when the means to
maintain it had yet to be established and the I.B.E.A. Company
had yet to be formed. It is also significant that at no time does
Mackinnon show any interest in acquiring territory west of Wadelai.
And Wadelai itself, although it remained a goal for Stanley's expedition and for the later expeditions under Jackson and Lugard
dispatched by Mackinnon to the interior, remained in fact something of a red herring, and it was never occupied by Mackinnon's
Company.

Leopold's objectives were more emphatically territorial. He wanted
to open up the north-eastern corner of the Congo State and obtain a
frontier on the Nile. But whatever his territorial ambitions west of the
Nile (and in the future they were to be considerable), Leopold never
really expected to acquire territory on the eastern bank.[3] Leopold's
idée fixe was a frontier on the Nile, and during 1887-9 he became
increasingly anxious that this frontier should adjoin the territory
under Mackinnon's I.B.E.A. Company without the interposition of
a third Power, particularly Germany.[4]

---

[1] The Congo offer to Emin is noticeably missing from the letter which Stanley
wrote to Mackinnon after he had met Emin describing in detail what had happened at their meeting. (Stanley to Mackinnon, 3 Sept. 1888, M.P., F. 4.).
Mackinnon never refers to it either in Stanley's letter or in his extensive correspondence with the F.O. (Mackinnon to Stanley, 5 Apr. 1889,
M.P., F.1.) Leopold never refers to the Congo offer in any of his letters to
Mackinnon. Leopold certainly knew of Mackinnon's proposal in 1889, when
Mackinnon sent a copy of Stanley's letter (cited above) to the King (enclosed
in Mackinnon to Leopold, 20 Apr. 1889, Palace Archives, Brussels, 82, no. 78).
[2] de Kiewiet, 'A History of the I.B.E.A. Company', p. 87.
[3] In Mar. 1893 King Leopold—always ready to step into the breach when there
was a chance of extending his territory—wrote to Gladstone offering to take over
the administration of Buganda and Bunyoro. The I.B.E.A. Company was
threatening to withdraw. The British Government was reluctant to take over.
This offer of Leopold's appears less as part of a serious and sustained attempt
to acquire territory east of the Nile than as another of the King's short-lived
inspirations. See W. L. Langer, *The Diplomacy of Imperialism*, 2nd edn. (New
York, 1951), p. 122.
[4] 'I am very anxious that no unoccupied territories should stand between your

A great deal was to happen between 1886, when the Emin Pasha relief expedition was organized, and 1888, when Stanley finally met Emin Pasha on the shores of Lake Albert. Behind the proposals of both Mackinnon and Leopold as they were conceived in 1886 lay the hope that if Emin were to be reinforced and maintained in Equatoria, Wadelai might become a terminus for the routes into the interior which Stanley's expedition was expected to open up from the Congo State on the one hand and from the East African coast on the other.[1] In territorial terms, therefore, the objectives of Leopold and Mackinnon with regard to Equatoria were not incompatible.

When it came to the enlistment of Emin and his garrisons, however, Stanley himself presented the proposals of Leopold and Mackinnon to Emin as mutually exclusive alternatives.[2] Whatever his attitude in 1886, it is clear that by 1888 Stanley personally favoured Mackinnon's scheme.[3] Leopold's treatment of him in the period 1884–6 was never quite forgotten, and Stanley's own experiences during the course of the expedition made him extremely sceptical of Leopold's ability to maintain a frontier on the Nile. At the end of the expedition Stanley declared to Mackinnon, 'I considered myself only as your agent.'[4] Possibly this declaration was made to counteract the charge of duplicity. It would, however, appear to reflect the true direction of Stanley's loyalty throughout the expedition. After 1886 Stanley's primary interest is in the future of British East Africa and Mackinnon's I.B.E.A. Company. Should a clash arise, this interest would not be subordinated to that of Leopold of the Belgians.[5]

There was a third important task which Leopold was to entrust to Stanley to carry out on behalf of the Congo State while on this expedition. At a second meeting in Brussels, on 15 January 1887, Stanley undertook to negotiate while he was at Zanzibar with the

stations and mine', Leopold to Mackinnon, 18 Apr. 1889, Palace Archives, Brussels, Dossier 82, no. 77. 'Our interests and those of the Congo State should never clash; their kingdom is so vast they can hardly wish to interfere in the East', Kirk to Mackinnon, 2 July 1888, M.P., 97.

[1] W. L. Langer, op. cit., p. 114.

[2] Emin's version of the proposals is to be found in his *Tagebücher*, iv. 100–19, May 1888 (Extracts X, pp. 204–7); and the conversation later reported by Euan-Smith, Euan-Smith to Salisbury, 14 Mar. 1890, F.O. 84/2060. See also Ch. VII, p. 157 below.

[3] See Ch. VII, p. 163 below.

[4] Stanley to Mackinnon, 19 Jan. 1890, M.P., F. 4. R. Anstey, *Britain and the Congo in the 19th Century*, p. 223.   [5] R. Anstey, op. cit., p. 223.

man Leopold was not yet strong enough to crush: the chief Arab
ruler of a large area of the eastern Congo, Tippu Tip. If the expedition were to take the Congo route, an arrangement with Tippu Tip
was essential. The expedition would have to pass through territory
where it would be dependent on the Arabs, with whom the Congo
State was on the brink of war. Further, Stanley wished to establish a
base camp on the Aruwimi in the heart of the Arab region near
Stanley Falls. Leopold had felt acutely the recent destruction of the
Stanley Falls station by the Arabs and would have 'pursued Tippu
Tip to the death if he were able'.[1] It is possible that Leopold's initial
hope was to utilize the Emin expedition for the recapture of the
station at Stanley Falls; this was certainly the fear of the British
Foreign Office.[2] But Stanley was determined to avoid Stanley Falls
and urged a policy of conciliation on the King.[3] Such a policy had
already been advised by two of Leopold's senior administrators in
the Congo, Wester and J. Becker.[4] Stanley had an immediate interest
in effecting such a policy and was himself in an excellent position
to act as mediator. In 1876 he had met and been assisted by Tippu
Tip during his journey down the Congo. Like Livingstone and
Cameron, Stanley had a favourable opinion of Tippu Tip. The news
had recently arrived that Tippu Tip was at this time in Zanzibar.
Stanley therefore undertook, when he was at Zanzibar, to negotiate
a peaceful settlement with Tippu Tip on behalf of the Congo State.
Since Tippu Tip was in effective occupation of Stanley Falls and the
Congo State was not yet in a position to displace him, the object was
to make him the ally, even the employee of the Congo State, and to
use him as a buffer against the lesser Arab 'warlords' in the area
above Stanley Falls.[4] The exact nature of the settlement to be arrived
at appears to have been left largely to Stanley's own initiative.
Stanley also planned to obtain particular assistance from Tippu Tip
for the expedition.

*   *   *

On 1 January 1887 Stanley was back in London. He at once
became immersed in organizing the expedition which was to leave
three weeks later—a task in which he was closely assisted by Sir
Francis de Winton, Colonel J. A. Grant, and Guy Dawnay of the

[1] F. Hird, *H. M. Stanley: the Authorised Life*, p. 226.
[2] See Gosselin to Salisbury, 21 July 1887, F.O.C.P. 5617, p. 49.
[3] F. Hird, op. cit., p. 228. Ceulemans, op. cit., pp. 98–9.
[4] Ibid. See also, J. Becker, *La Vie en Afrique*, ii. 46.

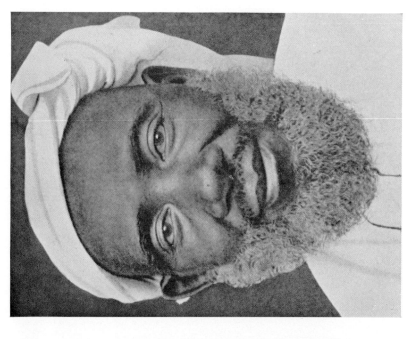

2b. TIPPU TIP

2a. H. M. STANLEY

War Office.[1] Telegrams had already been sent via the Foreign Office
to Holmwood instructing him to do everything to promote the
expedition. The support of the Sultan was obtained and Holmwood
was requested to recruit 400–500 porters to await Stanley's arrival
in Zanzibar.[2] Arrangements were made with Baring in Cairo for
the expedition to be equipped (without charge) with 400 Remington
rifles and ammunition; in addition, 100 loads of cloth and 200 loads
of ammunition were prepared for the expedition to take to Emin.[3]
Baring also recruited for the expedition sixty-one Sudanese soldiers—
many of whom had been on Wolseley's expedition to relieve Gordon
at Khartoum. Stanley was less concerned about the role of these
men as an armed escort than with their usefulness when the expedition reached Equatoria in reassuring Emin's men that the expedition
came from Egypt with the Khedive's orders.[4]

All Stanley's preparations were made on the assumption that the
expedition would take the Congo route. An open steel boat, 28 ft.
long and easily divided into twelve portable sections, was ordered.
Stanley hoped that this boat, named the *Advance*, would greatly
assist the conveyance of at least the equipment of the expedition
up the navigable portions of the Aruwimi. On the lower Congo,
Stanley and the Emin Pasha Relief Committee counted a good deal
on the services of the steamers belonging to the Congo State which
Leopold had promised. The major problem was the transport of
the expedition from Zanzibar round the Cape of Good Hope to the
mouth of the Congo at Banana. Stanley initially hoped that the
Admiralty would provide a ship—as they had done in 1877, when
H.M.S. *Industry* had transported Stanley's earlier expedition from
Loanda to Zanzibar after the crossing of the African continent.[5]
But the Admiralty were unable to provide a ship and so Mackinnon
made available one of the British India Steamship Company's
vessels, the *Madura*, to transport the expedition from Zanzibar to
the Congo. Eventually Mackinnon's Company found itself prevailed
upon to provide all the ocean-going transport for the expedition.
The P. & O. Line refused to transport the equipment of the expedition
to Zanzibar because this equipment contained a large amount of

---

[1] Report of the Emin Pasha Relief Committee, 1891, M.P., p. 14.
[2] Iddesleigh to Holmwood, 22 Dec. and 25 Dec. 1886, F.O.C.P. 5433, pp. 102,
104.
[3] Iddesleigh to Baring, 28 Dec. 1886, F.O.C.P. 5433, no. 76.
[4] *IDA* i. 68.
[5] Memorandum by Anderson, 5 Jan. 1887, F.O. C.P. 5617, no. 7.

ammunition. The *Navarino* was therefore offered to take the equipment and some of the officers to Aden and there the Postmaster-
General agreed to hold up the British India Steamship Company's
mail steamer *Oriental* to connect with the *Navarino* and complete
the transport to Zanzibar. Mackinnon's Company having provided
the ships, the Admiralty were prevailed upon by the Foreign Office
to provide 1,000 tons of free coal and loading facilities on the voyage
round Africa.

Other preparations were soon made. Hiram Maxim presented
Stanley with one of his recently invented Maxim guns (the first to
be taken to Africa). Mackinnon declared that 'merely exhibiting'
the gun during the course of the expedition was likely 'to prove a
great peace-preserver'; none the less, he persuaded the War Office
to provide plenty of free ammunition for it.[1] Fortnum & Mason's
packed forty loads of choicest provisions; Burroughs & Wellcome
presented nine fully equipped medicine chests; and the Eastern
Telegraph Company offered to transmit all telegrams connected
with the expedition at half rate.[2]

One of Stanley's major tasks was the selection of the officers who
were to accompany him on this expedition. By January he had received over 400 applications.[3] One of these came from Joseph
Thomson. Thomson had very much wanted to lead the expedition
himself. From Paris he had written to Brackenbury at the War
Office offering to lead any expedition which might be sent. 'I understand Stanley has offered himself', Thomson commented, 'but I
need hardly remind you that he is an American.'[4] Thomson later
asked Bates and Keltie at the Royal Geographical Society to intervene on his behalf.[5] When this was unsuccessful he approached the
Emin Pasha Relief Committee direct. In January he offered his
services unreservedly in any capacity. This was declined with thanks
'as the offer came so very late'.[6] There is no evidence to show that
on the question of the leadership of the expedition Mackinnon
ever considered anyone but Stanley.

---

[1] Mackinnon to Iddesleigh, 10 Jan. 1887, F.O.C.P. 5617, no. 16.
[2] Emin Pasha Relief Committee Minute Book, Jan. 1887, M.P.
[3] *The Times*, 17 Jan. 1887.
[4] Joseph Thomson to Brackenbury, 26 Nov. 1886, F.O.C.P. 5433, no. 48.
[5] Joseph Thomson to Bates, 25 Nov. 1886, 1 and 7 Dec. 1886, Royal Geographical Society Archives, Thomson Correspondence. (I am indebted to Mrs.
Middleton for this reference.)
[6] Emin Pasha Relief Committee Minute Book, 19 Jan. 1887, M.P.

Stanley eventually selected seven officers to accompany him, none of them exceptional. Captain R. H. Nelson of Methuen's Horse, Lieutenant W. G. Stairs of the Royal Engineers, Major Edmund Musgrave Barttelot of the 7th Fusiliers, and Mr. William Bonny were all army men, Bonny being engaged specifically in a lesser capacity as medical assistant. James S. Jameson had travelled extensively in Mashonaland and Matabeleland and was an amateur artist and natural historian. He was engaged to record and collect specimens of the flora and fauna during the course of the expedition. Like A. J. Mounteney-Jephson, he also made a subscription of £1,000 for the privilege of joining the expedition. Jephson had few obvious qualifications and some of the Committee objected that he looked too 'high class' for such an expedition. But the Countess de Noailles made the subscription of £1,000 on his behalf and Jephson was recruited. The fact that he was to be the only one of the officers in whom Stanley confided to any extent at all during the course of the expedition lends a particular value to his intelligent and sensitive record of the expedition.[1] The last of the seven officers recruited in England was John Rose Troup. He had only recently returned from the Congo where, for three years, he had been working for the Congo State under Sir Francis de Winton. de Winton's recommendation, and Troup's knowledge of present conditions on the Congo, led Stanley to hope that his services would be especially useful in organizing the passage of the expedition up the Congo. Stanley had hoped to recruit a Dr. Leslie as medical officer to the expedition, but Leslie objected to the terms of the contract,[2] and the place of medical officer was not filled until Dr. Thomas Heazle Parke, of the Army Medical Staff, was recruited in Cairo. While preparations for the departure of the expedition went forward, Stanley received widespread public acclaim. He was awarded the freedom of the City of London at the Guildhall—the first journalist ever to receive this honour. Accompanied by de Winton, he visited Sandringham and explained the route of the expedition to the Prince and Princess of Wales. On 12 January he was to have had a private interview with Lord Iddesleigh, but the Foreign Secretary dropped dead from heart failure earlier in the day.[3]

---

[1] This has recently been edited by Mrs. Middleton of the Royal Geographical Society and published by the Hakluyt Society (Cambridge, 1969).
[2] W. G. Barttelot, *The Life of Edmund Musgrave Barttelot* (London, 1890), p. 51.   [3] *IDA* i. 46.

In several public speeches Stanley outlined his plans for the expedition and the length of time he expected it to take. Similar statements were made by Mackinnon and the Committee in letters to the Foreign Office.[1] Travelling by Cairo and Zanzibar, Stanley expected the expedition to reach the mouth of the Congo towards the end of March 1887. With the assistance of the steamers and the employees of the Congo State, Stanley would then push on rapidly up the Congo to the point where the Aruwimi river branched off. Here he would establish a base camp before marching on with an advance column through unknown territory to Lake Albert. This march was expected to take only about thirty-five days and Mackinnon expected that Stanley and Emin would meet 'about the middle or end of July'. Whatever Stanley and Emin might then decide, it was expected that the expedition would form two separate parties for the return journey. The first would consist of the women and children belonging to the Egyptian employees in Equatoria who wished to return to Egypt. Their numbers were not expected to be large (calculations were based on an estimate of 100) and they were to return along the route through the upper Congo, which Stanley would have opened up, to the base camp on the Aruwimi. They were expected to arrive there between September and October 1887. From here it was to be left to the Egyptian Government to arrange with the authorities of the Congo State for a steamer to be sent to collect them and bring them down to the mouth of the Congo, whence they would be repatriated to Egypt. It was also hoped that a substantial amount of Emin's ivory could be brought out in this way. Since the Egyptian Government hoped that this would pay for the repatriation of the refugees, and the Committee hoped that it would cover the costs of the expedition, the question of how the proceeds from the sale of the ivory were to be shared formed the subject of prolonged negotiations between the Committee (who refused to deal with the Egyptian Government direct), the Foreign Office, and the Egyptian Government.[2]

The second party would return across the continent to the East African coast and Zanzibar. Stanley himself would lead this party

[1] Mackinnon to F.O. 10 Feb. 1887, F.O.C.P. 5617, no. 55. de Winton to F.O. 18 and 25 Mar. 1887, F.O.C.P. 5617, pp. 28–30.

[2] The correspondence between the Emin Pasha Relief Committee, the Foreign Office, and the Egyptian Government on the subjects of the repatriation of the expected refugees from Equatoria and the ivory is conveniently collected together in F.O.C.P. 5617, pp. 1–48.

and, whether or not Emin accompanied him, he hoped to enlist some of the soldiers who wished to leave Equatoria as an armed escort to assist him in the hostile territories he expected to cross. The whole expedition was expected to be over by December 1887, and to have cost no more than the £20,000 which had already been subscribed.

This programme was presented by the organizers of the expedition with confidence and optimism. The public reaction was, however, more sceptical. *The Scotsman* thought that Stanley was a man of sanguine temperament whose plans were 'covered with a roseate hue'. His programme allowed no margin for delays and even if the expedition met with no obstacles it was likely to take twice as long as Stanley estimated.[1] Others were more concerned with the excitement which the dispatch of the Emin Pasha relief expedition was likely to furnish the Victorian public for months to come. 'Africa, like the poor, is always with us', observed one correspondent, 'and with Mr. Stanley within her borders at the head of an army . . . we may expect to hear of stirring events.'[2] Stanley's mission to relieve Emin Pasha was compared with his earlier search for David Livingstone. But Livingstone had not wanted to leave Africa and there was considerable doubt as to whether Emin wanted to be rescued. Emin's continued presence in Equatoria was widely regarded in the classic mid-Victorian manner as 'a powerful check to the slave-trade there and a strong encouragement to legitimate industry and commerce';[3] to remove him 'would be a subject of poignant regret'. But 'It would be unfair to Mr. Stanley himself if a second time he had to return after hunting down his noble quarry without itself to show as the crowning evidence of his achievement.'[4] Whatever the outcome, the expedition set out with widespread public interest and goodwill. *The Times*, however, emphasized the fact that Stanley was leading 'no mere exploring or trading expedition . . . [but] the biggest non-military expedition that ever entered Africa'.[5] In a leader on 21 January 1887, the day Stanley finally left England, *The Times* observed, 'Polities and politics in Africa are like a pack of cards. The slightest movement which affects one section affects the whole . . . Mr. Stanley's arrival may anywhere precipitate a crisis.'

[1] *The Scotsman*, leader, 21 Jan. 1887.
[2] *The Times*, 'The Rescue of Emin Pasha' by a correspondent, 15 Dec. 1886.
[3] *The Times*, leader, 20 Jan. 1887.
[4] *The Times*, leader, 21 Jan. 1887.
[5] *The Times*, leader, 20 Jan. 1887.

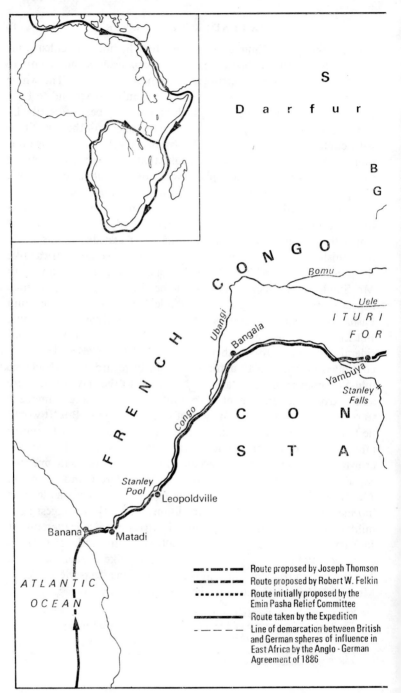

S

D a r f u r

B
G

C O N G O

Bomu

Uele

French Congo

Ubangi

Bangala

ITURI
FOR

Yambuya

Stanley
Falls

C O N

Congo

S T A

Stanley
Pool

Leopoldville

Banana

Matadi

ATLANTIC
OCEAN

▬ ▬ ▬ ▬	Route proposed by Joseph Thomson
▬ ▬ ▬ ▬	Route proposed by Robert W. Felkin
• • • • • •	Route initially proposed by the Emin Pasha Relief Committee
▬▬▬▬▬	Route taken by the Expedition
– – – – –	Line of demarcation between British and German spheres of influence in East Africa by the Anglo - German Agreement of 1886

FIG. 2. The route of the Emin

Pasha relief expedition 1887–9.

CHAPTER V

Cairo–Zanzibar–Congo: to Yambuya

STANLEY arrived in Cairo on 27 January 1887, on his way to Zanzibar. He was at once informed by Sir Evelyn Baring that the Khedive and Nubar Pasha (the Prime Minister) objected to the expedition adopting the Congo route. They estimated that it might take Stanley fifteen months or more to reach Emin by the Congo and doubted whether Emin could hold out for so long. Baring also reported that they feared that the expedition was becoming 'rather one of exploration than relief, and they somewhat demur to applying Egyptian money to the former object'.[1] The Egyptian Government appear to have threatened to withdraw their £10,000.[2] Baring felt that the objections of the Egyptian Government could be overridden if necessary and, in a personally drafted telegram, Salisbury ordered him in the most uncompromising terms to give Stanley his full support.[3] After Stanley himself had explained his reasons for adopting the Congo route to the Khedive and Nubar Pasha, they both 'expressed themselves thoroughly satisfied of the wisdom of Mr. Stanley's choice in adopting the Congo route in preference to that from Zanzibar'.[4] Nubar also agreed to permit the expedition to march under the Egyptian flag and urged that Emin should return to Egypt with as much ivory as possible.[5]

The instructions which the Khedive and Nubar gave to Stanley to convey to Emin and his garrisons left no doubt that the object of the expedition, as far as the Egyptian Government was concerned, was to bring about Emin's withdrawal from Equatoria and his return to Egypt. But, with all the appearance of an afterthought inserted at Stanley's request, Emin and his soldiers were also left with the choice of severing all connection with the Egyptian Govern-

---

[1] Baring to Salisbury, 23 Jan. 1887, F.O. 84/1878.
[2] d'Aunay to Flourens, 29 Jan. 1887. *Documents diplomatiques français*, vi, nos. 416, 431.
[3] Salisbury to Baring, 24 Jan. 1887, F.O. 84/1878.
[4] Baring to Salisbury, 2 Feb. 1887, ibid.
[5] *IDA* i. 52.

ment and remaining in Equatoria. In his letter to Emin, Nubar Pasha said:

> The expedition commanded by Mr. Stanley has been formed and organised in order to bring you the provisions and ammunition of which you must certainly be in want. Its object is to bring you, your officers, and soldiers, back to Egypt by the route which Mr. Stanley will judge most suitable. I have nothing to add to what I have just said about the object of the expedition. Only His Highness [the Khedive] leaves you, your officers, your soldiers and others entirely free to stay where you are, or to make use of the help he sends for your return.
>
> But it is well understood, and this must be made clear to your officers, soldiers, or others, if some do not wish to return they are free to remain, but at their own risk and by their own desire, and that they cannot expect any subsequent help from the Government. That is what I wish you to make clear to those who may wish to remain.[1]

The Khedive also wrote to Emin acknowledging the courage and determination with which the authority of the Egyptian Government had been upheld in Equatoria, approving the promotions which Emin had seen fit to make among the garrisons, and informing Emin that he himself had been promoted from the rank of Bey to Pasha.[2]

Whilst in Cairo, Stanley also met Mason Bey (who had first circumnavigated Lake Albert in 1877), Schweinfurth, and Junker. Junker had arrived in Cairo from Zanzibar earlier in January and both he and Schweinfurth had opposed the Congo route. Stanley's explanations, however, won them over and Junker presented Stanley with a map of his own recent travels in the Nepoko-Uele area of the Upper Congo.[3] Junker was also in a unique position to inform Stanley of Emin's actual circumstances, and this he appears to have done without reserve.

It is difficult to see how Stanley's romantic picture of Emin as an 'ideal Governor' at the head of loyal garrisons valiantly holding out against the Mahdist hordes could have survived the frank account of Emin's personality and position given to him by Junker in Cairo. After talking with Junker, Stanley reported that Emin was apparently

---

[1] Nubar Pasha to Emin Pasha, 2 Feb. 1887. English translation from the copy of the French original enclosed in Baring to Salisbury, 2 Feb. 1887, F.O. 84/1878.

[2] Khedive to Emin Pasha, 1 Feb. 1887. English translation of the copy in the Khartoum Archives, Cairint 1/11/56. The version printed in *IDA* i. 56–7 is inaccurate.

[3] W. Junker, *Travels in Africa*, vol. iii, p. 59.

'no fighter' but 'a cautious and prudent, painstaking administrator' who was a great linguist and extremely short-sighted.[1] His position was sadly reduced and the Equatorial province now consisted of only about 1,800 troops, distributed among eight stations in the southern part of the province. At Wadelai itself, Emin had a force of only about 250 men. His garrisons were inclined to be mutinous, and when Nubar Pasha's letter of May 1885 had arrived, it had been dismissed by Emin's followers as a forgery. Emin's orders had been disregarded and when he had attempted to bring about a withdrawal to the south, many of his men had been convinced that he intended to betray them and sell them as slaves to Kabarega or the Sultan of Zanzibar. Even today, observed Stanley prophetically, any letter from the Khedive or Nubar would not be believed. None the less, Stanley put vague hope in the possibility that the presence of a few Egyptians and Sudanese on the expedition 'who could talk and explain things' would bring about 'general satisfaction' when the expedition reached Equatoria 'and there would no doubt be a universal desire to return (to Egypt)'. Junker believed that Emin's own decision whether to stay or to withdraw would greatly influence his followers, but he warned Stanley that Emin would be most reluctant to abandon his men. Neglected by Egypt, forgotten in Europe, Emin had become greatly discouraged and depressed, and it was Junker's opinion that Emin desired to return to Egypt from Equatoria 'because of his conviction that no one cares about that part of Africa'. If Emin withdrew, Junker estimated that some 604 people would come with him—mainly Egyptians and northern Sudanese, their wives and children. But, concluded Stanley, in a letter intended for King Leopold: 'were he convinced that people were really anxious to support him in Africa, he would probably stay long enough to be relieved by some man ready to take his place', and some 700–800 of his Makaraka soldiers would probably stay with him.[1]

Before leaving Cairo, Stanley summed up the objects of the expedition as follows:

It is the relief of Emin Pasha that is the object of the expedition, the said relief consisting of ammunition in sufficient quantity to enable him to withdraw from his dangerous position in Central Africa in safety, or to hold his own if he decides to do so for such length of time as he may see

[1] Stanley to Comte de Borchgrave (reporting a conversation with Junker), 29 Jan. 1887, Palace Archives, Brussels, Dossier 102, no. 15.

fit . . . Junker does not think Emin will abandon the Province; the English subscribers to the fund hope he will not, but express nothing; the English Government would prefer that he would retire, as his Province under present circumstances is almost inaccessible, and certainly he, so far removed, is a cause of anxiety. The Khedive sends the above orders for Emin to accept our escort, but says, 'You may do as you please. If you decline our proffered aid you are not to expect further assistance from the Government'. Nubar Pasha's letter conveys the wishes of the Egyptian Government which are in accordance with those of the English Government, as expressed by Sir Evelyn Baring.[1]

Stanley left Cairo on 3 February for Suez accompanied by his European servant, William Hoffmann,[2] and the sixty-one Sudanese soldiers recruited and equipped for the expedition by Sir Evelyn Baring. At Suez they joined the *Navarino* along with Dr. Parke (who had been recruited in Cairo as medical officer), Jameson, Bonny, Jephson, Stairs, and Nelson. At Aden the entire company transferred to the *Oriental* which already had on board Major Barttelot and thirteen Somalis who had been recruited in Aden and whom Stanley was later to find very disappointing as an armed guard.[3] On 22 February the expedition arrived at Zanzibar.

During the next three days, while the European officers were fully occupied packing ammunition and stores for the expedition, loading the *Madura*, and equipping the 620 Zanzibari porters recruited by Holmwood, Stanley settled what he described as 'several little commissions'.[4]

The first and least-documented of these important transactions concerned the concession for a chartered Company on the East African mainland which Mackinnon had periodically been attempting to obtain from the Sultan of Zanzibar during the past ten years. Stanley's actions at Zanzibar in February 1887 did not initiate the revival of the Mackinnon concession (which was this time to result in the successful formation of the Imperial British East Africa Company), rather they encouraged the already existing predisposition of the Sultan to revive the matter.[5]

---

[1] *IDA* i. 52, 58.
[2] Hoffmann published in 1938 a little-known book, much of which is concerned with an account of his experiences on the Emin Pasha relief expedition. W. Hoffmann, *With Stanley in Africa* (London, 1938).
[3] *IDA* i. 153.   [4] Ibid. 68.
[5] The developments leading to the granting of the Mackinnon concession are related in the excellent study by Marie de Kiewiet, 'A History of the I.B.E.A. Company', Ph.D. thesis (London, 1955). In this work, however, Stanley's actions at Zanzibar in Feb. 1887 are strangely omitted. His own assertions that he

The signing of the Anglo-German Agreement over East Africa in 1886 had not been followed by any diminution in the assaults upon the dominions of the Sultan of Zanzibar. The French had claimed that their rights under the treaty of 1862 had been infringed. Portugal demanded from the Sultan the cession of territory in the Tunghi Bay area at the southern limit of his mainland dominions. Italy was beginning to exhibit an active interest in the coast to the north. The activities of individual Germans such as the Denhardt brothers, Karl Jühlke, and later Count Pfeil seemed to presage further German annexations on the mainland.[1] Sultan Barghash, desperately striving to hold his territories together amidst all these pressures on them, turned increasingly to the British Consul, Holmwood, for support and advice. On the day Stanley was due to arrive at Zanzibar, Holmwood was summoned to the Sultan's palace at 6 a.m. Here he 'found His Highness on the verge of distraction and, for the time, quite unequal to facing his difficulties'.[2] Barghash declared that if Holmwood would suggest a line of action which would prevent his dominions being broken up by the various European claims, 'he would follow the advice unhesitatingly'. Holmwood, after reviewing the position in the widest terms, suggested to the Sultan 'that his best chance at the present juncture was to proffer an unreserved acceptance of the concession scheme which had been suggested by Mr. Mackinnon'.[2] Holmwood stated that he was not in a position to say how far the British Government would support a revival of the Mackinnon concession, but by 8 a.m. Barghash had dispatched a telegram to Mackinnon, drafted by Holmwood, which affirmed the Sultan's readiness 'to agree to the concessions you formerly proposed if an influential association under your Presidency is found and the British Government approved'.[3] Stanley arrived in Zanzibar at 11 o'clock the same morning but did not meet the Sultan until the following day.[4] Thus, the first step towards what was to be the successful founding of the I.B.E.A.

persuaded the Sultan to sign the concession are exaggerations. See *IDA* i. 68, and H. M. Stanley, *Autobiography*, p. 446.

[1] de Kiewiet, op. cit., p. 74.
[2] Holmwood to Salisbury, 14 Mar. 1887, F.O. 84/1852, describing events of 22 Feb. 1887.
[3] Sultan of Zanzibar to Mackinnon, 22 Feb. 1887, F.O. 84/1851.
[4] W. G. Barttelot, *The Life of Edmund Musgrave Barttelot* (London, 1890), p. 56 (henceforth referred to as Barttelot, *Diary*); *IDA* i. 60; Holmwood to Salisbury, 25 Feb. 1887, F.O. 84/1851.

Company had already been taken, in response to the fear of further annexations (particularly by Germany) before Stanley arrived in Zanzibar.[1] Stanley, however, was in an excellent position to further the matter. He brought with him a letter from Mackinnon to the Sultan in which Mackinnon urged Barghash 'to communicate freely with Mr. Stanley on all points—as freely as if I had the honour of being there to receive the communications myself'.[2] Stanley pointed out to the Sultan that Englishmen would not be prepared to invest money in the development of the British 'sphere' in East Africa until some such concession was signed.[3] Holmwood urged the concession as a bulwark against annexations by other European powers. The day after Stanley left Zanzibar, Holmwood telegraphed to Lord Salisbury that the Sultan had agreed in principle to accept Mackinnon's concession scheme and was prepared to sign a charter at once if the British Government approved.[4] The charter was eventually signed on 24 May.[5] Thus, Stanley left Zanzibar convinced that Mackinnon's concession was assured. This knowledge was to play an important part in the development of Stanley's plans with regard to Emin Pasha and the future of Equatoria.[6]

The major part of Stanley's time at Zanzibar was taken up by negotiations with Tippu Tip. This remarkable Arab[7] was to play an important role in the Emin Pasha relief expedition and has left his own account of it in an autobiography in Swahili[8] and in several letters of great interest. A brief account of his position in central Africa at this time is therefore necessary.

* * *

[1] de Kiewiet, op. cit., p. 74.
[2] Mackinnon to Sultan of Zanzibar, 28 Jan. 1887, printed in *IDA* i. 61–2.
[3] Ibid. 69.
[4] Holmwood to Salisbury, 26 Feb. 1887, F.O. 84/1851.
[5] The events leading up to the final signing of the charter are given in de Kiewiet, op. cit., pp. 75–6.　　　　　　　　　　　　　[6] See Ch. VII, below.
[7] The term 'Arab' will be used throughout this book to cover the very mixed group of Swahili-speaking Arabs and Africans who lived and traded in East and Central Africa in this period. There is unfortunately no exact English equivalent to the more precise word 'les Arabisés' used in some of the literature in French on the subject.
[8] *Maisha ya Hamed bin Muhammed el Murjebi yaani Tippu Tip*, edited and translated by W. H. Whiteley, with an Introduction by Alison Smith. First published as a supplement to the *East African Swahili Committee Journals*, no. 28/2 (July 1958), and no. 29/1 (Jan. 1959); reprinted by the East African Literature Bureau (Nairobi, 1966) (henceforth referred to as Tippu Tip, *Autobiography*).

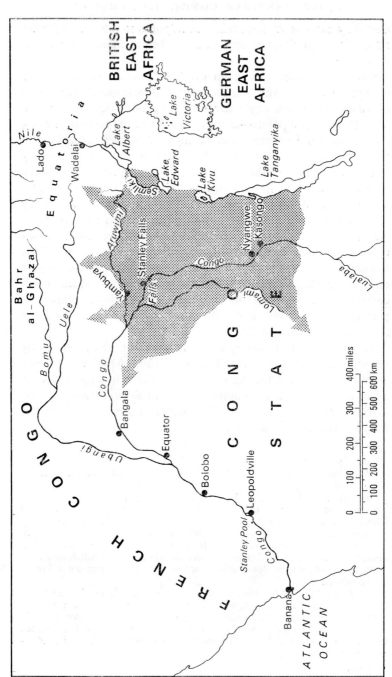

FIG. 3. The Arabs in the Eastern Congo 1886–90.

Tippu Tip was the son of an Arab from Muscat who had settled in Zanzibar and married an African woman from the coast. After accompanying his father on at least one trading expedition to Tabora, Tippu Tip was by 1860 leading caravans himself into the East African interior in search of ivory. He was particularly successful and he has left us in his autobiography a detailed account of how his power in the East African interior was established and then expanded. Behind the single biography of Tippu Tip it is possible to glimpse something of the more general process by which other prominent Arabs established their positions in the East African interior at this time.

The Arabs were not hoping to bring vast regions of the interior under the authority of the Sultan of Zanzibar, nor were they out to spread Islam. They were traders in search not of slaves but of ivory.[1]

The possession of firearms by the Arabs greatly facilitated their penetration of the interior. But the case of Tippu Tip indicates that Arab influence was often established peacefully through claims of kinship with, or patronage by, local African leaders, and through the distribution of trade goods. Once the Arabs had brought a certain region under their influence, numerous followers (some of whom had been on European exploring expeditions) attached themselves to the Arab settlements. These, along with local African leaders, then became agents for procuring ivory and slaves. These agents often picked up Arab ways and adopted Arab dress, with its turban and long white robe; many doubtless thought of themselves as Moslems. Thus, the 'Arab' trade in the interior was carried out less by pure Arabs than by half-caste and Arabized Africans. Some of these people established themselves independently in predatory bands beyond the areas of actual Arab occupation. The widespread suffering and destruction which accompanied their search for ivory and slaves is vividly described in the works of Livingstone and other early European travellers.[2]

The frontier of Arab settlement and trade in the interior moved rapidly west. By 1830 there were Arabs at Tabora; by 1840 at Ujiji on Lake Tanganyika. Tippu Tip himself occupied successive

[1] I am especially indebted to the following three works for this section: R. Slade, *King Leopold's Congo* (London, 1962), ch. v; R. Ceulemans, *La Question arabe et le Congo*; Alison Smith's Introduction to the *Autobiography of Tippu Tip*, cited above.

[2] See, especially, the *Last Journals of David Livingstone*, ed. H. Waller (London, 1874), vol. ii. ch. 6.

bases in Urua, Irande, and Utetera before he finally built up his greatest sphere of influence in the eastern Congo in the region between the Lomami and Lualaba rivers. Here he encountered a rival settlement of the Ujiji Arabs who were already established on the Lualaba at Nyangwe. Tippu Tip therefore made his settlement at Kasongo, up-stream from Nyangwe. This soon became a well-ordered centre, which greatly impressed the officers of Leopold's Congo State when they arrived there in the early 1890s. Immense fields of rice, sorghum, and maize were brought under cultivation, and many fruits and vegetables were introduced into the interior for the first time by the Arabs. Large villages of well-built houses were also established.[1]

From Kasongo Tippu Tip established a political structure in the Manyema area which extended rapidly as his power grew. Within this structure he appointed agents to act for him, to maintain order, and to extract tribute in the form of ivory and slaves from the African population. Around the edges of the political structure established by Tippu Tip, bands of independent 'war lords', equipped with firearms, raided and pillaged and brought devastation to the country. Arab penetration into the Manyema country was easy since the African population was small and too divided to offer much resistance. The dense tropical rain forest north of Nyangwe presented a more formidable barrier. Two or three attempts to penetrate the forest in search of new areas rich in ivory ended in disaster. Then, in October 1876, H. M. Stanley had arrived on his first great journey across Africa and had persuaded Tippu Tip to escort his expedition on the first part of its journey down the Congo.[2] Stanley's expedition blazed a trail and expeditions dispatched by Tippu Tip in search of ivory followed rapidly in its wake—a pattern which was to be repeated along the Aruwimi with the Emin Pasha relief expedition. When Stanley returned to establish a station at Stanley Falls on behalf of the *Association Internationale du Congo* at the end of 1883, he found that the Arabs were already active in the area and had extended their field of operations even further down the Congo to the north and west.[3] Stanley hoped that the Arab ivory trade

[1] Ceulemans, op. cit., pp. 40–1.

[2] This first encounter between Stanley and Tippu Tip is described in H. M. Stanley, *Through the Dark Continent* (London, 1879), 2 vols., vol. ii. chs. iv–vi: Tippu Tip, *Autobiography*, pp. 81–7.

[3] H. M. Stanley, *The Congo and the Founding of its Free State* (London, 1885), 2 vols., vol. i, ch. xxx.

might be diverted from Zanzibar to the west coast via the Congo,[1] but this was strongly opposed by the Arabs and by the Sultan of Zanzibar.

By the early 1880s, the area under the influence of Tippu Tip stretched from Lake Tanganyika to the Lomami river and north to the Aruwimi tributary of the Congo (see map). Between Tippu Tip's domain and the Indian Ocean only Mirambo had created for himself amongst the Nyamwezi a position of comparable influence in the interior.[2]

Tippu Tip's sphere of influence now came up against that of Leopold's Congo State. At first relations were peaceful. Stanley had left a Scotsman, Bennie, with thirty men at the newly established post at Stanley Falls with instructions to avoid hostilities. He was replaced in 1884 by the Swedish officer, Wester, who spoke fluent Swahili and maintained excellent relations with Tippu Tip. But the situation soon deteriorated. Once the *Association Internationale du Congo* had secured recognition as the Congo State, it was certainly in its interests to stem the Arab advance down the Congo. In addition, to prove itself worthy to administer the huge area of central Africa which Leopold had secured, the Congo State had both to occupy its territory effectively and to bring the slave-trade in the interior to an end. But in 1886 the infant State had neither the men nor the means to impose its authority in the eastern Congo. The station at Stanley Falls depended for its very existence on the goodwill of the Arabs. This rapidly disappeared when an Englishman, Deane, took over from Wester at Stanley Falls in February 1886. After a series of incidents for which both Arab and European sources lay heavy responsibility on Deane, the Arabs attacked the station in August. Deserted by their men, Deane and his Belgian companion fled, after setting fire to the station.[3] By the end of 1886 Stanley Falls was occupied by the Arabs and Bangala station marked the limit of the sphere of effective influence of Leopold's Congo State in the Upper Congo.

[1] Ibid.

[2] For Mirambo, see N. Bennett, 'Mirambo of the Nyamwezi', in N. R. Bennett, *Studies in East African History* (Boston University Press, 1963). For the relations between Tippu Tip and Mirambo, see the Introduction by Alison Smith to Tippu Tip, *Autobiography*, pp. 16–20, and also her chapter in the *History of East Africa*, eds. R. Oliver and G. Mathew (Oxford, 1963), vol. i, pp. 253–96.

[3] The incident is fully assessed, and the evidence of both sides is given in Ceulemans, op. cit., pp. 71–9.

Throughout these events at Stanley Falls Tippu Tip had been absent on one of his journeys to Zanzibar, where he periodically conducted large caravans to sell his ivory. In December 1886, while Leopold had been discussing the situation of the Arabs in the Upper Congo with Stanley in Brussels, Tippu Tip had engaged in long conversations on the matter with the British and Belgian Consuls in Zanzibar. On hearing of the events at Stanley Falls, Tippu Tip had at once realized the gravity of the situation. He told Holmwood that if the authorities of the Congo State engaged in reprisals against the Arabs at Stanley Falls, he would be unable to restrain the Congo Arabs from embarking on full-scale hostilities against Leopold's Congo State.[1] Holmwood urged Tippu Tip to send instructions to his representative at Stanley Falls to retire rather than be drawn into further hostilities with the Congo State.[2] Tippu agreed and seems to have been only too ready to follow the advice of the British Consul. At the same time, Tippu was incensed at the claims of the Congo State to areas which had been occupied by the Arabs long before the arrival of the Congo State authorities—whose behaviour he considered had been provocative. Holmwood confessed that he was unable to deny the justice of Tippu's claims and warned Stanley that Tippu was 'confident in his power to maintain his position'—a verdict which Stanley had already come to and had endeavoured to impress upon Leopold.[3] None the less, Tippu's overall attitude was conciliatory. Despite the apparent strength of the Arab position, it is clear that by 1886 Tippu Tip was convinced that in the long term the future lay with the Europeans.[4] Tippu had met many Europeans, including Livingstone, Cameron, and Stanley, and had been consistently esteemed by all of them—Stanley considered him to be one of the most remarkable men he had ever met in Africa.[5] As Tippu now declared to the Belgian Consul in Zanzibar, 'I have liked the Europeans ever since I was a young man; now, when I am a greybeard, why should I wish to make war with them? My interest has always been to be on good terms with them'.[6]

Hitherto, Tippu Tip had always declared that both he and his

[1] Holmwood to F.O., 24 Dec. 1886, F.O. 84/1777.
[2] Holmwood to Salisbury, 8 Jan. 1887, F.O. 84/1851.
[3] Holmwood to Salisbury, 3 Mar. 1887, F.O.C.P. C. 5617, pp. 33-4.
[4] Tippu Tip, *Autobiography*, Introduction, p. 21.
[5] H. M. Stanley, *Through the Dark Continent*, vol. ii, p. 74.
[6] de Cazanave to the Minister, 14 Feb. 1887, cited in Ceulemans, op. cit., p. 79.

territory were subject to the Sultan of Zanzibar.[1] In this he had been strongly supported by Sir John Kirk, who had sought to assert the Sultan's authority over the interior as a bulwark against European claims. But by 1887, as has been shown, the Sultan's position was crumbling and Kirk's policy was in ruins. Tippu Tip himself records a conversation he had with the Sultan at this time and reports the Sultan as saying to him: 'Hamed, I must beg your forgiveness. I no longer have any hope of keeping the interior. The Europeans here in Zanzibar are after my possessions. Will it be the hinterland they want? . . . you are yet a stranger to these events: but you will see how the land lies.' 'When I heard Seyyid's words', Tippu comments, 'I knew that it was all up.'[2]

* * *

It was in this situation that Stanley met Tippu Tip in Zanzibar in February 1887. As Stanley acknowledged, Tippu Tip was now a far more important figure in central Africa than he had been ten years previously when Stanley had first encountered him.[3] His influence also covered a much more extensive area, including that through which the Emin Pasha relief expedition would have to travel on the march between the Aruwimi and Lake Albert. Stanley also hoped to establish a base camp close to the Arab headquarters at Stanley Falls. As Stanley himself declared, he had as great an interest as Leopold in bringing about a peaceful settlement between the Arabs and the Congo State.[4]

So much depended on achieving this settlement that the possibility of switching the expedition from the Congo to the east coast route was left open until after Stanley arrived at Zanzibar.[5] If he was unable to bring about amicable relations with Tippu Tip, Stanley was determined 'to give him a wide berth; for the ammunition I had to convey to Emin Pasha, if captured and employed by him, would endanger the existence of the infant State of the Congo, and imperil all our hopes'.[6] This fear, that the ammunition conveyed by

---

[1] Tippu Tip, *Autobiography*, p. 109, para. 148.
[2] Ibid. 121, para. 168.
[3] *IDA* i. 63.   [4] *IDA* i. 119.
[5] See Mackinnon to F.O., 10 Feb. 1887, M.P. Also printed in F.O.C.P. C. 5617, no. 55.
[6] *IDA* i. 63–4. Also, the letter from Stanley published in *The Times*, 31 Mar. 1887.

the expedition would arouse the cupidity of the Arabs, or even incite them to attack the expedition, remained with Stanley throughout his passage through the Congo.

In his attempt to bring about a peaceful settlement between the Arabs and the Congo State, Stanley followed the broad outline which had been discussed between himself and Leopold at Brussels. His objective was to arrive at an arrangement with Tippu Tip whereby the Arab region and the area occupied by Leopold's Congo State could be mutually acknowledged as separate spheres of influence. The one point on which Leopold appears to have insisted was that the Congo State should extend up to Stanley Falls. This, Tippu Tip was unwilling to recognize. According to Holmwood, who assisted in the negotiations, Stanley's response was to state that if Tippu Tip persisted in this attitude the result might well be that the Congo State would gradually be ruined and would eventually be supplanted in the area by the French. The consequences of this intervention by a major European Power for the Arabs were then outlined to Tippu Tip by Stanley in what Holmwood described as 'a forcible exposition which seemed to convince his hearer'.[1] Eventually, with Holmwood's assistance, an Agreement was drawn up whereby Tippu Tip was appointed Governor of Stanley Falls under the Congo State. He was to receive a salary of £30 a month (which Tippu appears to have considered very small)[2] but he was also 'to be at full liberty to carry on his legitimate private trade in any direction and to send his caravans to and from any places he may desire'.[3] He was to fly the flag of the Congo State and maintain its authority in the region between Stanley Falls and the Aruwimi river in which region he was also to prevent both the Arabs and the local African population engaging in the slave-trade. Tippu Tip was also promised a European resident who would act as his secretary and assist in all communications with the Administrator-General of the Congo State.[4]

The proposal that Tippu Tip should be appointed Governor of

[1] Holmwood to Salisbury, 3 Mar. 1887, F.O.C.P. C. 5617, pp. 33-4.

[2] Tippu Tip, *Autobiography*, p. 123, para. 169.

[3] Agreement between H. M. Stanley and Tippu Tip, 24 Feb. 1887. Copy in the Van Eetvelde Papers, Archives du Royaume, Brussels, Dossier 132. The text of this Agreement is printed in W. G. Barttelot, *The Life of Edmund Musgrave Barttelot* (London, 1890), pp. 402-3.

[4] W. G. Barttelot, *The Life of Edmund Musgrave Barttelot* (London, 1890), pp. 402-3.

Stanley Falls under the Congo State was not a new idea—it had first been suggested by Vangèle in the spring of 1885—but at this point it exceeded the terms which had been discussed between Stanley and Leopold in Brussels. Before the Agreement was signed, therefore, Stanley telegraphed the King concerning its contents.[1] Tippu Tip also insisted that he must first discuss the matter with the Sultan of Zanzibar 'since both ourselves and our areas are under his authority'. The Sultan strongly urged Tippu to accept the terms, and when these were ratified by Leopold, the Agreement was signed.[2]

This Agreement caused a storm of controversy when it became known in Europe a month later. In Belgium the radical press described it as 'a violation of the principle on which the [Congo] Free State was founded, and a disgraceful compromise with a notorious slave-trader'.[3] In England, Stanley's action was compared with Gordon's intention to employ Zubayr in the Sudan and was similarly castigated as an open encouragement to the slave-trade.[4] Much of the controversy revolved around different interpretations of the 'legitimate private trade' which Tippu Tip was left free to undertake by the Agreement. In Europe, this was equated with the slave-trade; in fact Tippu's interest was primarily in ivory, and his methods of obtaining it differed little from those of the Sanford Exploring Expedition which was also on the Upper Congo for the purpose of extracting ivory at this time.[5]

In the circumstances of 1887 the Agreement was satisfactory to both sides. Tippu Tip knew that the Sultan's authority in the interior was declining and that the Europeans were the future masters of central Africa. To accept office as Governor under the Congo State of his present domain meant that in practice Tippu Tip retained a free hand over this territory and over the vast region above

---

[1] Ceulemans, op. cit., p. 68.

[2] Tippu Tip, *Autobiography*, pp. 122–3, para. 169. Holmwood to Salisbury, 3 Mar. 1887, cited above.

[3] Lord Vivian to Salisbury, 9 Apr. 1887, F.O.C.P. C. 5617, no. 87, reporting the reaction in Belgium to the news of the Agreement.

[4] *The Times*, 31 Mar. 1887.

[5] The activities of the Sanford Exploring Expedition, and of Roger Casement, who worked for it during what has hitherto been regarded as a rather obscure period of his life, are fully recorded in the Henry Sanford Papers (recently deposited in the Sanford Memorial Library, Sanford, Florida). There is a rather disappointing article based on this material by James P. White, 'The Sanford Exploring Expedition', in *J.A.H.* viii, no. 2 (1967).

Stanley Falls. The crucial question was how far he would be able to control some of the other Arab leaders who occupied the area and who, less foresighted and diplomatic than himself, were not so ready to co-operate with the Europeans.[1] Indeed, Tippu Tip's signing of this Agreement, followed as it was by repeated requests for European soldiers and guns to help him to maintain his position, may well have been a bid for greater power and prestige to bolster his already crumbling authority over the Arabs in the Manyema area. For the Congo State, a *modus vivendi* had been secured with the Arabs at a time when the State was not in a position to subdue them by force. The State stood to gain if the Agreement encouraged Tippu Tip to dispatch his ivory to the west coast. The Emin Pasha relief expedition could safely take the Congo route and Stanley could pursue his plans to establish a base camp on the Aruwimi in the Arab area. This Agreement also represents the attitude which Leopold was to follow consistently during the next few years with regard to the Arabs, an attitude whose essential objective was, as Leopold later declared, 'to get the Arabs, in return for money, to serve my policy'.[2]

Having concluded this Agreement on behalf of King Leopold, Stanley entered into a second Agreement with Tippu Tip regarding the provision of carriers in the Congo for the Emin Pasha relief expedition. It was widely believed in Europe that Emin had considerable stores of ivory in Equatoria and it had been the concern of Mackinnon, as of the Egyptian Government, that the expedition should bring out as much as possible of this ivory to defray the expenses of the expedition. While in Cairo, Stanley had learnt from Junker that this ivory amounted to something like seventy-five tons, the value of which was estimated at £60,000.[3] An excellent solution to the problem of bringing all this ivory out of Equatoria appeared to be at hand if the assistance of Tippu Tip could be obtained in the provision of porters. Stanley's plan was to engage Tippu Tip and several hundred carriers to assist the expedition in transporting the stores and ammunition for Emin on the overland journey through the eastern Congo to Lake Albert, and to carry the ivory back to the region of Stanley Falls on the return journey. From there a steamer could complete the transport of the ivory, along with the

[1] R. Slade, *King Leopold's Congo*, p. 95.
[2] Leopold to Van Eetvelde, 6 Oct. 1890, cited in Ceulemans, op. cit., p. 157.
[3] *IDA* i. 64.

refugees and their belongings, which Stanley expected to bring out of Equatoria, down the Congo.[1]

At Zanzibar, Stanley found in Tippu Tip a ready audience for this proposal. Tippu had long been aware of the position of Emin Pasha and his ivory in Equatoria, information which he appears to have first obtained from Oscar Lenz at Nyangwe.[2] On his way to the coast in 1886 Tippu Tip had met Dr. Tristram Pruen, an English traveller who was also a Fellow of the Royal Geographical Society, and a member of the C.M.S., at Mpwapwa, and Junker had accompanied him during the journey from Tabora. Both Europeans were surprised to discover Tippu's lively interest in the position of Emin in Equatoria and Junker records that Tippu 'showed himself inclined to head an expedition to that region, frankly stipulating, however, for a share of the ivory which Emin had accumulated there'.[3] On arriving at Zanzibar in December 1886, Tippu Tip had set about organizing his own expedition to go to Wadelai, but he had abandoned the project when news arrived of the events at Stanley Falls.[4]

The second Agreement which Stanley made with Tippu Tip at Zanzibar in February does not stipulate the number of carriers which were to be provided for the expedition by Tippu Tip, but the conditions on which they were to be employed are precisely defined.[5] Each man was to receive thirty dollars plus food for the round trip from Stanley Falls to Lake Albert and back, and Tippu Tip was to receive a commission of 1,000 dollars for providing the men. It is clear that Stanley expected these costs to be more than covered by the sale of the ivory which the carriers were to transport from Equatoria on the return journey to the Congo and that Tippu Tip himself expected a liberal share in Emin's ivory.[6] It is also clear that although the carriers were to be equipped with guns by Tippu Tip,

---

[1] Ibid. A lengthy correspondence was carried on between the Emin Pasha Relief Committee and the Foreign Office on the subject. This is conveniently collected in M.P., F. 6.   [2] W. Junker, *Travels in Africa*, vol. iii, p. 561.
[3] W. Junker, op. cit., vol. iii, p. 566. See also Tristram Pruen, *The Arab and the African* (London, 1891), p. 214. Junker had informed Emin of Tippu Tip's interest in Equatoria in a letter dated 8 Nov. 1886. See Emin to Mackay, 15 Apr. 1887, enclosed in Macdonald to Salisbury 26 Sept. 1887 and printed in F.O.C.P. C. 5617, p. 63.   [4] Holmwood to Salisbury, 8 Jan. 1887, F.O. 84/1851.
[5] The text of the Agreement, taken from the copy in the Zanzibar Secretariat archives, is printed in Sir John Gray, 'Stanley *versus* Tippoo Tib', *Tanganyika Notes and Records*, no. 18, Dec. 1944, pp. 26-7.
[6] Both Stanley (*IDA* i. 64) and Holmwood (Holmwood to Salisbury, 25 Feb. 1887, F.O. 84/1851) state that the number of carriers to be provided was 600. Tippu Tip (*Autobiography*, p. 123, para. 172) claims the number was 500.

Stanley was to be responsible for providing them with ammunition. Whether Tippu Tip was himself to accompany the carriers was not stated. His initial intention appears to have been to do so, but it was later agreed with Stanley that Tippu Tip should delegate one of his head men to accompany the expedition to Lake Albert in order to supervise the carriers.[1] It would also seem that Tippu Tip's original intention was to return to the Congo from Zanzibar by the overland route through East Africa by which he had come. Stanley, however, realized that this would take several months and insisted that Tippu Tip and his followers must accompany the expedition by sea round the Cape.[2] After 'a good deal of bargaining' the Agreement was signed on 24 February.[3] On the following day, Tippu Tip and his ninety-six followers joined the 620 Zanzibari porters already recruited for the expedition by Holmwood, 61 Sudanese, 13 Somalis, the European officers and their servants on board the *Madura*.

Before leaving Zanzibar, Stanley wrote a letter to Emin, to be conveyed overland via Bunyoro, in which he informed him of the arrangements concerning the expedition and its expected time-table. This had already been extended from the original plan made in England. Stanley now estimated that he would reach the Aruwimi and the site for a base camp there about 18 June. From there the overland march to Lake Albert was expected to take about fifty days. Emin would thus be reached by the end of August 1887, and the expedition was expected to be concluded by February–March 1888.[4]

Reporting the successful conclusion of Stanley's 'little commissions' at Zanzibar, and the departure of the *Madura* for the Congo on 25 February, Holmwood concluded optimistically: 'The relief party which has just left Zanzibar is in every way the most perfectly organised expedition that has hitherto entered tropical Africa.'[5]

* * *

On 18 March the expedition arrived at Banana at the mouth of the Congo. The telegraph cable had recently broken[6] and so Stanley's

---

[1] James S. Jameson, *Story of the Rear Column*, ed. Mrs. Jameson (London, 1890), p. 7. (Henceforth referred to as Jameson, *Diary*). *The Diary of A. J. Mounteney-Jephson*, ed. Mrs. D. Middleton (Cambridge, 1969), p. 110.
[2] J. M. Gray, 'Stanley versus Tippoo Tib', p. 13.   [3] *IDA* i. 64.
[4] *IDA* i. 62–3 (where the letter to Emin is printed) and p. 73. Barttelot, *Diary*, pp. 65–9.   [5] Holmwood to Salisbury, 25 Feb. 1887, F.O. 84/1851.
[6] *The Diary of A. J. Mounteney-Jephson*, ed. Mrs. D. Middleton, for the Hakluyt Society (Cambridge, 1969), p. 80 (henceforth referred to as Jephson, *Diary*). It will become clearer in later chapters how deeply indebted I am both to this work and to the constant co-operation of Mrs. Middleton.

cables and the instructions sent by Leopold from Brussels had failed to arrive.[1] Thus, Stanley found that the officials of the Congo State had made few arrangements to assist the expedition in its progress over 1,000 miles up the Congo river—indeed, the arrival of the expedition at some of the State stations came as a complete surprise.

The Congo State in 1887 was still in its infancy. Recognized at the Berlin Conference only two years previously, it covered a vast area, most of which was still unoccupied and unexplored. In June 1887 the total European population in the Congo—including missionaries as well as traders and administrators—amounted to a few hundred people, most of whom lived in the area below Stanley Pool.[2] This exiguous European presence was concentrated in a handful of stations scattered along the banks of the river Congo, some established by the State as administrative posts, some occupied by missionaries. Leopoldville was a collection of buildings overlooking Stanley Pool, many of which had fallen into ruin since the station had first been established by Stanley in 1881. The furthest station up the Congo in occupation by the Congo State in 1887 was Bangala, and this station consisted of two Europeans and about sixty African soldiers—most of them recruited from other parts of Africa.[3]

The area 'occupied' by the Congo State, even to the token extent of stations, had recently shrunk. Stanley Falls had been occupied by the Arabs and several stations between the Falls and Bangala had been abandoned for financial reasons the previous year. Although Leopold spent huge sums from his private fortune, the financial position of the Congo State, at least until 1890, remained extremely precarious.

At the heart of the problems of the infant Congo State, as elsewhere in Africa, lay the problem of communications. Stanley's assertion that the river Congo 'is and will be the grand highway of commerce to West Central Africa',[4] had excited great interest in

---

[1] Leopold's instructions to the officers of the Congo State concerning the expedition are printed in A. J. Wauters, *Stanley's Emin Pasha Expedition* (London, 1890, English edn., pp. 152–3.

[2] R. Slade, *King Leopold's Congo*, p. 71.

[3] Ibid. 173. The gradual recruitment of Congolese soldiers, beginning with Coquilhat's enlistment of some Bangala, is to be found in 'La Force publique de sa naissance à 1914' (Brussels, 1952), Institut Royal Colonial Belge, *Mémoires*, vol. xxvii.

[4] H. M. Stanley, *The Congo and the Founding of its Free State*, vol. i, p. vi.

Europe but, as with the Nile, the role of the river as a means of access to the interior could not be fully developed until the problem presented by its cataracts was surmounted. The building of a railway around the cataracts of the lower Congo had been regarded as a priority from the beginning. But in 1887 the financing and planning of this railway had barely begun, and all goods had to be transported between Matadi and Stanley Pool by porters recruited with increasing difficulty from the local African population.

One of the European officers of the Emin Pasha relief expedition, J. Rose Troup, who had had considerable experience in the service of the Congo State, had been dispatched direct from England to the Congo to arrange for porters to assist the expedition on this stage of the journey up the Congo. In this task he was assisted by a Baptist missionary, Mr. Ingham, and later by another European officer, recruited by Stanley for the expedition after he arrived in the Congo, Herbert Ward.[1]

From Banana, at the mouth of the Congo, to Matadi lay some 108 miles of navigable waterway and Stanley succeeded in chartering several small steamers from the Dutch and British trading companies at Banana to convey the expedition to Matadi, where it arrived on 21 March. Here the carriers recruited by Troup and Ingham took over and transported over 800 loads of stores and ammunition for the expedition overland to Leopoldville on Stanley Pool.

This overland march from Matadi to Leopoldville took a month. It is described in detail by several of Stanley's officers and these accounts give us what is perhaps the most complete picture in existence of Stanley's attitude towards the conduct of expeditions in Africa.[2]

The Emin Pasha relief expedition was organized on military lines, with European officers in charge of companies of men with orders to perform specific tasks. Jephson, for example, was responsible for the transport of the expedition's portable steel boat, the *Advance*— which was either carried overland in sections by forty men, or used to transport stores and the sick on navigable sections of the river. Barttelot was in charge of the Sudanese who, having been trained

---

[1] Troup's experiences on the Emin Pasha relief expedition are related in J. Rose Troup, *With Stanley's Rear Column* (London, 1890). Ward's less extensive account was also published: H. Ward, *My Life with Stanley's Rear Guard* (London, 1891).

[2] Jephson, *Diary*, pp. 80–95. Parke, *Diary*, pp. 34–44. Barttelot, *Diary*, pp. 74–88. Jameson, *Diary*, pp. 13–33.

as soldiers, greatly resented being treated as porters. Barttelot found them difficult, lazy, and mutinous, and Stanley became so exasperated with them that he abandoned his original plan of taking them to Wadelai and left them behind with the Rear Column on the Congo. 'His object', Barttelot wrote, on hearing of the decision, 'is personal dislike of me and hatred of the Sudanese.'[1] The other European officers were each in charge of a company of Zanzibaris. They were responsible for keeping their company together, for seeing that none of the men looted the African villages *en route* or deserted, and that none of the rifles or loads carried by the Zanzibaris were lost.

The pattern of daily life on the expedition was soon established. The day would begin early, since it was established practice in Africa to complete the day's march and establish camp by 2 p.m. On the journey up the Congo the expedition was so large—numbering about 1,000 men—that its different sections were seldom united. The various companies, under their European officers, often became scattered miles apart and frequently camped separately overnight. Essential equipment, such as tents and clothing, became dispersed, and the European officers soon went down with fever. Stanley himself had a severe attack of dysentery soon after the expedition left Matadi. Tempers became frayed, relations between Stanley and the European officers deteriorated, and Stanley himself exhibited outbursts of rage which shocked his subordinates.[2] His relations with Barttelot appear to have been particularly strained from the beginning. Stanley thought him headstrong and lacking in forbearance.[3] Barttelot was so incensed by Stanley's threats to ruin his career that he considered abandoning the expedition altogether and returning home.[4] Stanley's relations with his other officers were also by no means easy. He publicly insulted Jephson and Stairs on at least one occasion[5] and

---

[1] Barttelot, *Diary*, p. 91.

[2] One such instance is very fully recorded in Jameson, *Diary*, pp. 47–9; Barttelot, *Diary*, pp. 95–8.

[3] *IDA* i. 124.

[4] Barttelot, *Diary*, pp. 90–1. The MSS. of the diary (in the Barttelot papers) elaborates on the matter. General Brackenbury, under whom Barttelot had served in Egypt, later wrote: 'Had Major Barttelot by any chance consulted me, I should have advised him not to take service with Mr. Stanley. Knowing what I knew of the two characters, I should not have anticipated their getting on well together.' Brackenbury to Sir Walter Barttelot, 25 Oct. 1890, Barttelot Papers.

[5] See note 1 above. Jephson is reticent in his own account: see Jephson, *Diary*, p. 99.

put Jameson in an impossible position with his own men by humiliating him in their presence.[1] Stanley accused the other Europeans of conspiring together against him and repeatedly took the side of the Zanzibaris in disputes with their own officers.[2]

Stanley's impatience with his European companions was a feature of all his African ventures. Like most other European explorers in Africa, he appears to have got on much better with his African followers—towards whom he could adopt an uncompromising role as leader and master occasionally punctuated by exhibitions of paternal concern. Stanley's attitude towards the conduct of the expedition was founded on certain fixed assumptions from which he never deviated. As leader he considered it his place to remain aloof from his officers. On all his expeditions Stanley declared that though he was 'always willing to hear what my officers or men had to say' as a 'leader of men I could not hob-nob with my officers'.[3] Stanley kept his plans about the expedition strictly to himself until such time as he was ready to embody them in the written instructions which he issued periodically to his subordinates. While the other Europeans ate and slept together, Stanley kept to his own tent and had his meals alone. From his previous experience Stanley had come to the conclusion that the best way for Europeans to remain on amicable terms with each other whilst on expeditions in Africa was that 'each European should sleep in his own tent, and only meet at meal-times. Then disperse each man to his own tent or duty. It is by the prolonged discussion of trivial matters, and unnecessary conversation, that most quarrels begin.'[4]

The European officers, of course, did not expect to be on an equal footing with their leader and, coming from different social backgrounds, did not feel so even with each other. Jephson and Barttelot both had certain 'upper class' connections and pretensions which set them apart from the others. But Barttelot's experience had been in the army and this led him to admire Stairs; in personal terms, however, he appears to have felt a closer companionship with Jameson from the very beginning. Stairs and Nelson went together; they were army men, not very articulate, and both revered their

---

[1] Jameson, *Diary*, pp. 20, 24–6.
[2] Ibid. Also, Barttelot to Major Sclater, 19 July 1887 (Barttelot Papers).
[3] *The Autobiography of H. M. Stanley*, ed. D. Stanley (London, 1909), p. 351.
[4] Stanley embodied his experience and advice to other European explorers in Africa in his instructions to Captain Popelin in 1879, of which this is an extract. See H. M. Stanley, *The Congo and the Founding of its Free State*, vol. i, p. 47.

leader. Parke, as a medical man of obvious intelligence and maturity, is a more complex and isolated figure.[1] He was the only one to conduct his relations with Stanley on something approaching an equal basis and he did not hesitate to remonstrate with him when necessary and to speak firmly.[2] Stanley would seem to have respected him, an attitude enhanced perhaps by the fact that at least once on this expedition Parke undoubtedly saved Stanley's life. Troup and Ward were treated by the rest of the company as subordinates, and so was Bonny; their participation in the expedition was, in any case, largely restricted to the Congo.

Stanley's aloofness, one suspects, also stemmed from the fact that he found all human relations, outside the master–servant situation, extremely difficult. He never had any close friends. He himself later declared: 'I have had no friend on any expedition, no-one who could possibly be my companion, on an equal footing, except while with Livingstone . . . My only comfort was my work. To it I ever turned as to a friend.'[3] Stanley's meeting with Livingstone at Ujiji in 1871 had been one of the most profound experiences of his life. The experience had ended, however, in bitterness, when Stanley had returned to Europe to find that his meeting with Livingstone was widely disbelieved.[4] Stanley revered Livingstone but recognized in that great man a being of quite different qualities from himself. Livingstone's methods in Africa were, Stanley considered, 'almost Christ-like for goodness, patience, and self-sacrifice'. Stanley himself, however, believed that 'the selfish and wooden-headed world requires mastering, as well as loving charity'.[5]

Stanley attempted to dominate whatever situation he encountered. This is why his relationship with King Leopold during 1884–6, when Leopold had held the initiative, had been so intolerable to him. This is why he was to find the encounter with Emin Pasha so difficult. From poor, illegitimate origins, Stanley had raised himself to a position of great fame through what he considered to have been his mastering of successive situations. Only thus, Stanley believed,

---

[1] His account of the expedition is of especial value. T. H. Parke, *My Personal Experiences in Equatorial Africa* (London, 1891) (henceforth referred to as Parke, *Diary*).   [2] Barttelot, *Diary*, p. 83.
[3] *Autobiography of H. M. Stanley*, p. 351.
[4] For a careful study of Stanley's early career, see Ian Anstruther, *I Presume* (London, 1956). Stanley's own account of this episode was published as *How I Found Livingstone* (New York and London, 1872).
[5] Stanley's Notebook, quoted in B. Farwell, *The Man who Presumed*, p. 99.

could success be achieved. And, as Jephson soon observed, Stanley 'seemed to think that the only thing worth doing was to succeed, no matter how, in anything you undertook, and that success was everything . . . Stanley seems to have no sort of patience with anything which does not succeed'.[1] Stanley believed that his own success had stemmed from his recognition of the virtue of hard work, strict adherence to duty, and his genuine religious convictions.[2] A noticeable feature of all Stanley's actions is a certain ruthlessness, a quality which also pervades his writings. In this latter context, as the explorer Frederick Jackson perceptively observed, Stanley was 'a professional journalist trained in the "take-no-denial" school of American journalism, with a studied insight into the psychology of his readers'.[3]

Stanley's accounts of his African expeditions reached a far wider audience than those of any other Victorian traveller. But to accompany him on one of these expeditions cannot have been a particularly enjoyable experience. If you survived—and many soon did not expect to, and many did not—it would appear to have been in most cases due as much to your own efforts as to Stanley's concern and provision for your welfare. All the European officers on the Emin Pasha relief expedition repeatedly remark on Stanley's egotism and disregard for his companions. After a particularly wearing day on the march from Matadi, Jameson remarks: 'It is all very well for Mr. Stanley, who rides ahead straight on to the next camp, where we arrive hours afterwards, having done nothing all day but kick lazy carriers, and put the loads on to the heads of those who choose to fling them down.'[4] Again, on 3 April: 'The work was truly sickening, as every twenty yards one had to stop to put a load on a man's head who had flung it down, and very likely give him a good dose of stick before he would go on . . . The work must greatly resemble slave-driving.'[5] At the same time, Barttelot was having great trouble with the Sudanese. 'I felt like a brute, flogging the men to get them on', he wrote. 'We have been nothing but slave-drivers

[1] Jephson, *Diary*, p. 75.

[2] Stanley's religious convictions have, perhaps, been underemphasized by his biographers. I find the opinion of Sir John Gray, who declares that they were simple but deeply and sincerely held, entirely convincing: see Sir John Gray, 'Mutesa of Buganda', *Uganda Journal*, vol. i, no. i (1934), 32.

[3] F. J. Jackson, *Early Days in East Africa* (London, 1930), pp. 142–3.

[4] Jameson, *Diary*, p. 14.

[5] Ibid. 17.

since we started, and the trouble I have had to get the Sudanese along was something dreadful.'[1]

Over the whole progress of the expedition up the Congo there hung an atmosphere of despondency. 'It is all so serious', observed Jameson, 'a sort of gloom hangs over it all.'[2] Barttelot felt that he had 'never been on such a mournful, cheerless trip as this one. The harder we worked, the glummer Stanley looked. After a long march, no smile from him or word of any sort, except to say "You have lost a box", or some sneer of that sort'.[3] Stanley afterwards accounted for his attitude in a chill report to the Committee: 'I never permitted myself in Africa to indulge in laudation of any act however well done. To faithful performance of imperative duties I considered myself entitled; need or no need, it was what they each and all had pledged to do.'[4]

The progress of the expedition up the Congo was greatly hampered by the local conditions. It was the height of the rainy season, it poured with rain almost every day, and many of the swollen tributaries of the Congo had to be swum because of the lack of local canoes which could be appropriated to join the steel boat *Advance* as ferries. Food was desperately short as the entire area had been suffering from widespread famine for several months. Both Stanley and the Committee in London had been informed of this, but the decision to adopt the Congo route had been taken for 'principally political' reasons, as Stanley admitted,[5] and it had been taken too late to enable food to be stockpiled in the stations *en route*. Kept on very low rations, the Zanzibaris—most of whom were slaves or convicts[6]—lost no opportunity to loot villages or raid manioc plantations. There were some deaths and many more desertions and a month after the march had started, the expedition had lost fifty-seven men.[7] During this difficult and depressing march it was, as Jameson remarked, 'sometimes very hard to think of all the glory of relieving Emin Bey'.[8]

On 21 April the expedition arrived at Leopoldville, situated on Stanley Pool, nearly 350 miles up the Congo. Ahead lay 1,000 miles of navigable waterway on the Upper Congo to the rapids at

[1] Barttelot, *Diary*, pp. 79, 121.
[2] Jameson, *Diary*, p. 62.
[3] Barttelot, *Diary*, p. 120. See also Jephson, *Diary*, p. 159.
[4] Stanley to the Emin Pasha Relief Committee, 25 Mar. 1890, M.P. F. 4.
[5] *IDA* i. 63.   [6] *IDA* i. 93.   [7] *IDA* i. 92.
[8] Jameson, *Diary*, p. 15.

Yambuya on the Aruwimi where Stanley planned to establish a base camp.

It was at Leopoldville that the 'flotilla' of steamers belonging to the Congo State, which King Leopold had promised to make available for the expedition, was expected to be. It was soon apparent that this 'flotilla' simply did not exist. The only steamer in working order was the *Stanley*; there also existed two other vessels, both without engines. Stanley had had some intimation of this lack of transport, and he had made plans accordingly. There existed two other steamers on the Upper Congo, the *Peace* and the *Henry Reed*, both belonging to the missionaries. The *Peace* belonged to the English Baptist mission and before leaving England Stanley had written to Robert Arthington (popularly known as 'the miser of Leeds'), who had donated her to the mission, asking to loan or charter the vessel for the expedition. Arthington had refused, since he considered it 'improper' to associate a mission steamer with an enterprise led by H. M. Stanley, whose acts, he declared, he could not, 'dare not, sanction'.[1] Stanley, however, had taken the precaution of delaying the delivery of any letters to the Baptist missionaries on the Congo which he thought might contain Arthington's refusal.[2] When the expedition arrived at Stanley Pool, the missionary in charge decided to hand over the *Peace* to Stanley with a good grace.[3] Mackinnon had in any case telegraphed to Stanley at Banana urging him, with the aid of the officials of the Congo State, to requisition the *Peace* and the *Henry Reed* if necessary.[4]

Stanley was compelled to put Mackinnon's instructions into practice when it came to the *Henry Reed*. She was owned by the American Baptists, and the local missionaries refused to lend the steamer unless this was sanctioned by the authorities in Boston. After several efforts at persuasion had failed, Stanley enlisted the support of Liebrechts, the Governor of the Stanley Pool district, and requisitioned the *Henry Reed*, for which he then agreed to pay

---

[1] Arthington to Stanley, 15 Jan. 1887, printed in *IDA* i. 47. See also Arthington to Baynes, 15 Jan. 1887, cited in R. Slade, *English Speaking Missions in the Congo Independent State*, Académie royale des sciences coloniales, Mémoires, vol. xvi (Brussels, 1959) p. 87.

[2] Barttelot, *Diary*, p. 87. Jameson, *Diary*, p. 28.

[3] When Arthington heard of this he wrote: 'The *Peace* is in polluted hands . . . I should not be surprised, although I do not *expect* it—if it were dashed to pieces.' Arthington to Baynes, 30 June 1887, cited in R. Slade, op. cit., p. 89.

[4] Mackinnon to Stanley, 9 Mar. 1887, cited in R. Slade, op. cit., p. 88.

£100 per month.¹ Stanley also wrote a letter, which was published in *The Times*, justifying his actions and castigating the missionaries for their ingratitude for the services which he had rendered them in the past.² There was one other vessel at Stanley Pool which Stanley was also determined to obtain. This was the *Florida*, a new steamer being completed for the Sanford Exploring Company at Kinshassa under the manager of that company, Mr. Swinburne. Stanley knew Swinburne well from his previous time in the Congo and declared that 'under the sense of many life-long obligations from me, he could not refuse to give me the *Florida* as one way, to be sure, to pay his old debts'.³ Swinburne later simply stated that he was 'forced to give her or she would have been seized'.⁴ The steamer was without its engines and was used by Stanley as a barge. When it was returned in July, it was found to be badly battered and dented, and this led to a prolonged claim for damages by Sanford against the Emin Pasha Relief Committee. The affair caused Mackinnon, who knew Sanford personally, considerable embarrassment. But the Committee, who knew the desperate financial state of Sanford's venture, simply dismissed his claim as preposterous.⁵

The flotilla which Stanley had now got together consisted of three steamers and five barges, including the expedition's own boat, the *Advance*. But this was still insufficient to transport all the members of the expedition, let alone its vast quantity of stores and equipment. Stanley therefore left a large quantity of stores under the care of Troup at Leopoldville. A second deposit of 125 men and 600 loads of equipment were to be left under Ward and Bonny at Bolobo. Stanley's plan was that these two deposits should join the third and major settlement at Yambuya under Major Barttelot to form a Rear Column, while Stanley himself and a lightly equipped

---

¹ Stanley's account of these proceedings is given in *IDA* i. 90–2. Liebrecht's is in his memoirs, *Souvenirs d'Afrique* (Brussels, 1909), pp. 169–74. See also R. Slade, op. cit., p. 88.

² *The Times*, 17 July 1887. The letter, dated 26 Apr. 1887, is also printed in A. J. Wauters, *Stanley's Emin Pasha Expedition*, pp. 198–204.

³ Sanford to Mackinnon, 11 Mar. 1890, quoting a letter from Stanley, M.P., F. 8.

⁴ Jules Levita to Emin Pasha Relief Committee, 19 Oct. 1889, reporting a conversation with Swinburne, M.P., F. 8.

⁵ A. L. Bruce to McDermott, 9 Sept. 1890, M.P., F. 1. Details of the *Florida* affair are to be found in Sanford's letters to Mackinnon in M.P., 209, 211, 212, and in Mackinnon's replies in the Sanford Papers. Some of Sanford's letters to Mackinnon on this matter are in M.P., F. 8.

Advance Column pressed on through the unknown territory of the eastern Congo to meet Emin at Wadelai. Stanley's decision to divide the expedition in this way later came in for heavy criticism. He could have kept the entire expedition together by advancing in stages, as he later advised the Rear Column to do, but this would have greatly delayed his own advance. If Barttelot were established with the sick and weaker men and most of the impedimenta at Yambuya, Stanley believed that his own progress would be greatly improved. Stanley felt a sense of urgency about his mission, and had been frustrated by the slow progress of the full expedition on the overland march from Matadi. The decision to divide the expedition had in any case been at the back of Stanley's mind from the beginning.

When the expedition left Stanley Pool on 1 May, the State authorities and the missionaries were only too glad to see it depart. The arrival of such a large body of people in an area already short of food had imposed a severe strain on the resources of the State officials, the missionaries, and the local population alike. The missionaries especially felt so outraged at the devastation caused by 'Stanley's crowd, furious with hunger', that they wrote to the Emin Pasha Relief Committee describing the effect of the expedition on the area.[1] A year later, one of King Leopold's advisers on the Congo State, Van Eetvelde, expressed the hope 'that if any further expedition were to be sent to Emin Pasha's relief it might take the East Coast route, as the Government of the Congo had had nothing but trouble, anxiety and vexation (difficulties with the Arabs, missionaries and natives) since the departure of Mr. Stanley's expedition'.[2]

The voyage of the main body of the expedition from Stanley Pool to Yambuya took six weeks. During the day, the steamers, towing the barges, steamed monotonously up the Congo. At night, huge quantities of wood had to be cut by the Zanzibaris to provide the fuel for the following day. There were delays when the steamers ran aground or developed engine trouble. There were further rows between Stanley and the other European officers. Otherwise the voyage was uneventful.

[1] Bentley to Baynes, 24 May 1887, cited in R. Slade, op. cit., p. 88. G. Wilmot-Brooke to the Committee, 25 July 1888, M.P.

[2] Lord Vivian to F.O., 25 Nov. 1888, F.O. 84/1895, cited in R. Slade, op. cit. p. 89.

At Bangala, Barttelot was instructed to accompany Tippu Tip and his followers in the *Henry Reed* to Stanley Falls, while the rest of the expedition went on up the Aruwimi and began to build a station for the Rear Column at Yambuya. Stanley was careful to remove all the Zanzibaris from Barttelot's escort and replace them with Sudanese, since he feared that on arrival at Stanley Falls the Zanzibaris would desert.[1]

Stanley and the main body of the expedition arrived at Yambuya on 15 June—almost exactly the date which Stanley had anticipated in his letter to Emin.[2] At this point, where the first rapids occurred on the Aruwimi river, some ninety-six miles above its confluence with the Congo, Stanley had decided to establish the camp for the Rear Column of the expedition. Stanley had been the first European to discover the Aruwimi river in 1877, and in 1883 he had ascended it as far as the rapids at Yambuya and found the local inhabitants very hostile.[3] Now, he was determined to establish a base camp 'if not with the natives' goodwill . . . then by force'.[4] On 16 June Stanley and his party crossed to the south bank of the river, where the village of Yambuya was situated, and attempted 'to negotiate with the local people for leave to reside in their village'.[5] Not unreasonably, the request was refused. Mobilizing his full force in the two steamers, Stanley commenced an attack. The inhabitants fled into the surrounding forest and by 9 a.m. Stanley's expedition had occupied the deserted village.[6] This was soon made, under Stanley's directions, into a heavily fortified camp, surrounded by a ditch and a double wooden palisade. It soon became necessary, however, to try to reestablish relations with the evicted villagers. Although there were extensive manioc plantations immediately behind the camp, the Rear Column, consisting of some 271 people, would require meat and fish. It was Stanley's hope that these could be obtained by trading with the local people. He also expected that through this trade peaceful relations with the villagers might be established. But the displaced villagers refused to be forthcoming and apart from manioc the food supply for the Rear Column remained uncertain. 'There is not even a fowl to be had, and no big game', observed

---

[1] *IDA* i. 106.
[2] See above, p. 108.
[3] Stanley's account of this previous visit is to be found in H. M. Stanley, *The Congo and the Founding of its Free State*, vol. ii, ch. xxix.
[4] *IDA* i. 109.   [5] *IDA* i. 111.
[6] Ibid. 110–12. See also Jephson, *Diary*, pp. 107–8; Parke, *Diary*, p. 65.

Barttelot on his arrival, 'a pleasant look-out for Jameson and me, who are to be left behind'.[1]

It was now 22 June and Stanley was anxiously awaiting the arrival of Barttelot in the *Henry Reed* from Stanley Falls. Stanley distrusted Tippu Tip, who, he began to fear, had seized the *Henry Reed* and was holding Barttelot prisoner at Stanley Falls. Stanley even issued orders to Stairs to take the *Peace* and search for Barttelot and the other steamer and be prepared to attack Tippu Tip's settlement at Stanley Falls if necessary.[2] Before these instructions could be put into effect the *Henry Reed* appeared and Barttelot was able to report that all was well. The incident convinced Barttelot, however, that Stanley had no faith in Tippu Tip.

On his way to Stanley Falls, Barttelot (who was the first European to visit the station since its capture by the Arabs the previous year) had observed the devastation which had occurred as a result of the Arab victory and slave-raiding. Many of the villages along the Congo had been burnt down and their inhabitants had either taken to the forest or were living a precarious existence on the river in canoes. The arrival of the *Henry Reed* with a European on board was at first taken to represent the vanguard of an expedition to recapture Stanley Falls from the Arabs, but the presence of Tippu Tip was soon revealed and the reception was consistently hostile. Tippu Tip's assertions that he was now in the service of the Congo State and would bring the raids to an end were completely disbelieved.[3] At Stanley Falls, Barttelot found that the Arab settlement consisted of a stockaded village inhabited by about 4,000 persons, in which were three Krupp 7-pound guns (two of them defective), one heavy muzzle-loader without a carriage, and very little ammunition. Barttelot and his accompanying escort of forty Sudanese were treated with the most generous hospitality. The huge meals prepared for them were, Barttelot commented, far better than anything encountered on the expedition so far; wood was cut for the steamer by Tippu Tip's own people and Barttelot was given presents and some very welcome stores of provisions.[4] In return, at Tippu Tip's request, Barttelot agreed to write a letter to General Strauch in Brussels in which Tippu declared 'his loyalty to the King and his endeavours to create

---

[1] Barttelot, *Diary*, p. 111.   [2] *IDA* i. 114.
[3] Barttelot, *Diary*, p. 106.
[4] Barttelot to his parents, 1 June 1887, Barttelot Papers. Barttelot to Mabel Godman, 18 May–1 June 1887, B.P.

peace and order in his province'. Tippu Tip also requested the Congo State to provide him with soldiers and two European officers in accordance with the Agreement signed at Zanzibar.[1] Tippu Tip was to make this request repeatedly during the ensuing months and when it was not met, not even replied to, he felt that the State authorities had abandoned the Agreement.[2]

Tippu Tip also felt that Stanley had already broken faith with him over the second Agreement concerning the provision of carriers for the Emin Pasha relief expedition. The exact nature of Tippu Tip's grievance against Stanley is recorded in precisely similar terms by Barttelot and by Tippu Tip himself.[3] By Article 9 of the Agreement signed at Zanzibar, Tippu Tip had agreed to supply the carriers on condition that Stanley equipped them with ammunition. When Stanley had found himself compelled to leave most of the ammunition belonging to the expedition with Troup at Leopoldville, to come on later, he had asked Tippu Tip to equip the carriers himself, the understanding being that Tippu would be repaid later. Tippu Tip, Barttelot records at the time, 'thinks it a breach of contract, and also says his men have no powder'.[4] Tippu Tip also told Barttelot that the carriers would not come until the ammunition was provided.[5]

On his arrival at Stanley Falls, Tippu Tip appears to have done everything he could to make good Stanley's default.[6] Ammunition was highly valued and difficult to obtain in the heart of Africa, however, and Tippu Tip found that the stocks at Stanley Falls were very low. A caravan from the east coast was expected to arrive with new supplies very shortly (Tippu Tip had himself equipped and dispatched it whilst at Zanzibar.)[7] Until then the supplies available were both insufficient and expensive. Tippu Tip declared that, having learnt of this situation, he asked Barttelot's advice; but Barttelot 'said he was not able to order me to buy it' and therefore Tippu Tip 'did not buy it at so high a price, knowing Mr. Stanley to be a hard man'.[8] Before Barttelot left Stanley Falls for Yambuya, all he had been able to extract from Tippu Tip was a 'half promise

---

[1] Ibid.   [2] See Ch. VIII, p. 181 below.
[3] Barttelot, *Diary*, p. 108. Tippu Tip, *Autobiography*, p. 123, para. 172.
[4] Barttelot, *Diary*, p. 108.
[5] Ibid. 119.
[6] Tippu Tip to Holmwood, 21 July 1887, enclosed (in English translation) in Holmwood to F.O., 28 Mar. 1888, F.O. 84/1906. Tippu Tip, *Autobiography*, p. 123, para. 173.
[7] See Holmwood to F.O., 24 Dec. 1886, F.O. 84/1777.
[8] Tippu Tip to Holmwood, 21 July 1887, cited above.

to supply, at any rate, 200 men with ammunition, to be repaid'.[1] When Barttelot arrived at Yambuya he told Stanley that Tippu Tip felt that Stanley had broken faith with him concerning the ammunition. Stanley became furious and declared that he could do very well without Tippu Tip's aid or his men.[2] Stanley's Agreement with Tippu Tip at Zanzibar seems originally to have been made in the hope that the 600 carriers would accompany the Advance Column under Stanley's own leadership to Lake Albert. Two developments had compelled Stanley to alter this plan. First, the bulk of the loads to be transported to Lake Albert had had to be left behind at Leopold-ville. Secondly, it became clear, after Barttelot's return from Stanley Falls, that the 600 carriers would take several weeks to arrive at Yambuya if, indeed, they arrived at all. Rather than wait for them at Yambuya, Stanley decided to press on without them. The chief reason for this important decision, which was to affect the entire course of the expedition, was Stanley's own increasing obsession with the need to hurry. From the beginning, Stanley had tended to conceive his expedition to relieve Emin Pasha in terms of a mission to relieve a second Gordon at Khartoum. A sense of urgency haunted him.[3] Yet a delay of several weeks at Yambuya would be needed if they were to await the arrival of the sections of the expedition left at Leopoldville and at Bolobo, and—with luck—Tippu Tip's carriers. To Stanley this seemed intolerable:

Six weeks, probably two months, would pass before the entire force could be collected at Yambuya. If Emin was in such desperate straits as he had described, his total ruin might be effected in that time, and the disaster would be attributed to that delay—just as Gordon's death had been attributed to Sir Charles Wilson's delay at Metemmeh. To avoid that charge, I had no option but to form an Advance Column, whose duty would be to represent the steady progress of the expedition towards its goal.[4]

Stanley's plans for the Advance Column were quite clear. It was to push on following the course of the Aruwimi river through the unknown forest region as quickly as possible to the southern tip of

---

[1] Barttelot, *Diary*, pp. 108–9.
[2] Ibid. 113.
[3] *IDA* i. 77.
[4] *Autobiography of H. M. Stanley*, p. 355. A very similar assessment is given by Parke in a lecture given in Newcastle in 1890. A copy of the text of this is in the Barttelot Papers: 'Emin's cry was so urgent that Mr. Stanley preferred to risk a quick advance by forced marches with a light column rather than court disaster by delay, and repeat our too late experiences on the Nile.'

Lake Albert in the region of Kavalli's.[1] Here, a further base camp would be established, the portable steel boat *Advance* would be assembled, and it was hoped that contact would soon be established with Casati (who was believed to be at Kibiro on Lake Albert) and with Emin himself. Stanley had hoped that when Emin received the letter which Stanley had written to him at Zanzibar, he would come down to Lake Albert from Wadelai in one of his steamers and keep a watch for the arrival of the expedition. Having met Emin Pasha, Stanley assured Barttelot, 'we shall not be longer than a fortnight with him before deciding on our return to this camp [Yambuya], along the same route traversed by us when going east'.[2] Stanley estimated that according to this plan the Advance Column would arrive back at Yambuya after five months, that is, in November 1887.[3]

Whatever was decided at the meeting with Emin Pasha—whether he was to stay or to leave—it appears to have been part of Stanley's calculations at this stage that, after the return to Yambuya, a second journey to Lake Albert would have to be made with the stores and equipment (though not necessarily with all the men) assembled at Yambuya. This did not appear to present any very great problem since Stanley's plans rested on the belief that the march from Yambuya to Lake Albert through unknown territory could be accomplished in about two months without too much difficulty. If Emin were to remain in Equatoria he would need these supplies. If he were to leave, then Stanley would need a fair proportion of them on his overland march to Zanzibar.[4] Barttelot already knew of Stanley's intention to return eventually via the east coast route and suspected that Stanley's interest in exploration in the region of the Great Lakes

---

[1] Stanley apparently thought that the Aruwimi river itself probably emerged from the south-western corner of Lake Albert. See Barttelot to his father, 23 June 1887, copy in the M.P., F. 2.

[2] Barttelot, *Diary*, p. 136.

[3] See Instructions to Barttelot, printed in Barttelot, *Diary*, pp. 134–9. Barttelot sent a copy of these instructions to the Emin Pasha Relief Committee in London on 15 Aug. 1887 (Mackinnon Papers). This was printed in *The Times*, 28 Nov. 1887. Stanley's version of these instructions (*IDA* i. 114–17) is quite untrustworthy. It has been carefully edited and references to the return to Yambuya after five months have been omitted.

[4] In his instructions to Barttelot, Stanley emphasized the dependence of the Advance Column on the stores and ammunition left with the Rear. The stores would form 'the currency needed for transit through the regions beyond the lakes' and the ammunition would be needed for the fighting which Stanley expected to encounter there. Barttelot, *Diary*, p. 135.

formed as great a part of the purpose of the expedition as the relief of Emin Pasha.[1]

Stanley's plans for the Rear Column at this juncture are more difficult to disentangle from the *post factum* assertions and omissions with which he later overlaid them. The Rear Column was definitely to remain at Yambuya until Troup, Ward, and Bonny, with their men and loads, arrived on the return journey of the *Stanley* in August. Essentially, Stanley appears to have expected the united Rear Column to remain at Yambuya for a further three months until he returned from Lake Albert in October or November.[2] It was clearly unlikely that a force of 271 men, many of whom were sick, would be able to move with ammunition and stores which amounted to nearly 600 loads, on its own resources. If the Rear Column were to advance in Stanley's wake, it could only do so if carriers were provided by Tippu Tip. The fact that without these carriers the Rear Column would be unable to move from Yambuya was to be of crucial importance in the future for this section of the expedition. Did Stanley expect these carriers to arrive? The evidence suggests that he was extremely doubtful.[3] Stanley himself showed a consistent distrust of Tippu Tip and the Arabs, and warned Barttelot that far from assisting the Rear Column, 'the Arabs and their followers may, through some cause or other, quarrel with you and assail your camp'.[4] Even if Tippu Tip did keep the agreement to provide carriers, Stanley did not expect that they would arrive at once; he even declared his conviction that if they had not arrived by the time the *Stanley* returned in August, then they would not come at all.[5] In his plans for the Rear Column, therefore, Stanley placed no great hope in its being in a position to depend on anything other than its own resources. Barttelot understood that his instructions were to the effect that if Tippu Tip provided the carriers for the Rear Column, 'I was to move on with all the loads towards Wadelai, but if I was unable to transport all the loads I was to await Stanley's return'.[6]

---

[1] Barttelot to Major Sclater, 19 July–13 Aug. 1887. The original of this revealing letter is in the Barttelot Papers. An edited version is printed in Barttelot, *Diary*, pp. 118–21.

[2] Instructions to Barttelot, printed in Barttelot, *Diary*, pp. 134–9. Jameson, *Diary*, pp. 70–1. Stanley to de Winton, 19 June 1887, M.P., F. 4.

[3] *IDA* i. 117–23. Barttelot, *Diary*, pp. 120, 124–5.

[4] *IDA* i. 115.   [5] *IDA* i. 122.

[6] Barttelot to Major Tottenham, 19 June 1887, Barttelot Papers. Part of this

The idea of moving on in Stanley's wake instead of waiting for his return was, in any case, an afterthought. Stanley's initial instructions to Barttelot would seem to have assumed that the Rear Column would remain where it was.[1] The prospect of remaining isolated and inactive amidst the gloomy setting of Yambuya for five months appeared so bleak to Barttelot that he determined to try to persuade Stanley to allow him to advance, after the arrival of Troup, Ward, and Bonny, etc. in August.[2] Barttelot's attempts at persuasion appear to have been successful. In his final instructions, issued on 24 June, Stanley provided for the advance of the Rear Column under two contingencies.

First, if Tippu Tip supplied the full number of 600 carriers, then there would be no problem. Within a day or two after the arrival of the *Stanley* in August, the united Rear Column could set out to follow in Stanley's track. The two parts of the expedition would then be reunited either before Emin was reached, or on Stanley's return march towards Yambuya. Secondly, if Tippu Tip supplied some, but insufficient carriers (as Barttelot, on leaving Stanley Falls, expected), then Barttelot was left with the option of using his discretion as to what goods he could dispense with in order to enable the Rear Column to advance. But, warned Stanley, 'it would be better to make marches of six miles twice over, if you prefer marching to staying for our arrival, than throw too many things away'.[3]

Two aspects of these instructions must be emphasized. At no point is the case of Tippu Tip not providing any carriers alluded to —Stanley's claims to the contrary appear quite clearly to be later insertions.[4] Secondly, under all contingencies Barttelot was left with the option of remaining at Yambuya.

On 28 June 1887 Stanley left with the Advance Column for Lake Albert, leaving Major Barttelot in charge of the camp at Yambuya. 'Goodbye, Major', were his last words to Barttelot, 'I shall find you here in November when I return.'[5]

letter is printed in Barttelot, *Diary*, p. 91. Also Barttelot to Mackinnon, 27 Mar. 1888, M.P., F. 2. and Barttelot to Sir Redvers Buller, 1 June 1888, printed in Barttelot, *Diary*, p. 305. Stanley expected to take July and August to reach Emin Pasha and September and October to return to Yambuya. See Barttelot to Major Sclater, 19 Mar. 1888, B.P. Letter Book 3.

[1] Barttelot, *Diary*, pp. 111–12.
[2] Ibid. The full account of this initiative by Barttelot is to be found in a letter from Barttelot to his father, 23 June 1887, Barttelot Papers.
[3] Barttelot, *Diary*, p. 138.
[4] See *IDA* i. 122–3.   [5] Barttelot, *Diary*, p. 116.

CHAPTER VI

The Advance Column

STANLEY left Yambuya expecting to complete the march through the forest to Lake Albert in two months and to meet Emin Pasha by the middle of August.[1] But it was to be mid-December before he reached the lake, and not until April 1888 did he meet Emin Pasha. The events of these ten months, and especially the six months it was to take to traverse the Ituri rain forest to Lake Albert, altered the whole course of the expedition. The experiences undergone by the Advance Column during this time—graphically described in the accounts of Stanley and his officers—must surely rank amongst the most appalling of any nineteenth-century expedition in Africa. Of the 389 men who set out with Stanley from Yambuya, only 169 arrived six months later at Lake Albert. Two groups of sick and dying men had had to be left with Arab ivory-raiding parties *en route*, twenty men were simply 'missing', and 120 had been lost through death or desertion.[2] On more than one occasion during this march the whole fate of the expedition hung in the balance.

The Ituri rain forest had never before been traversed by Europeans. Information gathered from the Arabs, who were already penetrating the region in search of ivory, led Stanley to underestimate the extent of the forest region. He had been led to believe that after a march of a few weeks the forest would give way to open grassland where cattle and grain were plentiful, and where the Advance Column 'could swing along at the rate of from 10 to 15 miles per day'.[3] He made his calculations accordingly. In every respect they proved to be wrong.

The Ituri rain forest in fact covers a vast area, over 50,000 square miles. It is a region of dense forest and tangled vegetation through which rivers such as the Aruwimi (known in its upper reaches as the Ituri) rush from the plateau of the Nile–Congo watershed to join the Congo. The trees in the forest often reach great heights and form a screen through which the sun scarcely penetrates. The expedition

---

[1] Jephson, *Diary*, p. 144. Parke, *Diary*, p. 106.   [2] Jephson, *Diary*, p. 207.
[3] Statement by Stanley printed in *The Times*, 3 May 1890.

T. H. PARKE   R. H. NELSON   H. M. STANLEY   W. G. STAIRS   A. J. MOUNTENEY-JEPHSON

3. Stanley with the Officers of the Advance Column (taken in Cairo in 1890)

therefore marched for month after month in an atmosphere which was consistently wet and steamy—Jephson felt that he was 'drinking in malaria', Parke likened it to a Turkish bath.[1] Everything was saturated, even the four donkeys accompanying the expedition suffered from fever. The thick undergrowth made progress slow, the entire company lived in a perpetual state of near starvation, and these physical conditions brought about among the members of the expedition a state of mental gloom and despondency.

One of the most notable features of the progress of the expedition through this dismal region, and one of the reasons for its difficulties, was its lack of contact with the local inhabitants. All European-led expeditions in Africa depended on the assistance of the inhabitants of the areas through which they passed for food, for information, for survival. The population of the Ituri forest region, especially along the Aruwimi river, is very sparse and was at this time living in small scattered settlements amidst the unsettled conditions which had resulted from the recent Arab penetration of the area.[2] The region was a 'frontier' district beyond the area of organized Arab settlement, and most of the Arabs active in it owned no allegiance to men such as Tippu Tip. Equipped with firearms, they and their African followers had made their way, not up the Aruwimi, but direct from the Lualaba region of the Congo, and they had established themselves in recently constructed camps such as those of Ugarrowwa and Kilonga-Longa which Stanley was to visit. The devastation which accompanied their pursuit of ivory was always greater in these 'frontier' areas beyond the boundaries of the authority of men like Tippu Tip. Stanley's expedition encountered burnt and abandoned villages, an absence of cultivation (and hence of food for the expedition), and paths planted with poisoned wooden skewers which penetrated the feet of the Zanzibaris causing gangrenous sores and ulcers which would not heal. For five months, therefore the expedition marched through a devastated region where the remaining population was living in a state of war with all outsiders. Stanley's expedition was repeatedly taken for another Arab raiding party and attacked with poisoned arrows.[3] Every time it approached a village

[1] Jephson, *Diary*, p. 114. Parke, *Diary*, p. 73.
[2] The best studies of the peoples of this area are to be found in the *Ethnographic Survey of Africa*, ed. Daryll Forde (London and Brussels); *Les Bali*, by H. Van Geluwe, 1960; *Les Bira*, by H. Van Geluwe, 1957; *Mamvu-Mangutu et Balese-Mvuba*, by H. Van Geluwe, 1957.
[3] W. Hoffmann, *With Stanley in Africa*, p. 48.

the place was hurriedly abandoned, sometimes even set on fire; almost always such meagre stores of food as existed had been removed.

In its actions, Stanley's expedition soon came to differ very little from the Arab raiding parties. Villages were occupied, canoes were appropriated, and food was taken by the ravenous company throughout the march, with scant regard for human life and with immediate recourse to the use of the guns and ammunition with which the expedition was liberally equipped. Women and children were seized and held to ransom (for food or information or both). On more than one occasion sick and dying men were simply left behind.[1] The effect of all this on the sensitive and inexperienced Jephson is vividly recorded in his diary. On 5 July, for instance, the expedition entered an abandoned village. After collecting all the food available and seizing any other articles of interest, Jephson heard a shot from one of his company on the outskirts of the village. Hurrying to the spot he found that

one of my scouts, who had not come in with me, had seen two natives running away and had shot them both—I was awfully angry with the man for shooting men who were merely taking the liberty of running away from us in their own forest. One was shot in the side . . . and he was fast bleeding to death—the other, an oldish man, had his leg broken and would probably recover. Poor old fellow, he looked so emaciated and thin and wretched. Both looked at me with doglike eyes, like suffering animals. I felt sickenly [sic] sorry for them and awfully choky. It was such a cruel, ruthless, unnecessary thing, for neither were armed and both were running away, and here they were, lying all huddled up and bleeding to death, all we wanted was the food and that we could take—unjustly enough, though necessary—without shooting them.[2]

On such occasions Stanley himself showed scant regard for human life. On 16 July he wished to obtain some additional canoes to those he had already appropriated for transporting the expedition's equipment over a navigable stretch of the Aruwimi river. Jephson describes how one such canoe was obtained.

All day long we could see canoes ahead crossing and re-crossing the river, the natives were very much terrified and hardly seemed to know what to do. We harassed them all day long and Stanley pursued a canoe with four men in it, he shot one of the men and the other jumped ashore and got off. We towed the canoe to the other side of the river with the wounded native in it,

---

:e.g. Jephson, *Diary*, p. 148.   [2] Ibid. p. 118.

but he bled to death before we reached the bank and the men threw him overboard . . . The men then washed the canoe, which was covered with blood, and we manned and put loads into her.[1]

Stanley's methods were no less severe with his own men. As the expedition progressed, and food became desperately short, the Zanzibaris looted and stole and bartered even their rifles and ammunition for manioc, maize, or bananas. The bartering of guns or ammunition was punished by severe flogging. Even more serious were the large numbers of desertions. On 19 September, after the expedition had travelled for nearly three months and lost sixty-two men by death and desertion, Stanley felt compelled to 'adopt the strongest measures'. When three Zanzibaris, who had 'absconded with their rifles', were recaptured, Stanley had one of them hanged as an example; the others were later pardoned.[2] Stanley's officers marvelled that as conditions deteriorated the men did not resort to desperate measures against their European leaders. On 26 September Stanley himself recorded that 'the people were so reduced by hunger, that over a third could do no more than crawl. I was personally reduced to two bananas on this day from morning to night. But some of our Zanzibaris had found nothing to subsist on for two entire days.'[3]

On two occasions during this march Stanley's expedition was virtually saved by its arrival at Arab settlements. The first occasion was on 16 September, when the expedition stumbled into the settlement of an Arab called Ugarrowwa. Ugarrowwa in fact would seem to have been a Zanzibari. Stanley asserts that he was the same Uledi who had accompanied Speke and Grant as a tent carrier in 1860–3, before deserting them in Bunyoro.[4] Ugarrowwa had only recently established his settlement on the Aruwimi. He had arrived from the Lualaba area of the Congo after a journey through the forest of over 300 miles during which he had suffered considerable losses. It is doubtful if he was in any real sense a subject of Tippu Tip.[5] Jephson describes his settlement as consisting of about 300 people and possessing eighty guns.[6] At Ugarrowwa's, Stanley was able to obtain food for his starving men and to come to two arrangements.

The first concerned the dispatch of a letter to Barttelot.[7] Stanley's

---

[1] Ibid. 124.   [2] *IDA* i. 201–5.   [3] Ibid. 207.
[4] Ibid. 196.   [5] Ibid. 196–7.   [6] Jephson, *Diary*, p. 150.
[7] The text of this letter is printed in Barttelot, *Diary*, pp. 179–83. Barttelot himself never received it.

K

own experience had been such that he wished to warn the Rear
Column of the difficulties on the march. Ugarrowwa was short of
gunpowder; Barttelot's stores of it were considerable. In return for
3 cwt. of powder to be supplied by the Rear Column, Ugarrowwa
undertook to send a party of men to deliver the letter to Yambuya.
Ugarrowwa kept his promise, but his party turned back before
reaching Yambuya after being attacked by the local people and
suffering considerable losses.[1]

Secondly, Stanley arranged to leave fifty-six of his sick and dying
men at Ugarrowwa's with fifty guns (rendered useless by removal of
the breech blocks) to be picked up on the return journey from Lake
Albert to Yambuya. Stanley declares that arrangements were made
with Ugarrowwa for these men to be housed and fed at the rate of
$5 each per month (to be paid in goods from the stores of the Rear
Column), 'but', Stanley commented later, 'I doubted greatly whether
he would trouble his head about any of them'.[2] Ugarrowwa does not
seem to have done so: only fourteen of the fifty-six men who remained at his settlement survived.[3]

At Ugarrowwa's, Stanley also encountered the first of the dwarf
Mbuti people whom he was the first European to see and whose life
in the Ituri forest has recently been so engagingly described by Colin
Turnbull.[4]

On 19 September the expedition left Ugarrowwa's and soon encountered conditions even worse than those they had suffered
hitherto. Food was almost unobtainable. 'This hunger is terrible',
wrote Jephson, 'and it is terrible to see its ravages on the men and
feel its effects on oneself . . . The people are daily getting weaker and
weaker from hunger, for the one day on which they get a full stomach
they starve for three or four, and the consequence is that they are
going down hill very fast.'[5] Nelson became too ill to walk. Finally,
on 6 October, Stanley decided he would have to leave Nelson,
fifty-two men, and eighty-one loads behind, while he and the rest
of the expedition pushed on to obtain food at another Arab settlement which was believed to be a short distance ahead. This decision

[1] *IDA* i. 199.
[2] Report of Stanley to Euan-Smith, 19 Dec. 1889, published as *Africa No. 4*
(1890) (London), H.M.S.O., C. 5906.
[3] See Ch. VII, p. 169 below.
[4] Colin M. Turnbull, *The Forest People* (New York, 1961); *Wayward Servants*
(London, 1966).
[5] Jephson, *Diary*, p. 154.

by Stanley, to abandon Nelson and those unable to march, sorely tried the loyalty of the European officers. Jephson thought:

It was a terrible position for Nelson to be left in, he had food for only 2 days and will have to exist on what he can pick up in the shape of fungus and roots, or if there are any fish in the river he may be able to get a few; meantime we are going on with an exhausted and starving column to try and find food in a trackless wilderness . . . his position is very precarious and our chances of relieving him slight, he has worked with us in good fellowship all these months and now we are practically abandoning him.[1]

Parke, who never overstated anything, simply recorded that his parting from Nelson 'was altogether the most heart-rending good-bye I have ever experienced or witnessed'.[2] Only ten days later, after a time during which Jephson remarks that 'Stanley's anxiety has been frightful', and the fate of the expedition 'has been and is indeed hanging in the balance',[3] did the main body of the expedition arrive at Ipoto.

Ipoto was the second Arab settlement which Stanley encountered on the Aruwimi. Stanley was surprised to find that the Arabs had penetrated so far. As at Ugarrowwa's, the settlement had only recently been established, this time by a runaway Zanzibari slave called Kilonga-Longa, under whom was an armed force of about 150 Manyema. He too had arrived in the area from the Lualaba, but, hearing of Ugarrowwa's settlement downstream, he had established a separate base from which to send out parties seeking ivory and slaves outside the limits of Ugarrowwa's raiding circle.

At first, Stanley's expedition was received cordially enough, but this reception quickly evaporated when it became clear that the expedition had little to offer in return for the large quantities of food demanded. In order to obtain food the Zanzibaris sold their personal possessions, including their clothes. The European officers were compelled to do the same. Rifles and ammunition began to disappear at an alarming rate. When thirty rifles and 3,000 rounds of ammunition disappeared within two or three days, Stanley feared that the expedition was in danger of being disabled.[4] On his orders one man was hanged for selling his rifle to the Arabs for food and several others were flogged. There was now general discontent amongst

[1] Jephson, Diary, pp. 159–60.   [2] Parke, Diary, p. 117.
[3] Jephson, Diary, pp. 166–7.
[4] Report of Stanley to Euan-Smith, 19 Dec. 1889, published as Africa No. 4 (1890), C. 5906.

Stanley's followers about the lack of food and the wholesale flog-gings.[1] Stanley himself was unable to obtain much food for his followers, since the only way of paying for it was to give promises against the stores of the Rear Column—whose very existence the Arabs doubted. Only on 26 October was it possible to supply Jephson and forty Zanzibaris with sufficient food to set out to relieve Nelson. Jephson greatly feared that Stanley meant to push on ahead and leave him with Nelson at Ipoto 'without making any arrangement with the Arabs about supplying me with food etc. and I should just be stranded here, a dependant on the charity of slaves'.[1] Eventually it was decided that after returning from his mission to rescue Nelson, Jephson was to march on after Stanley and the main body of the expedition. Parke was selected to remain at Ipoto with Nelson and about thirty disabled men. Stanley could no longer spare forty men to carry the sections of the steel boat *Advance*, and so it was left behind along with the Maxim gun and a number of other loads of ammunition, etc., at Ipoto. Parke asked Stanley when he and Nelson could expect to be relieved; Stanley replied, after three months. But it was Parke's opinion that those who remained at Ipoto would in fact be held as hostages by the Arabs 'until redeemed by payment of cloth which is to be brought on by the rear column, and now due for corn etc. which the men have had'.[2] Jephson foresaw that

... this may mean a stay of nine months here ... for goodness knows when the expedition under Barttelot will be able to get up here; if we have experienced such frightful difficulties and troubles under Stanley, the troubles of the expedition under Barttelot will be ten times as great as he has no experience of the country and the men will not be likely to have the same faith in his leadership as in Stanley's.[3]

Leaving Ipoto on 26 October Jephson reached Nelson three days later. He found him in a dire condition. Of the fifty-two men left with him, only five remained, two of them dying; seventeen had died in the camp; the rest had deserted.[4] After burying thirteen boxes of ammunition and seven other loads of equipment which he was unable to carry and which he hoped to retrieve later, Jephson, accompanied by Nelson and the five remaining men, arrived back at Ipoto on 3 November. Stanley had already left with the main body of the expedition (now numbering only 147 men) on 27 October.[5]

---

[1] Jephson, *Diary*, p. 170.   [2] Parke, *Diary*, p. 128.
[3] Jephson, *Diary*, p. 172.
[4] Ten men arrived at Ipoto some months later. See Parke, *Diary*, p. 181.
[5] Ibid. 129.

Leaving Nelson and Parke with twenty-nine sick Zanzibaris and very little provision for their food and welfare with the Arabs at Ipoto, Jephson set out in pursuit of Stanley. He took with him a further forty-eight men and letters from Parke and Nelson which came close to reproaching Stanley for leaving them so poorly provided for at Ipoto.[1] On 16 November Jephson rejoined Stanley and the main body of the expedition.

The worst part of the march from Yambuya to Lake Albert was now over. Beyond Ipoto, the area affected by the Arabs gradually ended and after crossing the confluence of the Ituri and the Epulu rivers (the latter is called the Ihuru by Stanley),[2] the expedition entered a region of numerous well-populated villages with extensive clearings about them. In this country, inhabited by the Balese,[3] the expedition halted to recuperate for several days near the village of Ibwiri. Stanley was later to establish a permanent camp here. Describing the area, Jephson noted:

> The villages all round are like huge granaries of Indian corn, the clearings are all full of splendid bananas, we have as much goat meat and chickens as we can eat, flour and beans in plenty; such abundance I never dreamed of. This is the first village beyond the country conquered by the Manyema . . . directly one gets beyond their influence there is abundance of food.[4]

On 24 November the expedition marched on. The forest became less dense, food was plentiful, and ten days later the expedition emerged into open grassland. On 13 December the 169 men—all that remained of the Advance Column of the 389 who had left Yambuya —were looking down on Lake Albert. 'To say one experienced a feeling of relief or even joy on at last seeing the Lake would hardly describe what one felt', recorded Jephson. 'The Lake had ever been the goal held up before one's eyes since we had left Yambuya nearly six months ago . . . we had always looked to it as the haven where all our troubles would end.'[5]

But a new set of troubles was just beginning. Stanley had hoped that he would arrive at Lake Albert about the middle of August and that Emin Pasha, having received the letter which he had sent from

---

[1] These letters are printed in *IDA* i. 238–41.
[2] *IDA* i. 249.
[3] Stanley correctly names them. See *IDA* i. 253. For a detailed account of the life and country of the Balese, see H. Van Geluwe, *Les Mamvu-Mangutu et Balese-Mvuba*, Ethnographic Survey of Africa, ed. Daryll Forde, Part III (London, 1957).
[4] Jephson, *Diary*, pp. 192–3.   [5] Ibid. p. 207.

Zanzibar, would come down to the southern end of the lake in one of his steamers. Yet here was the expedition on the shores of Lake Albert in mid-December and there was no sign of Emin or his steamers. Indeed, the local people knew nothing about him—the last European they had seen had been Colonel Mason, who had paid a brief visit to the south end of the lake in a 'smoke-boat' ten years previously.[1] Stanley was completely nonplussed. 'A more heartless outlook never confronted an explorer in wild Africa than that which was now so abruptly revealed to us', he commented. 'From the date of leaving England . . . it never dawned on us that at the very goal we might be baffled so completely as we were now.'[2] The gulf between the position of Emin in Equatoria, as it was envisaged in Europe, and as it was in reality, was now gradually to be revealed. Stanley had come expecting to find 'an ideal Governor', loyally supported by his soldiers, administering an orderly province, and holding the Mahdists at bay. He took it for granted that his letter to Emin had arrived;[3] he expected to find in Equatoria a grateful Governor ready to fit in with whatever plans he would decide. Suddenly, on reaching Lake Albert, Stanley records that the chill thought struck him for the first time 'that, after all, our forced march and continual fighting and sacrifice of life would be in vain'.[4]

There is more to this remark than meets the eye. Throughout his march across the Congo, Stanley had kept to himself a fear that Emin Pasha would no longer be in Equatoria when the expedition arrived. As Stanley now revealed to Jephson and Stairs, the very last news which he had received from the Foreign Office had suggested that Emin was contemplating a withdrawal on his own account to Zanzibar via the east coast route through Bunyoro and Busoga.[5] This news had only reached England after the departure of the expedition, and Stanley himself had first heard it at Leopoldville in April, where Mackinnon's last telegrams had reached him. On hearing of Emin's plans at Leopoldville, Stanley appears to have seriously considered giving up the expedition altogether, but the other purposes for which it had been organized seem to have induced him to continue.[6] Everything that Stanley now observed by Lake

---

[1] Jephson, *Diary*, p. 212. *IDA* i. 310.   [2] *IDA* i. 311.
[3] Emin had never received the letter which Stanley had written to him at Zanzibar. Jephson, *Diary*, p. 250.   [4] *IDA* i. 305.   [5] Ibid. 313.
[6] This incident, omitted from Stanley's own account, is related in a letter written by Barttelot, reporting a conversation with Stanley. Barttelot to Major Sclater, 19 July 1887 (Barttelot Papers).

Albert confirmed the suspicion that Emin had gone. It is important to remember this in the context of Stanley's subsequent decisions.

The expedition was now in a wretched position. It was scattered over hundreds of miles in several settlements which had been hastily established and ill provided for between Yambuya and Lake Albert. The party arriving at Lake Albert—consisting of less than half of those who had set out from Yambuya—had with it very little of the expedition's equipment, barely sufficient ammunition for its own considerable needs, and scarcely any 'relief' to bring to Emin Pasha. The Maxim gun and, more immediately important, the portable steel boat, had been left behind at Ipoto, and there appeared to be no canoes which the expedition might utilize on Lake Albert. Wadelai was twenty-five days' march by land but, Stanley estimated rather optimistically, only four days by water.[1] After two days had been spent unsuccessfully looking for canoes, it was clear that there was no means of transporting the expedition by water. Stanley's relations with the people living between the edge of the forest and the western shore of Lake Albert were already so hostile—the expedition had seized livestock and burnt whole villages on an unprecedented scale[2]—that he felt his supplies of ammunition were inadequate for the expedition to embark on a land march which he envisaged would be accompanied by continuous fighting.[3]

The Advance Column was in fact no longer in a position to advance. Stanley and his officers were also increasingly anxious about the men and loads left behind. The conviction which had hitherto spurred on the progress of the expedition, and which had largely contributed to its present pass—that Emin Pasha must be reached quickly and at all costs—suddenly evaporated. It now seemed far more important to do something about the men and loads known to be in the rear, than to advance in search of an elusive Pasha whose very existence in Equatoria now seemed uncertain. Even if Emin still remained in the province, it is hard to avoid the conclusion that Stanley was reluctant to confront Emin in his present ill-equipped state. Stanley had set out to bring relief to Emin. Hard as it was for Stanley to face the fact, by December 1887 it was his own expedition which was in need of relief. By a curious process of wishful thinking,

---

[1] *IDA* i. 311.

[2] For details see *IDA* i. 289–309, where, under headings such as 'We disperse the natives', 'Peace arranged', and 'We keep the natives at bay', the destructive progress of the expedition between the edge of the forest and Lake Albert is charted. Also Jephson, *Diary*, pp. 194–204.   [3] *IDA* i. 311–12.

Stanley now came to anticipate that this relief would be forthcoming from the Rear Column and from Emin Pasha himself. Stanley came to hope, indeed to take it for granted, that the Rear Column would somehow have managed to move on after him, bringing with it all the stores and ammunition which he now so desperately needed, and would have survived intact the march through the forest which he had found so difficult. From Emin Pasha—if he still remained in Equatoria—Stanley came to expect not only supplies of food, but carriers to assist him in the future course of the expedition.

On 14 December Stanley decided to abandon, for the moment, the search for Emin Pasha. His plan was to march back to Ibwiri (where food was far more plentiful than by the lake and the people were less hostile) and construct a fortified camp there. Whilst the majority of the men would remain in this camp, a picked force would be sent back to bring on the boat along with Parke, Nelson, and the men left at Ipoto. A further expedition would be made to retrieve the men left at Ugarrowwa's and, it was hoped, to obtain news of the Rear Column. When the entire expedition was reunited at Ibwiri a further attempt would be made, with the aid of the steel boat, to establish contact with Emin Pasha.[1] All this would take many months, and Stanley's plan was strongly opposed by Stairs and Jephson who felt bitterly disappointed that the search for Emin Pasha should be subordinated to other considerations and that the expedition should 'turn back when we were on the eve of success'.[2] Jephson expressed astonishment that Stanley should abandon the whole purpose of the expedition so easily.[2] He urged Stanley to allow him to march northwards along the western shore of Lake Albert to a point opposite Kibiro; here he would seize a canoe and go across the lake and try to establish contact with Casati, Emin's Italian companion, whom Junker had reported to be staying at Kibiro. This had originally been Stanley's own intention and the purpose to which he had hoped to put the steel boat; now, however, Jephson records, 'Stanley said it was too risky'.[2] So, on 16 December, the expedition turned its back on Lake Albert and re-ascended the plateau on the march back to Ibwiri.

*   *   *

The village of Ibwiri had been abandoned by its inhabitants when the expedition arrived back on 6 January 1888. Food and building

---

[1] *IDA* i. 316.   [2] Jephson, *Diary*, p. 213.

materials had, however, been left behind. These were therefore appropriated and by 18 January a strongly stockaded camp called, by Stanley, Fort Bodo had been constructed on the site.

Stanley was very anxious about the fate of Nelson, Parke, and the men and goods left at Ipoto. Stairs was therefore dispatched with an armed force of ninety-eight men to bring them on to Fort Bodo; if the party had suffered any violence, Stairs was to embark on 'full and final retribution' against the Arabs at Ipoto.[1] Stairs returned on 12 February accompanied by Parke, Nelson, the Maxim gun, the steel boat *Advance*, and sixteen survivors. Eleven of the men left behind at Ipoto in October had died 'due to starvation'. The whole party had been kept in a state of near-starvation by the Arabs, whose chief interest was to obtain the guns and ammunition which the party possessed. Both Parke and Nelson had been seriously ill, and Stanley himself was shocked at the worn and haggard appearance of Nelson.[2]

Fort Bodo was now completed, stocks of ammunition had been replenished, and, most important, Stanley once more possessed the steel boat. Everyone in Fort Bodo was now in favour of a second advance to the lake, the launching of the boat, and a determined search for Emin Pasha.[3] Stanley, however, still hoped for the arrival of the Rear Column, and there were still the men and loads which had been abandoned at Ugarrowwa's since the previous September to be recovered. Before a second advance was made to Lake Albert, therefore, Stanley once again dispatched Stairs with a small force on a mission of retrieval. He was to return to Ugarrowwa's and bring on the men and loads remaining there to Fort Bodo. If no news of the Rear Column had been obtained before he reached Ugarrowwa's, he was to dispatch couriers all the way back to Yambuya with letters to Barttelot 'telling him to come on as fast as he could and warning him of the places where there was no food'.[4] Stairs left Fort Bodo on 16 February and was expected back by 25 March. It was then anticipated that a second advance would be made to Lake Albert.[5]

Two days after Stairs's departure Stanley became acutely ill.

[1] *IDA* i. 331.
[2] Ibid. 338–40, where the report of Parke is given. A full account of the months at Ipoto is to be found in Parke, *Diary*, pp. 129–97.
[3] *IDA* i. 340–1. Jephson, *Diary*, p. 227.
[4] Jephson, *Diary*, p. 227. The text of the letter from Stanley to Barttelot, dated 14 Feb. is printed in Barttelot, *Diary*, pp. 184–92.
[5] *IDA* i. 341.

His illness—probably due to an impacted gall-stone—was protracted and Parke more than once feared for his life.[1] For a whole month Stanley was completely incapacitated; he suffered acute pain, which Parke tried to relieve with repeated injections of morphine. Parke found Stanley as a patient irritable and 'very difficult to control; as he is very prone, under all circumstances, to do what he likes, regardless of advice'.[2] Any plans for an early start with the steel boat for the lake were naturally abandoned. Whilst Stanley lay ill, Jephson, Parke, and Nelson concentrated on improving the camp and supervising the planting around it of considerable quantities of maize, beans, and other food crops.

By the end of March, Stanley was sufficiently recovered to contemplate again an advance with the boat to Lake Albert, though he continued to hope that the Rear Column would somehow arrive before he once more set out to meet Emin Pasha. But by the beginning of April there was no sign of the Rear Column and no news of Stairs. On 2 April Stanley therefore left Fort Bodo without them and set out on his second advance to Lake Albert. He was accompanied by Jephson and Parke, the steel boat *Advance*, and 126 men. Forty-nine men, debilitated by ulcers, were left at Fort Bodo with Nelson, who had by no means fully recovered.[3]

The march to Lake Albert was uneventful and, on 14 April, whilst still some distance from the lake, the expedition received the first news of Emin Pasha. At first this came in the form of rumour. Some of the local Hima population approached Stanley and informed him, through interpreters, that two months after his previous visit to the lake a European (whom they called 'Maleju', the bearded one) had come to the southern end of the lake in a steamer. He had said he was expecting another European with many people and had asked if there had been any news of them. On hearing of Stanley's previous arrival and departure, Emin had left a letter and steamed away again.[4] Four days later this letter (carefully wrapped in oil cloth and a fragment of *The Times* for April 1886, describing the first Spring meeting at Newmarket)[5] was in Stanley's hands. Written in excellent English, this letter was a typical product of Emin's calm and precise intelligence.[6] Dated 'Tunguru, 25/3/1888', it

---

[1] Stanley's illness had a previous history; he also had a severe inflammation of one arm. See Parke, *Diary*, pp. 198–206.

[2] Ibid. 202.   [3] *IDA* i. 348.

[4] *IDA* i. 357–64.   [5] Parke, *Diary*, p. 216.

[6] *IDA* i. 368, where the only surviving text of this letter is given.

stated that Emin had heard rumours of Stanley's arrival and had come to investigate. On receiving the letter, Stanley was requested to stay where he was and send word to Emin by letter of his whereabouts. Emin would then come again in his steamer and take Stanley and his men to the station at Tunguru, situated on the western shore of Lake Albert to the north. Stanley was warned to avoid Kibiro; Casati was no longer there, having been expelled by Kabarega. The cool and dispassionate tone of Emin's message made it, as Stanley's servant Hoffman observed, 'a strange letter to receive from a man whom we had imagined to be in an agony of suspense for the relief to arrive'.[1]

The receipt of this first definite news from Emin was an immense relief to Stanley and immediately raised the spirits of all the members of the expedition.[2] Stanley at once made arrangements for Jephson, escorted by Parke and sixty men, to proceed to the lake with the steel boat, while Stanley and the main body of men camped where they were at Kavalli's. Jephson was to launch the boat and row up the lake to Mswa, the southernmost station established by Emin Pasha on the western shore, taking with him a small body of men and Stanley's reply to Emin's letter. From Mswa, Jephson would soon be in contact with Emin at Tunguru and the two men would then return to Kavalli's in Emin's steamer. Parke would meanwhile have returned to Kavalli's and sentries would be posted on the plateau to look out for the steamer. When it was sighted, Stanley planned to 'march down to the shore of the lake and deliver over the loads of ammunition to Emin Pasha'.[3] The scene was thus set for a rendezvous as dramatic as any which Stanley had made hitherto in Africa.

For once Stanley's plans went as anticipated. Jephson arrived at Mswa on 22 April. The station had been established by Emin the previous July when he first heard about the expedition and Jephson was immensely impressed by its order and neatness and by the polite reception accorded to him in Emin's absence by the garrison there. He also commented on the obvious affection and admiration exhibited by Emin's soldiers for their leader. 'It is wonderful with what love and affection his people speak of him', wrote Jephson,

[1] W. Hoffmann, *With Stanley in Africa*, p. 65.
[2] *IDA* i. 368. Jephson, *Diary*, p. 240. The receipt of this letter was, as Stanley later told Emin, the first intimation he had received that Emin was still alive and in Equatoria. *Tagebücher*, 29 Apr. 1888, iv. 99.
[3] Jephson, *Diary*, p. 241.

'what a difference from our leader with whom things are done by sheer brute force only.'[1] The order and equipment of Emin's soldiers also contrasted sharply with the sorry state of Stanley's expedition and of Jephson's own clothing and appearance:

They all looked so smart and clean compared with us who had arrived in rags—we looked as if we were in want of relief far more than they— I felt awfully dirty in my old worn out suit of Tweed beside the smart Nubian officer and even beside the servants who were all dressed in suits of fresh white cotton cloth which Emin Pasha's people weave.[2]

Hearing of Jephson's arrival, Emin set out from Tunguru with Casati and Vita Hassan in the steamer *Khedive*. On 27 April 1888 Emin and Jephson met at Mswa.[3]

[1] Jephson, *Diary*, p. 245.   [2] Ibid. 246.
[3] Jephson, *Diary*, p. 248, gives the date as 26 April; Emin, *Tagebücher*, iv. 97–8, as 27 Apr.—as do Casati and Vita Hassan. As Jephson's dating is unreliable throughout this month (see note by Mrs. D. Middleton in Jephson, *Diary*, p. 243), I have taken Emin's date.

CHAPTER VII

Equatoria 1886–1888

EMIN had first heard that an expedition was being sent from England to his relief through a letter from Mackay, the C.M.S. missionary in Buganda, which arrived on 9 April 1887.[1] With this letter, Mackay enclosed extracts from English and German newspapers published the previous November. From these sources Emin learnt that an expedition was being sent under the leadership of either H. M. Stanley or Joseph Thomson to bring ammunition and supplies to Equatoria. It was expected to consist of about 450 porters and to take a route inland from the East African coast avoiding Buganda. On hearing (falsely) that 'a rich London merchant' had donated £20,000 to the £10,000 allocated by the Egyptian Government for this expedition, Emin felt quite overwhelmed. 'I confess one must go to England to seek for such generosity', he commented.[2]

Now we must do our best to gain time for some two or three months until Stanley or Thomson are able to join us . . . I am delighted to see that the public in England take some interest in these countries and I hope that all shall yet end well. Mr. Stanley and Mr. Thomson certainly are entitled to our everlasting thankfulness for their generous offer to come to our help. I have always felt the greatest admiration for Mr. Stanley as an explorer; his intrepidity, his pluck, and his kindly regards for his followers have always commanded my hearty sympathies . . . I hope, nevertheless, that our letters may come in time and that a Protectorate over our territories at once may be established.[3]

Emin was amused to find that some British newspapers were already expressing the view that the expedition was to bring about his own

---

[1] *Tagebücher*, 9 Apr. 1887, iii. 337–8, where the letter from Mackay to Emin, dated 27 Feb. 1887, is given in full. Mackay himself had first received the news on 23 Feb. through letters from the Revd. R. P. Ashe, Bishop Parker, and Mr. E. Muxworthy, dated 29 Dec. 1886. See Mackay to Holmwood, 29 May 1887, enclosed in Macdonald to Salisbury, 25 Oct. 1887, F.O.C.P. 5617, p. 69.

[2] Emin to Mackay, 15 Apr. 1887, enclosed in Macdonald to Salisbury, 26 Sept. 1887, F.O.C.P. 5617, pp. 63–6.

[3] Emin to Mackay, 15 Apr. 1887, enclosed in Macdonald to Salisbury, 26 Sept. 1887, F.O.C.P. 5617, pp. 63–6.

withdrawal. 'If the people in Great Britain think that as soon as Stanley or Thomson comes I shall return with them they greatly err', Emin declared.[1] 'Even were Stanley to provide me with ammunition and supplies, I have no idea of ever leaving my post.'[2]

The news of the impending arrival of Stanley's expedition was warmly welcomed by Emin, but it in no way altered his resolve, firmly and consistently held, not to withdraw from Equatoria. Emin's ambition remained what it had always been: to stay in the Equatorial province and, he hoped, to administer it under new auspices. This determination of Emin not to abandon Equatoria needs some explanation, particularly as it was in direct opposition—as he himself acknowledged—to the instructions which he had already received from the Egyptian Government and was to receive again in the future.

In his hopes for the future of Equatoria, Emin Pasha held views which were closely similar to those of his predecessors, Gordon and Baker. He regarded the Egyptian presence in Equatoria as of dubious benefit to the area and its inhabitants. Emin had a profound concern for the development of the area of which he was Governor, a concern which was accompanied by a clear recognition of the lack of any such interest on the part of the Egyptian Government. He firmly believed that the development of Equatoria—as of the rest of the Sudan—would only be a very gradual process and that it would start only when Egyptian rule ended and a European occupation began. After the British occupation of Egypt, the rise of the Mahdi, and the fall of Khartoum, Emin became convinced that a British occupation of the Sudan—and of Equatoria—was 'only a question of time'. It was his great hope that he would survive long enough, with his impoverished administration, to bring about what he liked to describe as 'the reorganization' of the Equatorial province (which meant its expansion to its fullest limits and especially the reoccupation of the Mangbetu area) as part of the reorganization of all the provinces of the Sudan which he believed would take place when the Mahdists were defeated and the European occupation began. It was this hope, in addition to a personal predilection for the area which he had made his home and the scene for his consuming interest in natural history, which induced Emin to remain in

[1] Emin to R. W. Felkin, 17 Apr. 1887, printed in *E.P. in C.A.*, pp. 508-11.
[2] Emin to R. W. Felkin, 3 Sept. 1887, printed in Schweitzer, i. 263.

Equatoria during the years after 1884.[1] Once the British Government had annexed Equatoria, Emin would be quite happy to hand over his responsibilities to someone abler and younger than himself. 'Believe me', he wrote to Mackay, 'I in no way count upon or make any claim to receiving a Government situation in the English service, but I shall be content to withdraw when I am assured that my present countries are settled on a tolerably secure footing, and the government of them intrusted to excellent hands.'[2]

As has been seen, it was Mackay who had first led Emin to believe that if Egypt abandoned Equatoria, England might be ready to annex the province.[3] Mackay's influence on Emin throughout this period (1885-8) is of crucial importance. Emin had always believed that Equatoria should be separated from the rest of the 'Arab' Sudan. Mackay saw in Equatoria a 'nucleus of civilization' which he hoped might come to occupy the position of a counterweight to Buganda. By 1886 both Emin and Mackay looked to a future union of Buganda, Bunyoro, and Equatoria under British control.[4]

Emin had received every encouragement to believe that his hopes for the future incorporation of Equatoria within the British Empire would be supported from an even more important quarter than Mackay. In June 1887 Emin received two letters from Sir John Kirk. In the first, written in England the previous December, when Kirk was actively promoting the organization of the expedition for Emin's relief, Kirk acknowledged the receipt of Emin's important letter of 7 July 1886, in which Emin had offered the province of Equatoria to England. Kirk informed Emin of the details of the recent Anglo-German agreement over East Africa and stated: 'I am now doing all I can to make your position and your great and

---

[1] This passage is based on an extensive reading of Emin's Diary and of his many letters. Emin's hopes for the political future of Equatoria are stated most succinctly in a letter to Mackay, dated 7 Feb. 1887. This is enclosed in Macdonald to Salisbury, 27 Aug. 1887, F.O.C.P. 5617, pp. 55-62. Emin also felt that his collecting and investigations of the flora and fauna of Equatoria was far from complete. 'If ever I returned to Europe—though I do not expect it—I should be ashamed of submitting such patchwork to the public', he declared (Emin to R. W. Felkin, 3 Sept. 1887, cited above).

[2] Emin to Mackay, 6 July 1886, enclosed in Mackay to Kirk, 24 Aug. 1886, enclosed in Holmwood to Iddesleigh, 18 Oct. 1886, F.O. 84/1775.

[3] See Ch. II, p. 33 above.

[4] Mackay to C.M.S., 2 May and 22 Aug. 1886, F.O.C.P. 5433, pp. 93-100. See also Emin to R. W. Felkin, 22 July 1886, M.P., F. 7.

good work known and to secure you, not help to come away, but support to enable you to remain'.[1] In the second letter, dated 21 January 1887, Kirk was in a position to be even more explicit:

It has been decided to send Mr. Stanley with stores for your relief and support and I do trust you will be able to maintain your position until further supported. You may not know that an agreement has been come to between the British and the German Governments defining their respective spheres of influence in Africa, where the whole line inland from Mombasa on the East coast to the Victoria Nyanza and in a North West direction towards Uganda and your province have been assigned to us, while Germany has a free hand to the South and West in the direction of Tanganika. This agreement settles the rivalries of the two powers and gives each a right to act without offending the other. I hope that Mr. Stanley will be able to arrange with you some way in which this agreement of the two powers can be made advantageous to the country you have done so much to develop.[2]

These letters from Kirk reached Emin along with two others. The first was the letter which Holmwood had sent at the request of the Egyptian Government in December 1886.[3] This informed Emin that he had been promoted to the rank of Pasha and restated the instructions which had been contained in Nubar Pasha's previous letter to Emin. These instructions were quite explicit: the Egyptian Government wished to abandon Equatoria, Emin and his garrisons were ordered to withdraw, but 'any troops and refugees who desire to remain where they are, should be permitted to do so'.[4] Finally, there was a letter from Mackay in Buganda, of very recent date, which informed Emin that Stanley's expedition was taking the Congo route and was expected to arrive in Equatoria in July. Mackay was greatly relieved that Stanley had decided not to approach by the east coast route since although he was, of course, known in Buganda, Mackay still feared that once Stanley arrived in Equatoria there would be 'alarm in the air' in Buganda and the lives of the missionaries might be imperilled. The Kabaka's fear of a threat to his kingdom from the direction of Equatoria was so long-standing, and the Arab party at the court were becoming so hostile to the missionaries and to all Europeans, that Mackay told Emin of his own

[1] Kirk to Emin, 1 Dec. 1886, printed in *Tagebücher* under 27 June 1887, iii. 356.

[2] Kirk to Emin, 21 Jan. 1887, printed in ibid., under 27 June 1887, iii. 357.

[3] Holmwood to Emin, 1 Dec. 1886, *Tagebücher*, 27 June 1887, iii. 357. This letter transmits the instructions of the Egyptian Government as already related in Ch. III, p. 61.   [4] *Tagebücher*, iii. 355.

plans to withdraw from Buganda altogether.[1] Mackay concluded
by urging Emin to stick to his post until Stanley's expedition arrived.
'It is needless to say that my eyes turn towards Mr.
Stanley and yourself when you put your heads and hands together', wrote Mackay.
'Once more I implore you to do your utmost to get your province
firmly established as part of the British Empire.'[2] By June 1887
Emin needed no urging to adopt this course. Not only was he hoping
to place Equatoria under British control; he had shown a consistent
lack of interest in putting himself and his province either under the
Germans or under King Leopold's Congo State.[3]

Emin had also faced the possibility that Egypt would abandon
the province and England 'for political reasons will not annex it'.
In such an eventuality Emin hoped he might be able to govern
Equatoria independently along the lines of Rajah Brooke in Sarawak
—at least for the few years which might elapse before the British
occupation of the Sudan took place.[4] 'In order to do this', Emin
observed, 'funds and friends are necessary—friends who can place
implicit trust in me and who possess the money.'[5] Ever since 1883
Emin had appealed to his friends in England, R. W. Felkin and
Charles Allen, to endeavour to procure the approbation and support
of 'an influential circle' among their business acquaintances for the
development of Equatoria.[6] Their efforts had resulted in the abortive
attempts to form a Royal Sudan Company (on the lines of the British
North Borneo Company) between 1883 and 1885—an enterprise in
which both J. F. Hutton and H. M. Stanley had been involved.[7]
After 1886 Emin gave Felkin *carte blanche* to approach his business

[1] Mackay to Emin, 1 May 1887, in *Tagebücher*, iii. 359–60. Mackay withdrew
from Buganda to Msalala and then to Usambiro at the south end of Lake Victoria
in July 1887. It was there that Emin was to meet him for the first time in Aug.
1889. An interesting account of the situation in Buganda at this time, and of the
reaction of the Kabaka Mwanga to the distorted rumours of the approach of
Stanley's expedition (which Mwanga believed had been sent at least partly to
avenge the death of Bishop Hannington) is given in the article by Sir John Gray,
'The Year of the Three Kings in Buganda', *Uganda Journal*, xiv, no. 1 (1950),
pp. 17–18.   [2] Mackay to Emin, 1 May 1887, *Tagebücher*, iii. 359–60.
[3] See Ch. II, p. 35 above.
[4] See especially Emin to R. W. Felkin, 2 Oct. 1886, printed in Schweitzer,
i. xxx–xxxiv. The idea of 'sarawaking' the province of Equatoria had, according
to Felkin, been discussed between Emin and himself as early as 1879. See ibid. xxi.
[5] Emin to Felkin, 25 Oct. 1886, M.P., F. 7.
[6] Emin to R. W. Felkin, 22 July 1886, cited above. Emin to Charles Allen,
22 July 1886, A.S.S. 155/137.
[7] See Ch. IV, p. 75 above. The venture is described in R. Gray, *A History o
the Southern Sudan*, pp. 187–94.

friends on his behalf and to endeavour to come to 'a definite arrangement with a syndicate of English commercial men for the future development of Equatoria'.[1] Among Felkin's friends was Mackinnon, and, knowing of his interest in East Africa, it became Felkin's hope that Mackinnon might be persuaded to include Equatoria within the sphere of his East African concession, thus retaining the area for Britain.[2] As has been seen, Mackinnon was already interested in Equatoria as a possible alternative base of operations in the East African interior to Buganda. Emin's plight also appealed to his imagination and, like his friend King Leopold, the idea of a frontier on the Nile at Wadelai invoked a response in his impractical nature.[3] In 1888 Felkin constituted himself as Emin's agent in discussions with Mackinnon which resulted in an agreement whereby Equatoria became part of the sphere of the Imperial British East Africa Company, though a reserve clause allowed Emin to revoke the arrangement if he so wished.[4]

Felkin's chief concern was to act faithfully in Emin's own interests. His great fear was that his effort in England on Emin's behalf might be forestalled by offers to Emin from either the Germans or King Leopold. Felkin was acutely suspicious of Stanley and of the reasons which had led to the adoption of the Congo route by the relief expedition. He believed that Stanley was working primarily for Leopold and that Leopold was determined to annex Equatoria. Early in 1887, Felkin therefore wrote to Emin:

I trust you will go to work with extreme caution before signing any agreement with the Congo Free State or with the people who have set out for your rescue. If you hold out long enough, I am perfectly convinced that help will be brought you from England. At present people are holding back waiting to see the result of Stanley's expedition . . . I think hardly any doubt exists that at no very distant date the whole Congo State will collapse and fall a prey to France . . .

Felkin urged Emin not to be 'overcome by sentiments of gratitude,

---

[1] Emin to R. W. Felkin, 2 Oct. 1886, cited above. 'I place myself and all my Sudanese soldiers at your disposition and assure you that you can calculate fully on us.'

[2] See the Introduction by R. W. Felkin to Schweitzer, vol. i, pp. xxxvi–xl.

[3] See Ch. III, p. 53 above.

[4] The Agreement is printed in Schweitzer, vol. i, pp. xxxviii–xxxix. What appears to be the original document is in the Mackinnon Papers. That Emin received a copy of this Agreement (probably at Bagamoyo, in December 1889) is suggested by the existence of a copy of it in the Emin Pasha papers, State Archives, Hamburg.

or deference to the sophistries of those who are now going in search of you—always remember that the Relief Expedition has been publicly declared to be a work of philanthropy, not an expedition for the purpose of annexation'.[1]

The dispatch and receipt of these letters to and from Europe occupied a great deal of Emin's attention during the years 1886-8. Every letter from Wadelai had first to be taken to Kibiro on Lake Albert. This was a three-day journey by steamer from Emin's headquarters. But the real difficulties lay in the intrigues, obstacles, or delays which obstructed the transport of letters through Bunyoro and Buganda (whence they could be sent by the messengers dispatched regularly by the C.M.S. missionaries to the coast and Zanzibar—a journey of two to three months—and so to Europe). Only by a great deal of effort and persistence was Emin able to maintain this remarkable correspondence during this period. Of key importance was the role played by the Tripolitanian Arab, Muhammad Biri, who had met Junker at Kabarega's in February 1886.[2] He was assisted by Casati, who, after June 1886, remained at Kabarega's court ostensibly as Emin's agent, but chiefly to expedite the passage of mail and supplies to and from Equatoria.[3] After the middle of 1887, however, Emin's relations with Kabarega rapidly deteriorated. Partly this was brought about by Casati's tactless behaviour;[4] partly it resulted from Emin's allowing himself to be drawn into a conflict with Kabarega over certain districts in Acholi;[5] most of all, perhaps, it stemmed from Kabarega's growing fear of an alliance

---

[1] Schweitzer, op. cit. i. 311.

[2] See Ch. II, p. 30 above. See also H. B. Thomas, 'Muhammad Biri', *Uganda Journal*, xxiv, no. 1 (1960).

[3] Casati's account of his experiences in Bunyoro at this time is given in *Ten Years in Equatoria*, pp. 241-314.

[4] Casati attempted to establish the Egyptian flag and this probably reminded Kabarega of Baker's hostile actions fifteen years previously when he had claimed to have annexed Bunyoro to Egypt. Casati also seems to have aroused suspicion by his dealings with Buganda. In addition to Casati's own account (cited above), see Vita Hassan, *Die Wahrheit über Emin Pasha*, ii. 129; Emin's *Tagebücher*, 19 Jan. 1888, iv. 10; and the note by Sir John Gray in Extracts IX, pp. 82-3.

[5] The relations between Emin and Kabarega over the districts under Rionga and Kamisoa (Rionga's son and successor) and Anfina is a considerable story in itself. Essentially, Emin consistently supported these rulers against Kabarega, who was determined to expropriate them. There is an important account of the matter in a letter from Emin to Felkin, 25 Oct. 1888 in M.P. See also *E.P. in C.A.*, pp. 166-70. There is a relevant article by Sir John Gray, 'Rwot Ochama of Payera', *Uganda Journal*, xii, no. 2 (1948). The section in F. K. Girling, The *Acholi of Uganda*, H.M.S.O., 1960, is rather poor.

between Emin and Buganda against himself. Harassed by another attack on Bunyoro by Buganda, and steadily losing control over his own soldiers, Kabarega heard the first rumour of the approach of Stanley's expedition on 3 January 1888 through a messenger who arrived in Bunyoro from the south-west corner of Lake Albert.[1] Within a week Casati was evicted from Bunyoro amid circumstances in which he was lucky to escape with his life.[2] At about the same time Muhammad Biri was murdered.[3]

The period 1886-8 was also a time when Emin's diary records the steady disintegration of his administration and authority within Equatoria. By 1887 the province which Emin so invitingly offered to the British, and which Felkin wrote up as a potential El Dorado, was reduced to a riverain strip stretching for about 180 miles along the Nile northwards from Lake Albert. The outlying stations established to the north and west in 1879-81 had long since fallen away from Emin's authority; most of them had been abandoned altogether. Emin's move to the south in 1885 had been followed by the disintegration of his authority in the northern riverain stations, and by 1887 Lado was abandoned and the most northerly station in existence was at Rejaf. This was the headquarters of the first of Emin's two remaining battalions of troops. When Emin withdrew to Wadelai and surrounded himself with the soldiers of the 2nd battalion (based at Dufile), the 1st battalion felt abandoned and betrayed.[4] After 1886 Emin received very little news of events in any of the stations north of Dufile. There were internal plots and dissensions led chiefly, it would seem, by the Egyptian officers, and when Emin set out to visit the stations beyond Dufile in December 1887 he was forced to turn back at Kirri in the face of warnings of a threat to his life by the soldiers at Bedden and Rejaf.[5] Selim Bey, who was consistently loyal to Emin and who was to occupy an important role in the future,

[1] Casati, op. cit., p. 294.   [2] Ibid. 294-314.
[3] The precise circumstances of Muhammad Biri's death are not known. On 24 Feb. 1888, Emin was informed that he had been killed. (*Tagebücher*, 24 Feb. 1888, iv. 47; also H. B. Thomas, 'Muhammad Biri', *Uganda Journal*, xxiv, no. 1 (1960).) Kabarega may not have been directly responsible for his death. Mackay, on hearing of it, reported that the Arabs at Kabarega's court 'were intriguing against Md. Biri, as they were very jealous of his getting ivory from Wadelai while they had no permission to go there'. Mackay to Euan-Smith, 9 Aug. 1888, F.O. 84/1909.
[4] Statement of 'Uthmān Latīf, 9 July 1890, Khartoum Archives, Cairint 3/14/237.
[5] *Tagebücher*, 9-20 Dec. 1887, iii. 435-43 (Extracts VIII, pp. 214-15).

was kept 'a prisoner in his own house' at Rejaf by the rebel soldiers of the 1st battalion and it was only with some difficulty that he succeeded in escaping to join Emin in the south.[1] At the same time, Emin came to suspect that Hawash Effendi, the commander of the 2nd battalion at Dufile—whom he had consistently supported in the face of universal dislike—was secretly in collusion with the rebels at Rejaf.[2] Emin observed that 'the disagreement between the Sudanese and Egyptians becomes more marked every day, and hatred of the latter is openly expressed . . . This is certainly not undeserved, for the Egyptian gentlemen have always treated the Sudanese *en canaille*, in spite of all my warnings, but now the tables are turned.'[3] Most of Emin's soldiers refused to believe that Egypt had abandoned the Sudan and were strongly opposed to any suggestion of a withdrawal from Equatoria. Many of the Egyptians, however, were prepared to go, and Emin was only too ready to get rid of them; but they refused to contemplate any route to the south and persisted in planning an overland march north to Khartoum. Mackay wrote to Holmwood that most of these Egyptian officials were 'really Egyptian convicts, little inclined to obey any orders except their own will. Emin is, I fear, about as much in their hands as they in his'.[4]

All this is scarcely alluded to in Emin's own letters to Europe at this time. There is indeed a gulf between the daily realities which Emin records so dispassionately in his diary and the situation in the province as portrayed in his letters to Schweinfurth or Felkin. It would appear that this corresponds to the difference between things as they were and as Emin would have liked them to be. For the mass of illusions which people in Europe, including Stanley himself, had about Emin's position in Equatoria, and about the future possibilities for the province, Emin himself was considerably responsible. Probably this was not a deliberate deception on Emin's part. Rather, Emin simply closed his mind to those aspects of the situation which he found humiliating and painful and beyond his control.[5] One of the curious things about Equatoria is the way in which many of those who had personal experience of working amidst the hopeless

[1] Ibid.
[2] Ibid., 9 Dec. 1887, iii. 435.
[3] Emin to Schweinfurth, 15 May 1886, *E.P. in C.A.* 502.
[4] Mackay to Holmwood, 19 Apr. 1887, F.O.C.P. 5617, p. 55.
[5] 'To confess his own powerlessness, and censure his own errors, was repugnant to his proud mind', wrote Casati. Casati, *Ten Years in Equatoria*, p. 338.

conditions of the province managed to preserve their illusions about the area and went on to propagate them among other people. Baker, Gordon, Felkin, and Emin Pasha were all alike in this respect.

Between 1886 and 1888, Emin's chief concern was with events in the south. This was the part of the province which had always held his primary interest, and it was towards its future as a part of East Africa, separated from the 'Arab' Sudan, that Emin had now turned his attention. Communications with the stations north of Dufile were, in any case, greatly hindered by the cataracts in the Nile. But south of Dufile the river was navigable all the way to Lake Albert and the steamers *Nyanza* and *Khedive* plied to and fro between Wadelai and the other riverain stations, transporting wood and grain and messages. Occasionally, a steamer was sent under the direction of Vita Hassan to Kibiro on the eastern shore of Lake Albert to deliver and collect the mail for Europe which was expedited in Bunyoro by Casati. While in the rest of the Equatorial province since 1881 stations had been abandoned, in the south there had been a steady expansion. In 1887 Emin re-established the station of Mahagi in the north-western corner of Lake Albert and established two more stations (also on the western shore of the lake) further south at Tunguru and Mswa. These stations were founded with several purposes in mind. They would act as bases from which to keep in touch with Kibiro—the 'post-office' of the province on the eastern shore of Lake Albert (which was entirely under Kabarega). Secondly, Emin expected to hear through them more quickly of Stanley's expedition when it arrived. Emin also founded these stations in case of the more remote contingency of a further retreat to the south. Throughout this period there was at the back of Emin's mind the fear that the withdrawal of the Mahdist attack on the province since 1886 was only a temporary respite and that

one of these fine days the Danagla [Mahdists] will suddenly come down upon us in steamers . . . it is certain that they will not leave us in peace, and equally certain that they will occupy these districts again as soon as possible. They have men and weapons enough now, and the resistance of the Negroes will soon be broken down if a thousand or two of such scoundrels appear well armed.[1]

If a new Mahdist advance did take place, and Emin was unable to resist it, he planned 'to push forward . . . from the southern

---

[1] Emin to Schweinfurth, 3 Mar. 1886, *E.P. in C.A.* 499.

extremity of the Albert Nyanza direct to the northern point of [Lake] Tanganyika, to the English missionary station there'.[1] This idea had led Emin, through Mackay, to attempt to establish contact by letter with the African Lakes Company, a trading concern established on Lake Tanganyika by the Moir brothers.[2] Emin, however, never thought in more than the vaguest terms about this idea. The country between Lake Albert and Lake Tanganyika was completely unknown at this time and Emin undoubtedly underestimated both the distances and the difficulties which would have been involved.

At Wadelai itself Emin's life was quieter and less disturbed than it had ever been at Lado. The small garrison was loyal, the local Alur and Acholi were not hostile—or not particularly so—and communications had been established with Buganda, Bunyoro, and with Europe. The area was also far richer in interest for a naturalist than the district surrounding Lado. Emin experimented with various crops, grew orange trees from pips, employed his people in weaving cotton cloth and overhauling the two steamers. After a fire had seriously damaged the station in February 1887 (with the loss of much ivory, as had also happened at Lado), Emin rebuilt Wadelai 'on a neater plan' and in April he reported that 'we are living in peace and quiet, cultivating our gardens and fields, existing or rather vegetating'.[3] In March 1887 Emin suffered what was un-doubtedly a very grievous loss in the death of his Abyssinian wife. Writing to Mackay of his bereavement, he requested him to send a Bible.[4] Emin became inseparable from his little daughter, Ferida, and took refuge increasingly in his botanical and zoological collecting.

Periodically during 1887 Emin visited Lake Albert in one of the steamers. Partly these voyages were in connection with the dispatch and receipt of mail at Kibiro. Partly they were to find out if there was any news of the arrival of Stanley's expedition. It was while on a

---

[1] Emin to Junker, 20 Jan. 1887, printed in Schweitzer, i. 208-9.
[2] Mackay to Emin, 15 Nov. 1886, printed in the *Tagebücher*, 17 Jan. 1887, iii. 308. Emin to Mackay, 7 Feb. 1887, F.O.C.P. 5617, p. 57. In Dec. 1886, the Committee of the African Lakes Company in Glasgow, hearing of Emin's position, offered to organize an expedition to open a route between Lake Tanganyika and Lake Albert by which Emin could be reached regularly. Their scheme was abandoned in the face of Stanley's expedition. See Secretary of the African Lakes Co. to H. M. Stanley, enclosed in African Lakes Co. to F.O., 30 Dec. 1886, F.O.C.P. 5617, pp. 1-2. The best account of the African Lakes Company is that of F. L. M. Moir, *After Livingstone* (London, 1923).
[3] Emin to Junker, 15 Apr. 1887, printed in Schweitzer, i. 218.
[4] Emin to Mackay, 15 Apr. 1887, F.O.C.P. 5617, p. 66.

visit to the lake in July 1887 that Emin established Mswa as the most southerly station in the province. Mswa was five hours by steamer south of Tunguru and some nine hours steam from the southern end of the lake. Although Mackay had warned Emin to expect Stanley's expedition in July, there was no sign of its arrival in the vicinity of the lake. After July 1887 the outbreak of war between Buganda and Bunyoro halted all communications with Equatoria, and Emin was therefore without any information of the expedition's progress after January 1887. Emin returned to Lake Albert in November and again in January 1888. It was while he was at Tunguru on 15 January that Emin heard of the misfortunes which had overtaken Casati in Bunyoro. The following day Emin crossed the lake in the *Khedive* and rescued Casati near Kibiro.

Casati was able to report that a considerable mail for Emin (including, almost certainly, the letter which Stanley had written at Zanzibar) and many letters for Stanley and other members of the expedition had been lost during the recent disturbances in Bunyoro. Casati was also able to pass on to Emin the rumour that Stanley's expedition had arrived at the southern end of the lake.[1] Further rumours about a band of soldiers led by Europeans having arrived at the south-western corner of Lake Albert arrived during the following days. This party had repeatedly asked about the whereabouts of Emin Pasha and had made many raids on the cattle of the local inhabitants who were 'much afraid'. Emin was at first puzzled and thought that the party must have come from Kabarega or Tippu Tip 'as Stanley certainly does not make raids'.[2] Emin decided to go to the south of the lake and investigate, but he was delayed by repairs to the steamers and it was only on 28 February that he arrived at the south-western corner of Lake Albert. Here he received the first definite news of Stanley's arrival at the lake the previous December. A local leader told Emin that 'three Europeans with many people and much baggage' had arrived at the lake a few months previously. They had asked about Emin Pasha but had soon departed and reascended the plateau. Emin's informant concluded by saying 'all this story happened over five months ago and nobody knows where the strangers are, nor whether they are still there'.[3]

Emin was now in a quandary. He was quite unable to proceed in

[1] *Tagebücher*, 16 Jan. 1888, iv. 8–9 (Extracts IX, p. 77).
[2] Ibid., 14 Feb. 1888; 24 Feb. 1888, iv. 37, 47–8 (Extracts IX, pp. 80–1).
[3] *Tagebücher*, 28 Feb. 1888, iv. 60–1 (Extracts IX, p. 81).

search of Stanley's party as he had with him very few men and no equipment. He was also urgently needed in the stations at the northern end of the lake where conditions were unsettled as a result of the activities of Kabarega among the Alur and Acholi. Emin therefore decided to leave a letter for Stanley at Kavalli's, in case the expedition returned to the lake, and to return north to Mswa and Tunguru—where Casati had been left very ill with pneumonia. On 29 February Emin steamed away 'richer in experience; poorer in hopes', he records in his diary, 'so ends my first search for Stanley'.[1]

Two months later, on 23 April, while Emin was at Tunguru, he heard the news that Stanley's expedition had once more arrived at the south end of the lake.[2] The following day Emin received a note from Jephson, who had arrived at Mswa. Emin at once replied in terms of the warmest welcome. 'Nobody has slept, and today is full of rejoicing', he noted in his diary.[3] Emin was delayed by the absence of the steamer on a trip to Wadelai, but on 27 April it returned and that evening Emin met Jephson at Mswa.

*   *   *

Jephson found Emin in appearance 'a smaller man than his picture would lead one to suppose; he is very foreign-looking, speaks English very well but with a strong foreign accent'.[4] With great tact, Emin at once provided Jephson and his men with new clothes and several other things of which they were obviously in need. Jephson was overwhelmed by Emin's kindness and observed: 'One's heart really goes out towards such a man for one feels he is really sincere. It is such a pleasure to get someone quite new to talk with and that person such a clever and intelligent man.'[5] Emin, for his part, was polite and self-effacing; he was also, at this stage, deeply impressed by what he took to be the disinterested motives of those who had organized the expedition. 'How can you thank me for the few things I have given you and be shy about taking them', he said to Jephson, 'if I lived for a hundred years I could not thank the English people enough for their disinterested kindness in sending me help when I have been abandoned by my own government for so many years.'[5]

---

[1] Ibid., 1 Mar. 1888, iv. 66 (Extracts IX, p. 82).
[2] Ibid., 23 Apr. 1888, iv. 97 (Extracts IX, p. 202).
[3] *Tagebücher*, 24 Apr. 1888, iv. 97 (Extracts X, p. 202).
[4] Jephson, *Diary*, p. 249.
[5] Ibid. 250.

After spending a day at Mswa, Emin and Jephson, together with Casati, Vita Hassan, and a great stock of grain and livestock (which Emin had assembled to take to Stanley) set out in the *Khedive* for Stanley's camp at the southern end of Lake Albert. They arrived at dusk on Sunday, 29 April. After leaving the steamer at anchor, Emin rowed ashore with Jephson, Casati, and Vita Hassan in the *Advance*. Stanley's party was assembled to meet them on the shore— the Zanzibaris were so excited that they were 'firing off their guns and shouting in the maddest manner'.[1] Emin was conducted the few hundred yards to the camp where Stanley himself awaited him. 'It was', wrote Emin, 'a moment I shall never forget.'[2]

Emin's appearance came as a great shock to Stanley. Here was no harassed Governor, desperate for relief, but

a small spare figure in a well-kept fez and a clean suit of snowy cotton drilling, well-ironed and of perfect fit. A dark grizzled beard bordered a face of a Magyar cast, though a pair of spectacles lent it somewhat an Italian or Spanish appearance. There was not a trace on it of ill-health or anxiety; it rather indicated good condition of body and peace of mind.[3]

To celebrate the occasion Stanley opened three bottles of champagne —which he had brought all the way across the Congo—and the European officers and Emin Pasha sat talking far into the night.[4] 'We all hope that Emin Pasha will make up his mind to come out with us', wrote Parke in his diary at the end of the evening; but, he concluded, 'our duty will be finished when we have handed over the ammunition, which was what he required to protect himself.'[5]

*   *   *

The day after their meeting, Emin and Stanley moved a short distance along the lake to a better camp-site at Nsabe. The sight of Emin in full uniform of blue tunic with epaulettes and brass buttons, blue trousers with a red stripe and sword, and of his neatly dressed soldiers drawn up for parade, caused Stanley to reflect ruefully 'our Zanzibaris, by the side of these upright figures, seemed alto-

---

[1] Jephson, *Diary*, p. 251.
[2] *Tagebücher*, 29 Apr. 1888, iv. 98 (Extracts X, p. 203).
[3] *IDA* i. 374.
[4] Five bottles of champagne had been given to Stanley by one of the Europeans at Stanley Pool (*IDA* i. 375). Two had been opened to celebrate the first sight of Lake Albert (Jephson, *Diary*, p. 211). The three remaining bottles were now opened to celebrate the meeting with Emin Pasha. This, as Parke remarks, was a gesture typical of Stanley (Parke, *Diary*, pp. 223-4).
[5] Parke, *Diary*, p. 224.

4. The Meeting between Stanley and Emin Pasha

gether a beggarly troop, and more naked than ever'.[1] Emin at once did his best to supply food and clothing, tobacco, salt, and many other articles for the expedition sent from Europe for his relief. Thus were the rescuers rescued. Emin also sent the steamer to Dufile to recruit 130 Madi carriers for Stanley's depleted force.[2]

Stanley and Emin remained in each other's company at Nsabe for almost a month. During this time their discussions centred on Emin's plans and Stanley's proposals for the future. At first their discussions revolved around the instructions which Stanley had brought to Emin from the Egyptian Government. There was nothing of essential importance in the letters which Stanley had brought from the Khedive and Nubar Pasha which Emin did not know already.[3] And Emin did not consider that these letters contained clear instructions. Rather, they left him a choice between at least two alternatives. Either he returned with Stanley's expedition to Egypt (and continued in the employment of the Egyptian Government) or he remained as a free agent in Equatoria.[4] The evidence is conclusive that Stanley and the other European officers arrived in Equatoria hoping, indeed expecting, that Emin Pasha would withdraw from Equatoria and return with the expedition to the coast.[5] Partly, this was a reflection of their own misguided belief that Emin was in desperate straits. Partly, it would seem, the evacuation of Emin came to occupy in their minds the *raison d'être* for the expedition—the tangible symbol that the appalling march through the Congo had not been in vain. Stanley hoped that after a stay of about two weeks with Emin in Equatoria he would be able to return through the Congo forest and bring on the Rear Column to Lake Albert, together with the rest of the expedition's men and equipment. Meanwhile, Emin and those who wished to accompany him would have had time to prepare themselves to withdraw from the province. When Stanley rejoined them at Lake Albert with his reunited expedition, he anticipated that 'we could resume our march within a few days for Zanzibar'.[6] As so often during this expedition, however,

---

[1] *IDA* i. 375.   [2] Jephson, *Diary*, p. 251.

[3] The letters of Nubar Pasha, 27 May 1885, and Holmwood, 1 Dec. 1886, had already been received. See p. 30 and p. 144 above.

[4] *IDA* i. 377. The instructions are printed in Schweitzer, i. 277–9.

[5] *IDA* i. 377–81. Jephson, *Diary*, p. 254. Parke, *Diary*, pp. 224–5. Emin himself remarked: 'so far as I can see at present, all the gentlemen of the expedition are particularly bent upon getting me to withdraw to Egypt or to England'. *Tagebücher*, 2 May 1888, iv. 102 (Extracts X, p. 205.)

[6] *IDA* i. 377.

Stanley's plans were not to run so smoothly. 'Contrary to our expectations', Stanley later stated, 'we did not find the Pasha disposed to return to the sea, neither was Captain Casati; nor did any one impress us with his eagerness to return to civilisation. They all seemed content to remain.'[1]

By a curious repetition in Stanley's history, just as Livingstone had had no desire to be 'found', so Emin had no desire to be 'rescued'. What Emin wanted was what he had consistently asked for; ammunition and supplies to enable him to remain where he was, and a reliable route of communications with the outside world. It had been the objective of the expedition—as it was conceived by most people in England—to provide these. What had resulted was quite different. A collection of famine-stricken, tattered, and exhausted men had arrived at Lake Albert with only thirty-one cases of ammunition, two loads of half-spoiled clothes, and a bundle of letters for Emin Pasha which included the latest instructions from the Khedive. No route had been opened up to the east coast, and the experiences of Stanley's expedition finally brought to an end Emin's long-cherished hope that a route might readily be developed from Equatoria via the Mangbetu country with the Congo.

Stanley's mission came as a profound shock to Emin. In place of the British support which Mackay had so confidently led him to expect, Emin was confronted by an expedition which was in no position to bring him much 'relief', and whose leaders were determined to bring about his withdrawal. Emin had had some forewarning of Stanley's intention from Jephson. At Mswa Jephson had handed Emin a letter from Stanley in which the anticipation of Emin's withdrawal from Equatoria is revealed clearly enough.[2] After reading it, Emin noted in his diary, 'I have not many hopes, but my resolution is fixed. Go, I will not.'[3] When Stanley now put forward to Emin, repeatedly and very forcefully, the reasons why Equatoria should be abandoned, Emin refused to commit himself—though he acknowledged that the Egyptian Government was 'very anxious for me to leave here'.[4] Had he been so inclined, Emin could have withdrawn from Equatoria at almost any time and made his way to the East African coast accompanied by those who wanted to

---

[1] Report of Stanley to Euan-Smith, 19 Dec. 1889, *Africa No. 4* (1890), C. 5906.
[2] Stanley to Emin, 18 Apr. 1888, printed in *IDA* i. 369–70.
[3] *Tagebücher*, 27 Apr. 1888, iv. 98 (Extracts X, p. 203).
[4] Ibid., 28 Apr. 1888.

follow him—as Mackay had pointed out, and Junker had proved, before Stanley's expedition was ever started. But, like Gordon at Khartoum, Emin in Equatoria was determined to stay. His Egyptian officers and officials—numbering fewer than sixty—might be prepared to withdraw with Stanley's expedition, and Emin declared himself delighted that they should do so,[1] but the majority of his regular and irregular soldiers were southern Sudanese; they were not prepared to leave Equatoria, especially by a route to the south and east, and Emin himself—having 'no desire whatever to return to Egypt' or to Europe—was reluctant to abandon them to a situation which he thought would soon dissolve into anarchy and disorder.[1] Under these circumstances one can imagine Emin's impatience with the details, which Stanley now put before him, about whether and on what conditions he and his soldiers would receive their pay from the Egyptian Government. No one in Equatoria had received any pay for eight years (and only intermittently before that) and most had long since given up expecting any. Stanley had nothing new to tell Emin about the attitude of the Egyptian Government to Equatoria. What interested Emin was the attitude of influential people in England and of King Leopold of the Belgians.

It would appear that it was only after Emin had repeatedly confronted Stanley with the assurance that neither he nor the majority of his soldiers would withdraw from Equatoria and accompany Stanley's expedition back to Egypt that Stanley declared himself prepared, in the circumstances, 'to fulfil my promise to various parties' and put before Emin the propositions of King Leopold and Mackinnon 'although they appear somewhat conflicting'.[2] Stanley also asked Emin to keep them secret.[3]

King Leopold's proposition, whereby Emin was to remain in Equatoria as Governor of the province under the Congo State, was put forward according to the terms which had been agreed orally between Leopold and Stanley in Brussels.[4] Stanley produced a map of the Congo and a copy of the Delimitation Treaty with France

---

[1] Ibid., 4 May 1888, iv. 104–5 (Extracts X, pp. 205–6). *IDA* i. 386.
[2] *IDA* i. 386.
[3] *Tagebücher*, 4 May 1888, iv. 105 (Extracts X, p. 206).
[4] *IDA* i. 387. *Tagebücher*, 4 May 1888, iv. 105 (Extracts X, p. 206). Also, Euan-Smith to Salisbury, 14 Mar. 1890, reporting a long interview with Emin Pasha, F.O. 84/2060. That Leopold's instructions to Stanley were never written down is confirmed by a letter from the Comte de Borchgrave to Stanley, 26 Feb. 1887, Palace Archives, Brussels, Dossier 102, no. 17.

about the boundaries of the Congo State. He also showed Emin the sheet on which, immediately after his interview with Leopold in Brussels, he had noted the King's proposals. Emin observed 'it is evident from this that the King is most anxious to secure the Nile route'.[1] The possibility of annexing Equatoria to the Congo State was scarcely considered by Stanley as a serious proposition any longer. It had taken him nine months to struggle through the Congo to Lake Albert under conditions and over a distance which everyone, including the King himself, had greatly underestimated. It had cost also a great many lives. Stanley could not imagine that Leopold would have either the desire or the resources to make such expeditions a regular feature of his barely established Congo administration in order to sustain Emin Pasha in Equatoria and obtain a frontier on the Nile.[2] Emin later stated that after communicating King Leopold's offer to him, Stanley advised him 'instantly to refuse it'.[3] In any case, Emin, partly as a result of Felkin's influence, was extremely sceptical about the long-term future of King Leopold's Congo venture and at once refused the proposal.[4] Casati felt that the fate of Stanley's expedition in taking the Congo route to Equatoria 'was so eloquent as to render any reply needless'.[5]

Stanley's experiences in the Congo and the news, when he finally reached Equatoria, that the route via Bunyoro and Buganda to the East African coast was once again blocked, had in any case profoundly altered his view of the position of Emin and the future possibilities for Equatoria. The Egyptian Government was determined to abandon the province, the British Government 'would have nothing to do with it', and Stanley himself had come to the conclusion that, as far as any approach to Equatoria from the east coast was concerned, Emin's province was 'just 500 miles too far inland to be of any value, unless Uganda and Unyoro have been first brought under the law'.[6] With this important conclusion, later

---

[1] *Tagebücher*, 4 May 1888, iv. 105 (Extracts X, p. 206).

[2] *IDA* i. 391–2.

[3] This statement occurs in a letter by Emin published in the *Berliner Tageblatt*, 2 Dec. 1891. An edited version of this letter is published in French in the geographical journal *L'Afrique explorée et civilisée*, xiii. 9 (Geneva, 1892). (I owe this reference to Professor J. Stengers.)

[4] Euan-Smith to Salisbury, 14 Mar. 1890, F.O. 84/2060. Also F. Hird, *H. M. Stanley: the Authorised Life*, p. 247. In the *Tagebücher* Emin omits any discussion of Leopold's offer and merely states that it was made.

[5] Casati, *Ten Years in Equatoria*, p. 340.

[6] *IDA* i. 393.

employees of Mackinnon's I.B.E.A. Company, such as Jackson and Lugard, were reluctantly to agree.[1] Stanley was also convinced that after the experiences and expense of his own expedition to bring relief to Emin Pasha, 'no body of philanthropists would repeat these expensive outlays on behalf of a province so remote from the sea'.[2] Communications were the crux on which the plans of Stanley and Emin alike were now to turn with regard to the future.

The problem presented by the poor communications between Equatoria and the outside world had beset the province from its origins. Baker had written about it. Gordon had attempted to solve it by initiating the idea of an approach from the East African coast, but his calculations of the distances involved had been wildly wrong. Emin had followed Gordon in attempting to develop a reliable route through Bunyoro and Buganda. Until Stanley arrived on the scene and forced the issue, however, Emin had clung to the idea of retaining his headquarters at Wadelai. It is true that at various times since 1885 Emin had contemplated a retreat beyond the confines of the province: south to Lake Tanganyika, south-west through the Mangbetu country to the Uele and Nepoko rivers and so to the Congo, south-east to some undefined place on the edges of Buganda and Bunyoro. But these ideas had remained vague and undefined, retained against the event of a new Mahdist advance which had failed to take place. Now, under the influence of Stanley, Emin himself decided that he must abandon Wadelai and move to a new headquarters beyond the confines of the province.

On 1 May 1888 Emin had a conversation with Stanley in which he once again refused to commit himself to a withdrawal from Equatoria. 'I do not want to come to any conclusion until I have heard what my people have to say', Emin declared.[3] From his past experience, Emin knew only too well that 'his people' would refuse to withdraw. It would seem that consciously or unconsciously, Emin hoped to use this fact to persuade himself, and to persuade Stanley, that he would therefore have to remain as well.[4] But he would not

---

[1] See esp. M. Perham, ed., *The Diaries of Lord Lugard* (London, 1959), ii. 324-8.

[2] Report of Stanley to Euan-Smith, 19 Dec. 1889, *Africa No. 4* (1890), C. 5906, p. 8.　　　　　　[3] *Tagebücher*, 1 May 1888, iv. 101 (Extracts X, p. 204).

[4] Jephson has a different interpretation. He asserts that Emin first wanted to put the proposal of a withdrawal to his soldiers, so that 'in the event of the people refusing to leave and he comes out with us, it can never be said of him that he deserted his people', Jephson, *Diary*, p. 253.

remain in Equatoria. Recording this conversation with Stanley in his diary, Emin states that he told Stanley he would remain with his soldiers

provided that they follow me to some place whence communications with the world are practicable, which is not the case here, for, as soon as Stanley's expedition has retired, every connection with the outer world naturally ceases. In the course of conversation, Stanley asked what would I say if somebody found me a sufficient salary, and gave me enough yearly to pay and provide for my troops—would that be an inducement to stay? I said no; in the present state of affairs, victualling is impossible here, and to accept a subsidy of the kind under the circumstances would amount to robbing those who paid it.

Stanley rejoined by pointing out the possibility of occupying the north-eastern corner of the Victoria Nyanza, from which communications could be established immediately, and where the country was healthy; he thought a project of this nature would at once find support in England. The project appeared so extraordinarily practical and easy of execution that I entered into it heart and soul, and I was very pleased to see Stanley, who as a rule is fairly reticent, take a great interest in it too.[1]

Stanley's proposition was that Emin and a small band of his finest and most loyal soldiers should accompany the expedition as far as the Kavirondo region of Lake Victoria. There they would be established 'in the name of the East African Association'—as Mackinnon's I.B.E.A. Company was known at this time. Stanley's party would assist in the construction of a fort, the steel boat would be left with Emin's party, and Stanley would then proceed across the Masai land to the East African coast and then to England. There, Stanley would 'lay the matter before the East African Association, and obtain its sanction for the act'; he would also endeavour to obtain the assistance of Mackinnon's organization to maintain Emin permanently in the East African interior. 'I must explain to you that I have no authority to make this last proposition', Stanley told Emin, 'but I feel assured that I can obtain its hearty approval and cooperation, and that the Association will readily appreciate the value of a trained battalion or two in their new acquisition, and the services of such an administrator as yourself.'[2]

---

[1] *Tagebücher*, 1 May 1888, iv. 101 (Extracts X, p. 204).

[2] *IDA* i. 387–8. After Stanley had communicated this proposal and that of King Leopold, Emin states: 'I must incidentally do Stanley justice [by saying] that he in no way tried to win me over to either project, but left it to my free will' (*Tagebücher*, 6 May 1888, iv. 107, Extracts X, p. 207). This does not square with

EQUATORIA 1886-1888   161

Some months later, Stanley wrote a long letter to Mackinnon
telling him about the disastrous march through the Congo and of
Emin's refusal to commit himself to a withdrawal with the expedition.
'I have tried everything', wrote Stanley, but Emin was 'charmed with
his African life' and wanted to stay. Stanley continued:

Availing myself of this discovery, I suggested to him that he should settle
on the Victoria Nyanza somewhere nearer to the coast, in Kavirondo for
instance, and wait my communication with you. He jumped at this so
eagerly that . . . I have promised him I would take him there or elsewhere.

Stanley went on to explain to Mackinnon that in suggesting this plan
to Emin he had had in mind the possible usefulness of Emin and his
soldiers

as a colony of men amenable to law and discipline, by which your territory
could be governed and civilised, by which you would find a man and men
ready to your hand—a chain of stations kept by brave men from the Victoria Lake to Kilimanjaro. Examine this idea. Let Sir John Kirk know it.
Hear his views. The whole is quite plain what to do—to me.[1]

When Mackinnon replied to this letter from Stanley he said:

I feel that it would be out of place for me to advise you with regard to
the best mode of carrying out your own ideas in regard to Emin and the
arrangements connected with him. I have the fullest and most complete
confidence that whatever you do will be wisely done. I entirely approve of
everything you have done and all that seems to be in your mind to do with
regard to Emin and the territories between Mombasa and the centre of the
continent . . . you may rely on my complete support whatever your decisions
and arrangements with Emin may be.[2]

All this suggests that although the general idea of the possible
future employment of Emin and his soldiers in the East African
interior had been discussed by Mackinnon and Stanley before the
expedition set out, the precise proposal to establish Emin and his
garrison at the north-east corner of Lake Victoria was first clearly
formulated by Stanley after his meeting with Emin Pasha. Although

his later statement that Stanley at once advised him to reject Leopold's offer
(see p. 158 above). The rest of the evidence does not support the more generous
interpretation.
[1] Stanley to Mackinnon, 3 Sept. 1888, M.P., F. 1. (A copy of this important
letter is also in the Palace Archives, Brussels, enclosed in Mackinnon to King
Leopold, 20 Apr. 1889, Dossier 82, no. 78.)
[2] Mackinnon to Stanley, 5 Apr. 1889, M.P., F. 1. (Copy).
8216793   M

Mackinnon's reply to Stanley's letter did not reach Stanley until December 1889, Stanley was quite confident that Mackinnon would support his proposal. Emin understood that the mandate which Stanley had been given by Mackinnon in England authorized him

to settle him (Emin) and his followers at some place upon the eastern shores of the Victoria Nyanza where he should work and use all his influence in the interests of the Imperial British East Africa Company. Mr. Stanley, however, distinctly stated that he was not authorised to make any offer as to his pay or emoluments, or as to the administrative staff which the Pasha would be allowed to keep under his command.[1]

The idea of settling Emin with a garrison at the north-east corner of Lake Victoria would seem to have originated with Sir John Kirk,[2] and it was with Emin's letter to Kirk of July 1886 in mind—the letter in which Emin first offered Equatoria to England—that Stanley made the proposal. Emin would seem to have responded so enthusiastically to the proposal because it accorded so closely with his own previous plan for a possible retreat to some place on the edge of Buganda and Bunyoro.[3] To occupy a base in the Kavirondo region under Mackinnon's I.B.E.A. Company would not only give Emin direct access to the caravan route to the coast, it would also place him in an excellent position to undertake the re-establishment of Equatoria to its full extent under Britain when this became possible.

Ten days after Stanley and Emin had first met, their plan for the future had been settled. Emin had decided that whatever happened he would have to move his headquarters from Wadelai. While Stanley returned through the Congo in search of his Rear Column, Emin would travel about the remaining stations of his province in order to discover the wishes of his soldiers. If he found that the majority were prepared to go to Egypt, Emin himself was prepared to lead them there.[4] In fact Emin very much doubted if this would be the case. A small minority, including most of the Egyptians, might be prepared to leave with Stanley's expedition, but the majority of Emin's soldiers, like Emin himself, would remain. But, Emin noted, 'that I should remain here [i.e. in Equatoria] I could hardly promise, as I should have to find some spot admitting of our com-

---

[1] Euan-Smith to Salisbury, 14 Mar. 1890, F.O. 84/2060.
[2] *Tagebücher*, 7 May 1888, iv. 108 (Extracts X, p. 207). 'Stanley told me Dr. Kirk was the first to make this proposal.'
[3] Jephson, MS. Diary, 11 July 1888.
[4] *Tagebücher*, 4 May 1888, iv. 105 (Extracts X, p. 206).

municating with the world'.[1] By the end of May 1888, Emin later stated,

he had definitely decided to withdraw his men from the Equatorial Province, in accordance with the orders of His Highness the Khedive, and that having done this, he would then accept the second of the proposals put before him by Mr. Stanley, and would ask that gentleman to instal him, with as many of his men as would be willing to accompany him, at some place near Kavirondo, on the east shore of Victoria Nyanza, where he would regard himself as the representative, and work in the interests, of the Imperial British East Africa Company, the remainder of the Egyptian employés being sent down to the east coast with Mr. Stanley.[2]

It is clear that from the moment when Stanley first suggested it, Emin became set on the scheme to form a settlement at the northeast corner of Lake Victoria. What is equally certain—much as Stanley later tried to obscure the fact—is that at this time Stanley was equally enthusiastic. Jephson found that Stanley was 'heart and soul in the Kavirondo scheme and would much sooner the Pasha and his people adopted it instead of going to Egypt'.[3] In conversations over several days Stanley had talked to Jephson in terms of such a settlement becoming an important part of Mackinnon's future plans for East Africa.[4] These amounted to what Emin described as 'a characteristic project of English merchants and politicians'. There were plans for a railway to be constructed from the East African coast to Lake Victoria and for steamers to be launched on the lake.[5] 'A group of English merchants is simply awaiting your arrival to form a Company like the former East India Company', Stanley told Emin, '£400,000 have already been subscribed. They ask you to have confidence: all the rest will be seen to forthwith. A first caravan of supplies for you would immediately leave the coast.'[6]

One important fact about this whole scheme appears to have been curiously overlooked, or underrated, by both Stanley and Emin.

---

[1] Ibid.   [2] Euan-Smith to Salisbury, 14 Mar. 1890, F.O. 84/2060.
[3] Jephson, MS. Diary, 11 July 1888.
[4] Tagebücher, 3 May 1888, iv. 103 (Extracts X, p. 205).
[5] Ibid. See also the letter, describing these proposals, written by Emin to the German Consul at Zanzibar from Bagamoyo, 31 Mar. 1890 (in German). The original of this letter was found in the papers of the former German Consulate in Zanzibar. It was translated into English and published by Sir John Gray, 'Another Letter of Emin Pasha', Uganda Journal, xiv, no. 2 (1950), 219.
[6] Tagebücher, 4 May 1888, iv. 105 (Extracts X, p. 206).

This is that the employment which Stanley, on behalf of Mackinnon, offered to Emin and his soldiers under the I.B.E.A. Company was never considered in terms of the position of Governor and garrison *in* Equatoria. Emin and his soldiers were to withdraw from Equatoria altogether and establish themselves in the area of Busoga, between Mt. Elgon (called Mt. Masaba by Emin) and the Kavirondo gulf of Lake Victoria—an area little known in 1888. Emin undoubtedly considered such a withdrawal as a temporary move, as also, perhaps, did Stanley and Mackinnon.[1] But Emin appears seriously to have miscalculated in believing that even a small body of his soldiers, who had consistently opposed all attempts to get them to withdraw to the south or to Egypt, would follow him to Lake Victoria.[2] Between 1884 and 1888 Emin had tried several times to get his men to withdraw to the south. When his attempts had met with failure, he had resigned himself to the situation and thereby survived with a semblance of his authority. A Gordon or a Stanley would never have lasted so long. Now, inspired by Stanley, Emin was to try again; the result was to be disaster.

Whatever effect the arrival of Stanley's expedition had had on Emin Pasha, it had certainly had a negative effect on the situation in Equatoria, and on Emin's fragile authority. Throughout 1887 Emin had attempted to keep secret the news of the expedition's impending arrival in order not to create false hopes;[3] but he had by no means been successful. When it became known that the greatest of African explorers was leading an expedition to the relief of Equatoria, the news was greeted with suspicion and foreboding by Mwanga and Kabarega but with the very highest expectations amongst Emin's own southern garrisons. Emin himself had come to look to Stanley's arrival as the solution for all his difficulties and as the means by which his hopes for the future incorporation of Equatoria within British East Africa might be realized. The actual appearance of Stanley's ragged band in April 1888 was therefore an immense disappointment. The stories which Stanley's Zanzibaris passed on to Emin's men about their difficulties and sufferings on the march through the Congo lost nothing in the telling and served to reinforce

[1] See the report by Carl Peters of an important conversation with Emin at Mpwapwa, in *The Times*, 31 Oct. 1890.
[2] That Emin did believe that his soldiers would follow him to Lake Victoria is clear from his diary. See *Tagebücher*, 4 May 1888, iv. 105 (Extracts X, p. 206). Also *IDA* i. 399.
[3] Emin to Mackay, 15 Apr. 1887, F.O.C.P. C. 5617, p. 65.

the already existing prejudice against a march to the south. Emin's officers and soldiers were frankly incredulous that such a party of *washenzis* could possibly have come from Egypt. The Khedive's instructions were again dismissed as a forgery, and Stanley and his European officers were regarded as a bunch of adventurers.

To counteract the poor impression made by the expedition, Emin urged Stanley himself to accompany him on a tour of the stations as far as Dufile. Stanley, however, was anxious to set out in search of the Rear Column, and so Jephson was chosen to accompany Emin on a tour of the province. The rest of the expedition would meanwhile return to Fort Bodo, where Nelson, and probably Stairs, were awaiting them and where there was plenty of food. From Fort Bodo Stanley would set out on the long march back to Yambuya. The idea of transporting 'refugees' and ivory from Equatoria down the Congo was not considered. There were no 'refugees' and Stanley did not have sufficient carriers to transport any ivory. When he returned with the Rear Column, the united expedition would rejoin Emin and Jephson either at Fort Bodo or at Lake Albert. The whole procedure was expected to take 7-8 months.[1]

What precisely Emin and Jephson were expected to accomplish in the meantime is far from clear. Jephson felt that 'if by going round and addressing the people I can induce them to come out with us I shall have done good work'.[2] He was to read to Emin's soldiers a proclamation, written by Stanley, which announced that he had come with the Khedive's instructions to lead Emin's men out of Equatoria and to show them the way to Egypt. This, it was asserted, lay not to the north but to the south-east via Zanzibar and Suez. Emin's soldiers were to follow Jephson/Stanley if they wanted to get their pay. Finally, it was stated that although those who wished to remain in Equatoria could do so, they would forfeit their pay, and henceforth be abandoned by the Egyptian Government.[3] This piece of Victorian rhetoric and bombast was to be delivered by a strange European who spoke not a word of Arabic and was unaccompanied by any semblance of an expedition. Emin was to do his best to translate, but from the outset he was convinced that the whole performance—

---

[1] *Tagebücher*, 24 May 1888, iv. 119 (Extracts X, p. 210).
[2] Jephson, *Diary*, p. 254.
[3] The full text of Stanley's proclamation is printed in *IDA* i. 403-4. A similar version is in Jephson, *Diary*, pp. 432-3. The original, in Stanley's handwriting, and with a translation into Arabic is present on microfilm in the Sudan Archive, Durham, Jephson Papers, Box 14/1.

which was to be repeated at every station—would simply 'give offence and make the people refuse to undertake the journey'.[1] If it was not met with complete incredulity, it was most likely to lead Emin's soldiers simply to conclude that Emin Pasha had decided to withdraw from Equatoria in company with his new-found European friend for a destination unknown.

Eleven months had now passed since Stanley had left the Rear Column at Yambuya and in all that time there had been no information whatever about it. 'As the months rolled by without a word from them', Stanley wrote in his diary, 'my fears of what may have happened have accumulated until I am indescribably uneasy.'[2] Throughout his stay at Lake Albert, Stanley had been hoping that the couriers who had been dispatched from Fort Bodo in February in search of Barttelot and his men would have returned with some news. But they had not appeared. Stanley was therefore anxious to leave and begin the long march that was before him, but he was delayed until the arrival of the 130 carriers which Emin had recruited for him and on whom he was completely dependent. These arrived along with Selim Bey and Hawash Effendi on 22 May.[3] Two days later, Stanley, Parke, the main body of the expedition, and the 130 Madi carriers set out from Lake Albert for Fort Bodo. They left behind Jephson, three Sudanese soldiers, and Binza (the man who had been Junker's servant before joining Stanley's expedition at Zanzibar), who were to stay with Emin Pasha. Stanley expected on his return to find Emin and a body of soldiers ready to be escorted to Lake Victoria. The letters exchanged between the two men during the next few days suggest that they parted with every expression of goodwill and considerable respect for each other.[4]

* * *

On the first day of Stanley's march back to Fort Bodo the entire body of Emin's Madi carriers deserted him. Stanley was forced to halt and wait until Emin was able to retrieve some of them for him. Stanley wrote to Emin that these men should be 'tied by the neck in

---

[1] *Tagebücher*, 10 May 1888, iv. 112 (Extracts X, p. 208).
[2] This passage, probably transcribed straight from Stanley's diary, occurs in F. Hird, *H. M. Stanley: the Authorised Life*, p. 247.
[3] *IDA* i. 403.
[4] These letters are printed in *Tagebücher*, iv. 120–3, and in *IDA*, i. 407–8. They are collected together in the *Uganda Journal*, xxix, no. 2 (1965), 211–12, and ibid. xxx, no. 2 (1966), 199–200.

gangs of six'.[1] The purpose of this procedure was outlined by Jephson with disarming candour. Each 'gang of six' would be conducted back to Stanley and handed over. 'He will keep them tied up until he has gone some days march and placed two or three hostile tribes between them and the Lake, return will then be impossible for them and they will be obliged to follow him'.[2] Since more carriers would be needed on Stanley's return for the march to Lake Victoria, he urged Emin 'to take advantage of the period of our absence to make some slight chains for a set of 10 carriers with neck rings'.[3] The future of the carriers who now accompanied Stanley back through the Congo was indeed a miserable one: thirty-eight either died or deserted on the march back to Yambuya and thirty-one on the return journey. Only twenty-six returned, in a wretched condition, in December 1888.[4]

It was also on the first day after leaving Emin Pasha that Stanley caught sight, for the first time, of the Ruwenzori Mountains—the famous snow-covered Mountains of the Moon of Ptolemy.[5] It was during the course of the Emin Pasha relief expedition that these legendary mountains—so long believed to be the source of the Nile— were first seen by Europeans.[6] But, much as Stanley later tried to justify his claim, he was not the first European on this expedition to see them. The credit for this must, probably, be given to Parke— though he at once shared the experience with Jephson. On 20 April, it will be remembered, Parke and Jephson had set out with the steel

---

[1] Stanley to Emin, 24 May 1888, printed in *Tagebucher* iv. 120.

[2] Jephson, *Diary*, p. 255.

[3] Stanley to Emin, 24 May 1888, cited above.

[4] *IDA* i. 442; ii. 14, 105.

[5] Ibid. i. 405.

[6] It is possible that Baker, Stanley, and Emin Pasha had all seen the Ruwenzori before this date but had failed to recognize them for what they were. Baker's 'Blue Mountains' and Emin Pasha's 'Usongora Mountains' were both situated approximately in the position of the Ruwenzori, and were only seen hazily and at a great distance. From a distance the snow of the Ruwenzori is by no means their most obvious feature. In Jan. 1876 Stanley himself had reached the Kichwamba escarpment above Lake George, but he had been forced to turn back because his Baganda escort refused to accompany him further. Whilst there, he records 'we obtained a faint view of an enormous blue mass afar off, which we were told was the Great Mountain in the country of Gambaragara'. H. M. Stanley, *Through the Dark Continent* (London, 1899 edition), vol. i. p. 339. 'Gambaragara' is a word used in Ankole to denote Toro and the area of the Ruwenzori. It is therefore possible that Stanley himself had seen the Ruwenzori twelve years previously. See F. Lukyn Williams, 'Early Explorers in Ankole', *Uganda Journal*, ii, no. 3 (1935).

boat for Lake Albert, where Jephson was to launch the boat and go in search of Emin Pasha.[1] Parke noted in his diary that evening:

On the march we distinctly saw *snow* on top of a huge mountain situated to the south-west of our position. As this was a curious and unexpected sight, we halted the caravan to have a good view. Some of the Zanzibaris tried to persuade us that the white covering which decorated the mountain was *salt*; but Jephson and myself were quite satisfied that it was snow.[2]

Curiously enough, Jephson makes no mention of this event in his diary until much later.[3] Whilst Jephson went on to meet Emin at Mswa, Parke returned to Stanley's camp and reported his discovery to Stanley—whom he found 'a good deal interested'.[4] When Jephson later met Stanley he, too, mentioned the matter, but Stanley 'laughed at me and pooh-poohed the idea'.[5] Rather ungenerously, Jephson attempted to claim the discovery as his own and completely omits Parke from his account.[5] Now, Stanley tried to do the same thing. Whilst admitting that Parke and Jephson had reported the sight of a snow-covered mountain over a month previously, Stanley tried to dismiss their claims.[6] Since he was the leader of the expedition and his book about it was the first in print, and much the most widely read, Stanley has been remarkably successful in establishing his claim. Parke, the most modest of the three, let the matter rest. On the day on which Stanley—in the company of Parke—claims he first saw the Ruwenzori, Parke simply noted: 'We again saw the snow-capped mountain, which I first saw on the day I brought the boat to the lake with Jephson'.[7]

Stanley at once wrote a letter to Emin informing him of the discovery.[8] Nothing substantiates more strongly the generosity of Emin's character—to which all who met him bear witness—than Emin's immediate response. 'Allow me to be the first to congratulate you on your most splendid discovery of a snow-clad mountain', he replied.[9] 'It is wonderful to think how, wherever you go, you distance your predecessors by your discoveries.'[10] Emin himself was, of course, one of Stanley's predecessors. He had been in Equatoria for twelve years and had several times visited the south end of Lake

[1] See Ch. VI, p. 139 above.   [2] Parke, *Diary*, p. 217.
[3] Jephson, *Diary*, pp. 255–6.   [4] Parke, *Diary*, p. 220.
[5] Jephson, *Diary*, p. 255.   [6] *IDA* i. 406–7.
[7] Parke, *Diary*, p. 233.
[8] Stanley to Emin, 24 May 1888, *Tagebücher*, iv. 120.
[9] Emin to Stanley, 25 May 1888, *IDA* i. 408.
[10] Emin to Stanley, 26 May 1888, ibid.

Albert. But, like Baker, Gordon, Gessi, and Mason before him, Emin had never identified the Ruwenzori. The reasons are quite simple, and Stanley's scorn at the failure of his predecessors is quite out of place.[1] The Ruwenzori are probably the most elusive of all the mountains in Africa. They form a range in which several peaks achieve over 16,000 ft. and are perpetually covered with snow. They are situated to the south-west of Lake Albert and rise out of the foothills on the edge of the western section of the Great Rift Valley which runs in a south-westerly direction from the Red Sea and divides into two at Lake Rudolph. They occur in a situation of peculiar atmospheric conditions where the air is highly saturated and frequently misty. For most of the year the Ruwenzori are completely shrouded in mist; it is possible to spend weeks, even months, in their vicinity and never suspect their presence. It is only in the twentieth century that they have been successfully climbed (and then only rarely) and the strange nature of their flora and fauna revealed.[2] It is highly likely that none of Stanley's predecessors (except Parke and Jephson) had ever been in the vicinity of these mountains at a time when it was possible to see them clearly. It must also be remembered that Emin was extremely short-sighted. It is, perhaps, to be expected that the highest peak of these fascinating mountains has been named after Stanley; but a secondary peak was later named after Emin Pasha.[3]

Stanley arrived back at Fort Bodo on 8 June. Stairs had returned at the end of April after a journey to and from Ugarrowwa's which had taken twice as long as Stanley had anticipated. Stairs had brought with him only fourteen survivors; Stanley had expected at least forty.[4]

On 16 June Stanley left Fort Bodo to march back through the Congo forest in search of the missing Rear Column. Stairs and Parke

---

[1] *IDA* i. 406-7.
[2] See esp. R. M. Bere and P. H. Hicks, 'Ruwenzori', *Uganda Journal*, x, no. 2 (1946). Also H. B. Thomas, 'Ruwenzori and Elgon Footnotes', ibid., ii, no. 3 (1935). The fullest account of the Ruwenzori Mountains is that of the first expedition which explored them thoroughly. See Filippo de Filippi, *Ruwenzori: an Account of the Expedition of H. R. H. Prince Luigi Amadeo of Savoy*, (London, 1909).
[3] The main peaks of the Ruwenzori range are Mt. Stanley (consisting of two peaks—Margherita, 16,763 ft. and Alexandra, 16,703 ft.) Mt. Speke (16,042 ft.), Mt. Baker (15,889 ft.); Mt. Emin (15,740 ft.) and Mt. Gessi (15,470 ft.) Ordnance Survey of Uganda, 1961.
[4] *IDA* i. 428-30.

were left behind at Fort Bodo with Nelson and a small body of fifty-nine men—who, Stanley admitted, were 'not of the calibre requisite for a garrison in a dangerous country'.[1] They were to improve the fortifications, cultivate crops, and await the arrival of Emin and Jephson, who were expected to come to Fort Bodo after touring Emin's stations. The whole party was then to evacuate Fort Bodo and move closer to Lake Albert, where they would be in the safer and more friendly area adjoining Emin's province. Stanley would return direct to Lake Albert by a shorter route and then the whole expedition would move on to Lake Victoria to establish Emin and his garrison in a settlement there.[2]

Stanley set out in search of the Rear Column in a state of mounting anxiety and deepest foreboding. Stairs had heard not a word of information or rumour about the missing section of Stanley's expedition even in the vicinity of Ugarrowwa's, and Stanley feared that something had gone seriously wrong. Every conceivable disaster occurred to him.[3] Perhaps the steamer *Stanley* had foundered and Troup, Ward, Bonny, and all loads left at Leopoldville and Bolobo had failed to arrive at Yambuya. Perhaps Barttelot's Zanzibaris had deserted *en masse* to Stanley Falls. Even if they had not all deserted, perhaps Barttelot had lost over half his men through death and desertion as had Stanley's own party. Of two things Stanley became increasingly convinced. Tippu Tip had not fulfilled his agreement to provide 600 carriers, and the Rear Column had been unable to move from Yambuya. Stanley therefore set out expecting to march the whole way back to Yambuya. But if Troup, Ward, Bonny, their 128 men, and several hundred loads had for any reason failed to reach Yambuya, Stanley had decided to abandon them since 'to go down to Stanley Pool is totally out of the question'.[4]

Stanley took with him on this march his European servant, William Hoffman, 113 Zanzibaris, and ninety-five of Emin's Madi carriers.[5] Parke accompanied him with a small group of additional men as far as Ipoto in order to retrieve the thirteen loads which had been left there and bring them on to Fort Bodo. Stanley expected to return to Lake Albert by the end of December. The reason why he took with him such a large body of men is nowhere given by

[1] *IDA* i. 428–30.
[2] Instructions to Stairs, 13 June 1888. *IDA* i. 439–41.
[3] Ibid. 434–41. Also Instructions to Parke, 24 June 1888, Parke, *Diary*, p. 245.
[4] Stanley's Instructions to Parke, 24 June 1888, Parke, *Diary*, p. 245.
[5] *IDA* i. 442.

Stanley himself, but it would seem to be quite simple. Stanley believed that the Rear Column had been unable to move with all its loads from Yambuya because Tippu Tip had failed to supply the necessary carriers. Stanley therefore returned equipped with his own. Although he took the absolute maximum that could be spared, he doubted whether they would be sufficient and he hoped quite desperately that Barttelot would still have sufficient men left alive and able to march to assist him.[1] Stanley was urgently in need of the ammunition and stores with which only the Rear Column could supply him if he was to complete the march across East Africa. He was also seriously concerned at his dwindling numbers. As he wrote to Mackinnon, even his present depleted force would diminish further 'and I shall scarcely have 200 left when I turn my face homewards'. Unless Emin Pasha, on reaching Lake Victoria, decided that he would accompany the expedition to the coast after all, or was at least in a position to recruit more men for it, Stanley feared that he himself would not be in a position to do much treaty-making for Mackinnon 'in the Masai region, as my expedition has melted away so fast and will melt much more before I have done with the warlike peoples between the Albert Nyanza and Karagwe'. None the less, as far as treaty-making was concerned, Stanley assured Mackinnon, 'My soul is as keen for it as on the day I left you.'[2]

The march back through the Congo forest was almost as difficult as the march along the same track in the opposite direction had been the previous year. There were deaths and desertions (especially among Emin's Madi), there was very little food, the expedition was attacked more than once with poisoned arrows. Some of the loads and ammunition which had been buried in the ground on the previous march were retrieved, others had been discovered and appropriated by the local people. Ugarrowwa's was deserted—Ugarrowwa himself having set out for Stanley Pool to sell his huge stock of ivory. Stanley's party overtook him in August and found his expedition consisted of fifty-seven loaded canoes.[3] With Ugarrowwa were the survivors of the couriers sent by Stairs in search of the Rear Column six months previously. They told Stanley a heart-rending tale of their sufferings —with which Stanley duly delighted the Victorian public[4]—and they were warmly received back into the expedition; they may, of

[1] Parke, *Diary*, p. 244.
[2] Stanley to Mackinnon, 3 Sept. 1888, M.P., F. 1.
[3] Hoffman, *With Stanley in Africa*, p. 78.   [4] *IDA* i. 460-2.

course, simply have been deserters. Stanley also recovered all the letters which he and the other officers of the Advance Column had written to Barttelot. None of these had ever reached their destination; the Rear Column had therefore been entirely without news of Stanley's whereabouts for over a year.

Stanley was now less than ninety miles from Yambuya and he still encountered 'not a rumour of any kind' concerning the fate of the Rear Column. Stanley was in what he himself acknowledges was a 'nervous and highly-strung state . . . that old buoyant, confident feeling which had upheld me so long had nearly deserted me'.[1] Suddenly, on 17 August, without any forewarning, Stanley rounded a bend in the river Congo in the vicinity of a village called Banalya and observed a group of men in the charge of a single European. The European was Bonny, and he was about to tell Stanley what Stanley himself described as 'one of the most harrowing chapters of disastrous and fatal incidents that I ever heard attending the movements of an expedition in Africa'.[2]

[1] *IDA* i. 466.
[2] Report of Stanley to Euan-Smith, 19 Dec. 1889, *Africa No. 4* (1890), C. 5906, p. 9.

CHAPTER VIII

What Happened to the Rear Column

WHEN Stanley had marched out of the camp at Yambuya on 28
June 1887, he had left behind him a Rear Column consisting of
133 men plus the two European officers, Barttelot and Jameson, and
their personal servants. When Troup, Ward, and Bonny came up
with the 125 men and 600 loads in the second voyage of the steamer
Stanley in August, the Rear Column amounted to a force of some
271 men—over a third of the expedition—having with them the
bulk of the expedition's supplies and ammunition, including most
of that destined for Emin Pasha. When Stanley returned to Banalya
and encountered Bonny and the remains of this Rear Column over a
year later, he was confronted by disaster—the greatest disaster of any
of his African expeditions. Barttelot had been shot. Jameson was that
very day dying of fever at Bangala. Troup had been invalided home.
Ward had been sent over 1,000 miles down the Congo to telegraph to
the Committee in London. Of the Europeans, therefore, only Bonny
remained. 100 men had already died at Yambuya; thirty-three more
who were dying had been left there; ten had died on the march of
ninety miles from Yambuya to Banalya; and forty-five were on the
point of death in the camp at which Stanley had now arrived. Of a
Rear Column numbering 271 men, Stanley found only sixty who
'seemed in any way likely to survive'.[1] Scarcely a third of the loads
of stores and ammunition were left. 'I sat stupefied under a suffoca-
ting sense of despondency', says Stanley, as from Bonny's lips 'the
harrowing story moved on in a dismal cadence that had naught in it
but death and disaster, disaster and death.'[2]

The story of what had happened to the Rear Column during
Stanley's absence is minutely chronicled in all its depressing detail
in the diaries of its European officers and in their many letters to
friends and relatives and to the Emin Pasha Relief Committee
in London.[3] In addition, there are several accounts by other

---

[1] *IDA* ii. 2. [2] Ibid. i. 493.
[3] *The Life of Edmund Musgrave Barttelot*, from his letters and diary, ed. W. G.
Barttelot (London, 1890). (Henceforth referred to as Barttelot, *Diary*.) The

participants and observers, including those of Assad Farran, the Syrian interpreter, and Tippu Tip.[1] No disaster to a nineteenth-century African expedition is better documented.

The essential causes of the disaster to the Rear Column lay in two facts, both of which were known to Stanley before he ever set out from Yambuya. In the progress of the expedition up the Congo, it will be remembered, Stanley had encountered two set-backs which had forced him to reorganize his plans for the expedition. First, the 'flotilla' of steamers promised by King Leopold had not materialized —indeed, it did not exist. Although Stanley had managed to assemble a remarkable collection of boats, they had not been sufficient to transport the entire expedition to the furthest point of navigation on the Aruwimi at Yambuya. Stanley had therefore been compelled to split up the expedition. Troup had been left with several hundred loads of stores at Leopoldville. Ward and Bonny had been left with 125 men and a second deposit of equipment at Bolobo. A third camp had been made at Yambuya, and it was here that Stanley had planned to establish the united Rear Column when Troup, Ward, and Bonny came up with the rest of the men and equipment in the second voyage of the *Stanley* in August.

The second set-back had come over the agreement which Stanley had made with Tippu Tip in Zanzibar. By this agreement, Tippu Tip had agreed to obtain 600 carriers for the expedition on the condition that Stanley supplied them with ammunition. Because

original diary and letters are in the possession of the Barttelot family. I am grateful to Sir Brian de Barttelot for allowing me to consult them. Citation of the original diary is as Barttelot, MS. Diary. *Story of the Rear Column*, the letters and diary of James S. Jameson, ed. Mrs. J. S. Jameson (London, 1890). (Henceforth referred to as Jameson, *Diary*.) *With Stanley's Rear Column*, by J. Rose Troup (London, 1890). (Henceforth referred to as Troup, *Diary*.) *My Life with Stanley's Rear Guard*, by Herbert Ward (London, 1891). (Henceforth referred to as Ward, *Diary*.)

[1] Statement of Assad Farran before Stanley in Cairo, 4 Mar. 1890, published in *The Times*, 14 Nov. 1890. *Maisha ya . . . Tippu Tip*, ed. and trans. by W. H. Whiteley, (Henceforth referred to as Tippu Tip, *Autobiography*.) Tippu Tip to Consul Holmwood, 21 July 1887, enclosed (in English translation) in Holmwood to F.O. 28 Mar. 1888, F.O. 84/1906. A copy of this letter was forwarded by the F.O. to the Emin Pasha Relief Committee and is to be found in the Mackinnon Papers, F. 6. Tippu Tip to Mohammed Massoud, Aug. (n.d.) 1888. This letter to a relative of Tippu Tip's in Zanzibar found its way into the hands of the British Consul-General on 21 Dec. 1888. He sent an English translation of it to the F.O. (enclosed in Euan-Smith to F.O., 2 Jan. 1889). A copy of this translation is also in M.P., F. 6, and also in the Archives of the Ministry for the Colonies in Brussels (A.E. Box 75).

Stanley had had to leave the bulk of the stores and ammunition behind with Troup at Leopoldville, however, he found himself unable to keep his side of the agreement to equip the carriers. He informed Tippu Tip of this just before the latter left with Barttelot for Stanley Falls. Stanley asked Tippu Tip to obtain the necessary ammunition for the carriers himself at Stanley Falls, but when he arrived, Tippu Tip discovered that there was very little ammunition available, and he found it difficult to recruit the necessary carriers without it.[1] Barttelot's testimony suggests that Tippu Tip did his best to make good Stanley's default with regard to the ammunition; certainly Tippu Tip felt that Stanley had broken the agreement.[2] When Barttelot arrived at Yambuya in June 1887 he informed Stanley of this and said that Tippu Tip had stated that the carriers would not be sent until the ammunition arrived with Troup and the others in August.[3] Stanley, who was obsessed by the fate of General Gordon at Khartoum, and by the need to hurry to Emin's 'relief', had serious doubts whether these carriers would ever arrive. He therefore decided to set out at once without them and to leave Barttelot in charge of the camp at Yambuya. If the carriers turned up, then, after the arrival of the *Stanley* in August, the united Rear Column could march slowly on in Stanley's track towards Lake Albert. If the carriers did not arrive, or they proved insufficient, then the Rear Column was to remain at Yambuya until Stanley returned from Lake Albert in October or November 1887.[4] Stanley made it clear to Barttelot, whom he had appointed in command of the Rear Column, that he had no great faith in Tippu Tip, and that essentially he expected the Rear Column to remain at Yambuya until his return.[5] But the possibility of moving on after Stanley in August was eagerly anticipated by Barttelot and Jameson.[6]

Tippu Tip's sense that Stanley had betrayed him was not without

[1] Tippu Tip to Holmwood, 21 July 1887, enclosed (in English translation) in Holmwood to F.O., 28 Mar. 1888, F.O. 84/1906. Barttelot, *Diary*, pp. 108–9.

[2] Tippu Tip, *Autobiography*, p. 123. Barttelot, *Diary*, p. 108.

[3] Barttelot, *Diary*, p. 119.

[4] Instructions to Major Barttelot, 24 June 1887, printed in Barttelot, *Diary*, p. 137. See also Ward, *Diary*, pp. 36–7; Jameson, *Diary*, p. 99.

[5] The fullest account of this last important conversation between Stanley and Barttelot is in the Barttelot, MS. Diary under 25 June 1887, and in a letter to Major Sclater dated 19 July 1887, both in the Barttelot Papers. Stanley's version of this conversation (*IDA* i. 117–26) is quite unreliable.

[6] Barttelot to Mackinnon, 15 Aug. 1887, M.P., F. 2. Jameson, *Diary*, pp. 70–1. Also Jameson to Andrew Jameson, 7 Aug. 1888 in ibid., pp. 382–3.

some justification. Stanley had altered his original agreement in at least two important respects. First, he had failed to supply the ammunition. Secondly, he had changed the leader under whom the carriers were to serve. Tippu Tip had agreed to supply carriers to Stanley—whom he respected; now he was to perform the same services for Barttelot—whom he strongly disliked.[1]

Even if Tippu Tip had failed to supply the carriers, this would not have mattered if Stanley had returned, as he had expected, in November 1887. For Stanley planned to bring with him a large number of carriers recruited by Emin Pasha to make up for any deficiency on the part of Tippu Tip.[2] But Stanley had returned to his Rear Column not in November 1887 but in August 1888. In the interim, the Rear Column, unable to move without additional carriers, had wasted away in the camp at Yambuya where Stanley had left it, ill provided for, in June 1887.

*   *   *

The precarious conditions under which he had left his Rear Column seem to have caused Stanley himself some anxiety during the intervening months. Yambuya camp had been established in a village which had been obtained by force. The local inhabitants had been evicted, and thereafter they remained consistently hostile. The camp was heavily fortified and its inmates lived under the constant fear of attack. Yet the camp was in no respect self-sufficient and from the outset there was the greatest difficulty in obtaining food. Behind the camp there was an extensive manioc plantation and it had been Stanley's hope that this might be supplemented by trade in fish, corn, chickens, and goats with the local people. But Stanley's own attempts to initiate this trade with a hostile population by capturing women and ransoming them for food were not very successful. 'We release our captives at once, with small gifts and good words', Stanley assured the Committee in London, expressing the

---

[1] See Barttelot, *Diary*, p. 170. Bonny, Report on the Rear Column, published in *The Times*, 15 Nov. 1890. The original, dated July 1888, is in M.P., F. 2. Statement of J. Becker made at Anvers, 4 Dec. 1890, to W. G. Barttelot (reporting a conversation with Tippu Tip), B.P.

[2] Jameson, *Diary*, pp. 70-1. Stanley may well have envisaged at this stage utilizing these carriers to do in reverse the tasks he had first hoped to perform with the help of Tippu Tip's carriers, i.e. to transport the ivory he believed Emin to possess down the Congo and to transport the expedition's supplies and ammunition in the opposite direction on the return journey. Nowhere, however, is there any documentary evidence of Stanley's plans regarding the ivory after the expedition reached the Congo.

a

b

c

5. The Officers of the Rear Column

a. E. M. BARTTELOT
b. J. S. JAMESON
c. J. ROSE TROUP
d. H. WARD
e. W. BONNY

d

e

hope that his actions would provide the 'seedlings for future amicable intercourse. If Barttelot has but a little patience, long before we return there will be a prosperous community, friendly to all strangers.'[1] None of those who remained behind were nearly so optimistic. Jameson noted:

Here are Major Barttelot and myself left absolutely without one atom of meat, tinned or fresh, for several months, and no visible means of obtaining any. The natives have brought in nothing and have removed everything from all the villages within reach of this camp. There is not a pound of game meat, either bird or animal in the whole country round.[2]

In an attempt to re-establish friendly relations with the local people before his departure, Stanley persuaded Barttelot to undergo a simple ceremony of blood-brotherhood with a local leader. If Stanley and Barttelot took this seriously, the local people did not. In return for his fine gifts, Barttelot received a fortnight-old chick and a plaited cane bonnet—almost certainly expressions of contempt.[3]

After Stanley's departure, Barttelot was forced to resort to the methods which Stanley himself had used to obtain food: women and babies were captured and ransomed; foraging parties scoured the country around; trade was unforthcoming.[4] The manioc was plentiful but although a large part of the population of the Congo was used to a diet of manioc, most of the Zanzibaris on this expedition, coming from East Africa, were not. Manioc is a root crop consisting of tubers which have to be steeped in water, then dried and pounded into a sort of flour before it is palatable. In some varieties of manioc, if the tubers are eaten raw or even cooked without the process of steeping in water, they have a poisonous content of prussic acid. Unfamiliar with this diet, and unwilling to go through the extensive process of preparation, many of the Zanzibaris ate the manioc almost raw over a period of many months. Stanley is probably right in ascribing to this part of the cause of their rapid

---

[1] Stanley to Sir Francis de Winton, 19 June 1887, M.P., F. 4.
[2] Jameson, *Diary*, p. 76.   [3] *IDA* i. 130.
[4] A full account is contained in the letters which Barttelot wrote to his father, 1 June 1887 (a copy of this letter is in M.P., F. 2) and to Mabel Godman, 27 July 1887. The originals of these letters are in the Barttelot Papers. The difficulty of obtaining food in the Upper Congo at this time was a general one. The Becker and Van Kerckhoven expeditions were later to experience great difficulties in this respect and even the Arabs at Stanley Falls had to send to Kasongo for rice and livestock. See Ceulemans, *La Question arabe et le Congo*, p. 167; R. Slade, *King Leopold's Congo*, p. 99.

deterioration, illness, and death.[1] In addition, the members of the Rear Column, like those of Stanley's own party, were plagued with ulcers which, breaking out on the feet or legs, spread rapidly and soon penetrated to the bone.

It is evident that morale amongst both the officers and men left at Yambuya was never high, even at the outset, and that a process of steady demoralization soon took place. None of the men had anything like the confidence in Barttelot's leadership that they had in Stanley's. Ward felt that Barttelot 'personally disliked the Zanzibaris and lacked the proper influence over them'.[2] Bonny afterwards recorded that the Zanzibaris 'simply hated' Barttelot.[3] Certainly, as the months dragged by without a word or even a rumour concerning the whereabouts of Stanley and the Advance Column, the men at Yambuya 'became discouraged and depressed and, day after day, rumours circulated in the camp as to the disasters which had overtaken Stanley'.[4]

Matters were made worse by the attitude and the actions of Barttelot and the other officers. All of them were immensely disappointed at being left behind with little to occupy them in the gloomy camp at Yambuya while the rest of the expedition advanced through unknown country to 'rescue' Emin Pasha. Barttelot himself was not well suited to the position in which he had been left—a verdict which Stanley himself later admitted.[5] Whatever the arguments of seniority, it is clear that by the time the expedition had reached Yambuya, Stanley and Barttelot were on such bad terms that Stanley had been only too glad of this opportunity to leave Barttelot behind.[6]

Barttelot came from a prosperous Sussex land-owning family with a strong military tradition. His father was a baronet and M.P., and Barttelot himself had gone to Sandhurst and seen active service in Afghanistan and Egypt before joining Stanley's expedition. Like most of the other officers on this expedition he was only in his late twenties. Essentially, Barttelot was a soldier, and he regarded his

---

[1] *IDA* ii. 8–10. Emin Pasha also told Stanley of similar cases of manioc poisoning in certain areas of Equatoria. See Parke, *Diary*, p. 379. For a full discussion of the poisonous content of manioc, see W. O. Jones, *Manioc in Africa*, Stanford University Press (1959), esp. pp. 11–15, 103–111.

[2] Report by Ward, 13 Feb. 1890, printed in *IDA* i. 497.

[3] Bonny, Report on the Rear Column, published in *The Times*, 15 Nov. 1890.

[4] Statement by Ward in *The Times*, 9 Nov. 1890.

[5] See the statements by Stanley in *The Pall Mall Gazette*, 18 Nov. 1890, and *The New York Tribune*, 4 Dec. 1890.

[6] Barttelot, *Diary*, pp. 112–15.

participation in the expedition as a brief interlude in his military career. He was inexperienced as a leader and he tended to be over-bearing and hot-tempered when dealing with his subordinates. Ward recorded:

> He viewed things through the strict, stern, rigid spectacles of discipline, and with the autocratic manner of a British officer . . . He was a stranger to African manners and speech, with the ever-present suspicion of everyone and everything which this disadvantage must always excite . . . As a consequence of all this the black people with whom he was brought into contact were to Barttelot an unknown quantity, and the contempt and disdain natural to the highly-strung officer who believed nothing was equal to the British soldier, gained full and unfortunate sway . . . He was completely at sea when dealing with the black.[1]

'It did not take me long', says Troup, 'to discover that he had an intense hatred of anything in the shape of a black man, for he made no disguise of this, but frequently mentioned the fact.'[2] Although he formed a firm friendship with Jameson—who had a gentle, pleasant nature and whom everyone liked—Barttelot never got on well with the other officers. There seems little doubt that after several months of insufficient food and repeated attacks of fever, he became ill, depressed, and suspicious. Like other inexperienced officers on European-led expeditions in Africa, Barttelot had joined Stanley's expedition in the hope of living a life of action and adventure. Instead, he found himself in charge of a camp of men visibly wasting away in the forest and in a position of complete dependence on Tippu Tip for the carriers he needed if the Rear Column were to move. Ill and frustrated, Barttelot was anxious about the criticism which he felt Stanley was sure to heap on his handling of the difficult situation at Yambuya.

Stanley had impressed on Barttelot the need to 'spare no pains to maintain order and discipline in your camp, and make your defences complete'.[3] The attempts of the European officers at Yambuya to maintain order and discipline among their increasingly demoralized men led to floggings and some executions which were later heavily criticized. At first these floggings were chiefly in connection with night sentries found sleeping at or deserting their posts, and they were not, by military standards, excessive. But these incidents recur with dismal regularity. 'It is sickening, this continual flogging',

---

[1] Ward, *Diary*, pp. 30-1.   [2] Troup, *Diary*, p. 145.
[3] Stanley's Instructions to Barttelot, 24 June 1887, printed in Barttelot, *Diary*, pp. 134-9.

declared Jameson, 'but there is no help for it.'[1] As conditions deteriorated and hunger increased, stealing and desertion became more frequent and those caught were punished by floggings of excessive severity. One Sudanese, who had stolen half a goat from one of the European officers, deserted after receiving one of these floggings; he was caught, sentenced to death, and shot.[2] Another case involved a Zanzibari who was caught after deserting with Barttelot's rifle. He received a flogging from the effects of which he died two days later.[3] Stanley himself dealt with similar incidents in his party no less severely. But Barttelot was not Stanley, his men plainly disliked him and had no confidence in his leadership. On at least one occasion the Zanzibaris (who formed the overwhelming majority of the men at Yambuya) threatened to desert *en masse*.[4]

The death-rate at Yambuya was truly appalling. By March 1888 Jameson wrote to his wife:

> You can imagine how utterly helpless we are, and how utterly dependent upon Tippu Tip, when I tell you that we have already lost fully one third of our entire force at Yambuya camp from sickness, and that I do not believe we could produce 80 really sound carriers tomorrow, and yet we have between 600 and 700 loads there . . . It is horrible to watch these men slowly dying before your face and not be able to do anything for them.[5]

Ward felt that 'almost as many lives will be lost over this philanthropic mission as there are lives to save of Emin's people'.[6] Judging by Stanley's experience with the Advance Column, it seems likely that the Rear Column would have suffered a heavy death-rate even if it had been able to march in Stanley's wake through the forest to Lake Albert. But to Barttelot and the other Europeans at Yambuya, it seemed that the root cause for the steady deterioration of the Rear Column arose from the fact that it was unable to move.[7] The reason why it was unable to move was that Tippu Tip failed to supply sufficient carriers. Tippu Tip was later to be treated as a scapegoat for the disaster to the Rear Column and it was asserted that he deli-

---

[1] Jameson, *Diary*, p. 80.

[2] See Troup, *Diary*, p. 203; Jameson, *Diary*, p. 207; Statement of Assad Farran, 4 Mar. 1890, published in *The Times*, 14 Nov. 1890.

[3] A full account of this incident is given in Barttelot, *Diary*, pp. 228–31.

[4] Ibid., p. 229.

[5] Jameson to his wife, 17 Mar. 1888, printed in Jameson, *Diary*, pp. 224–5.

[6] Ward, *Diary*, p. 81.

[7] 'This hope deferred and weary waiting, month after month, with no brighter outlook is horrible work—far, far worse than any amount of hardship and fighting', wrote Jameson (*Diary*, p. 225).

berately conspired to prevent the Rear Column from following in Stanley's track. In fact all the officers with the Rear Column felt at the time that Tippu Tip did everything in his power to assist them. But Tippu Tip was simply unable to recruit large numbers of men in the vicinity of Stanley Falls at this time even for his own purposes, let alone for Stanley's expedition.

When Tippu Tip had arrived back at Stanley Falls in June 1887, after his long absence in Zanzibar, he had found himself in a difficult position.[1] He had hoped that as the newly appointed Governor under the Congo State he would receive reinforcements in the form of soldiers, arms, and at least one European assistant to bolster his already crumbling authority. Instead, it seemed that his new appointment had only weakened his position still further. Tippu Tip did not receive any reinforcements of men or equipment for over a year and he found himself completely ignored by the authorities of the Congo State. His letters were not answered; his goods, left behind at Leopoldville, were not forwarded to him; and no steamer visited Stanley Falls until June 1888. He felt abandoned and betrayed, and in a series of letters to the British Consul-General at Zanzibar— who had actively assisted in the drawing up of the Agreement between Tippu Tip and the Congo State in February 1887—Tippu Tip begged him to intercede on his behalf and to urge the King of the Belgians

to send those two or three Europeans and about forty or fifty soldiers to stay with me . . . If these people will stay with me my hands will be strengthened . . . [but if] the Europeans do not come now, I have no power.[2]

Now all the Arabs are my enemies. They say I am the man who gave up all the places of the mainland to the Belgian King. What I earnestly wish from the Belgian King is that he should not leave me alone. Oh, my friend! now, when all the Arabs have become my enemies, how can the Belgian King leave me on my own resources? This is not good on His Majesty's part . . . and I attribute what has happened to me to the English, who put me in the friendship of the Belgian King. And you know all about this.[3]

The difficulty of Tippu Tip's position at Stanley Falls had been

[1] The best general account of Tippu Tip's position in the Eastern Congo is in Ceulemans, *La Question arabe et le Congo*, esp. pp. 147–53, to which I am much indebted in this chapter.
[2] Tippu Tip to Holmwood, 21 July 1887, enclosed in Holmwood to F.O. 28 Mar. 1888, F.O. 84/1906.
[3] Tippu Tip to the British Consul at Zanzibar, 19 Mar. 1889, enclosed in Portal to F.O., 31 July 1889, F.O. 84/1979. (A copy of this letter is in M.P., F. 6, and also in the Archives of the Ministère des Colonies, Brussels, A.E. Dossier 75.)

recognized by Barttelot when he had accompanied Tippu Tip there
on his return. It had also been acknowledged by Stanley in a letter
to Mackinnon.[1] Whilst the Arabs immediately under Tippu Tip
himself (or under his nephew, Rashid, or his son, Sefu—who was at
Kasongo) acknowledged his new position, others did not. The
opposition was led by Sa'id bin Habib, who wanted to supplant
Tippu Tip at Stanley Falls and adopt an anti-European policy in
place of Tippu Tip's collaboration with the authorities of the Congo
State. Barttelot observed that Tippu Tip was 'a bit afraid of Sheik
Habib'.[2] Stanley feared that the attitude of Sa'id bin Habib would
'be a precedent for other Arabs' and urged that Tippu Tip should
be given the support he requested from the Congo State in order to
maintain his position at Stanley Falls—a position which Stanley
had played so large a part in bringing about. Stanley was confident
that 'with a small force of soldiers such as he asks for, and two
Europeans to supervise, advise and encourage him, Tippu Tip will
make the very best Governor that could be found for that distant
station'.[3] Stanley, of course, was not disinterested. It was vital to
the interests of his expedition, and more specifically to the existence
of his Rear Column, that amicable relations should be maintained
with Tippu Tip at Stanley Falls. This fact had governed a good deal
of Stanley's planning after the decision had been made to take the
Congo route and it had been a major objective behind the agreements made with Tippu Tip at Zanzibar. But it is highly likely that
Stanley's plans were made on outdated premisses. The Congo was
an area which Stanley thought he knew; but his knowledge dated
from the period 1884-5, when Tippu Tip was at the height of his
power, able to exact obedience and tribute from lesser Arab leaders
and Manyema over a very large area. Since the capture of Stanley
Falls by the Arabs (in Tippu Tip's absence at Zanzibar), the influence of Tippu Tip had declined. As guns and ammunition became
more widely distributed and more easily obtainable in the Eastern
Congo, and as the search for ivory penetrated further and further
afield, independent Arab 'war-lords', like Ugarrowwa and Kilonga-
longa, whom Stanley had met, and who owed no direct allegiance to
Tippu Tip, proliferated. Tippu Tip had been able to assist Stanley

[1] Barttelot to his parents, 18 June 1887, Barttelot Papers. (A copy is also in
M.P., F. 2.) Stanley to Mackinnon, 23 June 1887, M.P., F. 4.
[2] Barttelot to Major Tottenham, 19 June 1887, Barttelot Papers.
[3] Stanley to Mackinnon, 23 June 1887, M.P., F. 4.

very little in his march through the Eastern Congo. His ability to meet the increasing demands of the Rear Column was also very limited. The activities of the Arabs were widely scattered over a huge area at this time—the regions of the Lomami river and around Kasongo appear to have been of particular interest. Most of Tippu Tip's own men were perpetually away from Stanley Falls on expeditions in search of ivory in these areas and Tippu Tip himself was so short of men that he had to send to Kasongo for reinforcements.

None the less, the evidence is conclusive that, in spite of the fact that he felt that Stanley had broken faith with him, Tippu Tip did persist in his attempts to obtain carriers for the Rear Column. Shortly after Barttelot had left Stanley Falls, a considerable body of men was dispatched to the camp which Stanley had established on the Aruwimi.[1] Whether Tippu Tip himself accompanied them is not clear. These men set out up the Aruwimi river in canoes in search of Stanley's camp. But they were unable to find it and, seeing that the trees were blazed, they assumed that Stanley had already left with the entire expedition on his march through the forest. They became involved in a fight with the local people in the Basoko area, where a previous expedition from Stanley Falls had been completely cut to pieces.[2] After they had suffered severe losses and their ammunition ran out, the party dispersed. Most of the men returned to Stanley Falls and were then utilized elsewhere. One group, under a leader called Abdullah, arrived at Yambuya the day after Troup, Ward, and Bonny and company had come up in the steamer *Stanley* in August.[3] After establishing a camp on the opposite side of the river to Yambuya, Abdullah informed Barttelot that Tippu Tip would certainly send back some of the men who had returned to Stanley Falls and he offered to take letters to Tippu Tip himself. From him Barttelot learned, for the first time, that there was a good route overland to Stanley Falls.[4] Accordingly, Barttelot decided to send Jameson to Stanley Falls to see Tippu Tip about the carriers. Accompanied by Ward, and escorted by Abdullah, Jameson left Yambuya for Tippu Tip's headquarters on 23 August.[5]

[1] See Tippu Tip, *Autobiography*, p. 125. Tippu Tip to Holmwood, 21 July 1887, enclosed in Holmwood to F.O. 28 Mar. 1888, F.O. 84/1906. Barttelot, *Diary*, p. 122.   [2] Tippu Tip, *Autobiography*, p. 125.
[3] Barttelot, *Diary*, p. 131. Jameson, *Diary*, pp. 122–3. Ward, *Diary*, p. 39.
[4] Barttelot, *Diary*, pp. 150–5, 304.
[5] Details of their journey are to be found in Jameson, *Diary*, pp. 116–20; and Ward, *Diary*, pp. 40–3.

Tippu Tip received Jameson and Ward with all the courtesy and consideration he had previously shown to Barttelot. He explained what had happened about the carriers—Jameson was at first sceptical, but eventually became quite convinced—and at once promised to do everything he could to reassemble the men. He warned Jameson, however, that this might take some time, and that the numbers would be somewhat reduced as most of the men were now dispersed and the local people were unwilling to lend a large number of canoes and paddlers for another arduous excursion up the Aruwimi.[1]

Jameson had brought with him a letter to Tippu Tip from Barttelot in which Barttelot emphasized that the powder and ammunition promised by Stanley had not arrived; Tippu Tip was also informed that Stanley had gone on and that the carriers were now to be supplied to Barttelot.[2] While at Stanley Falls, Jameson and Ward were treated as honoured guests and introduced to Tippu Tip's nephew, Rashid, and one of Tippu Tip's chief men, Selim Mohammed— who was to accompany Jameson and Ward back to Yambuya, together with a vanguard of sixty men. When this party set out on 2 September, Tippu Tip promised to send more men and several loads of supplies when these arrived from Kasongo in the next few days.[3]

This news was greeted with great optimism by the officers at Yambuya. Tippu Tip himself was expected to arrive with the rest of the men in about ten days and it was confidently expected that within a fortnight the Rear Column would be in a position to set out in Stanley's track.[4] But the weeks dragged on and there was no sign of Tippu Tip or the carriers. Finally, Selim Mohammed—who had formed a camp with his men behind that of the Rear Column —informed Barttelot that he had received a letter from Tippu Tip stating that he was unable to recruit the necessary men, although a further forty would be sent to join those already with Selim Mohammed. Tippu Tip had sent to his son, Sefu, at Kasongo, in an attempt to recruit some Manyema (i.e. local Congolese) instead of Tippu Tip's own people.[5] Kasongo was a journey of thirty days from Stanley Falls, however, and even if carriers were forthcoming—which

[1] Jameson, *Diary*, p. 128.
[2] This letter, dated 19 Aug. 1887, is printed in Jameson, *Diary*, p. 387.
[3] Jameson, *Diary*, p. 129.
[4] Barttelot to Mackinnon, 21 Oct. 1887, M.P., F. 2. Troup to de Winton, 18 October 1887, M.P., F. 2. Troup, *Diary*, pp. 156–7.
[5] Jameson, *Diary*, pp. 123–6.

seemed unlikely—it was doubtful whether they would arrive at Yambuya much before Stanley's expected return in November. Barttelot therefore determined to go to Stanley Falls himself and attempt to put pressure on Tippu Tip to supply at least some of the carriers at once. Jameson was more resigned: he wrote, 'All our hopes of being able to go on after Stanley have been destroyed. We shall simply have to sit down for another two or three months and exist . . . I have very grave doubts as to whether we shall ever see Lake Albert Nyanza, and it is a pretty ending to our share in the relief of Emin Pasha.'[1]

Barttelot's visit to Stanley Falls accompanied by Troup in October achieved very little. Tippu Tip repeated that he had sent to Kasongo for the men and Troup observed that in the Stanley Falls area it was quite true that Tippu Tip had very few men whom he could recruit, most of his followers being away on ivory-hunting expeditions under Rashid in the direction of the Lomami river.[2] Barttelot and Troup were treated with every courtesy and Tippu Tip went to great trouble to apprehend some deserters from Stanley's Advance Column who had returned to Stanley Falls hoping to make good their escape. Tippu Tip handed these men over to Barttelot and from them Barttelot obtained some information about the difficulties Stanley was encountering. Barttelot concluded that Stanley was making far slower progress than he had expected, and doubted whether he would be back at Yambuya much before the New Year.[3] Before Barttelot and Troup left Stanley Falls, Tippu Tip himself departed for Kasongo. After his conversations with him, Barttelot felt that there was 'no chance, or at least very little chance, of getting any men' and he returned to Yambuya in a mood of resignation. 'I have done all I can now till Stanley puts in an appearance', he wrote, 'failing that, I shall not take any decided step till February; it will be weary waiting, but it must be gone through with . . .'[4]

With this dismal outlook the Rear Column settled down to several months of inactivity amidst conditions which became steadily more difficult. One after another the European officers went down with fever; Troup and Ward became so ill that they scarcely stirred from their tents for weeks at a stretch. They lay in a weak and delirious condition, suffering awful nightmares, and were unaware of what was happening in the rest of the camp. Even though food was

---

[1] Ibid. 141–2.   [2] Troup, *Diary*, p. 169.
[3] Barttelot, *Diary*, p. 159   [4] Ibid. 164–5.

very scarce, the officers refused to open the loads of European provisions, since Stanley had impressed on them that these must be retained for the march to the coast. The floggings and desertions of the men increased. Matters were made even more difficult by the proximity of Abdullah's camp across the river and that of Selim Mohammed's men behind that of the Rear Column. The Arabs attacked the local people while the officers of the Rear Column looked on helplessly; they also interfered with the meagre trade which had developed with the camp at Yambuya. The European officers came to feel threatened by the proximity of the Arabs and suspected a plot to attack the camp.[1] While an outright attack on the camp by the Arabs was, in fact, unlikely, it is very probable that Selim Mohammed and Abdullah and their followers were as interested in acquiring the loads of ammunition and the other stores at Yambuya by a process of attrition, as Ugarrowwa and Kilongalonga had been in obtaining the meagre possessions of Stanley's Advance Column. In November Ward was sent on a further journey to Stanley Falls to try to persuade Tippu Tip or his deputy to order Abdullah and his men to desist from interfering with the Rear Column. But Tippu Tip was still at Kasongo and Ward achieved very little.[2] Abdullah did eventually remove his camp some distance away, but whether this was as a result of Ward's mission or for quite other reasons is not clear. By the end of the year deaths were occurring almost daily among the men in the camp at Yambuya, and Barttelot was becoming increasingly anxious about the absence of news regarding Stanley.

By the middle of February 1888 Barttelot had decided that some course of action must be taken to move the Rear Column out of Yambuya and to find out what had happened to Stanley. Tippu Tip was expected back from Kasongo about the middle of February. On 13 February Barttelot put a series of proposals before the other European officers which he had been considering since December.[3] He suggested that in the first place he and Jameson should make a further visit to Stanley Falls immediately on Tippu Tip's arrival to find out if any carriers had been recruited for the Rear Column. If sufficient carriers were available, then the original plan would be implemented and the whole Rear Column would move on after Stanley.

[1] Barttelot to Major Sclater, 19 Mar. 1888 and 24 May 1888, B.P.
[2] For Ward's journey, see Ward, *Diary*, pp. 52–5.
[3] Troup, *Diary*, p. 179, reporting a conversation with Barttelot.

If, as seemed probable, there were insufficient carriers, then the Rear Column should be divided. Barttelot intended to try to recruit a body of 'fighting men' to accompany a lightly equipped flying column which would advance in search of Stanley and Emin Pasha —whom Barttelot felt, with increasing certainty, must have run into serious difficulties. Meanwhile, the rest of the Rear Column, with the bulk of the loads, would settle at Stanley Falls under one or more European officers and with the assistance of Tippu Tip.[1] How much these proposals were a reflection of Barttelot's own personal need of action is not clear. He himself had hoped to persuade Stanley to allow him to adopt a similar course of action after the Rear Column was united the previous August.[2] It was precisely such a course that Mackinnon was to recommend quite independently some months later.[3] Only by these means would any portion of the Rear Column be in a position to move on after Stanley. Barttelot asserts that the other European officers at Yambuya supported these proposals; some of them later declared that they had been highly critical of them, and had opposed them.[4] In any event, on 14 February Barttelot and Jameson set out once more for Stanley Falls accompanied by Selim Mohammed.

They arrived to find that Tippu Tip was still at Kasongo and was not expected back at Stanley Falls until the middle of March.[5] In his absence, one of his chief men, Bwana Nzige, looked after Barttelot and Jameson 'in every possible way'.[6] As nothing could be done without Tippu Tip, Barttelot now decided on the rather drastic course of sending Jameson on a month's journey to Kasongo by canoe. There he was to interview Tippu Tip and attempt to obtain from him 350 carriers and '400 extra fighting men' for which Barttelot and Jameson personally were prepared to guarantee payment.[7] Barttelot appears to have made this decision because he was now

---

[1] Proposals placed before the European officers at Yambuya by Major Barttelot, 13 Feb. 1888, M.P., F. 2.

[2] Barttelot to his father, 23 June 1887, B.P.

[3] Mackinnon to Barttelot, 13 July 1888, M.P. Letter Book. This letter was written in reply to Barttelot's letters to Mackinnon of 21 Oct. 1887 and 27 Mar. 1888 (M.P., F. 2.) at a time when Mackinnon was as ignorant as Barttelot of what had happened to Stanley. There is no evidence that it was ever received.

[4] See Troup, Diary, pp. 203–5. Much of this passage appears to be a later insertion.

[5] Barttelot, Diary, p. 200.   [6] Ibid., p. 203.

[7] Instructions to Mr. Jameson on his proceeding to Kasongo, 17 Mar. 1888, printed in Barttelot, Diary, p. 205.

convinced that Stanley had run into serious difficulties and he considered it pointless for the Rear Column to set out 'to try and relieve Mr. Stanley, if he be in a fix, with a force as small as the one he started with'.[1] The Arabs, including Tippu Tip himself, had heard no news of Stanley and the Advance Column and had repeatedly suggested that Stanley's small force might well have been cut to pieces by the peoples who were reputedly very hostile in the area between the edge of the forest and Lake Albert.[2] Barttelot therefore felt it imperative that his force should have, in addition to the carriers, a military escort of '400 fighting men' before it set out not only to follow Stanley but possibly to 'relieve' him. As for the carriers, Barttelot had already encountered a body of 150 men whom Tippu Tip had sent from Kasongo for the Rear Column on his way to Stanley Falls; and on 26 February Troup wrote to say that a further seventy men had arrived to join those who had been in Selim Mohammed's camp since the previous September.[3] Thus, a force of about 250 carriers had now been assembled for the Rear Column, but, Barttelot records, these were not to be handed over until Tippu Tip himself arrived.[4]

On 18 March Jameson left Stanley Falls for Kasongo, and a few days later Barttelot returned to Yambuya. There he set about completing arrangements for the division of the Rear Column into two sections. He hoped that with its armed escort the flying column would be able to take with it 325 loads (240 of which were to consist of ammunition) in the search for Stanley and Emin Pasha. The rest of the Rear Column, with the remaining loads, he intended to move to Stanley Falls and leave there in the charge of Troup.[5]

These plans were so obviously in contradiction of Stanley's orders, and fraught with such grave implications, that Barttelot decided to send Ward to telegraph to the Emin Pasha Relief Committee in London and obtain their permission.[6] This decision, meticulously correct in theory, had the most serious implications in practice. The nearest place from which a telegram could be sent was

---

[1] Barttelot to Mackinnon, 28 Mar. 1888, M.P., F. 2.
[2] See Ward to Mackinnon, 19 Aug. 1888, M.P., F. 2.
[3] Barttelot, *Diary*, p. 201. Troup, *Diary*, p. 215.
[4] Barttelot to Mackinnon, 28 Mar. 1888, M.P., F. 2.
[5] Barttelot to Mackinnon, 27 Mar. 1888, M.P., F. 2. Troup, *Diary*, p. 225.
[6] A further motive was to find out whether the Committee had received any news of Stanley by another route. Ward, Report on the Rear Column, 13 Feb. 1890, printed in *IDA* i. 497.

over 1,500 miles away down the Congo at São Thomé or St. Paul de Loanda. In order even to make use of the steamers belonging to the Congo State for part of the journey, Ward would first have to travel hundreds of miles down the Congo to Bangala by canoe. To send the telegram and then to accomplish the long journey back up the Congo again with the reply would take Ward several months. Yet this was the course which Barttelot was to adopt. It is hard to escape the impression that Barttelot made this decision to send Ward down the Congo partly for personal reasons and in an unbalanced state of mind. He was consistently down with fever at this time and when he had returned from Stanley Falls both Ward and Troup found him 'most awfully ill, highly-strung and excited'.[1] He exhibited signs of paranoia and suspected both Ward and Troup of acting behind his back.[2] Barttelot had never been on good terms with Ward,[3] and it would appear that this mission to telegraph to the Committee provided a convenient means of getting rid of him. Barttelot's later actions support this interpretation. Not only did he intend to start after Stanley, if this proved possible, before he received the Committee's reply, but he wrote after Ward in a manner which Ward found deeply insulting, ordering him not to return to Yambuya.[4]

Barttelot's telegram to the Committee in London turned out to be pointless.[5] Ward left Yambuya on 28 March and succeeded in making a remarkable descent down the Congo. He returned to Bangala in July with the Committee's reply. This simply referred the officers of the Rear Column to Stanley's instructions, forbade the engagement of 'fighting men' (Mackinnon consistently refused to consider the expedition as anything but a 'peaceful' venture) and ordered the Rear Column to remain at Yambuya until Stanley's arrival.[6] The one possibility that Barttelot had envisaged and provided for— that the Committee would order the recall of the entire Rear Column

---

[1] Ward, *Diary*, p. 96. Troup, *Diary*, p. 225.
[2] Barttelot, Diary MS, under 25–8 Mar. 1888.   [3] Ward, *Diary*, p. 30.
[4] Barttelot to Ward, 6 June 1888, printed in Ward, *Diary*, p. 119. See also Barttelot to Mackinnon, 27 Mar. 1888, M.P., F. 2. in which Barttelot states: 'Should Mr. Ward be too late to catch me, he will have to go to the Falls.' There he could relieve Troup and look after the stores belonging to the expedition whilst Troup, who was not well, went home on the first steamer.
[5] The text of the telegram is printed in Barttelot, *Diary*, pp. 216–17; also in Ward, *Diary*, pp. 95–6.
[6] Emin Pasha Relief Committee to Barttelot, 6 May 1888, printed in Ward, *Diary*, p. 119.

to England—was not mentioned.[1] Ward, having received Barttelot's letter ordering him to remain at Bangala, did so; henceforth he was separated from the events concerning the main sections of the ex-expedition and eventually, as Barttelot envisaged, he was recalled home.[2]

At Yambuya conditions continued to deteriorate. By the end of March, sixty-seven men had died in the camp and Barttelot estimated that fewer than eighty of the Zanzibaris were now fit enough to act as carriers.[3] Barttelot continued to cling desperately to the hope that Jameson would be successful in his negotiations with Tippu Tip at Kasongo because he saw in this the only hope of obtaining the men to enable the Rear Column to move. 'I cannot arrest the death-rate, nor force Tippu, as I am entirely in his hands and he knows it', Barttelot wrote to Mackinnon.[3] After Troup had left to accompany Ward on the first part of his journey and to obtain livestock for the camp, Barttelot and Bonny were the only Europeans remaining at Yambuya. Barttelot became obsessed by the idea that an attack on the camp and on his own life by the Arabs under Selim Mohammed was imminent, and he disarmed all the Zanzibaris because he feared that they would desert in a body to the Arabs at the first sign of trouble.[4] His relations with Selim Mohammed degenerated into a situation of open hostility and Barttelot determined to go yet again to Stanley Falls to try to persuade Bwana Nzigé to order Selim Mohammed's recall.[4] Barttelot left on 5 April, leaving Bonny— whom he regarded neither as an equal nor as an officer[5]—alone and in charge of the camp at Yambuya. It is to Bonny's credit that alone

[1] See Barttelot to Ward, 6 June 1888, cited above.
[2] See Ward, *Diary*, pp. 125 et seq.
[3] Barttelot to Mackinnon, 28 Mar. 1888, M.P., F. 2.
[4] Barttelot, *Diary*, p. 220. Barttelot to Major Sclater, 24 May 1888, B.P.
[5] In a letter to his fiancée, Mabel Godman, at this time, Barttelot describes Bonny as follows: 'Bonny is a good honest man, but rough, and not a man I could make a close friend of were I shut up for years alone with him . . . [he] is the queerest specimen you ever saw. A mixture of conceit, bravery and ignorance, born a gentleman, but by circumstances a non-commissioned officer in the Army, he purchased his discharge to come on this expedition. His continual cry is that he is every bit as good as we are, and must be treated the same. Stanley was very down on him, and he was very bitter about it. Since he has been with me I have done all I can for him. He is most useful with the natives and Arabs, of an unchanging slow temperament, he is just suited to them. He purchases all supplies for us and doctors the sick, for he was in the Army Medical Department. He is in charge also of the Zanzibaris. He is the third man who is going with me, Jameson being the other.' Barttelot to Mabel Godman, 26 May 1888, B.P.

and without even an interpreter he managed to avoid the outbreak of hostilities with the Arabs.[1]

At Stanley Falls Barttelot succeeded in persuading Bwana Nzigé to order Selim Mohammed elsewhere, and by the middle of May Selim Mohammed and his men had left the area. On the return journey to Yambuya, Barttelot met Troup—with whom he at once quarrelled and whom he accused of dishonesty.[2] When the two men arrived back at Yambuya in the middle of April, Troup was already very ill. From this date onwards Troup lay completely incapacitated in his tent and he and Barttelot were scarcely on speaking terms.[3] His health deteriorated so fast that Bonny and Barttelot feared for his life. As soon as the opportunity arose in June, he was invalided out of the expedition and sent back to Europe.

Nothing had been heard of either Ward or Jameson when, on 8 May, the steamer *A.I.A.*[4] belonging to the Congo State unexpectedly arrived at Yambuya. This, the first steamer to visit the Upper Congo for nearly a year, had been sent immediately after the arrival of Ward at Bangala. From Ward the officials at Bangala learned for the first time of the very existence of the camp at Yambuya—they had assumed that Stanley's entire expedition had left the Congo months previously.[5] On board the steamer were Van Kerckhoven and an engineer, Mr. Werner.[6] After a brief stay they left in the steamer for Stanley Falls, promising to call on their return to collect Troup, who was to be invalided home.

Shortly after the steamer had departed, Barttelot heard that Tippu Tip was at last returning from Kasongo. He therefore set out again for Stanley Falls on 14 May, leaving Bonny in charge of the camp. After catching up with the steamer *en route*, Barttelot arrived at Stanley Falls on 18 May. Four days later, Tippu Tip and Jameson arrived from Kasongo.

Jameson's arduous journey to Kasongo, accompanied by the

---

[1] The fullest account of these events is that which Bonny told to Troup and Troup recorded in his diary a few weeks later. See Troup, *Diary*, pp. 246–7.

[2] Barttelot, MS. Diary, under 16 Apr. 1888, B.P.

[3] Statement of Assad Farran in *The Times*, 14 Nov. 1890. Bonny, Report of the Rear Column, in *The Times*, 15 Nov. 1890. This, though not explicit, is also clear from the diaries of Barttelot and Troup.

[4] 'Association Internationale Africaine'.

[5] J. R. Werner, *A Visit to Stanley's Rear Guard* (London, 1889), Also 'The Camp at Yambuya', *Blackwoods Magazine*, Feb. 1889.

[6] Werner's book, cited above, includes a detailed description of the camp at Yambuya. See pp. 225–30.

Syrian interpreter, Assad Farran, would seem to have been rather unnecessary.[1] Jameson wrote to Mackinnon that he had found Tippu Tip 'as anxious as we are to see us start with all the men'.[2] 400 Manyema had been assembled under a headman (seemingly of very little standing) named Muni Somai. These men had arrived with Jameson and Tippu Tip at Stanley Falls. From Jameson and from Tippu Tip himself Barttelot learned that Tippu Tip had been encouraged in his endeavours to assist the Rear Column by letters which he had received from Consul Holmwood in Zanzibar.[3] But Tippu Tip was now extremely sceptical about the outcome of Stanley's expedition. He had been unable to obtain any information concerning Stanley's whereabouts, but he did not believe that Stanley was dead. He had recently heard rumours that Kabarega of Bunyoro was assisting Emin Pasha with the transport of his ivory to the East African coast and Tippu Tip suspected that Stanley had simply abandoned the Rear Column and was returning with Emin Pasha and the ivory to Zanzibar. Tippu Tip still felt that Stanley had broken faith with him and he was very reluctant to enter into any agreement with Barttelot, whom he distrusted and disliked.[4] It would seem that Tippu Tip experienced considerable difficulty in getting any men to go with Barttelot and the Rear Column. The early deserters from Stanley's party the previous autumn had brought back stories of a terrible march through the forest under oppressive conditions and a great shortage of food. Rumours of the conditions in the camp at Yambuya, the high death-rate, and the 'brutal treatment' by the Europeans had spread far and wide.[5] It was owing to these bad reports, Tippu Tip told Barttelot, that many of his men refused to come and this was why he had attempted to recruit fresh men from Kasongo.[6] Finally, the Manyema whom Tippu Tip had succeeded

---

[1] Jameson's journey to Kasongo is related in Jameson, *Diary*, pp. 226–301. See also the Statement of Assad Farran, cited above, and Tippu Tip, *Autobiography*, p. 125. It was during this journey that Jameson witnessed a cannibal feast (see Jameson, *Diary*, p. 291; and Jameson to Mackinnon, 3 Aug. 1888, published in *The Times*, 15 Nov. 1890). The incident aroused a long controversy in the British newspapers after the expedition was over.
[2] Jameson to Mackinnon, 15 Apr. 1888, M.P., F. 2.
[3] Barttelot, *Diary*, p. 239.
[4] Jameson to Mackinnon, 15 Apr. 1888, M.P., F. 2., reporting his discussions with Tippu Tip. Jameson, *Diary*, pp. 253–9.
[5] Tippu Tip to Mohammed Massoud in Zanzibar, Aug. (n.d.) 1888. Copy in the M.P., F. 6. Barttelot to Holmwood, 9 June 1888, M.P., F. 2. Jameson, *Diary*, p. 150.
[6] Barttelot, *Diary*, p. 272.

in obtaining expected to act as an armed escort, but it soon became apparent that their real task would be to act as porters. Because there were insufficient porters the loads were excessively heavy and Tippu Tip himself had to intervene and insist that if the loads were not reduced, the men would refuse to come.[1]

After Tippu Tip arrived back at Stanley Falls from Kasongo, a further development took place which acted as a new disincentive to sending such carriers as were available with Barttelot. Barttelot had arrived at Stanley Falls along with Van Kerckhoven—the first official of the Congo State to visit the station since Tippu Tip's appointment as Governor over a year previously. Before Barttelot had a chance to see Tippu Tip about the men for the Rear Column, Van Kerckhoven pointed to another purpose for which Tippu Tip might well employ his men.

Like all the other employees of the Congo State, Van Kerckhoven knew about and feared Tippu Tip's long-standing ambition to extend the Arab sphere of influence downstream as far as Bangala. As Stanley had made clear to King Leopold in Brussels, there was very little the Congo State could do to stop this. Stanley had seen in the appointment of Tippu Tip as Governor of Stanley Falls the chance to obtain a certain respite. Most of the officials of the Congo State believed that Stanley had been wrong and that his action, like his previous arrangement with Tippu Tip in 1877, had only opened the way for a more rapid Arab expansion.[2] Van Kerckhoven now found Tippu Tip deeply aggrieved at the complete failure of the authorities of the Congo State to recognize and maintain relations with him during the previous year. He also found that the Arabs, both those under Tippu Tip's authority and those outside it, were extending their activities further afield. Raschid was now firmly ensconced with a large following on the Lomami river. The repercussions of a widening Arab presence were being felt further and further downstream. Van Kerckhoven therefore tried a policy of diversion. The area into which he wished to divert Arab activity was that of the Ubangi river—a region which was reputedly rich in ivory and which lay on the ill-defined northern frontier between the Congo State and French Equatorial Africa. If Tippu Tip could be persuaded to occupy the area this would serve the double purpose of diverting him from Bangala and forestalling the French—of

[1] Ibid.
[2] See Ward, *Diary*, pp. 109–11.

whom Leopold was uneasily aware on his northern border.[1] Needless to say, such a project would attract far more support among Tippu Tip's men than any scheme to assist Barttelot and the Rear Column. As Barttelot observed: 'All the Arabs are dead against Tippu helping us—Tippu and all hating Stanley for his mean treatment of them when he crossed Africa [in 1877].'[2] Feeling himself betrayed by Stanley, and sceptical about the whole outcome of Stanley's expedition, Tippu Tip was by now reluctant to become any further involved with the fate of the Rear Column. Barttelot was probably right when he declared that as far as Tippu Tip was concerned, 'the whole business has become thoroughly distasteful to him'.[3]

None the less, during the next few weeks Tippu Tip continued to do what he could to assist Barttelot to move on with the Rear Column after Stanley. On 24 May he supervised and acted as witness to an Agreement between Muni Somai and Barttelot and Jameson, whereby Muni Somai agreed to serve as commander of the 400 Manyema who were to assist the Rear Column in the march to Lake Albert. For this service Muni Somai extracted an undertaking that he would be paid in goods to the value of the astonishing sum of £1,000 from the stores belonging to the Rear Column.[4]

Barttelot had arranged with Van Kerckhoven that all the stores which he would be unable to take with him on the march, amounting to nearly half of the total at Yambuya, were to be taken down to Bangala by steamer and stored there under the auspices of the Congo State rather than at Stanley Falls under Tippu Tip, as had originally been planned. Since Troup was being invalided home and Ward was downstream at either Boma or Bangala, there was now no need to divide the Rear Column into two sections. On his return to Yambuya on 30 May, Barttelot therefore made arrangements for the sick and debilitated to accompany Troup and the extra loads down the Congo, whence the men would be repatriated to Zanzibar.[5]

Barttelot's plans for himself, Jameson, Bonny, the essential loads, and the remaining Zanzibaris who were to form the flying column escorted by the 400 Manyema, were now described in a letter to

[1] Barttelot, *Diary*, pp. 239–40, 307–8. Also Barttelot to Mackinnon, 4 June 1888, M.P., F. 2.

[2] Barttelot, *Diary*, p. 308.   [3] Ibid. 279.

[4] The original of this Agreement is in B.P. Copies were sent both to Mackinnon and to Holmwood. Its terms are printed in Barttelot, *Diary*, pp. 282–4.

[5] Barttelot, *Diary*, pp. 273–4. Barttelot to Van Kerckhoven, 6 June 1888, M.P., F. 2.

Mackinnon and in a series of letters to other people in England. Apart from the Manyema, the Rear Column which was now to set off in pursuit of Stanley amounted to only 132 men and three Europeans.[1] With this force Barttelot intended to leave Yambuya during the second week in June. He would follow the same route as Stanley had taken and, if he received no prior news, he would proceed to Lake Albert. If he could obtain no news of the Advance Column in the region of Kavalli's, Barttelot would continue to Kibiro. Should Stanley 'be in a fix, I will do my utmost to relieve him', declared Barttelot, who believed that Stanley might be in difficulties but doubted whether he was dead.[2] If there was still no news of Stanley, Barttelot intended to 'go on to Wadelai and ascertain from Emin Pasha, if he be there still, if he has any news of Mr. Stanley, also of his own intentions as regards staying or leaving. I will persuade him, if possible, to come out with me, and, if necessary, aid me in my search for Mr. Stanley.'[3] Eventually Barttelot envisaged returning to the East African coast via Ujiji and Lake Tanganyika. First, however, he would have to return or send Jameson or Bonny back to the Congo with the Manyema, since Tippu Tip warned him that the Manyema would desert if he attempted to take them across East Africa. Barttelot expected the whole undertaking to occupy about a year.

But the rumours heard by Tippu Tip concerning Emin's departure for the east coast assisted by Kabarega, together with a conversation which Barttelot had had with Stanley on the voyage up the Congo the previous year,[4] had made Barttelot doubt whether Emin Pasha was still in Equatoria. 'I am nearly certain', he confessed, 'that should we accomplish our object and even reach Wadelai we shall find we have come on an empty quest, and that both Stanley and Emin are gone.'[5] Barttelot felt so apprehensive about the whole undertaking that he half hoped that a telegram of recall would result from the dispatch of the telegram which Ward had sent to the Committee in London.[6]

---

[1] Barttelot to Mackinnon, 4 June 1888, M.P., F. 2. Parts of this letter are printed in Barttelot, *Diary*, p. 270.
[2] Ibid. Barttelot to Mabel Godman, 4 June 1888, B.P.
[3] Barttelot to Mackinnon, 4 June 1888, cited above.
[4] See Ch. VI, p. 134 above.
[5] Barttelot to Mabel Godman, 25 May 1888, B.P. See also Barttelot to Major Sclater, 1 June 1888, B.P.
[6] Barttelot to Mabel Godman, 4 June 1888, B.P.

But an order of recall did not come, and on 4 June Tippu Tip arrived at Yambuya from Stanley Falls on the return voyage of the steamer *A.I.A.* The same day, another steamer, the *Stanley*, arrived from Bangala. On board the *Stanley* were Captain Van Gèle—who later reported about the mutinous state of the Zanzibaris in the camp[1]—and Lieutenant Alfred Baert. The latter was to remain at Stanley Falls during the ensuing weeks as Tippu Tip's European assistant and he has left a valuable record of events during this period.[2]

The two steamers remained at Yambuya for five days and during that time Muni Somai arrived with the 400 Manyema. Tippu Tip acted as intermediary between the Manyema and the Rear Column and greatly assisted in the arrangements for the departure of the expedition. The 250 men who had previously assembled in Selim Mohammed's camp had either dispersed or now refused to accompany the expedition. Tippu Tip told Barttelot that 'as they were subjects and not slaves he could not force them'.[3] He did, however, obtain a further thirty carriers for the expedition. The total strength of Barttelot's force was now about 560, of which only 132 came from the original Rear Column of 255 men which Stanley had left behind.[4] Barttelot had only about ninety carriers—formed from the few remaining Zanzibaris who were still fit enough—directly under his own control.[5] The 430 Manyema only agreed to come on the condition that they were to be under the orders not of Barttelot but of Muni Somai.[6] They also insisted that the loads they were to carry should be considerably reduced and several days were therefore spent opening and repacking cases of stores and ammunition.[7] When the cases of percussion caps were opened, it was found that the damp had rendered most of them ineffective and Barttelot was therefore obliged to obtain new ones from Tippu Tip, for which he paid him £48.[8]

The 430 Manyema which Barttelot had at last succeeded in getting together under Muni Somai were from the local Congolese population in the region of Kasongo. They were little Arabicized, the

---

[1] Report by Van Gèle, Brussels, 18 Sept. 1888. This was published in *The Standard*, 19 Sept. 1888 and in *The Daily News*, 22 Sept. 1888.
[2] Statement by Lt. A. Baert made at Ostend on 4 Dec. 1890 to W. G. Barttelot, B.P.   [3] Barttelot, *Diary*, p. 272.
[4] Barttelot to Mackinnon, 4 June 1888, M.P., F. 2.
[5] Barttelot to Mabel Godman, 4 June 1888, B.P.
[6] Tippu Tip to Mohammed Massoud, Aug. (n.d.) 1888. Copy in M.P., F. 6.
[7] Jameson, *Diary*, pp. 304–5. Werner, op. cit., pp. 269–71.
[8] Jameson, *Diary*, p. 306.

Arabs despising them, partly for their cannibal propensities.[1] The
Manyema were not slaves and they were usually recruited as armed
followers by the Arabs on their ivory-hunting expeditions. They
rarely acted as carriers and very much resented the task.[2] It seems
very likely that the Manyema who now agreed to assist the Rear
Column did so in order to follow up the route opened by Stanley
in search of ivory. Several expeditions had already left Stanley
Falls since the previous autumn for this purpose. Thus, Stanley's
march up the Aruwimi opened up a new area for Arab penetration
just as his descent of the Congo had done ten years previously.[3]
It seemed to some of the European officers at Yambuya, before ever
the Rear Column set out, that after a few days on the march the
Manyema might well abandon the expedition altogether. They were
undisciplined and Muni Somai had very little control over them.
It was also feared that their example might well induce the Zanzibaris belonging to the Rear Column to desert as well.[4] 'Our success',
wrote Barttelot, 'depends on these Manyema and how they behave,
for our own carriers are very few.'[5]

None of the Europeans at Yambuya thought that the outlook for
their expedition was promising, yet none felt that there was any
alternative to setting out to search for Stanley and Emin in company with such a large party of Manyema. 'I don't know what the
end of this is going to be, I am not over sanguine about it . . .',
wrote Barttelot on the eve of his departure.[6] On 9 June the two
steamers departed, taking with them Troup, the sick, and the extra
loads to Bangala. Tippu Tip remained behind to assist in the successful departure of Barttelot's expedition. On 11 June the camp at

[1] Cannibalism in this, as in certain other parts of Africa, did exist, but it was
never indiscriminate—despite many assertions to the contrary by fascinated
Europeans. Rather, it served a limited ritualistic purpose in specific circumstances.
[2] Statement by J. Becker, Anvers, 4 Dec. 1890, B.P. See also La Vie en Afrique
(Brussels, 1887), by the same author. Troup, Diary, pp. 8–9. When Tippu Tip
wished to recruit carriers to accompany his expeditions to Zanzibar, he had to
obtain Zanzibaris from amongst his own men as the Manyema refused to come.
Jameson, Diary, p. 129.
[3] Statement of J. Becker, 4 Dec. 1890, B.P. Bonny to his sister, 18 May 1888
(a copy of this letter is in M.P., F. 2.) Bonny, Report on the Rear Column,
published in The Times, 15 Nov. 1890. Letter by Lt. A. Baert to The Times,
13 Dec. 1890.
[4] Bonny, Report on the Rear Column, cited above. Ward, Report on the Rear
Column, 13 Feb. 1890, printed in IDA i. 497. Statement by Troup to The Times,
28 Oct. 1890.
[5] Barttelot to his father, 7 June 1888, printed in Barttelot, Diary, p. 301.
[6] Barttelot to Mabel Godman, 4 June 1888, B.P.

Yambuya was finally abandoned and Barttelot set out in company with 430 Manyema to march in search of Stanley.

The march of the Rear Column from Yambuya to Banalya—a distance of about ninety miles—took six weeks and took place amidst mounting chaos and disorder. The expedition became split up into several sections with the European officers separated from each other for days at a stretch; the road was difficult and the way was frequently lost; there was increasing hostility between the Zanzibaris and the Manyema and consistent disorder among both. Smallpox broke out among the Manyema and deaths occurred daily from this and other causes. There were threats to the lives of the three Europeans. Desertions occurred on a rapidly increasing scale and there was a great loss in loads and ammunition.[1] When twenty-five of his ninety Zanzibaris had deserted, Barttelot, fearing that the rest would soon follow suit, deprived them of their rifles and determined to obtain chains to keep them together.[2]

Within two weeks the march had come to a halt and Barttelot had decided that he would have to march back to Stanley Falls and obtain a further sixty men to make up for those who had deserted.[3] Whilst Jameson and Bonny struggled to reach Banalya by making repeated journeys to transport the loads, Barttelot returned to Stanley Falls and had a further meeting with Tippu Tip. Once again Tippu Tip did everything he could to meet Barttelot's demands. He wrote to Muni Somai, ordering him to keep a firmer control over the Manyema; he arranged for a further sixty men to be made available; he provided Barttelot with the chains which he requested.[4] On 17 July Barttelot rejoined Bonny and the main section of the expedition, including all the Manyema, at Banalya. Jameson, however, was still two or three days' march behind and so he was not present during the events of the next few days.

According to Bonny, Barttelot's return coincided with the celebration of a particular festival by the Manyema.[5] In any event, for

---

[1] The details of this journey are recorded in the daily log which was published in full in *The Times*, 17, 18, 19 Nov. 1890. See also Barttelot, *Diary*, pp. 326–34; Jameson, *Diary*, pp. 308–48.

[2] Barttelot to Jameson, 25 June 1888, printed in Jameson, *Diary*, pp. 389–90. Bonny to Mackinnon, July (n.d.) 1888, M.P., F. 2.

[3] Bonny to Mackinnon, July (n.d.) 1888, M.P., F. 2. Barttelot, *Diary*, pp. 328–9.

[4] Statement by Lt. A. Baert, 4 Dec. 1890, B.P. Barttelot to Major Sclater, 6 July 1888, B.P.

[5] Bonny, Report on the Rear Column, published in *The Times*, 15 Nov. 1890.

whatever cause, there was certainly a great deal of singing and danc-
ing in the camp, accompanied by an indiscriminate firing off of
rifles into the air. Barttelot, who was in a highly strung state, found
all this noise exasperating—as Jameson had done a week previously,[1]
and as Stanley was to do later.[2] There were several incidents, and
Barttelot tried to get Muni Somai to intervene, but Muni Somai
replied that he had no control over his men.[3] Early on the morning
of 19 July a Manyema woman commenced beating a drum and
singing. Barttelot, woken up by the noise, sent first his servant and
then some Sudanese to stop it. They were unsuccessful and one or two
Manyema began firing off their rifles. Barttelot was furious and,
though Bonny tried to persuade him to leave the men alone, he
got up, dressed and, taking his revolver, went out of his tent towards
the place where the woman was singing, shouting that he would shoot
the first man he caught firing his rifle. He was on the point of
striking the woman when a shot was fired from a near-by house and
Barttelot was killed instantaneously.[3]

The camp at once broke up in complete disorder. Amidst great
noise and confusion the stores were looted and scattered in the bush
and some of the Zanzibaris and most of the Manyema deserted.
With the small group of men who remained, Bonny succeeded in
gathering together the remaining loads of stores and ammunition
and arranging for the burial of Major Barttelot. He also wrote at
once to Jameson, urging him to come as quickly as he could, and
to Tippu Tip, informing him of what had happened.[3] During the
following weeks, Bonny also wrote to Barttelot's father and to
Mackinnon, giving a full report of the situation at Banalya.[4]

Jameson first heard of Barttelot's death two days after it had
occurred.[5] He reached Banalya on 22 July and found the camp
remarkably quiet. Over 100 Manyema had remained in the vicinity
in a separate camp but Muni Somai had gone at once to Stanley
Falls. Bonny had managed to recover nearly 300 loads but there
were now not nearly enough carriers to transport them. Jameson
therefore decided that he had no choice but to march all the way
back to Stanley Falls and there attempt to persuade Tippu Tip not

[1] Jameson, *Diary*, p. 333.
[2] *IDA* ii. 20.
[3] Bonny, Report on the Rear Column, published in *The Times*, 15 Nov. 1890.
[4] Bonny to Sir Walter de Barttelot, 20–9 July 1888, printed in *The Times*,
15 Nov. 1890. Bonny to Mackinnon, July 1888, M.P., F. 2.
[5] Log of the Rear Column, published in *The Times*, 18 Nov. 1890.

only to recruit more carriers, but to intervene personally to save the wreck of the Rear Column.[1] Leaving Bonny in charge of the camp at Banalya, Jameson set out on 25 July, never to return.

When he arrived at Stanley Falls on 1 August he found that the steamer *En Avant* had just arrived from Bangala. The captain told Jameson that Ward had succeeded in his task of dispatching the telegram to the Committee in London and had returned with the reply to Bangala—where he had received Barttelot's instructions not to proceed. Jameson was dismayed to find that the *En Avant* had brought no letters and not even the Committee's reply to the telegram—everything had been left at Bangala. Jameson noted in his diary: 'Now I am left here in a most serious position, not knowing what reply the Committee have sent, and I can only judge that it is not a recall from the fact that Ward did not send it on, and that, according to the last news from Europe, nothing is known of Mr. Stanley.'[2] Jameson at first concluded that it was his duty, in these circumstances, to do everything to make it possible for the Rear Column once more to advance. With this purpose in mind he went to see Tippu Tip.

Tippu Tip had been greatly shocked at the news of Barttelot's death[3] and had immediately sent men to find out more information and to arrest Sanga, the husband of the Manyema woman, who it was presumed had fired the fatal shot.[4] When Jameson arrived at Stanley Falls, Tippu Tip had already apprehended Sanga and after a summary court martial he was declared guilty and executed.[5] But the future of the Rear Column presented Tippu Tip with a serious problem. Jameson hoped that either Tippu Tip himself, or his nephew, Rashid, would agree to accompany the expedition in search of Stanley. Tippu Tip was very reluctant to do so himself and M. Haneuse, the Belgian officer who had arrived on the *En Avant* as Resident at Stanley Falls,[6] declared that in any case Tippu Tip had

[1] Jameson, *Diary*, pp. 340-1.
[2] Ibid. 346.
[3] 'I was stupefied and knew not what to do', wrote Tippu Tip to Mohammed Massoud, August 1888, M.P., F. 6. See also Statement of Lt. A. Baert, 4 Dec. 1890, B.P.
[4] Tippu Tip, *Autobiography*, p. 127. Jameson, *Diary*, pp. 346-7.
[5] The Proceedings are recorded in the Statement of Lt. A. Baert, cited above, and in Jameson, *Diary*, pp. 361-2. A copy of the proceedings, dated 6 Aug. 1888, is in the M.P.
[6] 'Tippu Tip was rather puzzled at the arrival of a Belgian chief of the Station, when he had himself been appointed chief.' Jameson, *Diary*, p. 349.

no right to go as he was an employee of the Congo State and his presence was needed at Stanley Falls.[1] Tippu Tip declared that there were only two men apart from himself who could effectively control the Manyema: Sefu, his son, and Rashid, his nephew. Sefu was at Kasongo and it would take a month at least to summon him, Rashid was at the Lomami river. Since Jameson strongly hoped that Rashid would agree to come, and was prepared to offer him a considerable sum from his own pocket if he would do so, Tippu Tip at once summoned him to Stanley Falls.[2]

When Rashid arrived on 6 August Tippu Tip made it clear that Jameson would have to arrange the matter himself with Rashid as the latter was a free man with his own interests and commitments. It soon became clear that Rashid was extremely unwilling to undertake the task. 500 tusks of ivory were expected shortly at his camp at the Lomami river and if he left there would be no one to look after his interests during his absence. He was, in any case, not very interested in rescuing Stanley's expedition. Stanley had said that he would return after a few months; he had now been away for over a year and no one knew anything of him.[3]

Tippu Tip now suggested that perhaps Selim Mohammed would agree to go; but after the near hostilities which had occurred between him and Barttelot at Yambuya, Jameson felt that he could not take him, even if he were willing to come.[4]

As a last resort, Jameson now tried to persuade Tippu Tip himself to come. The Belgian officers agreed not to oppose the possibility outright, but whether Tippu Tip ever considered the suggestion seriously is not at all clear. It was certainly a very extraordinary proposal. Jameson was by now quite desperate and he was prepared to guarantee Tippu Tip the sum of £20,000 (this figure would appear to have been demanded by Tippu Tip) if he would accompany the Rear Column to Equatoria in search of Stanley and Emin. Tippu Tip, however, insisted on several conditions. If a state of war existed between Buganda and Bunyoro, he refused to go near the area. A more southerly route was in any case to be adopted on the march to Lake Albert. If Stanley reappeared, or matters were settled satisfactorily in a shorter time than expected, Tippu Tip was still to

---

[1] Jameson, *Diary*, pp. 359–61. Tippu Tip, *Autobiography*, p. 127. Ward to de Winton, 16 Sept. 1888, M.P., F. 2.
[2] Jameson, *Diary*, pp. 348–57.
[3] Ibid. 358.
[4] Ibid. 358–9.

receive the full sum.[1] These conditions implied so great a contradiction to Stanley's orders that Jameson felt them to be unacceptable
without the sanction of the Committee in London. He was also
most anxious to learn the contents of the Committee's reply to the
telegram sent by Ward and, if the expedition was to continue, to
bring up the extra loads which were now at Bangala.[2] Jameson
therefore decided that he must go down to Bangala before he could
decide any future course of action. 'If I find the reply from the Committee to be "go on at all hazards", I will return at once and start
with your men myself', Jameson told Tippu Tip. 'If I find that it
does not tell me to go at all hazards, I will send Mr. Ward with a
telegram to Banana stating my present position, your proposals,
and asking for orders.'[3]

It is possible that Tippu Tip was simply using the conditions
outlined above to deter Jameson from his resolute determination to
proceed with the Rear Column. According to Jameson, Tippu Tip
told him on this occasion that 'he was afraid to let the Expedition
proceed': Barttelot had been shot; Jameson's own life had been
threatened; the Manyema were untrustworthy.[4] Tippu Tip certainly
feared that any further involvement on his part with the fate of the
Rear Column would only blacken his reputation with Holmwood,
the English, and Europeans generally.[5] In one of his last entries in
his diary before leaving Stanley Falls, Jameson exonerated Tippu
Tip from all blame regarding what had befallen the Rear Column
and declared that he had done 'all he could to help the expedition'.[6]

The steamer had already departed and so, on 9 August, Jameson
set out with about twenty people in canoes provided by Tippu Tip
on the journey of some 500 miles to Bangala. Tippu Tip promised to
see that everything would be done to safeguard Bonny, the men, and
the loads at Banalya. Jameson stressed in a letter to Mackinnon that
he did not think 'any blame can be attached to Tippu Tip for Major
Barttelot's death'.[7]

[1] Jameson, *Diary*, 359–63. Ward to *Mackinnon*, 19 Aug. 1888, M.P., F. 2.
Tippu Tip, *Autobiography*, p. 127. Tippu Tip to Mohammed Massoud, Aug.
1888, M.P., F. 6. The Agreement which Jameson drew up for himself and Tippu
Tip to sign is printed in Jameson, *Diary*, pp. 390–1.
[2] Jameson, *Diary*, p. 363. Ward to Mackinnon, 18 Aug. 1888, M.P., F. 2.
[3] Jameson, *Diary*, p. 363.
[4] Ibid. 353; also Jameson to Mackinnon, 3 Aug. 1888, M.P., F. 2.
[5] Tippu Tip to Mohammed Massoud, Aug. 1888, M.P., F. 6.
[6] Jameson, *Diary*, p. 361.
[7] Jameson to Mackinnon, 3 Aug. 1888, M.P., F. 2.

Jameson arrived at Bangala on 16 August unconscious and dying of haematuric fever. Ward—who had received the news of Barttelot's death only the previous day—was unable to do much for Jameson, who died the following day.[1]

All that was left of Stanley's Rear Column was now under the command of Bonny at Banalya. It was these sad remains which confronted Stanley when he arrived back at Banalya on 17 August—the very day that Jameson died at Bangala.

*   *   *

Characteristically, perhaps, Stanley's reaction to the account which Bonny gave him of what had happened to the Rear Column was one of anger and incredulity. Forgetting that originally he himself had expected the Rear Column to remain at Yambuya, Stanley now professed himself unable to understand why it had failed to move on after him, even slowly, by repeated marches. 'It was all an unsolved riddle to me', he declared, and from this position he never deviated.[2] The truth is that Stanley's own hopes and expectations had changed in the interim. Stanley had overcome difficulties and set-backs with almost superhuman determination, but this did not alter the fact that the fate of the Rear Column might have been very different if Stanley had returned, as he had expected, in November 1887. Conscious perhaps of his own part in the responsibility for what had happened to the Rear Column—a responsibility which he never acknowledged—Stanley lashed out in all directions. Believing that Jameson was still at Stanley Falls, Stanley wrote him a letter in which he accused him of deserting the expedition. 'I cannot make out why the Major, you, Troup and Ward, have been so *demented*', he declared, 'all of you seem to have acted like madmen.'[3]

When on 28 August Bonny received the letter which Jameson had written to him from Stanley Falls stating his intention of going to Bangala,[4] Bonny replied telling him of Stanley's anger and urging

---

[1] Ward, *Diary*, pp. 125–32. After Jameson's death, Ward went down to the coast once more to telegraph to the Committee in London. The Committee declined to sanction the Agreement which Jameson had provisionally drawn up with Tippu Tip. Ward and the loads at Bangala eventually returned to Europe. See Ward, *Diary*, pp. 133 *et seq.*

[2] *IDA* i. 494.

[3] Stanley to Jameson, 30 Aug. 1888, printed in Jameson, *Diary*, pp. 365–6. Jameson, of course, never received this letter. See also Stanley to Mackinnon, 3 Sept. 1888, M.P., F. 4.

[4] The text of this letter, dated 12 Aug. 1888, is printed in *IDA* i. 516–18.

him not to try and return to the expedition as Stanley had suggested. Stanley was particularly incensed, Bonny stated, to find that some of his personal possessions, including clothes, had been sent down with the other 'superfluous' loads to Bangala.[1] Not until August 1889 did Stanley hear of Jameson's death at Bangala.

Three days after his arrival, Stanley decided to move the remaining men and loads under Bonny from Banalya to a camp about fourteen miles upstream opposite an island in the river Aruwimi. Smallpox was spreading among the Manyema, and Stanley planned to establish them in a separate camp on the river bank while he, Bonny, the Zanzibaris, and the remaining Madi carriers brought from Equatoria camped on the island. The move, with all the loads, took three days to accomplish, and convinced Stanley of the 'utter unruliness of this mob of slaves',[2] as Stanley referred to the Manyema. During the following ten days Stanley reorganized the men and loads and spent much time writing letters to Mackinnon and others informing them of his meeting with Emin Pasha, the present situation with regard to the Rear Column, and his plans for the future of the expedition.[3] These letters, dutifully forwarded by Tippu Tip from Stanley Falls, eventually arrived in England and brought the first information about the expedition which had arrived for nearly eighteen months.[4]

Stanley also wrote to Tippu Tip himself.[5] Not a word of blame or reproach occurs in this letter. Stanley merely recounts his march to Lake Albert and back and his meeting with Emin Pasha as a tale of success and expresses the hope that he and Tippu Tip will meet 'face to face before many days'. Since Stanley was not prepared to go to Stanley Falls, and intended setting out shortly to return to Lake Albert, all he offered to do was to travel slowly for the first ten days so that Tippu Tip could catch up with him. Tippu Tip, it seems, did not find such a prospect inviting, nor feel himself obliged

---

[1] Bonny to Jameson, 28 Aug. 1888, M.P., F. 2.

[2] *IDA* ii. 13.

[3] Stanley to Mackinnon, 17 and 28 Aug. and 3 Sept. 1888. The first of these letters—which Stanley describes as a brief one—is missing; the other two are in M.P., F. 4. The second letter, written for publication, was published in *The Times*, 3 Apr. 1889. See also Bonny to Mackinnon, July–Aug. 1888, M.P., F. 2., published in *The Times*, 15 Nov. 1890, and Stanley to J. A. Grant, 8 Sept. 1888, M.P., F. 4.

[4] See Euan-Smith to Salisbury, 21 Dec. 1888, F.O. 84/1913. Also Tippu Tip to the British Consul at Zanzibar, 25 Aug. 1888, F.O. 84/1911.

[5] Stanley to Tippu Tip, 17 Aug. 1888, printed in Ward, *Diary*, pp. 138–9.

to fit in with Stanley's plans any longer—a view in which he was to be strongly supported by the authorities of the Congo State.

In reply to my enquiry as to the probable reason of Tippu Tip's refusal to accompany Mr. Stanley, M. van Eetvelde said that there seemed to him to be no reason for Tippu Tip's undertaking the journey. Mr. Stanley had no apparent need of his services, and all Tippu Tip's interests and duties lay in the district of Stanley Falls. Nothing had occurred to shake the confidence which the Government of the Congo State reposed in him . . .[1]

He had quite enough on his hands at Stanley Falls and he was shortly to set out on another prolonged expedition to Kasongo.[2] He did, however, send Selim Mohammed after Stanley to discover Stanley's plans. The two men met, on 4 September, and despite Bonny's inference to the contrary, Stanley concluded that Tippu Tip, Selim Mohammed, and the other Arabs had not deliberately set out to bring about the collapse of the Rear Column. While he would welcome Tippu Tip's help, Stanley was determined not to rely on it. He placed no faith in Selim Mohammed's declaration that he would return with a body of men within forty days, and suspected that it was Selim Mohammed's intention to incite the remaining Manyema to desert. Stanley sent Selim Mohammed back to Tippu Tip with a warning that when he reached Zanzibar he would institute court proceedings for the distraint of Tippu Tip's goods for breach of contract.[3] Thus Stanley and Tippu Tip finally parted company.

Stanley's force combined with what remained of the Rear Column and 170 Manyema now numbered 465 men, nearly half of whom were so debilitated that they were unable to march or to carry loads. Stanley could muster just enough carriers to transport the 230 loads which comprised all that remained of the 600 loads of equipment which had originally been stored at Yambuya.[4] The sick were at first transported up river by canoes whilst Stanley led the carriers on a land march following the course of the river. But the smallpox spread from the Manyema to Emin's Madi, who quickly succumbed; the Zanzibaris, having been inoculated on the voyage round from Zanzibar in 1887, were mostly immune, but many of them died

---

[1] Lord Vivian to Salisbury, 19 Jan. 1889, reporting a conversation with M. Van Eetvelde, F.O.C.P. 5867 (Zanzibar, 1889), no. 89.
[2] Tippu Tip, *Autobiography*, pp. 128–9. Report of Lt. A. Baert to the Governor General at Boma, 1888, published in *John Bull*, 20 Oct. 1888.
[3] *IDA* ii. 16–20.   [4] Ibid. 14.

from general debility. Forty-four deaths occurred in the first forty-nine days of Stanley's march back to Lake Albert.[1] For this march, Stanley adopted a more northerly route to that of his previous journeys. He hoped to avoid Fort Bodo altogether and march straight to Lake Albert; he also hoped to avoid the famine areas he had passed through before. But the experiences of this march were just as bad as on the previous ones and there were no Arab settlements encountered *en route*. In December the expedition came to a halt in a famine area less than ten days' march, as it turned out, from Fort Bodo. Surrounded by sick and dying men, Stanley was forced to send out most of those who were fit on foraging expeditions far afield while he and Bonny remained in a camp with the rest. After a week had passed, the foraging party had not returned and twenty men had died in the camp. Stanley became quite desperate and began to believe that his men had deserted him.[2] Finally, he decided that while Bonny remained in the camp, he would set out to find the foraging party. He later told Parke that he set out and followed them, 'bringing his revolver and a full dose of poison to destroy himself with in case he could not find them. He had never been in such a state of despair on any African expedition'.[3] But although the foraging party was found and the march continued, the experience made Stanley decide to make for Fort Bodo after all.

When Stanley had set out to search for the Rear Column the previous June, it had been expected that Emin and Jephson would have returned to Fort Bodo two months later, with those of Emin's men who wished to leave Equatoria. Stanley had left instructions that the Fort was then to be abandoned and its occupants were to march with Emin, Jephson, and their force to the plateau overlooking Lake Albert and there await Stanley's arrival.[4] When Stanley and his party finally approached Fort Bodo on 20 September they found the fort intact, surrounded by extensive fields of corn and vegetables. The fifty-nine men whom Stanley had left along with Stairs, Nelson, and Parke were now reduced to fifty-one but they were in greatly improved health. They had formed too small a body, however, to risk the march to Lake Albert without some reinforcements. Of Emin, Jephson, and events in Equatoria, no one had heard a word.[5]

[1] *IDA* ii. 35.
[2] See *IDA* ii. 59–63. Hoffmann, *With Stanley in Africa*, pp. 97–102.
[3] Parke, *Diary*, p. 345.   [4] See Ch. VII, p. 170 above.
[5] Report of Stairs, 21 Dec. 1888, printed in *IDA* ii. 103–4. Parke, *Diary*, pp. 240–333.

Once again Stanley's plans had gone awry. Until this moment it would appear that Stanley had expected on his return from bringing up the Rear Column to find Emin, Casati, Jephson, the men he had left behind, and a considerable body of Emin's Egyptian and Northern Sudanese soldiers ready and waiting to set out with him on the march to Lake Victoria, and possibly to Zanzibar. Now, Stanley became convinced that Emin had decided not to leave Equatoria.[1] The absence of any news from Jephson, however, suggested that, as with the Rear Column, something had gone seriously wrong during Stanley's absence. Three days after his arrival at Fort Bodo, Stanley determined to set out for the Lake to investigate. On 23 December Fort Bodo was abandoned and Stanley's united expedition moved on towards Lake Albert.

Stanley had lost 106 men on the march from Banalya to Fort Bodo, and his total force now numbered only 412—of whom 151 were Manyema.[2] Out of 412, 124 were ill and scarcely able to march, and the remainder were quite unable to transport all the loads. Stanley therefore decided that once again he would have to divide the expedition into two sections. By means of repeated marches he managed to get all the loads transported to the edge of the grassland a few days' march from the Lake. Here he decided to leave Stairs, Nelson, and Parke with the sick, and most of the loads, in a camp at a place called Kandekore while he pushed on with a small force in search of Emin and Jephson. On 11 January 1889 Stanley set out, and, on approaching Lake Albert five days later, he was met by messengers bringing him letters from Emin and Jephson. As he read these letters, Stanley states, 'a creeping feeling came over me', and for a time Stanley experienced 'complete mental paralysis'.[3] His worst fears were confirmed. There had been a rebellion in Equatoria, Emin and Jephson had been made prisoners by Emin's own officers, and the renewed Mahdist attack on the province, which Emin had long expected, had come about. Rejaf had fallen, the stations of Bedden, Kirri, and Muggi had been abandoned, and the remaining stations in the south were in complete disorder. Emin's fragile authority had finally collapsed.

[1] Stanley to Euan Smith, 19 Dec. 1889, *Africa No. 4* (1890).
[2] *IDA* ii. 105.   [3] Ibid. 109.

CHAPTER IX

Equatoria 1888–1889

WHEN Stanley had met Emin Pasha in May 1888 and had discussed with him the various proposals for the future, he had done so with certain preconceptions which he had brought with him from Europe. These preconceptions concerned Emin's position in Equatoria as Stanley, Leopold, and Mackinnon had envisaged it in 1886, and they bore little relation to Emin's situation as it actually was.

Like most people in Europe, Stanley had assumed that Emin's chief danger lay in external attack, that the Mahdists might again advance on Equatoria, and that what Emin needed was ammunition to defend the province against them. The siege of Amadi, as related by Emin in the letters which had been published in England, had created the picture of Emin as a valiant governor surrounded by loyal troops living among a population which, if not devoted to Egyptian rule, was at any rate not actively hostile. Equatoria was envisaged as an enclave of order, prosperity, and progress in the heart of an Africa threatened by 'barbarism' (i.e. the neighbouring African peoples, especially Kabarega of Bunyoro, and Mwanga of Buganda) and 'fanaticism' (the Mahdists). If this enclave, under its devoted Governor, could be supported and established as a part of the British Empire, then it might act as a nucleus from which 'civilization' might be extended to neighbouring territories. These preconceptions had lain behind the organization of the relief expedition in Europe and the proposals with regard to the future of Equatoria which Stanley had discussed with Emin in May 1888. Stanley would have us believe that when he set out to search for the Rear Column he did so with his preconceptions about Emin's position in Equatoria mostly intact.[1] But, as so often in his published works, Stanley is telling us less than the truth. In a long letter to J. A. Grant, written in September 1888, Stanley reported on the situation in Equatoria as he had found it. Stanley himself, of course, had never entered the confines of the province, but he had obtained a good deal of information from conversations with several of Emin's soldiers and officials

[1] *IDA* i. 399.

EQUATORIA 1888-1889   209

—especially Shukri Agha, the governor of Mswa station, and Selim
Bey, the governor of Labore—both of whom had visited him along
with Vita Hassan and Casati at the camp at Nsabe.¹ From them,
Stanley reported to Grant, he had learnt that 'Emin Pasha, though
living in comfort so far as provisions could supply his wants, was in
a much worse position than I believed he was when I set out from
England'.² Stanley's chief realization was that the dangers to Emin's
position stemmed less from the possibility of a further Mahdist
attack than from internal divisions within his own garrisons.
Shukri Agha told Stanley of the resolute opposition among most of
the soldiers to any scheme for a retreat to the south, and of the state
of rebellion against Emin's authority which already existed amongst
the northern garrisons consisting of men from the 1st battalion
based at Rejaf. Stanley further realized that rumours about the
approach of his expedition had only made matters worse. It had been
the news of Stanley's impending arrival which had led to the final
eviction of Casati from Bunyoro and a situation of open hostility
between Emin and Kabarega. It had been the rumours concerning
the advance of a 'European' expedition which had led the garrison
at Rejaf to attempt to capture Emin at Kirri in December 1887,
since they were convinced that this expedition would attempt to
bring about their evacuation to the south by force along the lines
which Emin had unsuccessfully been attempting since 1886.² Both
Emin and Shukri Agha had warned Stanley that any attempt to
persuade the members of the 1st battalion to retreat to the south
would be met by indignation and resistance.³ None the less, in May
1888 Stanley had left Jephson with only three men to accompany
Emin on a tour of all the stations during which he was to try to
persuade the garrisons to withdraw with Stanley's expedition to the
south. It was Emin's hope that Stanley's arrival would convince
the garrisons 'that there is another way to Egypt besides that to
the north, because they will see that you have succeeded in getting
here by it'. Emin also set great store by Stanley's reputation and the
fact that a few of Emin's own soldiers had met Stanley before, in
1876, when they had accompanied Linant de Bellefonds on a visit
to Buganda.⁴ Thus, Emin looked to Stanley, or rather to Jephson as
Stanley's representative, to succeed where he himself had consistently

¹ Ibid.
² Stanley to J. A. Grant, 8 Sept. 1888, M.P., F. 4.
³ Ibid. See also *IDA* i. 422.   ⁴ Stanley to Grant, 8 Sept. 1888.

210   EQUATORIA 1888-1889

failed. The evidence is conclusive that when Stanley departed from
Lake Albert in June 1888, leaving Emin and Jephson to set out on
their tour of the stations, the objective which all three of them
hoped to achieve was the evacuation of Equatoria and the establishment of Emin with his most loyal soldiers in a settlement in the
Kavirondo region. Stanley was 'heart and soul in the Kavirondo
scheme', declared Jephson, and Emin had told Stanley 'that the
Kavirondo scheme exactly chimes in with his [Emin's] own ideas of
what is best for the people'.[1] Yet not once during their tour of the
stations were either Emin or Jephson to make public the Kavirondo
proposal. This momentous omission was to have far-reaching consequences, especially as rumours concerning the plans made by Emin
and Stanley for the future soon spread far and wide. Why, then,
was the Kavirondo proposal never publicly discussed by Emin and
Jephson? 'I did not say anything about it', says Jephson, 'as I had
been strictly enjoined to understand that our first duty was to the
Khedive.'[2]

A similar sense of obligation to adhere strictly to what they conceived as their duty to the Khedive and the instructions which he had
sent appears to have affected Emin and Stanley. The Khedive's instructions presented Emin and his soldiers with only two alternatives, an
element of choice which was in itself to prove fatally unconvincing
to the garrisons: either they returned with Stanley's expedition to
Egypt, or they remained in Equatoria. If they remained in Equatoria,
then they ceased to be in the service of the Khedive and the Egyptian
Government abandoned all responsibility for them. Even if they
adopted the other alternative and returned to Egypt, Jephson noted
that 'neither the Khedive's nor Nubar Pasha's letters promise the
people much; all they promise them is that their pay shall continue
up to the time that they land in Egypt, they say nothing about future
employment'.[3] Emin felt that until he had discovered the response
among his soldiers to the two alternatives presented by the Khedive,
and in particular the response to the idea of a return to Egypt with
Stanley's expedition, he was not free to speak of the Kavirondo
project.[4] But this approach caused Emin some disquiet. As he noted
in his diary, if, after persuading his soldiers to follow him to Egypt

[1] Jephson, MS. Diary, under 11 June 1888.
[2] Jephson, *Emin Pasha and the Rebellion at the Equator* (London, 1890),
p. 53 (henceforth referred to as Jephson, *Rebellion*).
[3] Jephson, MS. Diary, 23 July 1888.
[4] Ibid. 11 July 1888.

'I then decide to go to the Kavirondo and stay there, all the Egyptians and a number of others will exclaim that it is treachery'.[1]

Stanley could have outlined the Kavirondo proposal in the proclamation which he asked Jephson to read after the letters of the Khedive and Nubar Pasha at every station. In this proclamation, Jephson observed, Stanley 'speaks more plainly than either the Khedive or Nubar Pasha . . . [and] represents very strongly that he has come expressly from the Khedive to bring the people out of Equatoria and lead them back to Egypt'.[2] Stanley deliberately omitted all reference to the Kavirondo proposal, Jephson comments, because he wished

to cover himself from blame, should the Pasha and his people decide on stopping at Kavirondo and by doing so anger the Khedive and lead him to say that Stanley had not done his best to bring the people to Egypt, as he was in duty bound to do, but had used the money Egypt had subscribed to further a scheme in which he had such a keen interest.[2]

Jephson considered that Stanley was certainly not open to the charge of false faith to the Khedive since at Nsabe, as in his proclamation, Stanley strongly urged Emin's people to return to Egypt, 'and his orders to me were to do my best to induce the people to go there'.[3] This was the course which Emin and Jephson were to adopt during their tour of the stations despite the fact that they, like Stanley, had from the outset 'a very good idea that the people do not care to go to Egypt'.[3] Thus, Emin and Jephson set out to try and persuade the best of the soldiers in the province to evacuate Equatoria and accompany Stanley's expedition to Egypt when the real objective, only to be revealed later, was to withdraw to the Kavirondo region, and there establish a settlement under the new auspices of Mackinnon's I.B.E.A. Company. From the beginning it had been understood that the Egyptian officers and clerks—whom Emin wished to rid himself of and who numbered no more than sixty—would return with Stanley to Egypt.

Emin and Jephson began their tour under very inauspicious circumstances. The northern stations, garrisoned by the officers and soldiers of the 1st battalion between Dufile and Rejaf, had been beyond Emin's authority for the past three years and Emin had also

[1] *Tagebücher*, 12 July 1888, iv. 138 (Extracts XI, p. 195).
[2] Jephson, MS. Diary, 11 July 1888. For the full text of Stanley's proclamation, see Jephson, *Diary*, pp. 432-3.
[3] Jephson, MS. Diary, 11 July 1888.

detected signs of incipient rebellion at the headquarters of the 2nd battalion at Dufile. Only in the few stations south of Wadelai, where he had gradually come to spend all his time, had Emin been able to maintain his position. But even in the south, Emin's position had declined as a result of the rapid deterioration in his relations with Kabarega. Casati's humiliating eviction from Bunyoro had led to a situation of open hostility between Emin and Kabarega. One of Emin's first actions after Stanley's departure was to order an attack on Kibiro, which was an important trade centre for Kabarega on account of its salt deposits. It would seem that Emin had been planning this attack for some time in revenge for Kabarega's treatment of Casati.[1] On 30 May Emin dispatched both steamers from Mswa to attack Kibiro. The place was burnt amidst considerable carnage. 'I do not thank you for the zeal you have displayed and the cruelty you have committed', Emin is reported to have said to the commander of this expedition on its return.[2] Later, Emin appears to have been ashamed of his own responsibility for the affair and to have removed from his diary the pages concerned with the attack on Kibiro.[3] Kabarega's response was to plan an attack on Emin's stations of Mswa and Tunguru, possibly in alliance with the Lango. But from this course he was prevented by the outbreak of new hostilities between Buganda and Bunyoro.[4]

But by 1888 the real threat to Emin's position lay in the situation in his own stations. It is clear that for some time before the arrival of Stanley's expedition Emin had possessed only a semblance of authority over his garrisons and that his position had declined steadily ever since his retreat from Lado. Not only had his orders been repeatedly disregarded, but the news which he had received and attempted to explain concerning events in Egypt and Khartoum had been disbelieved and his loyalty to the Khedive and Egypt had come to be doubted amongst his own men—all of whom were, Jephson noted, devoted to 'Effendina' (the Khedive). This devotion to the Khedive was strongest not among the Egyptians, but among the southern Sudanese soldiers who had never visited Egypt and who regarded the Khedive as a remote 'person in the clouds'.

---

[1] *Tagebücher*, 25 May 1888, iv. 121. *IDA* i. 408–9.

[2] Casati, *Ten Years in Equatoria*, p. 341.

[3] See the note by Sir John Gray on 'The attack on Kibiro' in *The Uganda Journal*, vol. xxx, Part 2 (1966), 196–7. Also Vita Hassan, *Die Wahrheit über Emin Pasha*, ii. 140–1. Jephson, MS. Diary, 5 June 1888.

[4] *Tagebücher*, 25 July 1888, iv. 143.

'They are told he is their Sultan and that the flag they are so fond of displaying on every occasion is his, but to them he is only a Mythical person who sends them fine words, but through all these years has neither helped them nor sent them their pay.'[1] The southern Sudanese soldiers, Jephson noted, also needed 'some tangible, real person to look up to, a person who will clothe them and give them food, that person is Emin Pasha, and I must say they seem to look up to him with both loyalty and devotion . . .'[1]

The situation was rather different amongst Emin's Egyptian and northern Sudanese officers and clerks. They had scant respect for Emin (whom they considered as a Christian) and they were highly suspicious of the intrigues which they felt he had entered into with Stanley and his expedition. The advent of Stanley's expedition had created the highest expectations amongst Emin's garrisons. 'The people understood that Mr. Stanley was bringing succour, and that they would be able to hold the Province', declared one official.[2] The actual appearance of Stanley's ragged and ill-equipped party at Nsabe therefore came as a great anti-climax. Casati records how

the people who had come with us looked with wonder, eyes wide open and dubious hearts, at this remnant of the Expedition, of which the Governor [Emin] had sung so many praises, and which he had taught them to consider a fount of comfort. Of what value were thirty cases of Remington cartridges? They had not in the least changed the situation of the Equatorial Province.[3]

Jephson found that Emin's officers 'were exceedingly sceptical about us, and did not believe we came from Egypt'.[4] No one had ever heard of an expedition from Egypt arriving from the southwest and the ambiguous nature of the Khedive's letter in itself inspired complete disbelief. Stanley, declared Emin's officers, 'is only a traveller, and not from His Highness the Khedive; he could not have sent such a letter'.[5]

Amongst Emin's officers, Stanley and Jephson appeared as the European agents of some English conspiracy to which Emin himself was a party. Their objectives were obviously not in the interests of

---

[1] Jephson, *Diary*, p. 263.
[2] Statement of Basili Boktor, printed in *The New York Herald*, 5 May 1890. A copy of this statement is also in the Khartoum Archives, Cairint, 1/11/56.
[3] Casati, *Ten Years in Equatoria*, p. 338.
[4] Jephson, *Rebellion*, p. 31.
[5] Statement of Basili Boktor, cited above.

the Khedive or of the garrisons themselves and they seemed determined to bring about the evacuation of the province and to sell the
soldiers 'as slaves to the English'. The garrisons refused to believe
that the Egyptian Government could possibly wish to evacuate
Equatoria, and Emin came to be regarded as a traitor to the Khedive.[1]
The fear of being sold to the English perhaps reflects the additional
general fear of an Islamic society *vis-à-vis* a Christian power.

Rumours about the proposals which Stanley and Emin had discussed at Nsabe soon spread amongst the stations. Although these
rumours soon became wildly exaggerated and distorted, they initially came very close to the truth. On three separate occasions
Jephson was approached and asked whether those who withdrew
from Equatoria with Stanley's expedition would in fact not be taken
to Egypt but would be settled in some hospitable region of the East
African interior within easier reach of the sea.[2] 'The supposition that
treaties were entered into for the cession of the Province to strangers
very soon appeared a certainty not to be doubted,' states Casati.[3]

These rumours created a mounting distrust of Emin's authority
and intentions amongst the garrisons. Initially, they had been used
with particular virulence to stir up feelings of revolt by two of Emin's
Egyptian employees, 'Abd al-Wahhāb (whom Emin describes as
Adjutant-Major of the 2nd battalion) and Ahmad Mahmūd, a
one-eyed clerk, both of whom had been exiled to Equatoria for
taking part in the Arabist rebellion in Egypt.[4] These two men were
in large part responsible for initiating the train of events which was
to break out in rebellion during the next few months. Full of some
unrecorded personal grievances against Emin, they had visited Stanley
at Nsabe and complained to him about Emin's administration and
the general state of disorder and unrest within the province. Stanley—
who never mentioned the matter to Emin—had told them to for-
mulate their complaints in a petition to the Khedive when they
returned to Egypt. The two men had then left for Tunguru some time
before Stanley's departure. When Emin arrived at Tunguru with
Jephson on 3 June, on the first stage of his tour of the stations, he
found that the two men had been spreading rumours to the effect
that Stanley and his expedition were nothing but a group of ad-

---

[1] Statement of Basili Boktor, cited above. Also Statement of Osman Effendi
Latif, 9 July 1890, Khartoum Archives, Cairint 3/14/237.
[2] Jephson, *Rebellion*, pp. 53, 74-5.
[3] Casati, op. cit., p. 342.   [4] *Tagebücher*, 5 June 1888, iv. 126.

venturers and that they had certainly not come from Egypt. The letters they purported to bring from the Khedive and Nubar Pasha were forgeries. It was untrue that Khartoum had fallen to the Mahdists or that the Egyptian Government wanted to evacuate Equatoria. Stanley and Emin had merely plotted together to deceive the garrisons and to take them out of the country in order to hand them over as slaves to the English.[1] Sulaimān Agha, the governor of Tunguru station, had been absent, and with the support of several of the Egyptian officers and clerks in the station the two men had succeeded in forming 'a nice little plot', the object of which was to join forces with the rebellious soldiers of the 1st battalion at Rejaf, depose Emin, and replace him with a government of Egyptian officials. Emin was seriously disturbed to discover from some of the loyal Sudanese officials at Tunguru what had been going on and he determined to act sternly and at once. 'If I allowed such rumours to reach the north we would all be lost', he declared.[2] Ahmad Mahmūd was sent as a prisoner on the steamer to Dufile; 'Abd al-Wahhāb and the other conspirators were reduced in rank and placed under house arrest. Emin then addressed the rest of the garrison and urged them not to be led astray by such people. But the damage had already been done. Before the arrival of Emin and Jephson at Tunguru, the conspirators had written letters to the governors of the stations of Wadelai, Dufile, and Fabbo, spreading their inflammatory rumours about Stanley's expedition and Stanley's and Emin's intentions.[3] Emin and Jephson visited Wadelai and Dufile themselves and so at these stations they were able to scotch some of the rumours. But they did not visit Fabbo, where Fadl al-Mūlā had complete control over the garrison and where the rumours therefore went unchecked.

While Emin and Jephson were at Tunguru, Jephson read the letters from the Khedive and Nubar Pasha (translated into Arabic, through an interpreter) and Stanley's proclamation to the assembled garrison. He has left us a vivid description of the occasion—which was to be often repeated at the other stations:

The people were all drawn up in a long line, their guns were all bright and clean and they all had on their smartest clothes and were really a very fine looking lot of men. The whole thing looked very well, there were five Turkish flags flying and the trumpeters standing together in their bright red

---

[1] *Tagebücher*, 5 June 1888, iv. 126. Jephson, Diary, 17 June 1888. Vita Hassan, *Die Wahrheit über Emin Pasha*, ii. 141–2.
[2] *Tagebücher*, iv. 126.   [3] Loc. cit.

suits gave the whole thing a very gay appearance. As Emin Pasha and I approached, the flags were dipped and the trumpeters played the Khedivial Hymn. I then spoke to them and made them a short address and told them how the Expedition was got up and a few of our experiences on the road, and the reason why Stanley had sent me to speak to them and so forth. I then called upon the clerk of the station to read the Khedive's and Nubar Pasha's letters, which were in Arabic, and after he had finished reading them, I read them Stanley's letter and then spoke to them again. Numbers of the men made short speeches all expressive of their loyalty and devotion to their Pasha. The burden of their song was always the same: 'We will follow our Pasha wherever he goes.'[1]

The following day Jephson interviewed the officers and chief officials of the station privately. Sulaimān Agha, the governor of the station, and the chief officers were questioned about their intentions with regard to the future in the light of the Khedive's instructions. Jephson states that

they unanimously said, in answer to my question as to whether they had made up their minds, 'We will follow our Pasha.' I then talked to them and told them it was all very well for them to say that now but would they be prepared to say the same thing when it was time to start and they had to leave their houses and a great many of their things; they said 'Yes'. I also told them the road would be long and difficult and probably at times we should suffer from hunger but they said they had thought about it all and were prepared to carry out their words.[2]

The same answer was given by all the others whom Jephson interviewed. But Jephson was not deceived. He was convinced that 'the feeling in the station is not for going to Egypt' and felt that this 'augurs well for our Kavirondo plan'.[2] The Egyptians, however, were a different matter, and 'Emin thought they would go out under any circumstances'.[3]

On 25 June Emin and Jephson left Tunguru to march by land to Wadelai. Casati, who had recently quarrelled with Emin, remained behind at Tunguru and states that as soon as Emin and Jephson had departed, Sulaimān Agha threw off his pretence of loyalty and entered into active collaboration with Fadl al-Mūlā and the garrisons at the neglected eastern stations of Fabbo and Fatiko urging them to join him in 'resistance to the Christians' and to prevent 'the evils which the Pasha was about to let loose on the Province'.[4]

Meanwhile, Emin and Jephson went on to Wadelai. Jephson

[1] Jephson, *Diary*, p. 262. [2] Ibid. 263.
[3] Jephson, *Rebellion*, p. 52.
[4] Casati, *Ten Years in Equatoria*, pp. 346-7.

describes the countryside between Lake Albert and Wadelai in lyrical terms as wooded and well-watered with numerous villages surrounded by fields of grain with herds of goats grazing in the valleys. The contrast between this peaceful scene and his experiences hitherto on Stanley's expedition struck him forcibly.[1] When they reached Wadelai on 27 June Jephson was impressed by the neatness of the station, the well-dressed soldiers and officials, and the home-like appearance of Emin's house, where he was 'glad to see two book cases full of books'.[2] Here he met Signor Marco—a Greek merchant who, arriving on a trading visit some years previously, had become an enforced resident in Equatoria—and Emin's small daughter, Ferida, aged about four. 'She was a pretty little girl, not darker in complexion than her father, and greatly resembling him', noted Jephson. 'She was dressed picturesquely like a little Arab girl, but looked exceedingly delicate.'[3] Emin was surprised to receive a letter from Hāmad Agha, the Major of the 1st battalion at Rejaf, inform-ing him that he was on his way to Wadelai accompanied by Farāj Agha Ajok.[4] Hāmad Agha wrote to say that he had come in response to Emin's summons to apologize for his past conduct and to declare his loyalty. It seems more likely that, hearing of the arrival of a European expedition in the south, he had come to assess the implica-tions of this new development. Hāmad Agha had replaced Rihān Agha as Major of the 1st battalion in May 1886 on the latter's death. Jephson states that he was basically loyal to Emin but 'was quite unable to stem the tide of rebellion which had been stirred up by the Egyptian officers, and had simply been swept along, against his will, with the flood',[5] a verdict substantiated by Hawash Effendi, the governor of Dufile and head of the 2nd battalion, who certainly bore him no goodwill.[6]

When he arrived at Wadelai, Hāmad Agha told Jephson of the 'very bad state' of things at Rejaf:

He deplored the influence the Egyptian officers and clerks had always exercised in the country, and said that the whole of the mutiny against the

[1] See Jephson, MS. Diary, under 2 July 1888. An abbreviated version is in *Rebellion*, pp. 53–9.
[2] Jephson, *Diary*, p. 266.   [3] Jephson, *Rebellion*, p. 61.
[4] *Tagebücher*, 27 June 1888, iv. 136. Farāj Agha Ajok is the Ferritch Agha Ajoke whom Baker had promoted to the rank of corporal in 1872–3. See Sir S. Baker, *Ismailia* (London 1874) 2 vols., i. pp. 81, 298, 349.
[5] Jephson, *Rebellion*, p. 66.
[6] Hawash Effendi declared that Hāmad Agha had 'no influence with his officers or soldiers'. Jephson, *Rebellion*, p. 87.

Governor in Rejaf had been stirred up by an Egyptian officer, a certain
Mustapha Effendi, who had been sent up to the Province for being concerned in Arabi's rebellion. He spoke very highly of Emin, and said he had
always been most self-sacrificing to his people, but that he was not firm
enough with them.[1]

Emin received Hāmad Agha very coldly and at first refused to accept
the profuse apologies and excuses which Hāmad Agha and Farāj
Agha Ajok proffered for their past behaviour. But Emin soon gave in.
'I know quite well that severity is of no use with these people and
that in the end I must show mercy to them. They have been led astray
and are not rebels', he noted in his diary.[2] Hāmad Agha now asked
Emin to allow himself and his family to retire from Rejaf and come
to Wadelai where he would like to remain. 'He does not want to go
to Egypt, where he has no place of abode', Emin noted, 'and he
thinks the greater part of the officers and people will likewise object
to going to Egypt.'[3]

After Jephson had addressed and talked to the garrison at Wadelai,
as at Tunguru, he formed precisely the same opinion.[4] He told the
Egyptians, however, 'that it was an understood thing that they would
return to Egypt and in speaking to the people generally what [he
had to say] referred chiefly to the Sudanese, who had no ties with
Egypt'.[5] Jephson was asked so often about the rumours concerning
a proposal to evacuate Emin and his soldiers 'to some good country
within reach of the sea, and settle them there',[6] that he considered
making the Kavirondo proposal public. Emin, however, wished to
wait until they had visited the northern garrisons before he unfolded
his plans.[7] 'Of course I know he [Emin] has decided on the Kavirondo
scheme', noted Jephson in his diary, 'but until I have got the answer
of all the people about going to Egypt, he is not free to speak of the
project.'[8] Nevertheless, Jephson was deeply interested in Emin's
considerable stores of ivory which he thought 'would come in so
useful for founding the new State' under Mackinnon's auspices in
East Africa.[9] At Wadelai, Jephson found that 'only a small portion'
of Emin's total stocks of ivory amounted to several tons and he

[1] Jephson, *Rebellion*, p. 69.
[2] *Tagebücher*, 7 July 1888, iv. 138 (Extracts XI, p. 195).
[3] *Tagebücher*, 9 July 1888, iv. 138 (Extracts XI, p. 195).
[4] Jephson, *Rebellion*, p. 76.
[5] Jephson, *Diary*, p. 268.   [6] Jephson, *Rebellion*, p. 74.
[7] *Tagebücher*, 9 July 1888, iv. 138 (Extracts XI, p. 195).
[8] Jephson, MS. Diary, 9 July 1888.
[9] Ibid. 11 July 1888.

estimated that the total value of the ivory stored in Emin's various stations was about £112,250.[1] But the difficulties of transporting all this ivory were enormous and Jephson feared that most of it would 'have to be abandoned, as we could never carry it down to the coast'.[1]

On 14 July Emin and Jephson left Wadelai in the steamer for Dufile where they arrived the following day. As one of the oldest stations in the province, Dufile had, as Jephson remarked, 'a well-established air about it'.[2] The houses, divided by broad streets, were built of brick and surrounded by fruit trees; there were boat-building sheds (still equipped chiefly with the materials brought up by Baker) and a wharf running out into the river. In the central square was a raised platform, shaded by a giant fig tree, under which Baker, Gordon, Gessi, Junker, Prout, and Emin had 'sat and talked and had their coffee and cigarettes as they settled the affairs of the Province'.[3] Here also Jephson found a mosque and a school in charge of an Imam who had been banished to Equatoria after being implicated in a murder case in Egypt.[3] Dufile was the headquarters of the 2nd battalion whose commander, Hawash Effendi—an Egyptian—had been consistently favoured by Emin and had incurred universal dislike. He greatly distrusted the officers and soldiers of the 1st battalion and warned Emin and Jephson to be careful when they ventured among the stations between Dufile and Rejaf. Emin agreed not to go directly to Rejaf, but to wait at Kirri, two days' march to the south, while Hāmad Agha and a company of men went on to report on the situation. On 17 July Emin and Jephson set out overland 'to visit the northern stations'.[4]

North of Dufile conditions deteriorated. Cataracts in the Nile prevented the passage of steamers and so communications were much worse than those in the south. Many of the stations were small (e.g. Khor Ayu had a garrison of only twenty-five soldiers and two officers)[5] and in disrepair. The delight in flag-flying and military parades and drill which was so characteristic of the Sudanese in the southern stations disappeared. The officers and soldiers in these northern stations were untidy and had long ceased to be effectively under Emin's control. They preyed upon the local inhabitants and their cattle constantly, and Jephson was surprised to find that in this,

---

[1] Jephson, *Diary*, p. 267. *Rebellion*, p. 76.
[2] Jephson, *Diary*, p. 269.
[3] Ibid. Jephson, *Rebellion*, p. 83.
[4] Jephson, *Rebellion*, pp. 87-9.
[5] Ibid. 95.

the oldest part of the province, relations between the garrisons and the local people were openly hostile.

At Labore, Emin and Jephson encountered Selim Bey. This 'great, easy-going' Sudanese, well over 6 ft. tall and 'enormously fat and broad'[1] was described in congenial terms by all the Europeans who ever met him. He is in fact almost the only one of Emin's southern Sudanese officials about whom we know a good deal, and he was to play a prominent role in the affairs of Equatoria until his withdrawal with Lugard in 1891. He had been one of those who had visited Stanley's camp at Nsabe, he was to prove consistently loyal to Emin, and, like Hawash Effendi, he distrusted the officers and soldiers at Rejaf. It was arranged that at Labore, as at Khor Ayu, Muggi, and Kirri, Jephson should defer speaking to the garrisons until his return from Rejaf. Spending only one night in each of these stations, Emin and Jephson arrived at Kirri, the station two days' march from Rejaf, on 19 July. Here they had decided to rest for several days while Hāmad Agha, and the other officers of the 1st battalion who had come to see Emin at Wadelai, went on and reported on the situation at Rejaf.

Emin was, in fact, adopting precisely the same procedure as that which he had followed on his last visit to the northern stations the previous December. On that occasion, it will be remembered, he had been no further than Kirri, since, while there, he had been informed of a plot by the garrison at Rejaf to capture him, possibly to make an attempt on his life.[2]

A closely similar sequence now took place. Whilst Emin and Jephson remained at Kirri, Hāmad Agha set out for Rejaf to inform the rebellious officers of the 1st battalion that Emin was at Kirri.

. . . if they came and made their submission, we would forgive them on condition they handed over to him the officers who first instigated them to rebel. Should they refuse to do this, he would leave them to themselves, and retire the garrisons of Kirri, Muggi, Labore and Khor Ayu to his southern station, preparatory to leaving the country on Stanley's return.[3]

Jephson considered that whether the officers responded or not, Emin's future course was clear: if they refused to come to Kirri then Emin would simply abandon them, but 'if, on the other hand they obey, he will have the leaders of the rebellion in his hands and can deal with them as he thinks fit'.[4]

---

[1] Jephson, *Rebellion*, p. 95.
[2] See Ch. VII, p. 148 above.
[3] Jephson, *Rebellion*, p. 101.
[4] Jephson, MS. Diary, 20 July 1888.

On 29 July Emin received a letter from Hāmad Agha at Rejaf smuggled out of that station in the turban of a boatman. In this letter Hāmad Agha informed Emin that he himself had been made a virtual prisoner by his own officers who, he declared, 'have conspired to retain your Excellency here, should you honour this place with your presence. They do not intend to permit you to return, but propose to start by way of Gondokoro to rejoin their Government, which they are convinced still exists at Khartoum.'[1] The leaders among the rebellious officers at Rejaf were two Egyptians, 'Ali Agha Jabor and Mahmūd al-'Adanī, both of whom had taken part in Arabi's rebellion. When Emin had visited Kirri the previous December, with the intention of going to Rejaf to inform the 1st battalion that Khartoum had fallen to the Mahdists and Stanley's expedition was expected to arrive shortly, it had been Mahmūd who had declared that the news of the fall of Khartoum was untrue, the Khedive's letter was a forgery, and that Emin was a traitor. He had urged the other officers at Rejaf to go to Kirri and seize Emin, declaring 'We have rebelled against the Khedive, why should we be afraid of Emin Pasha?'[2] On that occasion, Emin had at once left Kirri to return to the south. All might yet have been well if he had again acted in a similar manner and retired from the scene. This was Emin's own immediate inclination but Jephson, ever anxious to do what he considered to be his duty, 'counselled prudence (!)', and suggested that they should remain at Kirri for a few days in the hope that the Rejaf officers would come to their senses. 'Should they still remain impossible', declared Jephson,

I will go by myself to Rejaf and speak with the people and will read them the letters we have brought from Egypt and Stanley's proclamation and will endeavour to bring them down here with me to make their submission. Should they refuse, no harm will be done and I shall have done my duty in visiting all the stations and garrisons. It is possible they might use violence to my person, but I hardly think it.[3]

Emin was strongly against the idea of Jephson 'going down alone into that nest of rebels', but he agreed to remain at Kirri for a few more days.[3]

It soon became apparent that in Kirri itself there had long existed feelings of incipient rebellion against Emin. Some months previously

---

[1] Jephson, *Rebellion*, p. 107. *Tagebücher*, 29 July 1888, iv. 145.
[2] Jephson, MS. Diary, 28–30 July 1888. *Tagebücher*, 27 July 1888, iv. 144.
[3] Jephson, MS. Diary, 28–30 July, 1888.

nearly half the garrison had deserted to join 'Ali Agha Jabor, in setting themselves up as 'robber chiefs' in the Makaraka area—long since quite beyond Emin's control. More recently, letters had arrived at the station from Ahmad Mahmūd, the one-eyed clerk whom Emin had sent from Tunguru to Dufile as a 'prisoner'. These letters contained the same seditious rumours that had already been spread to Fabbo, Fatiko, and elsewhere. Jephson was accused of being a tool put up by Emin and Stanley to deceive the garrisons. Stanley's expedition, it was alleged, had nothing to do with the Khedive or Egypt but was merely a bunch of travellers who had come from Uganda; 'had the expedition come from the Khedive', it was asserted, 'he would have sent 300 and not three soldiers only'.[1] Jephson was exasperated. 'Were there ever such stupid people', he wrote in his diary,

here we have come to help them and have brought them letters, ammunition, etc. and still they refuse to believe us and say 'We don't know you and don't believe you have come from Egypt'; even supposing we hadn't, what can it matter so that we have brought them help . . . I am becoming sick of having to explain who we are, it was a difficulty nobody, neither the promoters nor the members of this expedition, could have foreseen.[2]

Like a good Victorian, Jephson believed that if only he could explain sufficiently to the garrisons then the truth would prevail, doubt and disaffection would melt away, and Emin's soldiers would respond with gratitude and devotion. He therefore addressed the garrison at Kirri, reprimanded the men, reminded them of Emin's long and faithful dedication to their welfare, and indicated the bleak future that lay before them if they insisted on remaining after Stanley's expedition departed. Their ammunition would run out, the local people would attack them, their clothes would not last long, and they 'would return to the state from which the Pasha took them years ago'.[3] Everyone expressed themselves deeply moved by his words and declared that they were ready to follow Emin and 'to move south whenever he ordered them; they also begged to be taken away from the reach of the officers at Rejaf'.[3]

But when Emin ordered the ammunition of the station to be taken out of the store-house next morning, preparatory to departing for

---

[1] Jephson, *Rebellion*, p. 103.
[2] Jephson, MS. Diary, 28 July 1888. It was, of course, of vital interest to the garrisons in Equatoria whether or not Jephson and his expedition had come from Egypt.
[3] Ibid. 29 July 1888.

Muggi and the south, he encountered resolute opposition. Emin and Jephson had in fact already left the station, expecting the men and the ammunition to follow them. A messenger brought the news that the soldiers had refused to let the ammunition leave the station. Emin sent him back with orders for the ammunition to be sent on at once. Jephson felt that Emin should have gone back and supervised the matter himself—'that's what Stanley would have done'.[1] In any event, Emin's orders were ignored and the next day the Governor of the station wrote to Emin that the soldiers had been 'deeply incensed at the Pasha endeavouring to take the ammunition and declare they will not now come out but will join the rebels at Rejaf'.[1] Two days later, the rebels at Rejaf came down to join the garrison at Kirri, seized the ammunition and planned to depart with it and some of the garrison back to Rejaf.[2] On receiving this news at Muggi, Emin was greatly distressed. Several pages of Emin's diary are curiously missing at this point,[3] but from Jephson's account it is clear that Emin was very agitated. He came to Jephson in the middle of the night and sought his advice. Jephson at first responded with a wild plan (later omitted from his book) whereby he and Emin should take a body of soldiers, return to Kirri, seize the rebellious officers and return with the ammunition to Muggi. Emin objected to this plan 'on the grounds that he could not be certain of his soldiers'.[4] It was therefore decided to send a party of soldiers back to Kirri with a letter from Emin urging those who wished to follow him to do so while those who did not could remain where they were. Very few of the soldiers at Kirri, and none of the officers, took the opportunity of following Emin and Jephson on their return to the south.

Emin now decided that the remaining stations between Kirri and Dufile should in turn be evacuated and burnt so that all the loyal soldiers could be concentrated in the southern stations on the navigable riverain stretch between Wadelai and Dufile and all communication with the rebels at Rejaf would be severed. At Muggi, he encountered a ready response to this plan, but this may well have been the result of a development from a quite new quarter.

While at Muggi, Emin received the first news of the beginnings of a new Mahdist attack on Equatoria. At first the news was scarcely

[1] Ibid. 31 July 1888.   [2] *Tagebücher*, 1 Aug. 1888, iv. 147–8.
[3] See the note by the editor, Stuhlmann, *Tagebücher*, iv. 150.
[4] Jephson, MS. Diary, 2 Aug. 1888.

a portent of what was to come. Hawash Effendi, the governor of Dufile and commander of the 2nd battalion, wrote to say that a party which he had sent to collect grain tax from the Acholi to the east of the Nile had returned with the information that a party of Danāqla had arrived in the Latuka country with a large band of armed followers. Hawash Effendi concluded his message to Emin by expressing the hope that this party might have come from the Khedive's government in Khartoum. 'Observe the awful stupidity of these people', expostulated Jephson; 'they cannot get it into their heads, or rather we cannot knock it into their heads, that Khartoum has fallen; Hawash Effendi has himself seen Stanley at Nsabe and heard from him all about affairs and yet he still harps on the subject of Khartoum.'[1]

Emin and Jephson were quite convinced that this news indicated a renewal of Mahdist interest in the area and greatly feared that if the party in the Latuka area formed a settlement, this would become 'an asylum for all the disaffected people in the province'. Emin, Jephson reported, 'thinks that the Rejaf officers are almost certain to go over when they hear the news, but he thinks the soldiers will not do so for in all probability their guns, women and children would be confiscated and they themselves made slaves'.[2]

Emin used the possibility of an impending Mahdist attack to urge the evacuation of Muggi. Before he and Jephson left for Labore on 12 August, most of the ammunition, women and children, and half of the garrison had already been sent ahead to Dufile.

It had been the intention of Emin and Jephson, after their arrival at Labore, to spend only two days there before hurrying south to Wadelai. Nearly three months had passed since they had parted from Stanley, and Jephson was anxious to send news to Fort Bodo and prepare the people in the south for Stanley's return. All this, however, now came to an abrupt halt. On 13 August Emin and Jephson assembled the garrison to address them in the manner followed in the other stations. We have several accounts of precisely what happened[3] and they all agree with that of Jephson, who wrote:

I read the Khedive's and Stanley's letters, and explained as usual everything connected with the Expedition. Whilst I was speaking I noticed that

[1] Jephson, MS. Diary, 4 Aug. 1888.
[2] Ibid. also *Tagebücher*, 4 Aug. 1888, iv. 149–50.
[3] *Tagebücher*, 13 Aug. 1888, iv. 150–1. Vita Hassan, *Die Wahrheit über Emin Pasha*, ii. 146–7. Statement of 'Uthmān Latīf, Khartoum archives, Cairint 3/14/237.

the soldiers were not as attentive as was generally the case, and that there was a good deal of whispering going on amongst them . . . there was an uneasy stir amongst them as if something unusual was going to happen. After I had finished speaking, Emin, as was his custom, added a few words to what I had said. Whilst he was speaking, a big bull-headed, sullen-looking Soudanese stepped out of the ranks, and exclaimed, 'All you have been telling us is a lie, and the letter you have read out is a forgery, for if it had come from Effendina he would have *commanded* us to come, and not have told us we might do as we pleased. You do not come from Egypt, we know only one road to Egypt and that is by Khartoum, we will either go by that road, or will live and die in this country.' Emin instantly sprang forward and seized him and, trying to wrench his gun out of his hand, shouted to his four orderlies to arrest the man and carry him off to prison. A struggle then ensued, and the mutineer shouted to his companions to help him . . . The soldiers, breaking from the ranks, dashed at Emin and me with loaded guns and surrounded us. Shouts of hate and execration were hurled at us as the mutineers hemmed us in with guns pointed at us . . . For a second it seemed to me that this was to be the ending of all our long struggle to rescue Emin Pasha . . .[1]

Selim Bey, the governor of the station, intervened and with the help of one or two other officers managed to quieten the men. He asked Emin and Jephson to withdraw outside the station, which they did. The life at the station soon returned to normal.

The first thing to be emphasized about this incident is that it was a spontaneous response by the soldiers of the station to the attempt by Emin to disarm one of their colleagues. This was made plain to Jephson when he interviewed the men later; it was Emin Pasha, they felt, who had precipitated the crisis.[1] But if the immediate cause had lain in Emin's unpremeditated action, the incident had also revealed a deep distrust of Emin's authority and a complete disbelief in everything that Emin and Jephson had to say about the situation in Egypt, the fall of Khartoum, and the purpose of the relief expedition. As far as the garrisons of Emin's remaining stations were concerned, nothing had changed since 1885. They continued to consider themselves as the employees of the Khedive; they still looked to steamers from Khartoum to bring them reinforcements and relief; they would certainly resist any attempt to make them withdraw to the south. Against this implacable disbelief and resolute opposition, the letters of Sir Evelyn Baring and Nubar Pasha, the repeated instructions of the Khedive, and the exhortations of Emin,

---

[1] Jephson, *Rebellion*, pp. 145-7. Also, Jephson, MS. Diary, under 13 Aug. 1888.

Q

Stanley, and Jephson were to be of no avail. From the point of view of the garrisons, all that had happened since 1885 was that a small band of travellers had arrived at Lake Albert from the west and had departed again, leaving one European and three soldiers with Emin Pasha. Emin Pasha was evidently very friendly with them and wished to leave the country by a route to the south. He did not command his garrisons to follow him, but left them the choice of remaining where they were; and that was what most of them intended to do.[1]

The day after the incident at Labore, Emin and Jephson left for Dufile, unaccompanied by most of the garrison. Selim Bey, however, had already had most of his goods transported to Dufile and Jephson felt certain that he would follow. About the others 'who, with the fairest words on their tongues, will be thinking and plotting the blackest things in their hearts' he felt 'terribly sceptical'.[2]

On the way to Dufile, Emin and Jephson stayed at the small station of Khor Ayu and it was here on the evening of 18 August that Emin received a letter from Hawash Effendi, announcing that a rebellion had broken out in Dufile. Led by Fadl al-Mūlā and two other officers, sixty soldiers had arrived from the station of Fabbo. They had liberated all the prisoners (including Ahmad Mahmūd), seized the stores and ammunition, and roused the soldiers at Dufile into rebellion. Fadl al-Mūlā had told them that they were fools to listen to Emin and Jephson, the letters from the Khedive were forgeries, there was only one route to Egypt and that lay to the north via Khartoum, etc. The officers and some of the soldiers at Dufile had readily joined in the rebellion and Hawash Effendi had been made a prisoner in his own house.[3] 'This is terrible news', declared Jephson, 'for here we are caught in a trap completely. Rejaf at one end, Dufile at the other and Labore in between, it is quite possible and indeed probable that we shall be made prisoners by these people.'[4]

Emin at once wrote to Selim Bey at Labore asking him to come immediately. Meanwhile, messengers were seen coming from Dufile and carefully avoiding the station of Khor Ayu on their way to Rejaf where Emin presumed that their object was to summon the chief

---

[1] For the situation as it was seen by some of Emin's troops, see especially Statement of Basili Boktor; statement of 'Uthmān Latīf; Report of the officers, soldiers and officials stationed in the Equatorial Province 1890. Khartoum Archives, Cairint 1/11/56.   [2] Jephson, MS. Diary, 14 Aug. 1888.
[3] *Tagebücher*, 17 Aug. 1888, iv. 153–4.
[4] Jephson, *Diary*, pp. 281–2.

rebel officers to Dufile.[1] Selim Bey arrived the following day and the decision was made to move on to Dufile. On 19 August, Emin, Jephson, and Vita Hassan, accompanied by Selim Bey and a small escort entered Dufile. The garrison was not drawn up as usual and Emin and his party entered the station in silence and made their way to Emin's compound. 'As soon as we entered our houses eight sentries were posted at the gate of our compound and so we are now prisoners', wrote Jephson.[2]

*   *   *

The rebellion at Dufile, like the incident at Labore, had an immediate cause which evoked a general response because it occurred in a situation of deep-seated and long-standing grievance. The immediate cause had been the arrival of Fadl al-Mūlā and the sixty soldiers from Fabbo and their whipping up of feelings of rebellion. They in turn had been aroused by the rumours concerning Stanley's expedition and Emin's future intentions which had been spread from Tunguru by 'Abd al-Wahhāb and Ahmad Mahmūd. Thus, the arrival of Stanley's expedition had precipitated a crisis in Equatoria. This crisis stemmed less from the sense of anti-climax and disappointment which the actual appearance of the expedition had aroused, than from the fact that Stanley's influence on Emin had been to force him to abandon the attitude of adapting himself to circumstances which had hitherto made possible his survival, and to oblige him to adopt a concrete plan of action with regard to the future. Ultimately, the rebellion was caused not by the general disbelief in Stanley's expedition and its credentials but by the fear that Stanley and Emin intended to compel the garrisons to withdraw from Equatoria. In the letter which he had managed to write to Emin from Dufile, Hawash Effendi put the case most clearly. He wrote

that he thought the people were afraid their Governor would compel them to leave the country, and that the mischief [i.e. the rebellion] had arisen from this misconception. He added, it had long been plain to him that, with the exception of a very few people, no-one really wished to leave the country; they were much too comfortable where they were.[3]

With this verdict both Emin and Jephson came to agree. There seems, nevertheless, to have been serious misjudgement on Emin's part in

---

[1] *Tagebücher*, 19 Aug. 1888, iv. 155.

[2] Jephson, *Diary*, p. 282. *Tagebücher*, 19 Aug. 1888, iv. 155.

[3] Jephson, *Rebellion*, p. 156. The text of the letter is given in German in *Tagebücher*, 20 Aug. 1888, iv. 156.

thinking that the garrisons would ever be persuaded to withdraw. He had known only too well of the implacable resistance with which his plans for a retreat to the south had been consistently met during the last three years. Yet until the very end he continued to believe that if only the Khedive's letter had been firm, clear, and less ambiguous, all would have been well.

The rebellion of his garrisons against him came as a genuine surprise and shock to Emin Pasha. For years he had cast himself in the paternal role of their guardian and adviser; he had kept from others, almost kept from himself, their many failings; he had devoted himself to their welfare and to the gradual development of Equatoria. Now, suddenly, he found himself regarded as an irrelevance. All the thought and planning and ambitions which he had had for the future had taken place in a context far removed from the reality of the situation in Equatoria where the essential factor was the refusal of the garrisons to move. Emin, as usual, suppressed his bitter feeling of disappointment even from his diary. But Jephson noted that he was 'terribly cut up at the idea of the people for whom he has worked so long turning against him in this way'.[1]

> He has with despair and indignation seen all his best efforts for the good of his province clogged and nullified by the shameful policy of his government at Khartoum and for the last five years since he has been cut off from Egypt it has been all he could do to hold his own against his enemies and to clothe and look after the people under his care . . . He is now in such a state of nervous exhaustion that he is unable to sleep and his heart gives him a great deal of trouble and anxiety. Unless he goes to a colder climate he says he does not give himself more than three years of life—he is now only 48.[2]

The rebellion at Dufile, though precipitated by the arrival of Stanley's expedition, had other long-standing causes. There is little suggestion of any personal animosity against Emin himself—the evidence is rather to the contrary.[3] But there was deep dislike for certain officers who had been consistently favoured and promoted by Emin. The chief target was Hawash Effendi, the erstwhile governor of Dufile and commander of the 2nd battalion, but there were others of lesser positions, and Vita Hassan was singled out and accused of spying on the garrisons and spreading lies about them.[4] There is no

[1] Jephson, MS. Diary, 18 Aug. 1888.   [2] Jephson, *Diary*, p. 276.
[3] Jephson, MS. Diary, 20 Aug. 1888.
[4] *Tagebücher*, 19 Aug. 1888, iv. 155–6.

doubt that Hawash Effendi was intensely disliked—accusations and vituperation against him occupy a prominent place in the statements that we have by Emin's officers and soldiers.[1] He was accused of using his position for personal aggrandisement, of seizing women, cattle, and other property unlawfully. Emin had long known of his unpopularity and had received repeated accusations against him but he had refused to take any action against him.

The day after Emin and Jephson arrived at Dufile, Emin was presented by the rebels with a list of three demands. First, Hawash Effendi was to be dismissed; second, 'the people are not willing to leave here'; third, the prisoners (including Ahmad Mahmūd) whom the rebels had released, were to be reinstated in their former positions.[2] Emin was forced to accept these demands. During the following days Hawash Effendi's house was rigorously searched, he was stripped of all but the most basic possessions, and he himself was kept a closely guarded prisoner—but not, it seems, otherwise ill treated.[3]

Emin's party was not ill treated. Their movements were restricted (Emin never left his house) but Vita Hassan and Selim Bey acted as frequent go-betweens for Emin and Jephson with the rebel officers. Jephson was left free to wander about the station, but he was unable to obtain much information as he spoke no Arabic; Binza, the young man who accompanied Jephson as a servant on Stanley's expedition, had previously worked for Junker, and he acted as an active informant. The rebel officers, states Jephson, 'said they had personally nothing against me, except that I was an envoy of Stanley, and was helping the Pasha and him to carry out their plans of forcing the people to leave the Province, but they supposed I was only obeying orders'.[4] During the ensuing weeks Jephson was to make great play of Muslim hospitality and of his status as a 'guest'.

Having arrested Emin and Jephson, the immediate action of the mutineers was to summon the rebel officers at Rejaf to a council to be held at Dufile. Messages were also sent ordering the governors and chief officers of the southern stations to come to Dufile, but none of them appears to have responded. The rebel officers of the 1st Battalion at Rejaf set out for Dufile at once. There is some evidence that

[1] See especially the Statements of 'Uthmān Latīf and Basili Boktor, Khartoum archives, Cairint 3/14/237 and 1/11/56.
[2] Tagebücher, 20 Aug. 1888, iv. 156 (Extracts XII, p. 156).
[3] Jephson, MS. Diary, 20 Aug.–5 Sept. 1888.
[4] Jephson, Rebellion, p. 164.

conditions at Rejaf had in any case become so precarious that the officers were only too ready to seize the opportunity to move their headquarters to the south. Rejaf was in the Bari country; relations with the local people had been consistently hostile and, in the past, food supplies had had to be brought from Lado. Since Emin's move to the south, food had been obtained from the Makaraka area (also in rebel hands) but this source had proved erratic and unreliable. At the same time, attacks on the station by the Bari had increased.

Before the officers arrived from Rejaf, however, news was received at Dufile from Tunguru and Mswa that Stanley had returned with his expedition to Lake Albert. This news arrived on 26 August and it eventually proved to be quite false. But it brought about an immediate effect on the rebels. Stanley was rumoured to have returned with a great force, including three elephants and a large boat! At first the rebels considered sending an expedition 'to seize Stanley and take all his guns and ammunition', but they were deterred by rumours of the strength of Stanley's force.[1] It was decided to defer action until the arrival of the party from Rejaf. Selim Bey managed to pass on the gist of this news to Emin and Jephson, who were greatly excited and at once discussed the strategy they would adopt when the council met.[2]

The party from Rejaf arrived at Dufile on 31 August. Amongst the people were Hāmad Agha (commander of the 1st battalion who had left Emin and Jephson at Kirri), Farāj Agha Ajok, Bakhīt Agha (the governor of Muggi station), and Surūr Agha (governor of Labore), together with several Egyptian clerks and sixty soldiers drawn from the northern stations.[3] The next day, the council—which was to go on intermittently for many weeks—began.

This council consisted of the long-rebellious officers of the 1st battalion, and the more recent rebels of the 2nd battalion led by Fadl al-Mūlā. The two groups appear to have combined their forces with little difficulty and to have shared similar objectives with regard to the future. The council included all those named above, although Hāmad Agha appears to have occupied a somewhat ambiguous position. He intervened several times on Emin's behalf but he was aligned too emphatically and too consistently with the deliberations of the rebels to merit the judgement that he was simply swayed by

[1] Jephson, MS. Diary, 26–9 Aug. 1888.
[2] Ibid. Also *Tagebücher*, 29–30 Aug. 1888, iv. 159–60 (Extracts XII, p. 157).
[3] Jephson, *Diary*, p. 283.

their influence. Of great importance in the whole proceedings were the Egyptian clerks. While most of the officers were Egyptian or northern Sudanese, very few of them were literate, and they were therefore dependent on the clerks. Emin had always regarded these clerks as Jephson now did, as 'the curse of the province'. They were mostly convicted murderers or felons, the scum of Egyptian society, who had been deported to Equatoria and through their skill in reading and writing had managed to establish for themselves a privileged position there which they would never have held in Egypt. They were therefore deeply opposed to any scheme for their repatriation and Emin seems to have been seeking a fulfilment of his own wishes rather than representing their actual inclinations when he had consistently urged their return to Egypt.

The council was thus chiefly composed of officers and clerks. A word needs to be said about the position of the soldiers. Unlike most of the officers and clerks, the soldiers were overwhelmingly southern Sudanese. The rebellion had been provoked and led by a handful of disaffected Egyptian and northern Sudanese officers and clerks. The soldiers played almost no active part in the entire proceedings. Most of them acquiesced, a few resisted, practically all of them deeply disliked the rebel officers and refused to recognize the powers and positions they now gave themselves. Many of the soldiers appear to have been genuinely devoted to Emin, as the representative of the Khedive, but they distrusted Stanley's mission, suspected the influence of Emin's new-found European friend, and had no wish to evacuate Equatoria. They had fought valiantly and much more determinedly against the Mahdists than their officers had done, and they were to do so again. So long as the rebel officers left them alone, the soldiers acquiesced in the proceedings at Dufile; but when pressure was put on them they threatened to desert to their home areas, and when some of their number were arrested and imprisoned at Dufile, they demanded and obtained their release.[1] As time went on, the rift between the officers and soldiers at Dufile widened, and on this Emin and Jephson built most of their hopes for the future.

One of the first actions of the council was to interrogate the two soldiers belonging to Stanley's expedition who had accompanied

---

[1] Jephson, MS. Diary, Aug.–Sept. 1888. *Tagebücher*, Sept. 1888, iv. 160–5. Vita Hassan, *Die Wahrheit über Emin Pasha*, ii, ch. xii. Report of the officers, soldiers and officials stationed in the Equatoria Province, 1890, cited above.

Jephson on his tour of the stations. The rebel officers accused them of being not soldiers at all but merely vagabonds whom Stanley had picked up in Uganda. The two soldiers replied that they were the Khedive's soldiers and could prove it by being put through their drill. On being tested, they acquitted themselves well. Jephson was then interviewed, his chief interrogators being Fadl al-Mūlā and ʿAli Agha Jabor; neither Hāmad Agha nor Selim Bey were present. During the course of this interview Jephson obtained a fair indication of the main grievances of the rebels. Foremost was their hatred of Hawash Effendi; they were incensed against Emin for having upheld him for so long but declared that 'except for this, they had nothing against him'.[1] Emin's attempt to remove the ammunition from Muggi and evacuate the station had, however, aroused the greatest fears among the officers of the 1st battalion that this was a plot by Emin in alliance with Hawash Effendi 'to carry away all the ammunition and leave them stranded and helpless in the country at the mercy of the natives'.[2] To counter this, Jephson produced the Arabic versions of the letters from the Khedive, Nubar Pasha, and Stanley, and handed them to one of the clerks to read aloud 'so that the people might see that there was no wish on the part of Effendina or their Governor to force them to leave the country if they preferred to remain where they were'.[3] After comparing the Khedive's signature with that on other documents, the officers appeared convinced and they told Jephson that as Stanley was reported to have returned, they planned to send the steamer down to Lake Albert and 'invite Stanley to come up with his officers to Dufile and they would then hold a consultation with him'.[4] Jephson feared that this was simply a ruse to lure Stanley into a trap and he pointed out that Stanley would never agree to come unless he or Emin were there to reassure him. After much debate it was decided that whilst Emin remained at Dufile, Jephson would be allowed to accompany the steamer to the south to inquire after Stanley's whereabouts. Jephson was confident that if he could only join forces with Stanley, Stanley could seize the steamer, hold the rebel officers on board it as hostages and 'concert measures for the safety and delivery of the Pasha'. Jephson felt that Stanley's 'white hair and firm, inscrutable face will be as good as a regiment of cavalry'.[5] Emin was greatly relieved to hear that

---

[1] Jephson, *Diary*, p. 284.   [2] Jephson, *Rebellion*, p. 178.
[3] Ibid. 177.   [4] Jephson, *Diary*, p. 285.
[5] Jephson, MS. Diary, 1 Sept. 1888.

Jephson was to be allowed to go to the south but felt the greatest foreboding for his own future and for that of Vita Hassan who was also to remain at Dufile.[1]

On 3 September the *Khedive* departed for Wadelai and the south with Jephson on board alongside eight officers, one clerk, and sixty-five soldiers, and Stanley's steel boat, the *Advance*, which was to be left at Wadelai. Jephson was ill with fever, the heat was intense, and he found the voyage 'a very hell' but the following day the steamer reached Wadelai. Here the rebel officers did not receive a very enthusiastic reception. When they tried to take the ammunition from the store-house for transport to Dufile, they met with strong opposition. There were conferences and quarrels, and in the end half the ammunition was left at Wadelai. Jephson was occupied packing up Emin's journals and collections 'ready to take them to Stanley'. Some of the Wadelai soldiers came and told him that they would all 'be glad when Stanley comes and alters the position of things'.[2] Kodi Agha, the governor, was, however, cowed by the rebel officers and when they, together with Jephson, left Wadelai on 8 September for Lake Albert, he accompanied them. At Tunguru Jephson met Casati, who had little to report and who was greatly depressed at the news of events at Dufile. Since their quarrel in June, Emin and Casati had neither spoken nor communicated with each other, but Jephson now found that 'Casati seemed to forget all about it now that Emin was in trouble'.[3] No further information had been obtained about the alleged arrival of Stanley, and it was now assumed that the rumour had been quite false. Jephson was so ill with fever that he was left at Tunguru with Casati whilst the rebel officers went on in the *Khedive* to visit Mswa. When they returned on 17 September they brought with them the thirty-one boxes of ammunition which Stanley had brought for Emin Pasha and two boxes of ammunition for Winchester rifles which Stanley had asked Emin to store at Mswa until his return.[4] Jephson was unable to do anything about the former but he managed to reclaim the latter; as the rifles used in the province were Remingtons this was not much of a loss to the rebels.

Before leaving Tunguru the rebel officers addressed the garrison, proclaiming a new government and the deposition of Emin Pasha. 'The crowd applauded', wrote Casati, 'but more for the change,

---

[1] Ibid. Also *Tagebücher*, 1 Sept. 1888, iv. 160.
[2] Jephson, MS. Diary, 5 Sept. 1888. [3] Jephson, *Rebellion*, p. 195.
[4] Jephson, MS. Diary, 17 Sept. 1888.

which opened the way to individual licence, than on account of sincere conviction.'[1] When Sulaimān Agha, the governor, remonstrated with the rebels, he was removed from office, beaten and imprisoned. Shukri Agha, the governor of Mswa, had been rather more astute. On hearing of the impending arrival of the rebels, he had left the station under the pretext of going to collect grain tax from the surrounding population, telling his clerk to let him know when the rebels had gone.[2] On 18 September the whole party, together with Jephson and Casati, set out on the journey back to Dufile.

At Dufile, Jephson found Emin fairly well, but in very low spirits. He had been kept virtually ignorant of what was happening in the station, but from the noise had guessed that the rebels had spent most of the time drinking.[3]

On 24 September, the council resumed. All the government books had been assembled and copies of the letters and reports which Emin had sent, or retained in the hope of sending to Khartoum, were read out. 'The people expected to find that he had written badly of them and were considerably surprised to find that he had only written of his people in the highest terms', observed Jephson.[4] When Emin's personal accounts were investigated, everything was found to be scrupulously correct. At no point was Emin accused of abusing his position. This, however, did not prevent the clerks from drawing up a document accusing Emin of betraying the Khedive, conspiring with Stanley and the English, and forging letters and instructions from Egypt. On 27 September Emin was compelled to sign a paper which declared that he was deposed and no longer held any appointment in the province. Hāmad Agha was appointed chief administrator of Equatoria in Emin's place; 'Abd al-Wahhāb became commander of the 1st battalion and Selim Bey commander of the 2nd.[5] Hāmad Agha, Selim Bey, and 'Uthmān Latīf none the less appear to have continued to intercede on Emin's behalf with Fadl al-Mūlā and the chief rebels.[6] Many of the soldiers at Dufile

---

[1] Casati, *Ten Years in Equatoria*, p. 361.

[2] Jephson, *Rebellion*, p. 201.

[3] *Tagebücher*, 3–23 Sept. 1888, iv. 162–3. See also Vita Hassan, *Die Wahrheit über Emin Pasha*, ii. 160–9.

[4] Jephson, MS. Diary, 24 Sept. 1888.

[5] *Tagebücher*, 25–7 Sept. 1888, iv. 163–4. Jephson, *Rebellion*, pp. 214–15.

[6] Hāmad Agha, Jephson wrote, 'though he is, I know, the nominal head of the present government, never leaves his house hardly and strongly expresses his disapproval of what is going on to the officers, but is powerless to do anything'. Jephson, MS. Diary, 8 Oct. 1888.

refused 'to have anything to do with the new order of things', but Emin was convinced that 'all the Egyptians, clerks, etc. are against me'.[1] Emin feared that the rebels would send him as a prisoner to Rejaf and he threatened to kill himself if they attempted to do so.[2] In a mood of deepest despondency Emin made his will providing for the care of his daughter, Ferida, and entrusted the document to Jephson.[3] But having deposed Emin and confiscated the property of Hawash Effendi, the rebel council soon lost its way in dissension. 'The people now have become completely demoralised, each has an idea of his own and nobody obeys orders from anyone; it is all anarchy and confusion', wrote Jephson in October.[4] The soldiers became increasingly restive and some of them came out openly in support of Emin Pasha, declaring that if he 'was not again reinstated, they would take their weapons and go home' to their own areas.[5] It was amidst this confused situation that, on 15 October, a soldier arrived from Rejaf with the news of a new Mahdist attack on Equatoria.[6]

* * *

After Karam Allāh had withdrawn from Equatoria and the Bahr al-Ghasal in 1885, the Mahdi, and his successor the Khalifa, had shown no further interest in the south. They were occupied with the internal changes within the Mahdist state in the Sudan which took place after the Mahdi's death and with campaigns against Abyssinia and Egypt.[7] The evidence in the Mahdist archives suggests that the event which reawakened a Mahdist interest in Equatoria in 1888 was the arrival of Stanley's relief expedition in the south.[8] The news that 'a strong expedition led by Europeans' had arrived in Equatoria alarmed the Khalifa and aroused fears of an attack on the Mahdist state from

[1] *Tagebücher*, 29 Sept.–1 Oct. 1888, iv. 165 (Extracts XII, pp. 159–60).
[2] Ibid., 10 Oct. 1888, iv. 168. Jephson, *Diary*, pp. 291–2.
[3] A typescript copy of this, translated from the Arabic, is in the Jephson Papers, the Sudan Archives, Durham, Box 14/1 on microfilm. For a note about this and Emin's later will, see Sir John Gray in *The Uganda Journal*, vol. xxxi, no. 2 (1967), 167–8.   [4] Jephson, *Diary*, p. 293.
[5] *Tagebücher*, 7 Oct. 1888, iv. 167 (Extracts XII, p. 161). Jephson, MS. Diary, 7–8 Oct. 1888.
[6] Ibid. 15 Oct. 1888.
[7] See P. M. Holt, *The Mahdist State in the Sudan*, pp. 117–56.
[8] I am greatly indebted in the following pages to the work of R. O. Collins, *The Southern Sudan 1883–1898* (Yale University Press, 1962), esp. ch. 2.

the south.[1] He therefore ordered that an expedition under the command of 'Umar Sālih should be dispatched to Equatoria. The objective, as in 1884–5, was to end the last vestige of the Khedive's government in the area—which others might seek to utilize and to develop—and most particularly to capture Emin Pasha. The sending of the expedition under 'Umar Sālih was, as Collins observes, a political decision based on reports that Europeans had returned to Equatoria and not a religious decision to spread Mahdism in the southern Sudan.[2]

In October 1888 'Umar Sālih wrote to the Khalifa from Equatoria

We will do our best to capture Emin, no matter how much he tries to escape, we will either kill him or capture him . . . As Emin and his Arab and Christian followers are the main concern, I have postponed the question of the negroes . . . who are not completely loyal at the moment and their country is very large and they are very well armed . . . When we get hold of Emin we will treat the question of the negroes.[3]

There is no suggestion that the ivory which was known to exist in Emin's stations played any part in the Khalifa's deliberations. Nor would the Mahdists appear to have obtained large numbers of slaves for the *jihadiya* from Emin's province. Rather, Equatoria soon took on the role for the Mahdists which it had occupied under the Turkiyya. Slatin wrote that after the capture of Rejaf it 'became a colony for the deportation of convicts and of persons whose presence in Omdurman was considered dangerous by the state'.[4]

Leaving Omdurman on 11 June 1888 with three steamers, six barges, and 1,500 *ansār* (armed followers), 'Umar Sālih experienced great difficulties in transporting his expedition to the south.[5] Near Shambe a block in the river had induced a section of the expedition to march overland into the Latuka country and it was about the

[1] See especially Statement of Mohammad Bornawi, 17 Feb. 1889, Khartoum Archives, Cairint 1/11/56, and Report on Emin Pasha by H. G. Dunning (of Wingate's Intelligence Dept. in Cairo), 17 Feb. 1889, Cairint 3/10/191.
[2] R. O. Collins, op. cit., p. 56.
[3] 'Umar Sālih to the Khalifa, Safar 21, 1306 (27 Oct. 1888), Khartoum Archives, Mahdiya 1/33/12. I am most grateful to Miss Maymouna Mirghani Hamza of the Sudan Research Unit, Khartoum, and to Mr. Kamal Abu Deeb of the Oriental Institute, Oxford, for this and other translations from the Arabic.
[4] R. Slatin, *Fire and Sword in the Sudan* (London 1896), p. 470, cited in R. O. Collins, op. cit., p. 58.
[5] A member of the expedition, Mohammad Bornawi, later gave an account of its progress to General Wingate's Intelligence Dept. in Cairo. This account, dated 17 Feb. 1889, is at present in English translation in the Khartoum Archives, Cairint 1/11/56.

activities of this party that Emin and Jephson had heard rumours in August.[1] When 'Umar Sālih and his force had finally reached Lado on 11 October, they found it completely deserted. Unable to proceed further south by steamer because the river was very low,[2] 'Umar Sālih decided to send three *ansār* to Dufile with letters calling on Emin to surrender.[3] These letters arrived at Dufile on 17 October in the hands of three peacock Dervishes (so called by Emin's people because of their distinctive dress of a long white *jibba* covered with coloured patches.[4]

The news of a new Mahdist advance on the province threw the council at Dufile into a panic. The rebel officers now became 'paralysed with fear and knew not what to do'. Some appeared ready to submit to the Mahdists; others planned to go off to the Makaraka country. The soldiers refused to fight under their officers unless Emin was reinstated. Jephson felt that the situation was 'well nigh desperate unless Stanley returns very quickly for the Pasha does not think the soldiers will stand a second war with the rebels, they will merely run'.[5]

The letters from 'Umar Sālih addressed to Emin were at first held by Fadl al-Mūlā, and the three peacock Dervishes from 'Umar Sālih were imprisoned and tortured. The soldiers at Dufile, however, were 'in an intensely excited state and went in a body to the rebels' compound and insisted on Fadl al-Mūlā's appealing to the *mudir* [Emin] to help them in their need'.[6] Convinced at last that Khartoum really was in Mahdist hands, that the way to the north was closed, and that much might depend in the future on obtaining the help of Stanley's expedition, Fadl al-Mūlā and the chief rebel officers went to Emin with the letters from 'Umar Sālih and sought his advice.

The chief letter, a very long one from 'Umar Sālih himself, follows typical Mahdist lines. It consists of a record of the successive Mahdist victories, expressed in the stereotyped phraseology used for propaganda, and a summons to Emin to join the ranks of the

[1] See p. 224 above.
[2] The Nile in the summer of 1888 reached the lowest level on record. This was noted by Emin and Jephson in Equatoria and by many officials in Cairo. In England there were a series of letters to *The Times* about it. See *The Times*, 9, 17, 25 Oct. 1888.
[3] 'Umar Sālih to the Khalifa, n.d. (1888), Mahdiya 1/33/22. R. O. Collins, op. cit., p. 60.
[4] For a detailed description of their dress see Jephson, *Rebellion*, pp. 243-4.
[5] Jephson, MS. Diary, 15-17 Oct. 1888.
[6] Jephson, *Rebellion*, p. 245.

faithful. Emin was reminded, in language reminiscent of Ecclesiastes, that 'the world is a house of change and decay, and everything in it must one day perish'. For the benefit of his future life he was invited to submit his present one at once to the Mahdi (who was now dead) whom 'Umar Sālih declared 'we have found . . . more compassionate to us than a pitying mother'. Emin was informed that the Khalifa (the Mahdi's successor) 'out of compassion for your forlorn state, left alone in the hands of the negroes—for there has been no news of you for a long time, and you must have lost all hope—has sent us to you with an army . . . to take you out of the land of the infidels, to join your brethren, the Muslims'. Concluding his appeal, 'Umar Sālih urged Emin to 'submit, therefore, with gladness to God's wish, and come at once to see me . . .'¹ With this letter came others from Slatin and Lupton, who, it was declared, 'now live a life of the greatest ease and enjoy the most perfect comfort' as the prisoners of the Mahdists at Omdurman. In his letter, which was probably written under duress, Slatin advised Emin, 'when the army of the Mahdi comes against you, submit at once, for in doing so you save yourself and yours from destruction'.²

After reading these letters, Emin was asked by the rebel officers for his advice as to what course of action should be adopted. At first Emin refused to have anything to do with them as he had been removed from his post.³ Eventually, however, he was prevailed upon and he then suggested the three things which had formed the basis of his own policy at the time of the fall of Amadi: the letter should be ignored; surrender was not to be thought of; there should be a complete withdrawal from all the northern stations to Dufile and ultimately, if necessary, to Tunguru which, being on a peninsula in the lake, could easily be defended.⁴ The rebel officers, possibly influenced by the soldiers—who declared they would never surrender to the Mahdists—decided to follow Emin's advice. But little was done for several days and on 22 October news arrived that the

---

¹ 'Umar Sālih to Emin Pasha, 12 Oct. 1888. A copy of the original Arabic text, together with an English translation and useful notes is on microfilm in the Jephson Papers, the Sudan Archives, Durham, Box 14/1. A similar version is given in Jephson, *Rebellion*, pp. 245–53. The dramatic way in which Jephson obtained this copy is related in Jephson, *Rebellion*, p. 255.

² Slatin to Emin, 31 May 1888. The original in Arabic, signed by Slatin, together with an English translation, is in the Sudan Archive, Durham, Box 438/651.

³ *Tagebücher*, 18 Oct. 1888, iv. 169–70 (Extracts XII, p. 162).

⁴ Jephson, *Rebellion*, pp. 253–4.

Mahdists had captured Rejaf after the local Bari had joined with them in an attack on the garrison. A force, under Hāmad Agha, was immediately sent from Dufile to attempt to retake the station, but it suffered from massive desertions *en route*. All the northern stations were gradually being abandoned in confusion, many of the soldiers deserted to the Makaraka country from which they had originally come, some of the officers joined the Mahdists, a stream of refugees —chiefly women and children—began to arrive at Dufile from the northern stations.[1] At last preparations were begun to fortify Dufile but Jephson was dismayed to discover that a great deal of attention was devoted to manufacturing silver bullets (the Mahdists were thought to be impervious to ordinary bullets) out of the silver dollars confiscated from Hawash Effendi.[2] Fadl al-Mūlā asked Jephson whether he wished to retire to Lake Albert on the next steamer to be out of danger. 'I told him, of course, I had no wish to run away when danger came', noted Jephson, 'that I was in the same box with them and was perfectly ready to fight along with them and that it wasn't usual for Englishmen to clear out when fighting was expected.'[3] None the less, Jephson earnestly hoped that by some miracle Stanley would return at this time when the rebels were so preoccupied with the Mahdist attack that 'Stanley could easily seize the Pasha and take him away'.[4]

On 30 October Casati, who had recently gone on the steamer to Wadelai, returned to Dufile. He reported that in the southern stations there was rising discontent with the rebels and great confusion prevailed.[5] At Dufile it was now decided to send Emin and Jephson, together with all non-combatants, to Wadelai. The first party left at once on the *Khedive*. It was at this time that Jephson wrote a long letter to Stanley describing what had taken place in the province and warning him 'to be careful how he approached the country'.[6] He sent this letter to the south to await Stanley's arrival.

During the first two weeks of November, there was little activity at Dufile. Everyone was waiting to see the outcome of the attempt to retake Rejaf. On 16 November the news arrived that it had met

---

[1] Jephson, MS. Diary, 22 Oct. 1888. *Tagebücher*, 22–6 Oct. 1888, iv. 171–3. Vita Hassan, *Die Wahrheit über Emin Pasha*, ii. 169–73.
[2] Jephson, MS. Diary, 24 Oct. 1888.
[3] Ibid. 25 Oct. 1888.   [4] Ibid. 26 Oct. 1888.
[5] Ibid. 30 Oct. 1888.
[6] Jephson, *Diary*, pp. 298–9. The letter, dated 7 Nov. 1888, is printed in *IDA* ii. 111–13.

with disaster. Hāmad Agha, 'Abd al-Wahhāb, 'Ali Agha Jabor, and three of the other rebel officers had been killed, together with many men. Most of the remaining soldiers in the northern stations had deserted, only about fifty men returned to Dufile.[1] Once again the rebel officers approached Emin in a panic. Emin was quite certain that they only came to him because 'they were no longer sure of the soldiers who were unwilling to fight for officers who maltreated them and misled them by misrepresenting that Khartoum remained in the hands of Egypt'. In addition, the death of several of the chief rebels at Rejaf and stories of Mahdist cruelties greatly demoralized the rebel party.[2] Selim Bey now took charge. Emin's wish to leave Dufile for the south was granted and it was arranged that Emin and Jephson, together with Casati and Vita Hassan, should leave at once for Wadelai. Dufile was fortified and a large body of soldiers was concentrated there.[3]

On 17 November Emin and Jephson left in the *Khedive* for Wadelai. Their main object was to go on to Tunguru and Mswa and try to get in touch with Stanley, whose return to the Lake was imminently expected. It would seem that the rebels also looked to Stanley to assist them. Before leaving Dufile, Emin was asked to do his best 'to interest Stanley on their behalf when he arrived'.[4]

Free again, and heading towards the south, Emin was, states Jephson, in 'tremendous spirits'; at Wadelai he received a rapturous welcome. 'Everyone seems glad to have him back, and the utmost contentment prevails. The few faithfuls who have stuck to him, in spite of threats, etc. from the rebels, go about with grinning faces, showing their delight that the bad days are over. The Pasha's return here is decidedly triumphant.'[5] Emin refused, however, to be reinstated in a position of authority. Jephson was very glad about this.

It is much the best that he should not accept authority again, for if he does so, he accepts an immense responsibility as well, and as things have happened he now is in no way responsible for anything. If Stanley comes tomorrow he can, without the slightest blame being attached to him, leave the country as a private man, leaving the people who have thrown him over,

---

[1] Statement of Basili Boktor. Jephson, MS. Diary, 16 Nov. 1888.
[2] *Tagebücher*, 15–16 Nov. 1888, iv. 178–81 (Extracts XII, pp. 165–6). Vita Hassan, op. cit. ii. 171–2.
[3] Basili Boktor states the number as 1,200, but this is almost certainly an exaggeration.
[4] *Tagebücher*, 15 Nov. 1888, iv. 179 (Extracts XII, p. 165).
[5] Jephson, *Diary*, p. 302.

and taking with him only such people as have been faithful to him through-out. When once people have said they don't want him, his duty to them entirely ceased . . . All he has now to do is to get out of the country with the faithfuls and not trouble his head about the rest . . . I repeat, he has now no more responsibility.[1]

This is a very revealing passage. As Emin makes clear, throughout his stay in Equatoria Jephson had never ceased to try to persuade Emin to abandon most of his garrisons and to withdraw with a small party of his most loyal soldiers with Stanley's expedition.[2] These had been Stanley's clear instructions to Jephson; Jephson himself was convinced of their widsom and was determined to bring them to a successful conclusion by the time of Stanley's return.[3] But, despite all that had happened at Dufile, this was still completely at variance with Emin's own wishes. Like Gordon at Khartoum, Emin in Equatoria wished to stay. 'I protest against the fact that the expedition has come to "rescue" me', he declared.

In all my letters to Europe I only asked for help for my people and never mentioned myself personally. It is, to say the least, ungenerous repeatedly to tell me, as Jephson does, what sacrifices people have made in leaving England and coming to join me and what great difficulties and losses the expedition has had to endure—as if *I* had proposed the route through the Congo, or *I* had even invited the gentlemen to come.[4]

Emin had his own shrewd explanation of why Stanley was so deter-mined to banish him from Equatoria.

For him, everything depends on whether he is able to take me along, for only then, when people could actually see me, would his expedition be regarded as totally successful. To Stanley's chagrin, when he went on the expedition to find Livingstone, he experienced what it meant to leave behind in Africa the main object of his expedition.[5] This time, he would rather perish than leave without me! Therefore, Stanley urged Jephson, during his own absence, to try everything to persuade me to leave. So, here again, we have only egoism under the guise of philanthropy.[6]

Emin resented, and intended to obstruct, Stanley's determination to cast him in the role of a mascot for his expedition. He was now

---

[1] Jephson, MS. Diary, 18 Nov. 1888. See also Jephson, *Rebellion*, pp. 293-4.
[2] See especially *Tagebücher*, 27-30 Jan. 1889, iv. 208-13.
[3] Jephson, MS. Diary, 11 Aug. 1888.
[4] *Tagebücher*, 30 Jan. 1889, iv. 213.
[5] When Stanley had returned to Europe after his meeting with Livingstone, he had found his account of his meeting was widely disbelieved. See Ian Anstruther, *I Presume: H. M. Stanley's triumph and disaster* (London, 1956).
[6] *Tagebücher*, 14 Jan. 1889, iv. 202.

convinced 'that when the time for departure comes, our people will not want to go to Zanzibar or to Egypt, but will prefer to settle at the first place which appears suitable to them; but', he concluded with sinister presentiment, 'perhaps after they have taken all Stanley's arms and ammunition'.[1]

Whilst Emin and Jephson were at Wadelai, they received on 4 December the news that all the northern stations, including Muggi, Labore, Khor Ayu, and Fabbo, had fallen to the Mahdists, who had then attacked Dufile. Both Selim Bey and 'Umar Sālih have left vivid accounts of this attack on Dufile.[2] Sulaimān Agha, who was at Dufile, said that Selim Bey had acted with great fortitude but that most of the soldiers had shown 'the utmost cowardice' and had fled in the face of a small party of Mahdists who had succeeded in entering the station.[3] The first object of the Mahdists had been to capture Emin 'but unfortunately', reported 'Umar Sālih to the Khalifa, 'we found that Emin had gone to Wadelai, accompanied by some Christians'.[4] Selim Bey had finally succeeded in rallying some of his men and had re-entered the station. The three peacock Dervishes had been clubbed to death. After the Mahdists had suffered considerable losses, they had retired to Rejaf to await reinforcements from Omdurman.

At Rejaf considerable stores of ammunition and ivory had fallen into the hands of the Mahdists, along with copies of the letters from the Khedive and Nubar Pasha, acknowledging the abandonment of Equatoria by the Egyptian Government, which had been brought by Stanley. These were sent down to Omdurman by 'Umar Sālih along with a remarkably accurate description of the arrival of Stanley's expedition in Equatoria in 1888 and the subsequent upheavals in the province.[5] 'Umar Sālih concluded his report to the Khalifa by stating that 'as for the great European who is known as Mr. Stanley, he went back having promised Emin to return with more arms and support . . . but up to now he has not come'. Emin's

---

[1] *Tagebücher*, 11 Dec. 1889, iv. 192. Sir John Gray's translation of this passage in Extracts XIII, p. 67, seems to me to be incorrect.

[2] Selim Bey to Emin Pasha, n.d., printed in Jephson, *Rebellion*, pp. 327–30. A facsimile of the Arabic original is in Casati, *Ten Years in Equatoria*, pp. 366–7. 'Umar Sālih to Khalifa, n.d., Khartoum Archives, Mahdiya 1/33/6–1. Part of this letter is printed in R. O. Collins, op. cit., pp. 65–6.

[3] Jephson, MS. Diary, 15–17 Dec. 1888, reporting a conversation with Sulaimān Agha.

[4] 'Umar Sālih to Khalifa, n.d., cited above.

[5] R. O. Collins, *The Southern Sudan*, pp. 60–1.

soldiers had refused to go with Stanley's expedition to Egypt and 'Umar Sālih confidently predicted that 'very soon we shall capture Emin and the Christians with him and all the steamers'.[1] The Khalifa later sent these captured copies of the letters from the Khedive and Nubar Pasha, as well as a copy of 'Umar Sālih's report, to General Grenfell at Suakin. Owing largely to a misinterpretation of 'Umar Sālih's report by 'Uthmān Diqna, the Mahdist *amīr* besieging Suakin, Grenfell and hence the British Government came to believe that Emin and 'another European traveller who was with him' had been captured by the Mahdists, and rumours circulated in Britain that Stanley's expedition had met with disaster.[2]

*   *   *

It was while Emin and Jephson were at Wadelai that they heard the first rumours from the people near Mswa, in the extreme south, that Stanley's expedition was once more approaching Lake Albert.[3] Emin and Jephson, fearing that the Mahdists would again attack Dufile and might soon penetrate even further south, decided to leave at once for Tunguru and Mswa and from there to go on to Fort Bodo.[4] Jephson reluctantly agreed to destroy Stanley's steel boat, the *Advance*, which they were unable to take with them. He also improvised a hammock for Emin's daughter, Ferida, out of two blankets slung across bamboo poles. It was on this hammock that she later travelled all the way to the coast.[4] Emin, with a heavy heart, prepared to make his final departure from the station which had served as his headquarters for the past three years. It was impossible to transport any of the ivory and Emin was forced to abandon many of the cases of specimens, etc., which he had gathered with such care and industry over the years. 'All my collections, all my books, all my instruments must be left behind', he noted sadly.[5]

The evacuation of Wadelai began on 6 December. Despite their protestations of loyalty, many of the soldiers refused to accompany

[1] 'Umar Sālih to the Khalifa, n.d., 1888, Khartoum Archives, Mahdiya 1/33/19.
[2] Details of this matter are collected together in the 'Paper respecting the reported capture of Emin Pasha and Mr. Stanley' presented to Parliament in Dec. 1888 and published as *Africa No. 9 (1888)* C. 5602. See also R. O. Collins, op. cit., p. 61.
[3] *Tagebücher*, 22 Nov. 1888, iv. pp. 183 *et seq.* Sir John Gray's dating here (Extracts XIII, p. 66) is incorrect.
[4] Jephson, MS. Diary, 4 Dec. 1888.
[5] *Tagebücher*, 4 Dec. 1888, iv. 186 (Extracts XIII, p. 66).

Emin and though a large number of women and children did set out with Emin and Jephson for Tunguru, many of these later returned to Wadelai. Jephson found the march to Tunguru an appalling business. It was 'awfully pathetic to see these poor half-savage people toiling along with their loads stuffed with all sorts of the most useless rubbish and dragging or carrying their poor unfortunate little children'.[1] Where streams had to be crossed, the path became churned into a deep mire and women and children were trampled under foot. 'People in Europe have a queer idea of what evacuation means in these countries', Jephson observed; 'they tell one to "evacuate" just as they would tell one to eat one's dinner and evidently don't seem to think that the one is much harder than the other . . .'.[2]

Immediately after Emin and Jephson left Wadelai, they later discovered, the soldiers entered and plundered their houses. 'I cannot conceal from myself that my enemies will make the best of my flight from Wadelai and that perhaps very difficult times may arise for me', wrote Emin. 'God grant that Stanley will come during the next few days and then all will end well.'[3]

It is not clear precisely what Emin expected to happen when Stanley arrived back at the Lake. Emin's greatest fear at this time was that the Mahdists would return to the attack on Dufile with reinforcements and that they would soon succeed in taking the station. After this a further advance into the south could easily follow since none of the southern stations, certainly not Wadelai, was readily defensible. The one exception was Tunguru which, if a ditch were dug, could be turned into an island in the lake and, if the steamers were held there, could remain almost impregnable. Emin therefore decided to remain at Tunguru until Stanley arrived. It is clear from the letter which Emin wrote to Stanley at this time that he still hoped that since 'nobody thinks . . . of going to Egypt, except, perhaps, a few officers and men', he might still be settled in the Kavirondo area and take new employment under Mackinnon's I.B.E.A. Company.[4] Jephson, however, had changed his own opinion. 'I had such hopes of the Kavirondo scheme, but alas, that I fear now will never come to pass, this rebellion has made it impossible', he wrote in his diary.[5]

---

[1] Jephson, *Diary*, p. 308.   [2] Ibid. 309.
[3] *Tagebücher*, 7 Dec. 1888, iv. 191.
[4] Ibid. 7–28 Dec. 1888, iv. 190–9. Emin to Stanley, 21 Dec. 1888, printed in *IDA* ii. 110–11.
[5] Jephson, *Diary*, p. 305.

He had become so sceptical of Emin's people that, in spite of the Khedive's instructions, he now declared:

> I would rather they were caught by the Danāqla [Mahdists] than that they should come out with us; it would only be a just punishment for their treachery and ingratitude. It is far better that they should be swallowed up in the Soudan, where they cannot do much harm, than that we should take them out of Egypt and let loose such a lot of worthless blackguards on society again.[1]

Jephson considered that the organizers of the relief expedition had been completely misled by Felkin, Junker, and Emin himself about the situation in Equatoria. 'From the Pasha's letters all Europe thought his soldiers were heroes'; Emin had said nothing about

> one half of his people being in open rebellion against him and many of the others being disaffected in his letters. We were led to believe that either he and his soldiers would follow us out of the country, or that they would receive us with a certain amount of gratitude, accept what we had brought them in the way of ammunition, clothes, etc. and, after perhaps staying a short time with them, we should go on our way to the coast, wishing them well and having their good wishes with us also. But we did not expect, nor had anyone given us the slightest reason to expect, that after getting through the dangers and overcoming the difficulties on the road—and their name was legion—that the greatest danger of all awaited us, when we reached this country, in the shape of a plot, formed by the very people we had come to help, to seize and rob us of all that we had and then to turn us adrift.[2]

Throughout the rest of December and January, Emin and Jephson remained at Tunguru anxiously awaiting Stanley's arrival. Steamers brought letters from Selim Bey at Dufile reporting on the progress of events there and 'protesting his devotion to Emin Pasha and saying that he hoped that Emin Pasha would be able to resume his authority shortly'.[3] But Selim Bey had never managed to establish his own authority fully at Dufile, and by December it is clear that those supporting him were succumbing to the faction headed by Fadl al-Mūlā. Selim Bey, following Emin's proposals, urged that Dufile should be abandoned and the remaining men and ammunition concentrated in the south. Fadl al-Mūlā's party, however, resisted

---

[1] Jephson, MS. Diary, 1 Dec. 1888.
[2] Jephson, *Diary*, pp. 313–14.
[3] Statement of Basili Boktor.

this, and when news arrived that Emin had abandoned Wadelai for the south, they called a meeting in which Emin was accused of deserting the garrisons. It was suggested that he should be brought back to Dufile in chains and that Jephson, Casati, Vita Hassan, and Signor Marco 'should be hanged for having incited the troops to abandon Wadelai on purpose to cause the ruin of the soldiers who were at Dufile'.[1] Selim Bey's position steadily declined as it became clear that he was prepared to remain in contact with Emin and 'wished to join the Pasha and leave the country with him' when Stanley's expedition returned.[2] Fadl al-Mūlā's followers, consisting of those already most compromised in the rebellion against Emin, were adamant in their resolution not to withdraw from Equatoria and declared that it was better to surrender to the Mahdists than 'to infidels like the English'.[3]

The people who had accompanied Emin and Jephson to Tunguru were few and consisted chiefly of those who had been unpopular with the rebels and some 'seven or eight soldiers who remained faithful'.[4] Along with Casati, Vita Hassan, and Signor Marco were Hawash Effendi, 'Uthmān Latīf, and their households. A consistent and devoted ally of Emin's throughout this period was Shukri Agha, the governor of the station at Mswa. When news arrived in January 1889 that Dufile was being evacuated and all the officers and soldiers were retiring to Wadelai, he wrote to Emin at Tunguru suggesting that he should retire to Mswa, preparatory to going on to meet Stanley at Kavalli's. Emin, however, delayed and on 26 January letters arrived at Wadelai announcing Stanley's arrival at a point one day's march from Lake Albert.

Stanley had received the letters which Emin and Jephson had sent to Kavalli's informing him of the rebellion in the province and of their own eventual withdrawal to Tunguru. In reply he had written to both Emin and Jephson. The letter to Emin is brief and formal. Stanley announced that he had arrived with a second delivery of ammunition and gunpowder and a few stores, and demanded 'a definite answer to the question—if you propose to accept our escort and assistance to reach Zanzibar—or if Signor Casati proposes to

---

[1] Casati, *Ten Years in Equatoria*, p. 370. Statement of Basili Boktor. See also the letter which Fadl al-Mūlā's party wrote to Selim Bey on 10 Dec. 1888, printed in Jephson, *Rebellion*, pp. 343-6.
[2] Jephson, Report to Stanley, in *IDA* ii. 124.
[3] Ibid. See also Jephson, MS. Diary, 9 Dec. 1888.
[4] Jephson, Report to Stanley, ibid.

do so or whether there are any officers or men disposed to accept of our safe conduct to the sea'.[1]

Stanley's two letters to Jephson express Stanley's complete exasperation at the successive disasters which had befallen his expedition, his belief that Jephson, like the officers of the Rear Column, had deliberately failed to obey his orders, and his vexation that his plans had repeatedly gone awry. Stanley gave a full account of his journey in search of the Rear Column, the wreck he had found at Banalya, and his return to Fort Bodo and the Lake. 'The difficulties I met at Banalya are repeated today near the Albert Lake', wrote Stanley. 'If you are still victims of indecision—then a long good night to you all—but while I retain my senses, I must save my expedition.' If Emin was unable to receive the second delivery of ammunition which had been brought, then Stanley declared that he would have to destroy it before his expedition, which 'has no further business in these regions', retired. 'You must understand that we are perfectly unable to assist Emin Pasha by force. My people are mere porters incapable of standing before a volley of Remingtons.' Jephson was ordered to come at once to Kavalli's, to bring with him supplies of food for Stanley's party and forty-two tusks of ivory with which he could pay his Manyema carriers. Stanley wrote that he was quite prepared to assist Emin and whoever wished to follow him to withdraw from Equatoria, 'but I must have clear and definite assertions followed by promptitude according to such orders as I shall give for effecting this purpose, or a clear and definite refusal as we cannot stay here all our lives awaiting people who seem to be not very clear as to what they wish'. Jephson was instructed to make clear to Emin, in an obvious attempt to get him to withdraw, 'the bitter end and fate of those obstinate and misguided people who decline assistance when tendered to them'. 'I could save a dozen Pasha's if they were willing to be saved', declared Stanley.[2]

Jephson, who was ill with fever at the time, was very upset by Stanley's letters.[3] He rightly observed that with regard to events in Equatoria, as with the fate of the Rear Column, Stanley was not at

---

[1] Stanley to Emin Pasha, 17 Jan. 1889, printed in *Tagebücher*, under 26 Jan. iv. 206–7. In the version given by Stanley himself (*IDA* ii. 118–19) Stanley has greatly exaggerated the amount of the second delivery of 'relief' which he had brought.

[2] Stanley to Jephson, 17/18 Jan. 1889, printed in Jephson, *Diary*, pp. 321–7. The version printed in *IDA* ii. 114–18 is heavily edited (i.e. censored).

[3] Jephson, *Diary*, p. 329. See also *Tagebücher*, 27 Jan. 1889, iv. 208–9.

all just. When all allowances are made the letters still remain self-righteous and arrogant in tone, and exhibit a devastating lack of understanding, on Stanley's part, of any situation other than his own. Emin was also deeply offended by Stanley's peremptory message. In a cool, somewhat despondent reply, he thanked Stanley for what he took to be his 'good intentions, and those of the people who sent you', and praised Jephson for the courage and unfaltering kindness and patience he had shown 'under the most trying circumstances'. About his own intentions, however, Emin remained equivocal. 'Concerning your question if Signor Casati and myself propose to accept your escort and assistance to reach Zanzibar', Emin wrote, 'I have to state that not only Signor Casati and myself would gladly avail us of your help, but that there are lots of people desirous of going out from the far Egypt [sic], as well as for any other convenient place.' But it is doubtful whether Emin still really believed this. In concluding his letter to Stanley, Emin wished him and his expedition 'a happy and speedy homeward march' and declared his belief that he would not see Stanley again.[1]

Emin deliberately kept these farewell remarks from Jephson who, it was arranged, would leave at once for Mswa and Kavalli's to meet Stanley. Jephson, therefore, when he left Emin was convinced that once he had joined forces with Stanley he would be able to induce the Pasha to leave Equatoria and withdraw with the expedition. But, as has been indicated, Emin had no wish to return to Zanzibar, Egypt, or Europe as the trophy of Stanley's expedition. All Emin's hopes had been fixed on the Kavirondo proposal. Jephson was now convinced that this was impossible. The Kavirondo scheme had not even been mentioned by Stanley in his letter to Emin; Stanley's offer was now an escort to Zanzibar or Egypt. The fact is that Stanley, like Jephson, had changed his mind. From the moment when he had received the letters from Emin and Jephson reporting the rebellion in Equatoria and the downfall of Emin's authority, Stanley had completely abandoned the Kavirondo idea, and in his written communications with Emin he never henceforth refers to it again. Emin was deeply mortified by this change in Stanley's attitude and rapidly came to suspect that Stanley had never intended to bring about the scheme which Emin had taken so seriously. Weary and dejected, Emin would seem to have decided early in 1889 on the course which he was to follow from 1890 until his death in October

[1] Emin to Stanley, 27 Jan. 1889, printed in IDA ii. 127-8.

1892: he wished to remain, preferably without political responsibilities, a lone wanderer in the African interior until his death—which he sensed was near. The comparison with the aged Livingstone is striking. But from such a course Emin was to be temporarily prevented by the brusque, determined, indefatigable Stanley.

CHAPTER X

The Withdrawal and the March
to the Coast

After a difficult journey, Jephson reached Stanley at his camp on the plateau above Lake Albert on 6 February 1889. For the first time on the expedition Stanley invited one of his officers to take his meals with him and Jephson was able to give Stanley a full account of all that had happened.[1] As for the course of action which was now to be adopted, Jephson declared emphatically to Stanley that the principal obstacle to the 'rescue' of Emin Pasha was Emin himself. Jephson advised that the only way to overcome this obstacle was for Stanley to march his expedition along the plateau to a point above Mswa, then Jephson would 'descend into the station and take the Pasha and his loads up and simply walk off with him'.[2] Stanley, who now came once again to regard his relief expedition as a 'rescue' mission, declared that he was prepared to use force if necessary to bring about Emin's withdrawal from Mswa. He therefore wrote a letter to Emin in which he outlined his proposals as to how this was to be achieved. Jephson was so certain that the tone of Stanley's letter would be deeply offensive to Emin that Stanley was persuaded to redraft the letter. The version which was eventually dispatched was written in a style which Stanley felt even Chesterfield would have approved.[3] It is, indeed, a masterpiece of Stanley's journalistic skill. With smooth words and flattering cadences Stanley expressed his respect and admiration for all that Emin had managed to achieve for his people; his distress on hearing of the base ingratitude and insensate conduct of a few misguided miscreants in the province; his determination to lay himself and his expedition completely at Emin's disposal 'to perform any pact you can suggest to me'. Meanwhile, Stanley gave his own very concrete

---

[1] This account was written down at Stanley's request as a Report. Dated 7 Feb. 1889 it is printed in *IDA* ii. 121-7.

[2] Jephson, MS. Diary, 7 Feb. 1889.

[3] *IDA* ii. 130-1; Jephson, MS. Diary, 8 Feb. 1889.

instructions. With the help of Shukri Agha, Emin was to seize and detain a steamer and go by water if possible, by land if necessary, to Mswa. Once there, he and Stanley would be able to act 'in concert'.[1]

By the time Emin received Stanley's letter he had already come with the two steamers, Casati, Vita Hassan, and a small following to Mswa. He then steamed on to a point near Kavalli's. On 13 February Stanley and Jephson received a note from Emin announcing his arrival accompanied by twelve officers and forty soldiers who had come, Emin declared, to request Stanley to give them some time to assemble their relatives and any others who wished to leave Equatoria with Stanley's expedition. About his own intentions, Emin made no mention.[2] In a later note to Stanley, Emin simply expressed the hope that 'my being somewhat African in my moods may not interfere with our friendly relations'.[3] On 17 February Emin Pasha and a party of about sixty-five people, headed by Selim Bey, arrived at Stanley's camp. The following day, Stairs, Parke, Nelson, and the rest of the expedition also arrived at Kavalli's from their camp at Kandekore.[4] For the first time since June 1887 the expedition was once again united.

Stanley now interviewed Selim Bey and the officers who had arrived with Emin. It was only with some difficulty that Selim Bey and those who had accompanied him had managed to leave Wadelai. After the evacuation of Dufile in January Wadelai had become the headquarters of Fadl al-Mūlā's party. When news rived at Wadelai of Stanley's return, there was great confusion. The strength of Stanley's expedition was greatly exaggerated and the rebels feared that when Stanley heard of the rebellion in the province he would advance on Wadelai from the south, while the Mahdists might at any moment come from the north. It was therefore agreed that Selim Bey should set out to join Emin and find out the intentions of Stanley and the expedition.[5] Selim Bey and his party of officers and soldiers had met Emin at Tunguru. There they had begged him to accompany them on a visit to Stanley's camp as their interpreter! Emin, who had shown no clear intention of going to

---

[1] Stanley to Emin, 7 Feb. 1889, printed in *Tagebücher*, under 11 Feb. 1889, iv. 218–20.
[2] Emin to Stanley, 13 Feb. 1889, printed in *IDA* ii. 134–5.
[3] Emin to Stanley, 15 Feb. 1889, ibid. 137–8.
[4] See Ch. VIII, p. 207 above.
[5] Statement of Basili Boktor. Also Jephson, MS. Diary, 8 Feb. 1889.

join Stanley of his own volition, refused to assist Selim Bey and his followers in this capacity. After they had beseeched him once again to act as their Governor and assist them, Emin was prevailed upon to accompany them to Stanley and intercede with him on their behalf.[1] This, it would seem, was the immediate purpose behind Emin's departure from Tunguru for Mswa and Kavalli's on what was to be his final withdrawal from the province. Selim Bey and his party had protested to Emin, as they now did to Stanley, that they were united in their desire to follow Stanley out of the country. Emin, like Stanley, was only partly convinced.[2] Selim Bey presented Stanley with a letter signed by all the chief rebel officers, including Fadl al-Mūlā, acknowledging that Stanley had come as the representative of the Khedive and asserting a general desire 'to be very soon with you'.[3] In his reply to this letter, Stanley ordered those who were willing to withdraw with his expedition to come with a minimum of baggage (they would have to provide their own carriers) to his camp at Kavalli's, where he would prepare for immediate departure.[4] On 26 February Selim Bey and his party departed with this letter for Wadelai, despite the arrival the previous day of what Emin describes as 'an arrogant letter' from the rebel officers stating that Selim Bey had been deposed from his position as commander of the troops and that Fadl al-Mūlā had promoted himself to the rank of Bey.[5] Before leaving, Selim Bey declared that he and his party would only stay at Wadelai long enough to assemble their families before setting out to rejoin Stanley and withdraw from Equatoria with the expedition. It was Stanley's fervent but undeclared hope that Selim Bey would succeed in bringing with him at least sixty of Emin's loyal soldiers whom Stanley could then add to his sadly depleted force as an armed escort for the march to the coast.[6]

There now began a period of several weeks during which Stanley remained with his expedition at Kavalli's while the party of Emin's officers and soldiers who were to accompany the expedition assembled. During this time the camp at Kavalli's grew to be almost a

[1] Statement of Basili Boktor; Casati, *Ten Years in Equatoria*, pp. 377–82; *Tagebücher*, 3–19 Feb. 1889, iv. 214–18.
[2] *Tagebücher*, 18 Feb. 1889, iv. 225.
[3] The letter is printed in English translation in *IDA* ii. 140.
[4] Stanley's letter, dated 19 Feb. 1889, is printed in *IDA* ii. 142. A copy of the original Arabic version is in the Sudan Archives, Durham, Box 101/25/1.
[5] *Tagebücher*, 25 Feb. 1889, iv. 229–30 (Extracts XIII, p. 72). *IDA* ii. 146.
[6] Jephson, MS. Diary, 1 Mar. 1889.

town. Nearly 1,000 people were eventually collected there in over 190 huts. The problem of feeding all these people was a business which Stanley tackled rigorously and without compunction. Raiding parties were sent out every few days under European officers, and these scoured the surrounding countryside in every direction. They returned with herds of cattle, hundreds of goats and chickens, and a considerable number of female slaves, and they left a trail of burnt-out villages and devasted fields behind them.[1] Stanley was presented with a more intractable problem over the transportation of the immense amounts of baggage which Emin's people brought with them from the lake-shore to his camp. This involved a difficult march of some eighteen miles up on to the plateau over 2,000 ft. above Lake Albert.[2] Emin's people provided very few carriers of their own, and Stanley at first felt obliged to send daily fatigue parties of his own Zanzibaris to assist them. The European officers were appalled by the mountains of baggage, including bedsteads and grinding stones, which Emin's people brought with them, and the Zanzibaris, who had to struggle up the escarpment with these excessive loads, were brought to the brink of mutiny for the first and last time on the expedition. Stanley acted firmly without losing the loyalty of the Zanzibaris. This was, as Parke remarked, a great tribute to Stanley's extraordinary powers of leadership.[3] Stanley now developed a new method of obtaining carriers to do the work. A herd of cattle would be seized from the local people, who would be informed that they could secure their return by carrying a number of loads up from the lake. Jephson thought this scheme was 'rather hard on the natives but it is the fortune of war . . . it is one of those high-handed acts which African travellers are obliged to resort to . . .'.[4]

Throughout February and March Emin and Stanley were a good deal in each other's company, and during this time their relations were quite cordial. Emin obviously found much in Stanley which he respected, even admired: Stanley was a good leader and most obliging, declared Emin, and 'much more practical than I am'.[5] Stanley, on the other hand, became more exasperated with Emin's lack of decisiveness and personal sensitivity. It is hard to imagine

[1] For a detailed account of one of these raids, see Jephson, MS. Diary, 21 Mar. 1889.

[2] Parke, Diary, p. 374.

[3] Ibid. 381. See also Jephson, MS. Diary, 10 Mar. 1889.

[4] Ibid. 18 Mar. 1889.

[5] Tagebücher, 15 and 22 Mar., 2 Apr. 1889, iv. 237–45.

two men less suited to act 'in concert' and march together on an African expedition than Emin and Stanley. As Stanley himself admitted, 'their natures were diametrically opposed'.[1] While Emin was sensitive, vacillating, and quick to take offence, Stanley was brusque and decisive. But the fact is that Stanley wanted Emin to act decisively in a direction which Emin did not want to take. Stanley and the European officers had always hoped that Emin would withdraw with the expedition.[2] Since a rebellion against Emin's authority had taken place in Equatoria, it was now taken for granted that Emin could not remain and would wish to accompany the expedition to Zanzibar, possibly to Egypt. The motley group of Egyptians and Sudanese who had come to join Emin in Stanley's camp consisted of only a few soldiers and chiefly of petty clerks and officials who wanted to return to Egypt. The majority of the people were, in any case, women and children—only 126 out of a total of over 500 are listed as men.[3] These were not people who could form an effective force and be settled, under Emin's command, in the Kavirondo area as an outpost of Mackinnon's I.B.E.A. Company. Emin knew this and he later stated, 'He did not therefore feel himself in a position to reopen the subject of his employment under the Imperial British East Africa Company, and Mr. Stanley preserved a complete silence regarding this proposal.'[4] Stanley had, in fact, completely abandoned any thought of implementing his former proposal. As he wrote to Mackinnon, Emin 'had no force to do anything for him, for you, or for me . . . Nolens Volens the Pasha had to come' out of Equatoria with the expedition and withdraw to the coast.[5] In a conversation with Emin on 26 March, Stanley suggested that Emin might possibly find future employment with King Leopold as Governor of the Lower Congo, or with Mackinnon's I.B.E.A. Company as Governor of Mombasa at an assured yearly income of £700–£800.[6] But Emin could summon no enthusiasm for the prospect of a withdrawal from the area and the people he had come to know so well, although he readily admitted the truth of all that Stanley and the others had to say about the

[1] IDA ii. 245.   [2] See Ch. VII, p. 155 above.
[3] IDA ii. 187.
[4] Euan-Smith to Salisbury, 14 Mar. 1889, reporting a conversation with Emin Pasha, F.O. 84/2060.
[5] Stanley to Mackinnon, 31 Aug. 1889, M.P., F. 1.
[6] Tagebücher, 26 Mar. 1889, iv. 242 (Extracts XII, p. 73). See also Parke, Diary, p. 395, reporting a conversation with Emin the following day.

impossible position he would be in if he remained.[1] At no point did Emin express a firm intention to withdraw with Stanley's expedition, rather, as the choices before him diminished, he simply accommodated himself to circumstances—and these soon came to be dominated by the more forceful personality of Stanley.

On 5 April Stanley finally lost patience with Emin's vacillation and took matters into his own hands. After a furious row with Emin—which Emin describes as like 'a scene in a mad-house'—Stanley stormed out of Emin's house 'in a desperate rage', shouting 'I am resolved, Pasha, I am resolved.' The whole camp was assembled in great alarm, Emin's people were driven out of their huts with clubs by the Zanzibaris, and Stanley ordered those among them who were not prepared to follow him to stand on one side. Since many feared that they would be shot if they showed any such inclination, none did so; all protested that they were ready to leave with the expedition on 10 April, the date arranged by Stanley. After a furious harangue Stanley gradually calmed down and the camp returned to normal.[2] Stairs, Jephson, and Parke all thought that Stanley's forceful demonstration had been most effective. Emin considered that Stanley had 'passed every limit of courtesy', and never forgave him for his rude and insulting behaviour; Emin also thought that the whole matter could have been managed 'with fewer scenic effects and journalistic rhetoric'. 'Stanley is created to converse with Zanzibaris', he commented, 'he should never include Europeans on his expeditions.'[3] From this date onwards relations between Stanley and Emin steadily deteriorated. The chief result of this confrontation between them was that henceforth Stanley took all matters concerning the expedition entirely into his own hands. Emin was issued with instructions, rarely consulted, and treated as a subordinate. The days of being treated as Stanley's 'guest' were over.

This confrontation between Stanley and Emin had been sparked off by the Zanzibaris reporting that Emin's people had attempted to steal their rifles during the night. This confirmed Stanley's conviction that a conspiracy existed among Emin's people to seize the rifles

---

[1] Ibid. 25 Mar. iv. 241.

[2] *Tagebücher*, 5 Apr. 1889, iv. 247–8; Jephson, MS. Diary, 5 Apr. 1889; Stairs, MS. Diary, under 12 Apr. 1889. I am most grateful to Professor G. Shepperson for photo-copying extracts from the Stairs diary for me from the State Archives, Halifax, Nova Scotia. Stanley's version of these events (*IDA* ii. 179–88) is unreliable.

[3] *Tagebücher*, 5 Apr. 1889, iv. 247–8.

and ammunition belonging to the expedition 'and so deprive us of the power of returning to Zanzibar'.[1] Jephson had long suspected such a plot among the rebel officers in Equatoria and he had communicated his suspicions to Stanley. Stanley became convinced that Selim Bey and his followers were implicated and were in secret correspondence with those of Emin's men who were now at Kavalli's. 'Uthmān Latīf who, like Shukri Agha, had been loyal to Emin during the rebellion and was to withdraw with the expedition, told Stanley that neither Selim Bey nor Fadl al-Mūlā had any intention of assembling with their people to withdraw from Equatoria; they were simply waiting for an opportunity to attack the expedition.[2]

It is not clear whether there ever was a plot amongst Emin's people to disrupt Stanley's expedition. Certainly it is likely that the rebels, like the Congo Arabs, had coveted the arms and ammunition carried by the expedition,[3] but they also went in some awe of Stanley's strength and were far from united themselves. When Selim Bey had returned to Wadelai with Stanley's order that those who wished to withdraw from the province should come to Kavalli's, he encountered increasing opposition from the party of Fadl al-Mūlā. None the less, the steamers were used to transport people from Wadelai to Lake Albert, where most of those who wished to leave had been concentrated by the end of March.[4] But they were a few in number and there is no indication that Fadl al-Mūlā or the majority of Emin's garrisons ever really contemplated withdrawing from Equatoria, particularly as the Mahdist threat under 'Umar Sālih had once again receded.[5]

On 26 March a letter arrived at Kavalli's from Selim Bey in which he declared that he was proceeding with the evacuation as he had promised but that he was experiencing great difficulties. On receipt of this letter, Emin told Stanley that Selim Bey could not possibly accomplish his task by 10 April—the date Stanley had set for the departure of the expedition—and begged him to allow a little more time. Stanley and the European officers, who despised and were highly suspicious of Emin's people, refused to consider any further delay and so it was decided that the expedition would depart for the coast on 10 April whether or not Selim Bey and those accom-

---

[1] *IDA* ii. 162.
[2] Ibid. 160–6.
[3] See Ch. IX, p. 230 above.
[4] Statement of Basili Boktor.
[5] Ibid. See also *Tagebücher*, 4 Apr. 1889, iv. 246.

panying him had arrived at Kavalli's.[1] Letters were dispatched to Selim Bey at Wadelai, and Shukri Agha at Mswa, informing them of this.[2] Jephson comments that 'Emin was evidently not pleased with our decision and in so many words said so'.[3] Stanley once again became exasperated with Emin and told him that 'he had absolutely no confidence in his people'. The letter which Selim Bey and his friends had just written

meant something very different from what they really intended doing, he [Stanley] could read between the lines and could see what was meant, which was, that they had it in their hearts to come here with all their soldiers, as they found their position at Wadelai was untenable, they might march with us for a few days and then settle down in a good country and take from us all our guns, ammunition etc. and turn us adrift.[3]

Stanley's suspicions were shared not only by his own officers but to some extent by Emin himself.[4]

It is very doubtful whether Selim Bey and those who were with him had any intention of withdrawing with Stanley's expedition all the way to Zanzibar or Egypt. Those who were prepared for this were already with Emin in Stanley's camp at Kavalli's and few of them were southern Sudanese soldiers. The wishes of Selim Bey were probably in close accord with those of Emin himself. What Selim Bey probably intended is what he eventually achieved: this was to withdraw from Equatoria beyond the grasp of Fadl al-Mūlā and his party to some near-by convenient place and to settle there. This is what Emin had anticipated for his most loyal soldiers in 1888 and Lugard was to bring about in 1891, when he returned to Kavalli's and evacuated Selim Bey and his remaining soldiers to Uganda.[5] There is little evidence to suggest that Selim Bey ever plotted to seize Stanley's arms and ammunition. It was the opinion of Emin and Shukri Agha, and later of Lugard also, that throughout these events Selim Bey was consistently loyal and attempted, amidst great difficulties, to collect together his men and bring them to Stanley as he had promised.

---

[1] IDA ii. 158–63. Jephson, MS. Diary, 26 Mar. 1889. Tagebücher, 25–6 Mar. 1889, iv.

[2] IDA ii. 163.

[3] Jephson, MS. Diary, 26 Mar. 1889.

[4] See Ch. IX, p. 242 above, where the relevant passage from the Tagebücher, 11 Dec. 1889, is quoted.

[5] The full story of Lugard's relations with Selim Bey is related in M. Perham, ed., The Diaries of Lord Lugard (London, 1959), esp. ii. 300–49.

On 10 April Stanley's expedition left Kavalli's to begin the march to the coast. Initially, it was a long column consisting of about 1,500 people including many women and children. Of Stanley's original expedition a mere 230 remained, but to these had been added 130 Manyema. There were about 570 of Emin's people, only 126 of them men (chiefly Egyptians and northern Sudanese), the rest consisting of their women and children. In addition, over 500 local people had been persuaded or impressed—by means of what can only be described as slave-raids—to accompany the expedition as carriers.[1] The desertions amongst the carriers and Emin's people were so large and continuous that further 'raids' to obtain new carriers were repeatedly made *en route*. During the first few days the deserters numbered between 50 and 100 every day. Large numbers of loads had simply to be abandoned. The only ivory which was brought out of Equatoria with the expedition was the forty-two tusks which Selim Bey had dutifully brought to Kavalli's, on Jephson's instructions, in February to enable Stanley to pay the Manyema carriers he had brought from the Congo. During the evacuation of the stations from Lado to Wadelai something like 6,000 *kantars* of ivory had been looted, destroyed, or thrown into the river.[2] Two days after the expedition had set out, Shukri Agha, the governor of Mswa, arrived to join it accompanied by only two soldiers and three women. All the rest of his garrison had refused to come. He reported that the greatest confusion existed in all the remaining stations and that Selim Bey was still at Wadelai.[3]

The following day Stanley became acutely ill with gastritis and for nearly a month the entire expedition came to a halt at a place called by Stanley Mazamboni's. Parke attended him with great care and intense anxiety, and during the latter part of Stanley's long illness both Parke and Jephson also became seriously ill with fever.[4] Emin and Vita Hassan did a great deal during this time both for Stanley and his incapacitated officers and for the rest of the camp.

During this period letters passed between Shukri Agha and some of the others in Stanley's camp and Selim Bey. These letters were never delivered and they later fell into Stanley's own hands. Shukri Agha's letter—which Stanley described as containing 'not a syllable

[1] Slightly dissimilar figures are given in *IDA* ii. 192. Parke, *Diary*, p. 406. Jephson, *Diary*, p. 343.
[2] Statement of Basili Boktor.
[3] Jephson, *Diary*, p. 344.
[4] Parke, *Diary*, pp. 411-21; Jephson, *Diary*, pp. 345-6.

in it that was otherwise than sterling honesty'[1]—urged Selim Bey to hurry after the expedition which had been delayed. Other letters, from less reputable characters, led Stanley to believe that a conspiracy was still afoot between Selim Bey and those of Emin's followers who were in Stanley's camp.[2] Stanley at once ordered all the mainsprings to be removed from the rifles in the possession of Emin's men and made ready for immediate departure. Emin was outraged at this latest affront to his men and to his own authority, and begged Stanley to wait and allow Selim Bey to join the expedition.[3] An advance party of four soldiers arrived with a letter from Selim Bey on 8 May with the news that after overcoming great difficulties, Selim Bey and his party were now only a few days march behind. Everything they had to tell to a sceptical Stanley was later corroborated and undoubtedly represents what actually happened after Emin had withdrawn with Stanley's expedition beyond the confines of the province.

At Wadelai, Selim Bey's position had rapidly declined in the face of the party led by Fadl al-Mūlā. Finally, Fadl al-Mūlā 'had suborned the greater part of the troops and with them, in the dead of night, he marched to the magazines, possessed himself of all the ammunition, and left Wadelai for the hills'.[4] Selim Bey and his followers, consisting of some 200 officers, soldiers, and clerks, now withdrew to Mswa. Here, however, they learnt that Stanley's expedition had already left. On 22 April Selim Bey wrote to Stanley begging him to wait for his arrival. Stanley replied that he was not prepared to wait any longer but that after crossing the Semliki river the expedition would travel slowly and this would enable Selim Bey to overtake the expedition if he were determined to do so.[5] This was the last communication that passed between Stanley's expedition and Selim Bey.

Selim Bey was now in a difficult position. He had almost no ammunition and so was unwilling to risk a march after Stanley's expedition through country which the depredations of Stanley's party had rendered very hostile; he could not return to Wadelai, which was in the hands of Fadl al-Mūlā, and his men began to disperse. It was at

---

[1] *IDA* ii. 199.
[2] Ibid. Also Parke, *Diary*, pp. 420–1.
[3] *Tagebücher*, 8 May 1889, iv. 280–1.
[4] Report of twenty-one officers, etc., from Equatoria, June 1892. Sudan Intelligence Report No. 3, Khartoum Archives, Cairint 1/35/205. A copy is also in the Sudan Archives, Durham, Box 253. See also R. O. Collins, *The Southern Sudan*, pp. 69–70. [5] *IDA* ii. 206.

this point that some deserters from Stanley's expedition pointed out the place at Kavalli's where Stanley had buried twenty-five boxes of ammunition and eighteen boxes of gunpowder which he had been unable to transport. The news of this find soon reached Fadl al-Mūlā who sent a party to Kavalli's to seize it. This they succeeded in doing, although Selim Bey's dwindling followers managed to retain five boxes. Selim Bey himself was ill treated and imprisoned, but he eventually escaped and, with a body of about ninety soldiers and many women and children, he established himself at Kavalli's. Here he planted the Egyptian flag and hoped that relief would eventually be sent to him from the coast. He had no further communication with Fadl al-Mūlā, who established himself at Wadelai, and later went on to negotiate with both the Belgian officers of the Van Kerckhoven expedition and the Mahdists before he was killed in a battle near Wadelai in January 1894.[1] A remnant of Fadl al-Mūlā's soldiers was later evacuated to Uganda and served under the British authorities there.[2]

In July 1891 Emin Pasha, now in German service, returned to Kavalli's and once again met Selim Bey. Selim Bey refused to have anything to do with him, stating that by going off with Stanley's expedition Emin had simply abandoned him, and that in taking service with the Germans Emin had betrayed the Khedive.[3] A month later, shortly after Emin's departure, Lugard (in the employment of Mackinnon's I.B.E.A. Company) arrived at Kavalli's. He was greatly impressed by Selim Bey and his garrison of devoted men and highly critical of Stanley's expedition and the way it had abandoned Selim Bey. Lugard noted:

It was a sight to touch a man's heart to see this noble remnant, who were fanatical in their loyalty to their flag and their Khedive, scarred and wounded, many prematurely grey, clad in skins, and deserted, here in the heart of Africa, and I do thank God (as I said in my speech) that it has fallen to my lot to come to their relief as well as that I have been able to secure so fine a body of men for the Company's service.[4]

[1] Report of the twenty-one officers, etc., from Equatoria, cited above. See also Selim Bey's report to Lugard in M. Perham, ed., *The Diaries of Lord Lugard* (London, 1939), ii. 320–31. Stanley knew a good deal of the information up to May 1889; see *IDA* ii. 204–6. For the later career of Fadl al-Mūlā see R. O. Collins, *The Southern Sudan*, pp. 92–117.

[2] See A. B. Thruston, *African Incidents* (London, 1900), pp. 164–6.

[3] See F. Stuhlmann, *Mit Emin Pascha ins Herz von Afrika* (Berlin, 1894), pp. 338–62.

[4] M. Perham, ed., *The Diaries of Lord Lugard*, ii. 332.

Selim Bey and his garrison welcomed Lugard warmly, but at first they refused to entertain the idea of enlisting under Mackinnon's Company, declaring that their loyalty was to the Khedive. When Lugard explained that the Khedive's permission would first be requested, Selim Bey and his men eventually agreed to withdraw with Lugard to Uganda.[1] Here they were of great service to Lugard, to Mackinnon's Company, and to the future Uganda Protectorate. After the Sudanese mutiny of 1893, Selim Bey was arrested and, Lugard and others considered, quite wrongly convicted. He died at Naivasha on his way to the coast.[2]

* * *

The expedition finally set out from Mazamboni's for the coast on 8 May, the day after the arrival of the last letter from Selim Bey. At first Stanley was still so weak that he had to be carried in a hammock made out of hide. Jephson, Stairs, and Parke all suffered from very severe attacks of fever during the early weeks of the march and the progress of the expedition was slow.

During the next three months the expedition passed through a part of Africa which had never been traversed by Europeans before. It is an area of quite exceptional geographical interest and during this march Stanley's expedition made discoveries of major significance.

South of Lake Albert, the western arm of the great Rift Valley—which runs in a south-westerly direction from the Red Sea to Lake Tanganyika—is bifurcated by the great mountain range of the Ruwenzori. As has already been related, it was during the course of the Emin Pasha relief expedition that these mountains were first clearly seen by Europeans.[3] The Ruwenzori (Stanley gave it this name, which derives from an Ankole word meaning 'the place whence the rain comes')[4] is a range of mountains over seventy

[1] Ibid. 320–8.
[2] F. D. Lugard, The Rise of Our East African Empire (Edinburgh and London, 1893), ii. 478–9. There is an extensive literature on the subject of the Sudanese troops in Uganda. I am particularly indebted to Mr. O. Furley's unpublished paper 'The Sudanese Troops in Uganda' given at a meeting of the East African Institute of Research at Makerere in Jan. 1959. There are also a number of Selim Bey's letters (in Arabic original and with English translations) hitherto little known, in the Khartoum Archives, Cairint 1/35/206.
[3] See Ch. VII, p. 167 above.
[4] R. M. Bere, 'The Exploration of the Ruwenzori', Uganda Journal, xix, no. 2 (1955), 124.

miles in length and the largest snow-capped range in sub-Saharan Africa.[1] The whole of the drainage of these mountains is into the Nile, by a system of lakes and rivers which this expedition was the first to chart. The Congo–Nile watershed lies some distance away in a range of much smaller hills to the west of the Semliki valley. The Semliki valley represents the western arm of the bifurcation of the Rift Valley; the eastern arm is much less consequential. The two arms unite once more at the southern tip of the Ruwenzori range. Between 6–7 June 1889 Stairs, accompanied by a small party of volunteers, made a first ascent of the Ruwenzori, approaching from the western side. He succeeded in ascending through the bamboo forest of the lower slopes to the heath belt. Here he encountered English blackberries and the giant tree-heather and he was able to collect some specimens of the strange flora of the region, which Emin later classified. Stairs found, however, that he was separated from the volcanic peaks, which form the summits, by a series of ravines. After spending a very cold night in the open, Stairs and his party returned to Stanley's camp, after reaching a height of 10,677 ft.[2]

To the south of the Ruwenzori Mountains Stanley discovered two lakes, both much smaller than Lake Albert. He named them Lake Albert Edward (known as Lake Edward) and Lake George. These two lakes are joined together by the Kazinga Channel (which Stanley maps rather inaccurately) and they are in turn joined to Lake Albert by the Semliki river. This river flows out of the northwest corner of Lake Edward and after wandering for some 155 miles to the west of the Ruwenzori, during which it drops nearly 1,000 ft., it enters Lake Albert. This important water system not only carries all the drainage of the Ruwenzori (Ptolemy's Mountains of the Moon), it also plays a vital role in the hydrology of the Nile. It can rightly be claimed, therefore, that it was during the Emin Pasha relief expedition that Stanley solved the last remaining problem of that greatest of Victorian quests in Africa: the origins of the Nile.

Ever since Baker had discovered Lake Albert it had remained an open question whether another reservoir for the waters of the Nile existed further to the south. In 1876 Stanley had finally proved the

[1] I am much indebted to the excellent section on the geography of this area in *A Handbook of the Uganda Protectorate* (H.M.S.O., 1921), ch. 2.

[2] Stairs's full account of this ascent is in his MS. Diary in the Stairs Papers, the State Archives, Halifax, Nova Scotia. Stairs's report to Stanley is printed in *IDA* ii. 254–8.

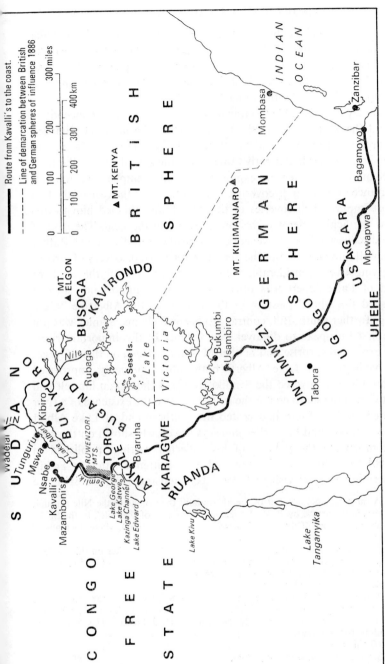

FIG. 4. The March to the Coast.

Source

The sketch-map was constructed by superimposing the contemporary map from T. H. Parke, *Experiences in Equatorial Africa* (London, 1891)—which is a compression of the map in H. M. Stanley, *In Darkest Africa* (London, 1890)—on to a modern base-map of the area.

accuracy of Speke's 'hunch' concerning the size and role of Lake Victoria as a source of the Nile. Now, in 1889, he was to reveal the astonishing nearness to the truth of Ptolemy's map of *circa* A.D. 150 in which the western branch of the Nile is shown as originating in a group of lakes fed by the Luna Montes.[1]

Stanley was also able to clear up his own previous misconceptions about the Muta Nzige [Lake Edward] which he had first glimpsed from the east in 1876, and to substantiate the claims of Mason and Gessi that Baker had greatly exaggerated the size of Lake Albert.[2]

Stanley was never an explorer who underemphasized the importance of his own discoveries. Frequently, as in the case of the two most important discoveries of this expedition, this led him to dismiss the achievements of his predecessors in the field. The case of the discovery of the Ruwenzori has already been discussed.[3] Rather less well known is that of the Semliki river.[4] The discovery of a river, carrying a very considerable volume of water, entering the southern end of Lake Albert was obviously of major importance since it pushed the whole question of the sources of the Albertine Nile a stage further south. But, contrary to his own claims, Stanley was not the first European to discover the existence of this important river. He expressed surprise that neither Mason nor Gessi on their voyages of navigation of Lake Albert (both rather hurriedly improvised affairs) had discovered the Semliki river and that Emin himself had not visited the south end of the lake and noted the existence of a river there.[5] In fact, Emin had visited the southern end of Lake Albert several times, and his earlier journeys are clearly shown on the map accompanying the volume of his collected writings published in 1888.[6] In October 1886 Emin had also written a letter to Felkin describing a recent visit to Lake Albert and reporting the existence

[1] A most succinct account of the ideas about the origins of the Nile through the ages is the article by B. W. Langlands, 'Concepts of the Nile', in the Speke Centenary number of the *Uganda Journal*, xxvi, no. 1 (1962), where the maps of Ptolemy and others are reproduced.

[2] There is a long and interesting letter from Stanley to Baker on this subject, dated 14 Feb. 1890, in the Valentine Baker papers, File 5; also Gessi to Baker, 24 Apr. and 22 Aug. 1876, in the same collection.

[3] See Ch. VII, p. 168 above.

[4] The name Semliki was given to the river by Stanley. This bears no relation to any of the local names by which the river was known. In this respect, Emin's Duéru would be more applicable. See Sir H. H. Johnston, *The Nile Quest* (London, 1903), p. 261.

[5] *IDA* ii. 220.

[6] See *E.P.* in *C.A.* (London, 1888).

of a river entering the southern end of the lake which can only be the Semliki. 'The chief result of my work', Emin had written to Felkin,

is the discovery of a new river flowing from the Usongoro mountains. It is of considerable size, and flows into the lake at the south. The river, which is called Kakibi by the Wasongoro, and Duéru by the Wamboga, contains a large island near its junction with the lake. On account of numerous cataracts, however, it is very difficult to navigate; but, on the other hand, it pours into the lake throughout the whole year a large volume of water.[1]

It was also during this march that Stanley visited Lake Katwe, one of a group of small crater lakes of volcanic origin close to Lake Edward which contain the most important salt deposits in the northern part of the East African interior.[2] A thriving salt trade, far more extensive than that at Kibiro, had long existed at Katwe, and traders came from as far afield as Usagara and Ruanda. The actual possession of the salt deposits seems to have changed several times even during the nineteenth century and at the time of Stanley's arrival one of Kabarega's chief men, Rukara, accompanied by a following of banasura had occupied the area. Stanley burnt their settlement and put them to flight and so won the respect and gratitude of the neighbouring Banyankole.[3]

This was not the first time during the march that Stanley had come into conflict with Kabarega's banasura. Whether the previous skirmishes were a series of isolated incidents, or part of a determined attempt by Kabarega to disrupt Stanley's expedition, is not clear. Stanley certainly believed that Kabarega was out to attack the

[1] Emin to R. W. Felkin, 26 Oct. 1886, printed in *E.P. in C.A.*, p. 507. See also ibid., pp. 167–8, 171. In Mar.–Apr. 1876 Gessi had been the first to circumnavigate Lake Albert and to discover the Muzizi river. In June 1877 Mason had sailed round the lake in the opposite direction to that taken by Gessi. Neither of them, however, had observed the existence of a river entering the south-west corner of the lake. See R. Gessi, 'The Circumnavigation of Lake Albert', *Bulletin de la société Khediviale de géographie du Caire*, Ser. ii, June 1885; A. M. Mason, 'Report of a Reconnaisance of Lake Albert', *Proc. Royal Geog. Soc.*, Old Series, vol. 22 (1877–8); A. M. Mason, 'The River at the Southern End of Albert Nyanza', *Proc. Royal Geog. Soc.*, New Series, vol. 12 (1890). See also B. W. Langlands, 'Early Travellers in Uganda', *Uganda Journal*, xxvi, no. 1 (1962). Sir Harry Johnston was probably correct, therefore, in suggesting that Emin was the first European to discover the Semliki river, H. H. Johnston, *The Nile Quest* (London, 1903) p. 251.
[2] For an account of Lake Katwe, see E. J. Wayland, 'Katwe', *Uganda Journal*, i, no. 2 (1934).
[3] *IDA* ii. 316–18.

expedition and that all those—including some isolated bands of pyg-
mies—who obstructed the progress of the expedition were therefore in
league with him.[1] This is extremely doubtful. What is certain is that
from the outset of the expedition Stanley had expected to encounter
serious fighting on his return march across East Africa to the coast.
It was a reasonable expectation, but it was scarcely realized. In
his book about the expedition, written for a popular audience,
Stanley felt no compunction about enlivening his narrative of the
march with accounts of a few dramatic skirmishes. This was, after
all, what his audience had come to expect from their reading of the
encounters between Europeans and Indians in North America. But
the more pedestrian accounts of the same march by Parke, Jephson,
Stairs, Emin, Casati, and Vita Hassan have about them a greater
ring of truth. Also, Stanley himself later described this march to the
more select audience of the British Consul-General at Zanzibar as
'one of the most peaceful and happy marches any expedition ever
made in Africa. Four hundred miles of an absolutely new region,
untravelled and unvisited by any white man . . . were travelled by us
without meeting with a single instance of tribal hostility.'[2]

It was during this peaceful progress that Stanley would have us
believe that he signed a number of treaties with the rulers, or their
representatives, of the areas through which the expedition passed.
These 'treaties' were presented to the I.B.E.A. Company by Stanley
in April 1890, after his return to England, and were later used by
Mackinnon in his attempts to forestall the Germans in the hinterland and secure the territory lying between Lake Albert and Lake
Tanganyika for Britain.[3] It is quite evident that whatever arrangements Stanley came to whilst passing through this area in 1889 it
was only after the expedition was over that these arrangements
came to be regarded as treaties. By these 'treaties', it was asserted,

---

[1] *IDA* ii. 248.

[2] Stanley to Euan-Smith, 19 Dec. 1889, *Africa No. 4* (1890), C. 5906. This,
of course, is exactly what Euan-Smith would want to hear and so is also probably
an exaggeration.

[3] The subject has attracted considerable attention among diplomatic historians:
see esp. W. R. Louis, *Ruanda-Urundi 1884–1919* (Oxford, 1963), pp. 11–15,
18–29. G. N. Sanderson, *England, Europe and the Upper Nile, 1882–1899*,
pp. 56–7. D. R. Gillard, 'Salisbury's African Policy and the Heligoland Offer
of 1890', *English Historical Review*, vol. lxxv (1960), pp. 631–53. The fullest
analysis of the question whether Stanley ever in fact made these treaties is Sir
J. Gray, 'Early Treaties in Uganda 1888–1891', *Uganda Journal*, xii, no. 1 (1948),
to which I am especially indebted. See also H. B. Thomas, 'More Early Treaties
in Uganda', *Uganda Journal*, xiii, no. 1 (1949).

various rulers had ceded to Stanley 'all rights of government' over their country in return 'for the protection he [Stanley] has accorded to us and our neighbours against Kabba Rega and his Warasura'. It was these 'rights' which Stanley made over to Mackinnon's Company and which Mackinnon tried to utilize with the British Foreign Office in a way not dissimilar to that adopted by Carl Peters with the German Foreign Office five years previously. It had, of course, been part of the original plan of Mackinnon and Hutton that the Emin Pasha relief expedition should be utilized to obtain such treaties.[1] By 1889 Mackinnon was more eager than ever that his Company should secure treaties with local rulers in the hinterland.[2] But it is clear that Stanley's 'treaties' were initially no more than oral agreements. On 5 February 1890 Stanley wrote to Mackinnon from Cairo:

> About friendly arrangements west of Victoria Nyanza I have made several verbally but no written, as the Pasha and Casati were there and I have witnesses, Ankori, Usongora and Ukarija—east of the Semliki were given to me on the same terms as Treaties are made—and all my rights, of course, I turn over to you—but all this will be drawn out properly on arriving in London.[3]

Accordingly, on 29 April 1890, the I.B.E.A. Company received six 'treaties' drawn up by Stanley and witnessed by three of his European officers.[4]

These 'treaties' are perhaps best regarded not as treaties at all but as *post-facto* memoranda constructed by Stanley out of certain

---

[1] See Ch. III, p. 55 above.
[2] See Mackinnon to Stanley, 5 Apr. 1889, M.P., F. 1. Mackinnon to Nicol (an I.B.E.A. employee), 1 Aug. 1889, forwarded to Stanley 5 Nov. 1889, F.O. 84/2036. Part of this letter is printed in W. R. Louis, op. cit., p. 12. These letters, clearly indicating Mackinnon's designs on the German 'hinterland', later fell into the hands of the Germans. See F. F. Müller, *Deutschland—Zanzibar—Ostafrika* (E. Berlin, 1959), p. 475.
[3] Stanley to Mackinnon, 6 Feb. 1890, M.P., 218.
[4] Copies of these 'treaties' were forwarded to the F.O. by the Secretary of the I.B.E.A. Company on 2 May 1890 with the request that the British Government 'may be pleased with as little delay as possible' to declare a British Protectorate over the territories 'ceded to the Company in virtue of the Treaties', F.O. 84/2081. The texts of the treaties were later published, first in the Government Paper *Africa No. 4* (1892), later in Sir Edward Hertslet, *The Map of Africa by Treaty* (London, 1896), H.M.S.O.—2 vols. vol. i. pp. 167–8. These treaties were utilized in the negotiations which resulted in the Anglo-German Agreement over East Africa in July 1890. See W. R. Louis, op. cit., pp. 15–29.

ceremonies of friendship and blood-brotherhood which he, or one of his officers, had undergone with representatives of the rulers of the areas through which the expedition passed. In two cases such ceremonies were certainly performed. In others it is doubtful if the rulers or their representatives, cited by Stanley in each case as the other party to the 'treaty', ever met him, and the dates of some of the agreements are definitely false.[1]

The best-documented case of the events from which Stanley later constructed a treaty is that of Ankole. At the beginning of July 1889 Stanley, having skirted round Lake George and ascended the Kichwamba escarpment, arrived on the borders of Ankole. Here he had to decide which of three routes the expedition was to adopt for the remainder of the march to the coast. It could go direct across Buganda; south-west via Ankole to the southern tip of Lake Victoria and then to Bagamayo via the 'southern' route; or it could take the much longer way via Ruanda and Lake Tanganyika. Ruanda was little known, and Buganda was known to be in a state of great unrest. After a discussion with his officers (which they found largely a formality, as Stanley had already made up his mind), it was decided that the expedition should adopt the second route via Ankole and the south end of Lake Victoria.[2]

Stanley approached Ankole with some apprehension. The ruler of the country, Ntare, had utilized the position of Ankole—astride the southern trade-route from the east coast via Karagwe—to acquire guns; Stanley also believed he possessed a very considerable army of spearmen, a small section of which would be quite large enough to stop the expedition. But he also hoped that the exchanges between the expedition and Kabarega's *banasura*, and especially the release of the salt deposits at Katwe, would incline Ntare to treat the expedition favourably.[3] Stanley's fears proved groundless. The Banyankole feared Stanley and his expedition quite as much as he feared them. Both parties were suspicious of each other and anxious to form some pact of non-aggression.[4] At first the messengers dispatched by Stanley to Ntare returned with the message that Ntare was away and the Queen Mother was indisposed. This was almost

[1] See Sir John Gray, op. cit., pp. 31–2. See also the personal communications of Sir John Gray and H. B. Thomas cited in W. R. Louis, op. cit., pp. 11–12.

[2] *IDA* ii. 330–2. Jephson, *Diary*, p. 375. Parke, *Diary*, pp. 449–50.

[3] *IDA* ii. 331.

[4] F. Lukyn Williams, 'Early Explorers in Ankole', *Uganda Journal*, ii, no. 3 (1935).

certainly a ruse to keep Stanley and his large following away from the royal capital.[1] Eventually a prince of the royal clan (not Ntare's son, as Stanley claims) was sent to perform a ceremony of *omukago* (blood-brotherhood) with Stanley. This was eventually performed on 24 July at Byaruha (Stanley calls the place Viaruha) in Ruampara.[2] What was performed was certainly not the full rite of *omukago* but a much abbreviated version, and all that this appears to have secured was permission for Stanley and his expedition to cross Ankole. There was no mention of a treaty by which Stanley acquired 'all rights of government' over Ankole. What the Banyankole who were present at the occasion chiefly seem to remember is that for many of them this was their first encounter with Europeans. They were also astonished and terrified by a demonstration of the devastating effectiveness of Stanley's Maxim gun.[3]

It was also whilst the expedition was in Ankole that Stanley received two visits from representatives of the Christians from Buganda who had recently fled to Ankole as refugees during the disturbances in Buganda. They were able to tell Stanley of the recent events in Buganda. The Muslim party at the court had eventually succeeded in deposing Mwanga in September 1888 and had replaced him first by Kiwewa and then by Kalema. The missionaries had all been expelled from the country and had established themselves to the south of Lake Victoria in two settlements: Mackay and the C.M.S. missionaries were at Usambiro; the French Roman Catholics were at Bukumbi. During a widespread persecution of Christians throughout Buganda, over 2,000 had fled to Ankole. Among those who had fled from Buganda had been Hamu Mukasa and Apolo Kagwa—who were later to be of such importance in the country's history. Mukasa had tried to persuade Mackay and the missionaries to become involved in an attempt to restore Mwanga to his throne and thereby to bring about the re-establishment of the missionaries in Buganda. Mackay, however, had refused, since he believed that such an intervention would expose all missionaries in the African interior to serious danger. Charles Stokes, an English trader who had married an African woman, had been more ready to intervene on Mwanga's behalf. He had arrived at Usambiro with a caravan of supplies sent

---

[1] Ntare School History Society. 'H. M. Stanley's journey through Ankole in 1889', *Uganda Journal*, xxix, no. 2 (1965).
[2] *IDA* ii. 348–9.
[3] See F. Lukyn Williams, 'Blood Brotherhood in Ankole', *Uganda Journal*, ii, no. 1 (1934). Also H. F. Morris, *A History of Ankole* (Kampala, 1962), p. 14.

by the I.B.E.A. Company for Stanley's expedition. He also possessed considerable stocks of guns and ammunition, and a boat. These he had used in an unsuccessful attempt to reinstate Mwanga in May 1889. After this defeat, Mwanga had taken refuge in the Sese Islands on Lake Victoria. From there he had once again implored Mackay to assist him. He had also written a letter (which he sent with another letter from Stokes) to Frederick Jackson, the leader of the expedition which the I.B.E.A. Company had dispatched from the coast and which Mwanga knew was approaching Buganda across the Masai land. In this letter, which was to fall into the eager hands of the German, Carl Peters, Mwanga requested help 'to put me on my throne'.[1] Mwanga had also learnt that Stanley, having met Emin Pasha, was making his way from Lake Albert through Ankole at the head of a considerable expedition. Rumours about Stanley's Emin Pasha relief expedition had reached Buganda in 1887 and had led to great apprehension. It had been believed that 'there is a *Muzungu* [European] coming here with a thousand guns' and Mwanga had at first been convinced that Stanley's real purpose was to attack Buganda in revenge for the murder of Bishop Hannington. By June 1889, however, Mwanga's views had mellowed, and he had come to see in Stanley's expedition a possibility which he might turn to his own advantage. He had instructed the Christian refugees in Ankole to approach Stanley and to invoke the assistance of his expedition to restore Mwanga to the throne of Buganda.[2] Accordingly, on 9 July, Stanley was approached by Samwiri Mukasa and Zakariya Kizito at Katera in Ankole. Stanley, however, refused to become embroiled in the affairs of Buganda—to the great disappointment of Mwanga—although he allowed five of the Buganda Christians to accompany the expedition to the coast.[3]

Throughout July and August Stanley's expedition marched across Ankole and Karagwe. During this part of the journey considerable numbers of Emin's followers either deserted or were left behind, along with several Zanzibaris and the pygmy woman who had been brought with the expedition all the way from the Ituri forest. Some of these people were abandoned under the most pathetic circumstances. It is impossible to know what became of them. By the time

[1] See Carl Peters, *New Light on Dark Africa* (London, 1891), Chs. IX and X. Also F. F. Müller, op. cit., p. 473.

[2] See Sir John Gray, 'The Year of the Three Kings in Buganda 1888–1889' *Uganda Journal*, xiv, no. 1 (1950).

[3] Ibid. Also *IDA* ii. 337–41, 350–3.

the expedition reached Karagwe, Stanley states that its numbers were reduced to about 800.[1]

In August Jephson was deputed to visit the ruler of Karagwe, whose capital lay six miles from the route of the expedition. When he arrived at the 'royal enclosure', Jephson encountered a boy, about eighteen years old, who was the grandson of Rumanika. Jephson was rather disappointed by what he found and used the occasion to contrast in his diary the different ways in which he and Stanley described such incidents. Jephson found the royal capital to consist of 'nothing but a collection of dirty miserable huts surrounded by untidy courtyards and the king himself is just like any ordinary native, he lives in the same way and has the same kind of hut to live in, only that it is a little larger'.[2] Stanley, Jephson considered, wrote about such places in an

absurdly exaggerated style. All this talk of kings and emperors and princes of the royal blood, with their residences, courts and palaces sounds all very fine in books of travel, but it is nothing but bosh and it conveys a very false idea to the people for whose instruction the book is published.[3]

During this peaceful march, Emin became increasingly withdrawn and absorbed in his natural history collecting. His diary is uninformative. He was rather depressed. His relations with Stanley and the other European officers, as with Casati and Vita Hassan, were very strained. After another row with Stanley in June, Emin asked Stanley simply to leave him to stay with his people where they were. Stanley 'in an outburst of fury more brutal than that at Kavalli's', told Emin he regretted that he had ever come with the expedition to 'relieve' him and declared that Emin was 'a most thankless and ungrateful man'.[4] Emin later apologized to Stanley for his apparent ingratitude and declared his appreciation of what Stanley and the expedition had done for him. None the less Emin still wished to be left behind in the East African interior, and Stanley continued to refuse to allow Emin to go his own way.[5] Emin adopted an increasingly passive role and appears as a passenger on an expedition in the conduct of which he now had almost no say at all.

On 15 August the expedition came in sight of Lake Victoria—the

[1] Stanley to Euan-Smith, 19 Dec. 1889, *Africa No. 4* (1890), C. 5906.
[2] Jephson, *Diary*, pp. 389–90.   [3] Ibid. 390.
[4] *Tagebücher*, 13 June 1889, iv. 315 (Extracts XIII, p. 78). Jephson, *Diary*, pp. 361–2. Parke, *Diary*, p. 439. Parke's dating is incorrect.
[5] *Tagebücher*, 15 June 1889, iv. 317.

south-west corner of which Stanley now charted and proved to be much more extensive than had been thought hitherto.[1] On 28 August the expedition arrived at the mission station which Mackay, the C.M.S. missionary, had built at Usambiro after his withdrawal from Buganda. Stanley and the expedition remained with Mackay for almost three weeks and during this time a number of important developments took place, which Stanley completely omits from his account. It was on this occasion also that Emin first met Mackay— the man who had exercised such an important influence on him during the years since 1885, and who had played such a crucial role in the sending of the expedition. Emin's diary, also, is curiously uninformative. Fortunately, both Stanley and Emin wrote a number of letters while they were at Usambiro and these have survived. In his book, Stanley presents the stay at Usambiro as a welcome period of rest and recuperation after the long march from Lake Albert, amidst the attentions of the missionaries Mackay and Deekes and the supplies sent by the I.B.E.A. Company.[2] This it certainly was. But even more important is the fact that it was here that the expedition received the first news of developments in Europe and East Africa since leaving the Congo.[3] 'Our first question', says Parke, with that almost unbelievable sense of Victorian patriotism, 'was whether her Majesty the Queen was still alive.'[4]

Of more immediate relevance was the news of the developments in East Africa. Mackinnon's I.B.E.A. Company had received its charter the previous year and had begun to prosecute and extend its claims in the East African interior.[5] Its methods followed closely those of its immediate German rival, the German East Africa Company under Wissmann, although the latter obtained considerably more encouragement from its Government. Expeditions had been sent inland from the coast to make treaties with local rulers which reserved exclusive rights to the English Company. Mackinnon had

[1] Stanley states that this discovery made Lake Victoria 'just 1,900 square miles larger than the reputed "exaggerations" of Captain Speke'. Stanley to the British Consul at Zanzibar, 11 Nov. 1889, enclosed in C. S. Smith to Salisbury, 28 Nov. 1889, F.O. 84/1981.   [2] *IDA* ii. 388–91.
[3] Most of the letters sent to Stanley and the other officers had been dispatched to Buganda and so were lost. But Mackay had been in regular correspondence with Europe and the I.B.E.A. Company and there were many newspapers and some letters for Emin.   [4] Parke, *Diary*, p. 475.
[5] I am much indebted to the work of Marie de Kiewiet, 'A History of the I.B.E.A. Company', unpublished Ph.D. thesis (London, 1955) in the following section.

even sought to enlist missionaries such as Mackay in this activity and thereby save the Company considerable expense. By the end of 1889 the Anglo-German rivalry at the coast had become extended into a fierce competition for the interior. In this competition first Equatoria then Buganda came to occupy the focal role. The intense interest now shown by both the English and the German Companies in the province which he had just abandoned came as a great surprise to Emin and had not altogether been expected by Stanley. Stanley learnt that his expedition to 'relieve' Emin Pasha (who was now claimed as a German subject) had come to be regarded with the greatest suspicion by the Germans. In July 1887 Lord Salisbury had been obliged to instruct the British Ambassador in Berlin to assure the German Government that there 'was no cause to apprehend' that the Emin Pasha relief expedition would be 'used as a means of interference with the territory under German influence'.[1] Since the Anglo-German Agreement of 1886 had left the question of the western delimitation of the British and German 'spheres' in East Africa open, the German Carl Peters had succeeded, despite the Anglo-German Hinterland Agreement of 1887,[2] in organizing an expedition to extend German claims in the interior under the guise of a mission to relieve Emin Pasha.[3] Despite the fact that an English expedition had already been sent under Stanley to achieve this object and that both Wissmann and the German Government—at least for the moment—disowned him, Peters had set out in 1889.[4] By the time Stanley and Emin arrived at Usambiro, Carl Peters was already at large in the interior, heading towards Buganda.

This rapid rise in German interest in the interior had aroused mounting alarm and Germanophobia in Mackinnon and those members of the 'Mackinnon Clan' and the Emin Pasha Relief Committee now closely involved with the I.B.E.A. Company. After its departure from Stanley Pool in April 1887 nothing had been heard of

---

[1] See Hertslet, *The Map of Africa by Treaty*, vol. ii, p. 626.

[2] In July 1887 Salisbury had agreed to a request from Bismarck that he should 'discourage British annexation in the rear of the German sphere of influence, on the understanding that the German Government would equally discourage German annexations in the rear of the British sphere', ibid., p. 627.

[3] Carl Peters, *New Light on Dark Africa*, esp. ch. 1, F. M. Müller, *Deutschland—Zanzibar—Ostafrika*, esp. ch. xv.

[4] The British Consul at Zanzibar remarked, 'Although in theory the leading officials of the German Government in Zanzibar have washed their hands of Dr. Peters and his expedition, it is no secret that in practice this is by no means the case.' Portal to F.O., 10 Aug. 1889, F.O. 84/1980.

Stanley's expedition until December 1888, when the news of Stanley's return to the Rear Column and the disasters which had befallen it had become known. By this time it had become clear that Stanley's expedition had encountered a series of set-backs and by the beginning of 1889, when Stanley's letters from Banalya had finally arrived, both Mackinnon and King Leopold had come to the conclusion that the various objectives which they had each sought through Stanley's expedition were unlikely to be achieved. The Egyptian Government seems to have been less concerned, although the reported capture of Emin and Stanley by the Mahdists led Sir Evelyn Baring to engage in a fascinating correspondence with Lord Salisbury about the possibility of ransoming them from the Khalifa.[1]

Both King Leopold and Mackinnon had responded to the situation by attempting to safeguard their interests by other means. Leopold initiated the train of events which led to the Becker mission to Tippu Tip and the Van Kerckhoven expedition to the Nile.[2] Mackinnon, in a series of letters which fell into the hands of the Germans, had written to both Stanley and Mackay urging them to do everything to extend the Company's claims in the interior, even behind the German 'sphere', and thus make it possible for Mackinnon's Company to join hands with that of Cecil Rhodes in an all-red route from Capetown to Cairo.[3]

Mackinnon had also seen fit to dispatch another expedition to 'relieve' Emin Pasha and possibly Stanley as well. Led by Frederick Jackson (Lugard had been approached but he was still occupied in the Lake Nyasa region) this expedition had left Mombasa for the interior in November 1888. Like the German expedition under Carl Peters, its objective was the Equatorial province, but Jackson had been instructed to avoid Buganda—a fact which was to give a considerable but ultimately fruitless advantage to Carl Peters in 1890.[4]

[1] See Salisbury to Baring, 14 Dec. 1888 and Baring to Salisbury, 15 Dec. 1888, F.O. 84/1903. Also Baring to Salisbury, 16 Dec. 1888 and enclosures. Salisbury Papers, A 53/no. 74. (Another version of this letter is in F.O. 633/6/137.)

[2] For both of these see Ceulemans, *La Question arabe et le Congo*, pp. 153–71, 283–8. Also R. O. Collins, *The Southern Sudan 1883–1898*, ch. 3, and G. N. Sanderson, *England, Europe and the Upper Nile*, ch. v.

[3] The letters, dated Apr.–Nov. 1889, were found by the Germans when they captured Abushiri, the leader of a rebellion in German East Africa. Copies are to be found in F.O. 84/2036 and F.O. 84/2086. Copies of the letters to Stanley are also in M.P., 218. See also D. R. Gillard, 'Salisbury's African Policy and the Heligoland Offer of 1890', *English Historical Review*, lxxv, (1960), 297.

[4] For the accounts of these two expeditions, see F. J. Jackson, *Early Days in East Africa* (London, 1930), and Carl Peters, op. cit.

YET ANOTHER CRIME

How will the disaster at Uganda affect the position of Emin Pasha and Mr. Stanley? Uganda is claimed as a Mahomedan country. If our troops had gone on to Khartoum it is certain these events would not have happened. Another beautiful illustration of Mr. Gladstone's foresight and statesmanship!

Ghost of General Gordon—IF STANLEY AND EMIN NEVER RETURN *YOU* ARE AGAIN RESPONSIBLE!

(From Judy: the London serio-comic journal, 23 January, 1889)

6. The expedition as seen in England in 1888–9

Mackinnon had further attempted to safeguard his Company's interests in Equatoria by entering into negotiations with R. W. Felkin during the summer of 1888. Emin, it will be remembered, had given Felkin *carte blanche* to act in his interests even before Stanley's expedition had set out.[1] Felkin had hesitated to use these powers but, like Mackinnon, he feared the Germans, and when it became known that Carl Peters was organizing an expedition to go to Wadelai in 1888, Felkin acted firmly and at once. In June 1888 Felkin wrote to Emin telling him about the negotiations he had recently entered into with Mackinnon and the I.B.E.A. Company whereby Emin was to remain in Equatoria as an employee of the Company. Felkin assured Emin that he could put complete trust in the Company and urged him to co-operate with it.[2] A copy of the Agreement which Felkin had drawn up on Emin's behalf with the I.B.E.A. Company was also sent, along with a letter from Sir Francis de Winton.[3] In this letter, de Winton explained the reasons for the Agreement, requested Emin's co-operation, and outlined the steps the I.B.E.A. Company intended to take with regard to the future of Equatoria, although 'Mr. Stanley will no doubt have discussed with you many points bearing on this most important question'.[4] With regard to all these arrangements, Emin was left with the option of refusing the Agreement drawn up on his behalf by Felkin; but it would be hard to imagine a more precise implementation of all the hopes and ambitions which Emin had so optimistically outlined for the future of the Equatorial Province between 1885–8.

But by the end of 1889 the collapse of Emin's position in Equatoria and events in Buganda had led to a shift in interest in both English and German circles from Equatoria to Buganda. Henceforth Buganda replaces Equatoria as the focus of Anglo-German rivalry in the interior.[5]

[1] See Ch. VII, pp. 145–6 above.
[2] Felkin to Emin, 10 June 1888. This and other letters from Felkin to Emin at this time are included as an appendix to the last published volume of Emin's diary by the editor Stuhlmann. See *Tagebücher*, iv. 439–45. There is no evidence that Emin ever received these letters but it is highly likely that he did so after reaching the coast in Dec. 1889. See also Felkin's account of these events in Schweitzer, vol. i, pp. xxxvi–xli.
[3] A copy of this Agreement, together with an outline of I.B.E.A.'s general plans with regard to Emin and Equatoria, is in F.O. 84/1908.
[4] de Winton to Emin Pasha, 9 June 1888, printed in *Tagebücher*, iv. 445–8. Copies of Felkin's and de Winton's letters are also in M.P., F. 1.
[5] de Kiewiet, op. cit., p. 180.

This was soon made apparent to Stanley and Emin at Usambiro in August 1889 by Mackay. By the summer of 1889 Mackay was urging the I.B.E.A. Company to act in Buganda in a manner, indeed in language, which closely resembles that of Holmwood's dispatches to the British Government about Equatoria three years previously. In letters to Mackinnon and to the British Consul at Zanzibar, Mackay declared

... the Company's true course is to make themselves masters of Buganda. The present state of matters there will aid them if taken advantage of, and such an opportunity may not occur again for many years to come ... If they could join hands with Emin Pasha and by aid of his troops set Mwanga on the throne of Buganda, he would be entirely in their hands and they will secure the key to the whole Lake region.[1]

Three days before Stanley and Emin arrived at Usambiro Mackay had written a long letter to Emin Pasha, which later fell into the hands of Carl Peters. In this letter, Mackay told Emin of the recent events in Buganda and of the dispatch of the expedition under Frederick Jackson by the I.B.E.A. Company from the coast. This expedition may have set out with the intention of reaching Wadelai but, wrote Mackay, 'Now is the time to strike a strong blow for the right to win Uganda.' Since Mackay believed that Emin and Stanley had left Equatoria with a considerable number of Emin's troops, Mackay now proposed that they should join forces with Jackson's expedition to march on Buganda, expel Kalema and the Muslim party, and put Mwanga back on the throne 'not, as before, as an independent sovereign, but as an agent of the British East Africa Company'.[2] Judging by the letter which Mwanga himself wrote to Jackson, imploring his assistance, Mwanga would have been only too happy to participate in such a scheme.[3] Rather prematurely, Mackinnon's Company had already published a statement in which it was declared 'it is probable that the Company's caravans have already joined hands with Emin Pasha and Mr. Stanley'.[4] When Stanley and Emin arrived, rather unexpectedly, at Usambiro on 28 August it became Mackay's objective to unite Stanley's expedition with that of Jackson and for this combined force to intervene in Buganda. Stokes was

[1] Mackay to the British Consul at Zanzibar, 31 July 1889, F.O. 84/1981. See also Mackay to Mackinnon, 2 Sept. 1889, M.P.

[2] Mackay to Emin, 25 Aug. 1889, printed in Carl Peters, *New Light on Dark Africa*, pp. 313-17.

[3] This letter is printed in F. J. Jackson, *Early Days in East Africa*, p. 222.

[4] Prospectus for the I.B.E.A. Company, 14 Aug. 1889. A copy is in the M.P.

expected to return with news of events in Buganda shortly after the arrival of Stanley's expedition. Mackay at once sent a message to Jackson urging him to come to Usambiro. On 30 August, Emin noted, 'it is to be hoped that we will then all go to Uganda, annex it and return home'.[1]

Stanley, however, was implacably opposed to any involvement of his expedition in the affairs of Buganda, a position he had consistently taken ever since he had first been approached to lead the expedition.[2] He was also incensed to discover that so little confidence had been placed in his remarkable abilities that Mackinnon had seen the necessity to dispatch a second expedition under Jackson. In a letter to Mackinnon Stanley declared that this was 'totally contrary to what was agreed to before I left England', and warned Mackinnon of the dangers Jackson would encounter between Buganda and Equatoria and the situation that existed at Wadelai. Stanley blamed Mackinnon bitterly 'for sending Jackson to relieve me at Wadelai', before it was even known 'that I needed relief'.[3] The news of the dispatch of Jackson's expedition and of the attacks on his own expedition which he now discovered had already begun in the British press, exasperated Stanley. After all he had been through, after the successive set-backs and frustrations, to have emerged with his expedition to encounter such little faith in his abilities and so much criticism was just too much. It was almost to be expected that Stanley would vent his feelings of exasperation on Emin. Emin was dismissed as a sensitive, intelligent, and courteous man who was completely impractical and whose people were scarcely worth the enormous cost their 'rescue' had entailed. Emin should be found a quiet corner somewhere, where he could 'study insects, collect birds, classify them, and stuff them for preservation. His industry in small things is immense; but it is in a small circle, as narrow as his range of sight, which is just about 10 yards.'[3]

Emin, however, was not to be dismissed so lightly. The whole subject of the Kavirondo proposal would seem never to have been discussed by Emin and Stanley on the march to Usambiro, although Emin had more than once expressed his desire to be settled with his

[1] *Tagebücher*, 30 Aug. 1889, iv. 366. Mackay's plan is further outlined in Mackay to Consul Berkeley, 31 July 1889, F.O. 84/1981.
[2] Mackay to I.B.E.A. Company, 2 Sept. 1889. Zanzibar Secretariat Archives, cited in Sir John Gray 'The Year of the Three Kings in Buganda', *Uganda Journal*, xiv, no. 1 (1950), 42.
[3] Stanley to Mackinnon, 31 Aug. 1889, M.P.

followers somewhere in the interior whilst Stanley went on with the rest of the expedition to the coast. Once the expedition had arrived at Usambiro, Emin, like Mackay, saw new possibilities in the proximity and objectives of Jackson's expedition. He approached Stanley and asked him to allow him and some of his followers to join Jackson's expedition and establish themselves at some point on Lake Victoria.[1] It is clear that Emin hoped that from this base he would be able to assist the I.B.E.A. Company in the conquest of Buganda and Bunyoro, which Stanley had rightly stressed as a precondition for the eventual re-establishment of Equatoria under British auspices.[2] Stanley, however, refused to sanction such a proposal and declared in no uncertain terms that Emin was to accompany his expedition to the coast. Emin later stated that he was thus 'compelled to march with him [Stanley] to the coast, whereas originally the question was only that of a transfer of my capital from Lake Albert to Lake Victoria'.[2] It is quite clear from Stanley's letter to Mackinnon that by the time the expedition reached Usambiro, Stanley had decided that Emin had no future usefulness for Mackinnon's company. There is, however, another reason why Stanley was so emphatically determined to take Emin with him to the coast. If Emin were left at large in the East African interior, with however small a following, he would be free and available to work for the interests of anyone who might approach him with an attractive proposal. Emin had been born a German and the news that Carl Peters was somewhere in the vicinity with a German expedition and with the avowed objective of reaching Wadelai and staking out claims for Germany in the interior, caused Stanley profound disquiet. After the immense trouble he had taken to lead an English expedition to 'rescue' Emin Pasha, Stanley was certainly not prepared to risk the possibility that Emin would at once return to Equatoria under the auspices of the Germans. As Stanley wrote to Mackinnon, '*Nolens volens*, the Pasha had to come' with Stanley's expedition to the coast.[3]

[1] Euan-Smith to Salisbury, 14 Mar. 1890, reporting a recent conversation with Emin Pasha, F.O. 84/2060.

[2] Carl Peters, *New Light on Dark Africa*, p. 545, reporting a conversation with Emin Pasha at Mpwapwa.

[3] Stanley to Mackinnon, 31 Aug. 1889, M.P., F. 1. Stanley's fear of Emin's German sympathies are best documented by Emin himself. See esp. *Tagebücher*, 2, 5, and 16 Nov. and 3 Dec. 1889, iv. 417–20, 426–7, 438. See *IDA* ii. 107 for Stanley's suggestion in 1887–8 that a German expedition had been sent to Equatoria from the east coast. See also the comment of John Flint in R. Oliver and G. Mathew, eds., *A History of East Africa*, i. 377.

Emin at least succeeded in persuading Stanley to delay his departure from Usambiro for several days in the hope that news would arrive of Jackson's caravan. During this time both Emin and Stanley wrote a number of letters which were at once dispatched to the coast. These described in detail the whole progress of the expedition since leaving the Congo and the events in Equatoria which had culminated in Emin's withdrawal.[1] Emin also wrote two more personal letters which are of some interest. One was a letter to Mackinnon. It is a masterpiece of restraint in which Emin expresses his appreciation of 'the generous help you have sent us' and asks for his thanks to be conveyed to the subscribers to the Emin Pasha Relief Fund whose donations had financed the expedition. As for Stanley and his officers, 'to speak here of [their] merits would be inadequate' and with regard to the events which the arrival of their expedition had helped to bring about, Stanley's 'graphic pen will tell you everything much better than I could'.[2] Emin also wrote a much more intimate letter at this time to his closest friend in Britain, R. W. Felkin. It is a sad and weary epistle permeated by a sense of resignation to circumstances—perhaps to Stanley's more forceful personality. In it Emin describes the events which had led to his withdrawal from Equatoria in company with Stanley's expedition and his arrival at Usambiro. 'Amongst those who are with me', Emin concluded,

many have gangrenous sores, and have suffered so much that I fear by the time we reach the coast my party will be a small one. Concerning the journey, excuse me [not] writing to you; others will be able to do this better than I. All my hopes are shattered and I return home half blind and broken down. I indeed hope that I shall not be judged too hardly.[3]

By 17 September news had still not arrived from Stokes, Jackson,

---

[1] Stanley to the Emin Pasha Relief Committee, 5 and 17 Aug. 1889, printed in *The Standard*, 25 and 26 Nov. 1889. Stanley to de Winton, 31 Aug. 1889, printed in ibid. 31 Dec. 1889. Stanley to Marston, 3 Sept. 1889, printed in ibid. 25 Nov. 1889. Stanley to the British Consul at Zanzibar, 29 Aug. 1889, enclosed in Portal to Salisbury, 2 Nov. 1889, F.O. 84/1981. Emin to Portal, 28 Aug. 1889, enclosed in ibid. Emin to the President of the Council in Cairo (in French), 28 Aug. 1889, F.O. 84/1972. A letter from Stanley to Jackson, dated 4 Sept. 1889, later fell into the hands of Carl Peters. It was through this letter that Peters first heard of Emin's withdrawal with Stanley's expedition from Equatoria. This letter is printed in Carl Peters, op. cit., p. 360.
[2] Emin to Mackinnon, 23 Aug. 1889, printed in the Report of the Committee to the subscribers of the Emin Pasha Relief Fund, 1891 (never published), p. 101, M.P. The original letter is not, I believe, extant.
[3] Emin to Felkin, 28 Aug. 1889, printed in Schweitzer, vol. i, pp. xli–xliii.

or the coast and so the expedition left Mackay's station on the final march to Bagamoyo. Stokes was in fact occupied with affairs in Buganda where, after an abortive attempt in October, Mwanga was finally reinstated as Kabaka in February 1890 with the assistance of the Christian party. Mackay, however, was never to return to Buganda, for in that very month he died at Usambiro.[1]

* * *

When Stanley's expedition left Usambiro for the coast, its numbers were little more than 700—less than half of the total which had set out from Kavalli's.[2] About 100 men were sick; ten had to be left with Mackay. Carriers were now so few that some more had had to be obtained from Mackay and others were recruited on the march to the coast. During the rest of September and October the march was fairly uneventful, although the expedition exchanged hostilities with the Sukuma in which the Maxim gun was used with deadly effect and 'some 200 cattle and about the same number of goats and sheep' were captured.[3]

On 17 October the expedition was joined by two of the French Roman Catholic missionaries stationed at Bukumbi. Father Girault was suffering from cataract and, accompanied by Father Schynse, he had visited Mackay's station to consult Emin. Emin had recommended him to return to Europe for an operation. The two men decided to accept the escort of Stanley's expedition to the coast. In a little-known work Father Schynse has left us a fascinating account of the state of the expedition at this time and of the attitudes of its various members towards each other and towards the expedition as a whole.[4] Schynse was struck by the great difference between the characters of Emin and Stanley. Emin he describes as a man of very simple tastes, a great linguist, and a devoted scientist, whose nature was fundamentally different from that of Stanley 'whose character is so energetic'.[5] Emin was frequently ill and ate very little. Most of his time was spent on his scientific work; what remained he gave to

---

[1] See R. Oliver and G. Mathew, eds., *A History of East Africa*, pp. 401–2, for a brief outline. One awaits with great interest the detailed study of Buganda in this period by John Rowe.

[2] Stanley to the British Consul at Zanzibar, 29 Aug. 1889, enclosed in Portal to Salisbury, 2 Nov. 1889, F.O. 84/1981. Also, *IDA* ii. 407.

[3] Jephson, *Diary*, pp. 402–5.

[4] Père Schynse, *A travers l'Afrique avec Stanley et Emin Pasha* (Paris, 1890).

[5] Ibid. 140.

his little daughter, Ferida, who on the march was carried in front of him in a hammock, close enough for Emin to see her with his bad eyesight.[1] Schynse found the European officers bitterly disappointed at the outcome of the expedition. They had set out believing Emin to be a soldier at the head of 2,000 well-disciplined troops whom they had only to supply with ammunition in order to secure Equatoria for England, and open a route to Mombasa. A host of men had died; vast sums had been spent; and what had been achieved? Stanley's officers declared, 'We are bringing a lot of useless, rotten Egyptian clerks, Jews, Greeks and Turks out of the interior; people who don't so much as thank us for doing so . . . and the Pasha, although an honourable man, is, after all, merely a scientist.' As for the expedition, Schynse remarks 'outwardly it is a success, of course, and it will be acclaimed in Europe accordingly; but at heart the officers of the expedition are grievously disappointed with the result and quite admit it'.[2] Being the only other member of the expedition who spoke German, Schynse conversed a good deal with Emin Pasha. He found that Emin had lost all his illusions about the true purposes behind the expedition. Mackinnon, Emin observed, had never even heard of him before 1886. Why, then, should this shrewd Scottish businessman suddenly conceive the idea of spending large sums of money to 'rescue' an Egyptian employee? Emin was convinced that it was not for himself, but for the province of which he was governor and for his ivory that the expedition had really been sent. If things had remained as they were, the considerable stocks of ivory accumulated at Wadelai would not only have covered the cost of the expedition, but would have provided capital for several years.[3] The expedition, however, had failed to obtain any of the ivory in Equatoria. On 22 November Emin received a letter from a representative of a Hamburg trading firm offering to take over all his ivory. 'I haven't got any!' he noted ruefully.[4]

On 31 October the European members of the expedition were astonished to meet a caravan of Nyamwezi, who greeted them in German. Stanley's expedition was, of course, approaching the coast through what was now the German 'sphere'. Everywhere there were

---

[1] Ibid. 206.

[2] Ibid. 160–1.

[3] Ibid. 200–1.

[4] *Tagebücher*, 22 Nov. 1889, iv. 430. See also Schynse, op. cit. p. 295, and the comment of Sir Percy Anderson on a letter from the British Consulate at Cairo, Clarke to Salisbury, 29 Nov. 1889, F.O. 84/1972.

signs of the German presence in the interior. Now Emin received the first of a series of letters from Wissmann, the German Commissioner. Wissmann welcomed Emin as Germany's 'distinguished son' and told him of the efforts of Carl Peters on his behalf. Wissmann promised to take the mail which Emin and Stanley had forwarded from Usambiro with him to the coast, and expressed a great interest in the large quantity of ivory which Emin was reputedly bringing with him. 'The Emperor William II . . . wishes me to keep him fully advised concerning yourself and Mr. Stanley', wrote Wissmann; meanwhile Emin would find Lieutenant Schmidt at Mpwapwa ready to receive the expedition and 'under orders to accompany you to the coast if you desire it'.[1]

When the expedition duly arrived at Mpwapwa on 10 November, Emin found himself welcomed as a hero and soon felt 'quite at home'.

Schmidt is extremely obliging; he had repeatedly hinted that at Berlin they would try to make use of me for East Africa . . . I don't quite know whether all this is simply a matter of conjecture. He tells me that the German East Africa Company will probably be taken over by the Government at no distant date.[2]

The welcome Emin received from Schmidt and Wissmann was but the beginning of a determined attempt by the German authorities, and especially by their representatives in East Africa, to win Emin Pasha for the German colonial cause. Emin was quite aware of this and made a shrewd assessment of the current state of Anglo-German rivalry over East Africa. It will be remembered that Emin had a rather sceptical view of Germany's African ventures and it would seem that his immediate inclination was still to seek future employment with the English Company.[3] But the effect of the reception which Emin now received from the Germans on Stanley and the English officers of the expedition, and of the 'German' surroundings in which they found themselves, was noted by Emin with some amusement. 'The gentlemen of the expedition see me for the first time acknowledged by my countrymen', wrote Emin, 'and are now most eager to be polite.'[4] Stanley became most friendly and eager to please. But his mounting anxiety over Emin's future intentions is

---

[1] Wissmann to Emin, 14–15 Oct. 1889, printed in Schweitzer, i. 316–18.

[2] *Tagebücher*, 10 Nov. 1889, iv. 423. (I have here used the translation in Schweitzer, i. 319.)

[3] See Euan-Smith to Salisbury, 14 Mar. 1890, relating a long conversation with Emin Pasha, F.O. 84/2060.

[4] *Tagebücher*, 2 Nov. 1889, iv. 417.

revealed in a conversation which he had with Emin on 16 November about the future of the Madi carriers, who had come from Equatoria, when the expedition reached the coast. Emin states that Stanley

questioned me as to what I intended to do with my Madi porters, suggesting that the very best thing would be to hand them over to the English East African Company, since all this time they had been fed at Mackinnon's expense. Of course it was merely a 'hint', and I should do as I liked; after all, being a German at heart, I might perhaps desire to transfer the people to the Germans, to which he had no objection. Only I ought to bear in mind that England had sent the expedition, whilst Germany had not thought of me till the eleventh hour. In my present position, of course, I could not raise any objection, but I told him that I reserved to myself the disposal of my servants.[1]

When Stanley informed Emin that he had written to the English Consul-General at Zanzibar to have quarters, etc., arranged for all the members of the expedition 'so that we should not be in the position of shipwrecked people on a foreign island', Emin commented, 'A true Yankee ending to the expedition',[2] and promptly wrote to ask for a house at Bagamayo from the Sultan of Zanzibar for his own use 'as I want to be independent'.[3] 'Stanley', Emin observed, 'plays at being a cosmopolitan but he cannot rid himself of his English prejudices. In unguarded moments when we are alone, he reproaches me for being in sympathy with Germany.' Stanley's officers plainly despised the Germans and insisted that although Bagamayo was the chief port in the German 'sphere', the expedition, being an English affair, must be transported to Zanzibar by an English steamer. 'And then', writes Emin, 'they talk of German narrow-mindedness and prejudice!'[4]

On 29 November the expedition, now only a few days' march from the coast, was met by two newspaper correspondents and a party of other people, chiefly Germans, led by Baron von Gravenreuth. The newspaper correspondents represented *The New York Herald* and *The New York World*. It had been in the service of the former newspaper that Stanley himself had been sent on his expedition to find Livingstone. Now, the enterprising editor of that newspaper, Mr. James Gordon Bennett, ever eager for a *coup*, had sent Edmund

---

[1] Ibid., 16 Nov. 1889, iv. 426–71 (I have again used Schweitzer's translation, but with some alterations. See, Schweitzer, i. 320.)
[2] *Tagebücher*, 16 Nov. 1889, iv.
[3] Ibid. 18 Nov. 1889, iv. 428.
[4] Ibid. 25 Nov. 1889, iv. 433.

Vizetelly to find Stanley. A reward of £2,000 had been offered for the first news of Stanley's arrival. Since *The New York Herald* was prepared to pay more for the first news of Stanley's emergence after three years in Africa than *The New York World*, Stanley was able to abide by his former loyalty and hand over to Vizetelly a dispatch, already written and prepared beforehand by the great explorer himself, to announce his impending return to 'civilization'.[1] Stevens, the reporter from *The New York World*, who had already sent off at least one account of Stanley's expedition based entirely on surmise and wrong in every particular, had to content himself with interviewing the other officers on the expedition, including Emin. His findings were later published and they corroborate the less flamboyant account of Father Schynse.[2]

On 4 December the expedition was met by Wissmann, who had come to welcome Emin, congratulate Stanley, and escort the expedition into Bagamoyo. Stanley handed over the command of the rest of the expedition, which was to follow on more slowly, to Stairs and he and Emin accompanied Wissmann on a triumphal march into Bagamoyo. The British and German Governments had been informed of Stanley's and Emin's arrival, arrangements had been made for their reception, and the English naval vessels *Turquoise* and *Somali*, and the German warships *Sperber* and *Schwalbe* had been ordered to stand by to transport the expedition from Bagamoyo to Zanzibar. But the end of the expedition was also to take an unexpected turning.

On the evening of the day the expedition arrived at Bagamoyo, a banquet was held. About thirty people were present, including all the European members of the expedition, Wissmann, the captains of the English and German ships, the two missionaries who had come to the coast, and representatives of the English and German East Africa Companies. The banquet, which had been arranged by Wissmann, was a remarkably lavish affair for Bagamoyo, and it was seemingly much enjoyed by all who attended. There were speeches of welcome and congratulation by Wissmann and votes of thanks

[1] *Tagebücher*, 30 Nov. 1889, iv. 437, where Emin is reporting a conversation with Parke.
[2] T. Stevens, *Scouting for Stanley in East Africa* (London, 1890). A previous letter written by Stevens to a Mrs. May Sheldon, dated 21 Oct. 1889, is in the archives of the Royal Geographical Society. (My thanks are due to Mrs. D. Middleton for sending me a copy of this letter.) See also *Tagebücher*, 30 Nov. 1889, iv. 436–7; Schynse, op. cit., p. 274; *IDA* ii. 410–11.

by Stanley and Emin. Emin was, by all accounts, in a very lively and gay mood and had been deeply impressed by the special message of welcome which had been awaiting him from the Emperor William II.[1] Emin moved about the gathering talking to the various guests. No one noticed him wander into an adjoining room. Suddenly, a servant came in and told Stanley that Emin had fallen into the street and was unconscious. Emin was extremely short-sighted, he had been accustomed to living in single-storey houses, and it would seem that he had mistaken a low window for a door on to a veranda and had fallen from the first floor into the street below. Although his fall had been partially broken by the sloping roof of an outhouse, Emin was seriously injured; his skull was fractured, two ribs were broken, and he was severely bruised. He remained unconscious until the next day and also developed broncho-pneumonia. Not until the end of January 1890 was he able to walk about and write again.[2] During this time Emin lay in the German hospital at Bagamoyo attended by both Parke and Dr. Brehme—until Parke himself became seriously ill with haematuric fever and had to be sent to the French hospital at Zanzibar.

Many reports about Emin's fall at Bagamoyo were made by eye-witnesses immediately after the event. All of these concur in their description of what happened, and all express the conviction that it was an accident.[3] The suggestion that Emin had attempted to commit suicide was only put about by others much later and it seems to me to be quite groundless.

Stanley professes himself to have been profoundly affected by Emin's accident, but perhaps the strangest feature of the events which succeeded it is the fact that after bidding Emin a curt goodbye, Stanley left Bagamoyo for Zanzibar two days later and never saw him again. Stanley later declared that when Emin entered the hospital at Bagamoyo 'a shadow came between him and me' and went on to make the sinister suggestion that this estrangement was deliberately brought about by the German doctors and officials in East Africa in

---

[1] Schweitzer, ii. 1–2. Vita Hassan, *Die Wahrheit über Emin Pasha*, ii. 237.

[2] See Parke, *Diary*, pp. 504–5. Schweitzer, op. cit. 2–11.

[3] See esp. the Report of Lt. Cracknell (the captain of one of the English ships) enclosed in Euan-Smith to Salisbury, 14 Dec. 1889, F.O. 84/1982; and the statement of Captain Hirschberg (commander of one of the German ships), 17 Dec. 1889, printed in Schweitzer, ii. 2–4. See also, *IDA* ii. 416–19; Parke, *Diary*, pp. 503–5; Jephson, *Rebellion*, pp. 473–4; Hoffmann, *With Stanley in Africa*, pp. 162–4.

order to win Emin for the German colonial service.[1] While there is no doubt that Wissmann and the others who had welcomed Emin so warmly put pressure on him during the following weeks to bring to an end his connections with Egypt and his inclinations to work for the British Company, this is by no means the only aspect of the matter. It is clear from Emin's later letters that he was deeply mortified and offended by the way Stanley had treated him on the march to the coast and by the invectives which Stanley wrote about him after his return to Europe. He also suspected, as did Wissmann, that the chief purpose behind Stanley's attempts to take Emin with him to Cairo and Europe was to remove him from the influence of the Germans and parade him as the trophy of his expedition.[2] Emin had no desire to return to Europe or to be relegated to a subordinate position in some inconsequential place in Egypt. As he wrote to one of his old student friends in Breslau, 'my sphere of action now lies on African soil, and I suppose I shall leave my bones here'.[3] When, therefore, Stanley sent first Stairs and later Jephson on special visits to Bagamoyo from Zanzibar later in December in attempts to persuade Emin to come to Cairo, Emin saw and talked to them but refused to accompany them. Both parted from him with feelings of genuine affection and with repeated expressions of gratitude from Emin for all they had done.[4]

By the beginning of 1890 the members of the Emin Pasha relief expedition had dispersed. The Zanzibaris who had survived the march across the continent were paid and dismissed or, as was the case with many of them who were slaves, returned to their masters. The European officers were very distressed about this and attempted to get the British Consul-General to intervene. He, however, was afraid of arousing Arab hostility and declared that 'existing Zanzibar customs' must be maintained—despite the Sultan's proclamation banning the importation of slaves into Zanzibar the previous year.[5] The matter was taken up in London by that determined campaigner for humanitarian causes, Mr. Alfred Pease. He tabled a question in the House of Commons which caused the Government some embar-

[1] *IDA* ii. 425–7; Stanley, *Autobiography*, pp. 373–4.
[2] See Schweitzer, ii. 5–28, where Emin's letters of Jan. and Feb. 1890 are printed.   [3] Ibid. ii. 29.
[4] Jephson, *Diary*, pp. 475–8; Emin to Stairs, 1 Apr. 1890, Stairs Papers, State Archives, Halifax, Nova Scotia.
[5] Euan-Smith to Salisbury, 16 Jan. 1890, F.O. 84/2059. F.O. to Euan-Smith, 3 May 1890, F.O. 84/2067; Euan-Smith to F.O., 4 May 1890, F.O. 84/2069.

rassment, and discussed with Charles Allen of the Anti-Slavery Society the possibility—eventually abandoned—of demanding a full parliamentary inquiry into this aspect of the expedition's affairs.[1]

The Egyptians and Sudanese and their families who had come with the expedition from Equatoria were sent, along with Vita Hassan, by steamer to Egypt. Later in the year, Captain Williams, an employee of Mackinnon's I.B.E.A. Company, enlisted a number of the men, chiefly Sudanese, as soldiers in the Company's service and seventy-five of these accompanied him on his march to join Lugard in Buganda in 1891.[2] Shukri Agha and a few of the most able soldiers had already taken employment with the I.B.E.A. Company and had left with Lugard for the interior.[3] Casati returned to Italy; the other European officers returned to England;[4] and Stanley settled down at the Villa Victoria in Cairo to answer hundreds of letters and telegrams and to accomplish the astonishing literary feat of writing his 900-page book about the expedition in fifty days.[5]

Emin Pasha remained at Bagamoyo until April 1890, except for occasional visits to Zanzibar. His recovery from his fall was slow, his spirits were rather low, and he felt humiliated by the off-hand manner in which the Khedive wrote to him and failed to make adequate financial provision for even his modest needs. 'You may imagine the frame of mind I was in', Emin later wrote to a friend, 'anxiety about my own future, anxiety as to the preservation of my people [servants], sickness, the indifference of the Egyptian Government, Stanley's invectives . . .'.[6] At the end of February Emin finally resigned from the Egyptian service. He still hoped that there might

[1] Alfred E. Pease to Charles Allen, 24 Nov. 1890, A. S.S., C. 64/156, British Empire MSS., s.18. See also C. 64/159 in the same collection. (I am indebted to Mrs. S. Miers for this reference.)
[2] See Note by H. B. Thomas in The Uganda Journal, xix, no. 2 (1955), 209–10. There is a good deal of material concerning the difficulties of the Egyptian authorities in settling those from Equatoria who remained in Egypt, or later arrived there, in the Khartoum Archives, Cairint, 1/11/56, 1/12/75, and 1/35/205.
[3] Shukri Agha features prominently in Lugard's account of later events in Buganda. See M. Perham, ed., The Diaries of Lord Lugard, esp. vols. i. and ii.
[4] Their future careers are succinctly outlined in the Epilogue by Mrs. D. Middleton in Jephson, Diary, pp. 414–22. Four years after the expedition Stairs, Nelson, and Parke were all dead.
[5] For an account of Stanley's life in Cairo during the writing of the book, see E. Marston How Stanley Wrote 'In Darkest Africa' (London, 1890).
[6] Schweitzer, ii. 12.

be some chance of his being employed by Mackinnon's Company. But his experience with Stanley had greatly disillusioned him about working for the English. Emin also felt that England was no longer interested in Equatoria.

For some time after the conclusion of the expedition, Mackinnon did consider the possibility of employing Emin in the service of the I.B.E.A. Company. Stanley, however, was strongly against the idea and ridiculed Emin in public as a short-sighted and scholarly little man, more suited to natural history collecting than to colonial administration. Euan-Smith, the British Consul-General at Zanzibar, considered that 'Per se, Emin Pasha would, I think, be for the British Company as barren an acquisition as the islands of Manda and Patta.' None the less, he toyed with the possibility of getting Mackinnon to employ Emin 'in order that . . . he may not fall into the hands of the Germans'.[1] The possibility of Emin's employment by Mackinnon's Company was cleared with the British Foreign Office and with the Egyptian Government, but Mackinnon was dilatory, and, before Stanley arrived in Europe, Emin's services had been secured by Wissmann.[2]

That Emin turned to the rival German Company is, in fact, scarcely surprising. During the months after his arrival at the coast, those who expressed admiration for Emin and accorded him respect were chiefly Germans. Emin received gold medals from German Geographical Societies, an honorary degree from his old university at Königsberg, and large numbers of letters from German friends and acquaintances with whom he had been out of touch for nearly thirty years. He also re-established contact with his family in Neisse. More immediately, Emin was surrounded by an almost exclusively German circle of Europeans in Bagamoyo, at the head of which was Wissman. Wissman was determined to recruit Emin to serve German colonial interests in East Africa and by the end of February he had obtained formal permission from Berlin to offer Emin a definite appointment.[3]

---

[1] Euan-Smith to Salisbury, 25 Mar. 1890. Salisbury Papers, A/80/7.
[2] The correspondence between Euan-Smith, Mackinnon, Salisbury, and Baring is to be found in M.P. 14; F.O. 84/2057, F.O. 84/2060, F.O. 84/2061, F.O. 84/2069; and in the Salisbury Papers A/80. Copies of some of the correspondence which passed between Wissmann, Emin, and Bismarck on the subject of Emin's employment by the German Company, taken from the Zanzibar archives, exist amongst the papers of the late Sir John Gray in the Cambridge University Library and in the library of the Royal Commonwealth Society in London. Further correspondence, relating to the German side, exists in the archives at Potsdam.   [3] Schweitzer, ii. 23.

After considerable hesitation and much heart-searching—much of it done in the company of the British Consul-General[1]—Emin accepted this offer of employment. In England the news that Emin Pasha had taken service with the Germans was greeted with dismay and national indignation. The *St. James's Gazette* declared:

> The expensive and superfluous relief of Emin has brought no advantage either to the rescuers or to the rescued. On the contrary, the rescuers now find that their money and their enthusiasm have seriously prejudiced national interests. Although, perhaps, it may have been worth while to relieve Emin in order to afford Stanley an opportunity of still further adding to his great deeds as an explorer, it was certainly not worth while to relieve him for the purpose of presenting the German Government with a new and experienced leader of expeditions calculated to open a route into the centre of Africa. If Emin succeeds in re-establishing himself in his old province, the consequence will be that the frontiers of Germany in Africa will be considerably advanced to the north-west.[2]

It soon became clear that Emin, under Wissmann's instructions, was preparing to lead a new expedition to extend German claims in the interior. Emin bought a small estate near Bagamoyo where he settled his daughter, Ferida, with a nurse and where he hoped to retire himself on his return. On 26 April 1890, at the beginning of the rainy season, Emin Pasha set out at the head of a small expedition which was eventually to return to the province from which he had just been so expensively and so laboriously withdrawn by H. M. Stanley.

[1] See esp. Euan-Smith to Salisbury, 14 and 18 Mar. 1890, F.O. 84/2060, reporting two conversations with Emin Pasha.
[2] Printed in Schweitzer, ii. 24–5.

CHAPTER XI

Epilogue

WHEN Mackinnon had first approached Stanley in the autumn of 1886 with the proposal that he should organize and lead an expedition to the relief of Emin Pasha, he had envisaged a quite modest affair. Even as late as the middle of 1887 he had continued to hope that Stanley's expedition would 'reach Emin Pasha about the middle of July and would have returned to Zanzibar by the end of the year'.[1] The whole project was not expected to cost more than £20,000, half of which had already been contributed by the Egyptian Government, the rest by Mackinnon and his friends. In return for organizing the expedition, Mackinnon hoped that Stanley would be able to make treaties on behalf of the projected I.B.E.A. Company in the interior, treaties which might include a specific arrangement whereby Emin would remain in the interior (Mackinnon envisaged at Wadelai) as the representative of the British company. Stanley stated that when he set out on the expedition he did so

to assist . . . an ideal Governor who had fixed himself in my imagination as a man eminently worthy of assistance. He was a lieutenant of Gordon's but had been sent far into Equatoria, was besieged as I thought by the Mahdists, and I hoped that a little ammunition would enable him to hold out until the effect of further light upon his position would be a more general desire to assist him.[2]

At the time that the expedition had left England, therefore, both Stanley and Mackinnon had envisaged that the result of their expedition would be to enable Emin not to withdraw from Equatoria (this he could already have done) but to remain there under new auspices.

The British public would seem initially to have supported Stanley's venture as a mission to 'rescue' Emin Pasha from what they conceived to be some ill-defined 'hordes' representing 'barbarism' and 'fanaticism'. As Anglo-German rivalry over the East African interior

[1] Mackinnon to Sanford, 30 May and 5 July 1887, Sanford Papers.
[2] Stanley to F. A. Brockhaus, 27 May 1890. Brockhaus was the editor of the German edition of Stanley's book about the expedition and this letter appears only in the German edition, *Im dunkelsten Afrika* 2 vols. (Leipzig, 1890). An extract from it is printed in Jephson, *Rebellion*, p. viii.

increased during the course of the expedition, the public, like Mackinnon, Holmwood, Kirk, and Mackay, came to see in Emin's position in Equatoria a unique opportunity for the establishment of British influence in the interior, and came to hope—with increasing fervour —that Stanley's expedition would somehow bring this about. In December 1888 *The Times* declared confidently, 'We may feel assured that Mr. Stanley will have done all it is possible to do to secure the influence of the British East Africa Company over the province of Emin and the Lake Region generally; and the influence of the Company means the interests of England.'[1]

In 1886 Mackinnon and Hutton had seen in Emin's position in Equatoria an opportunity for taking over what, from a distance, appeared to be a flourishing concern.[2] The wealth of the province, the peace and prosperity created by Emin's administration, the bravery and devotion of his soldiers, and the picture of Emin himself as 'an ideal Governor', a 'second Gordon', were all fostered by Emin's friends in Britain and not least by Emin himself. Equatoria appeared as a nucleus of order and administration, troops and trade, in the heart of Africa. Most of this was an illusion, but in the partition of Africa, as in human affairs generally, illusions occupy an important role.

Neither Sir Evelyn Baring nor Lord Salisbury had any such illusions about the position of Emin Pasha or the value of Equatoria. Yet both wished to see Emin removed from his post and the last vestiges of Egyptian claims to Equatoria abandoned. Baring and Salisbury therefore supported the expedition to bring about Emin's withdrawal. Mackinnon, Hutton, Stanley, and King Leopold (assisted by that dubious and amorphous body called public opinion) hoped—for diverse and conflicting reasons—that the expedition would enable Emin to stay. In this they were in fact (if not always consciously or in intention) supporting the wishes of Emin himself.

Some of the illusions which had surrounded the dispatch of the expedition crumbled when confronted with the reality. Stanley found that Equatoria was no nucleus of order and 'civilization' but the remnant of a province which, under Egyptian rule, had consisted of a number of garrisons living off the country and oppressing and enslaving the local population. The area seemed poor in communications and resources and prone to Madhist attacks. As such it was of

---

[1] *The Times*, 25 Dec. 1888.
[2] R. Gray, *A History of the Southern Sudan*, p. 203.

little use, either to Leopold or to Mackinnon until their already established 'spheres' in Africa were much more developed and advanced. Emin and the best of his soldiers, however, had at first appeared ready and able to be utilized elsewhere. Stanley's proposal that they should be enrolled in the service of Mackinnon's Company in the Kavirondo region had met with an immediate response from Emin, but both Stanley and Emin had seriously misjudged the situation in thinking that Emin's soldiers would agree to the withdrawal from Equatoria which this would entail and which they had previously resisted. The very arrival of Stanley's expedition precipitated the train of events which were to lead to the final collapse of Emin's position in Equatoria. The state of Stanley's party brought to an end the hopes which Emin and his garrisons had shared that Stanley's expedition would in some way solve the problems of their situation and that Equatoria would be established on a more secure basis with regular supplies and a good route of communications to the East and West African coasts. Emin's garrisons had, in fact, existed in a state of suspended animation since the retreat of the Mahdists in 1885. Stanley's arrival forced Emin to revive and actively to promote the proposal for a withdrawal from the province which he had earlier abandoned. Emin's action, together with the doubts and uncertainties surrounding the origins and intentions of Stanley's expedition, provoked a crisis in Equatoria which left Emin under no illusions about the true nature of his tenuous authority over the garrisons among whom he had lived for so long. One further illusion had had to be abandoned as the expedition progressed. This was Emin's belief in the disinterested motives of those who had sent the expedition, and his hopes that its arrival would in some way strengthen his position and lead to the establishment of Equatoria on a permanent basis as part of the British Empire.

Some illusions, however, persisted in spite of the realities which Stanley's expedition had revealed. The experience of Stanley's march through the eastern Congo in no way altered King Leopold's *idée fixe* of a frontier for his Congo State on the Nile, and his belief that Equatoria and the Bahr al-Ghazal might prove possible and profitable acquisitions. Until 1891 Wadelai remained the goal for Mackinnon's later expeditions under Jackson and Lugard.

Those who had embarked on the Emin Pasha relief expedition with illusions either preserved them or became disillusioned men. Those who had had few illusions achieved their objectives. Baring succeeded in placing Equatoria beyond Egyptian responsibilities. Salisbury succeeded in achieving Baring's objectives through the auspices of someone else's expedition. The Egyptian Government paid £14,000 to bring Egyptian responsibilities in Equatoria to an end. Mackinnon and his associates paid a similar amount in pursuit of a chimera.

Stanley's expedition took twice as long, and cost nearly twice as much, as had originally been expected; and the death-rate was truly appalling. Of the 703 people who had set out with Stanley from Zanzibar in February 1887, only 246 returned in December 1889.[1] Stanley himself admitted that at least 311 of those lost during the course of the expedition had died: the rest had either been left behind or had deserted.[2] The losses among the inhabitants of the areas through which the expedition had passed, and with whom Stanley had had repeated 'skirmishes', will never be known, but they were certainly considerable.

Emin's followers from Equatoria had also suffered great losses on the march from Kavalli's to the coast. Their precise numbers are more difficult to calculate on account of the large numbers of women and children. Stanley estimates that the 570 who were in his camp at Kavalli's five days before his departure had been reduced to 555 by 2 July, and that by the time the expedition reached the coast, the total number was only 290. The loss *en route* was therefore nearly half; many of the people, unable to keep up with the expedition, were simply left behind; at least eighty perished 'from ulcers, fevers, fatigue and debility'.[2] Only 251 of those who arrived at Bagamoyo from Equatoria finally reached Cairo in January 1890. Stanley himself handed them over to the Egyptian authorities, together with a report on each head of household.[3]

Stanley's expedition for the relief of Emin Pasha was the largest and the last of all his African expeditions. Its cost, in lives and resources, greatly exceeded that of any of his previous expeditions.

---

[1] These are Stanley's own estimates in Stanley to Euan-Smith, 19 Dec. 1889, published as *Africa No. 4* (1890), C. 5906. Jephson estimates that the numbers were 708 and 210 respectively (Jephson, *Diary*, p. 207). A comparison of these figures with those calculated by Euan-Smith himself (in Euan-Smith to F.O., 9 Dec. 1889, F.O. 84/1982) suggests that Stanley's estimates are approximately correct, if allowance is made for those whom Barttelot sent down the Congo in June 1888, many of whom, including Assad Farran, eventually returned either to Zanzibar or Cairo.

[2] Stanley to Euan-Smith, 19 Dec. 1889, *Africa No. 4* (1890), C. 5906.

[3] This Report is in the Khartoum Archives, Cairint 1/12/75.

Quite apart from the removal of Emin Pasha from his province, its achievements in the sphere of geographical discovery were considerable. The Congo rain forest had been traversed for the first time and the Aruwimi river had been found not to drain from the 'Muta Nzige' lake as Stanley had half expected. This lake (i.e. Lake Edward) and the adjoining Lake George had been charted, together with the Semliki river, and the final problem of the Albertine sources of the Nile had been solved. The Ruwenzori Mountains had been discovered, the Nile–Congo watershed had been defined, and Lake Victoria had been revealed as more extensive in its south-western corner than had been expected. Stanley had led an expedition which had traversed Africa from west to east. In the face of these geographical achievements, the 'Quest, Rescue and Retreat of Emin Pasha'—as Stanley subtitled his book about the expedition—seemed altogether of secondary significance.

That Stanley ever succeeded in reaching Emin Pasha and then returning with his reunited expedition to the East African coast is in itself a remarkable achievement and an impressive demonstration of his extraordinary powers of leadership and determination. As the Emin Pasha Relief Committee modestly acknowledged, the expedition had completed a remarkable journey 'after surmounting difficulties and escaping dangers which were little anticipated at the time of its departure'.[1] The European officers who had accompanied Stanley might find him scarcely a gentleman, and impossible to consider as a friend, but they all felt compelled to respect and admire him and none of them believed that the expedition would have survived in the hands of a lesser man.[2]

On his return from the expedition, Stanley at first met with a public acclaim such as neither he nor any previous African explorer had ever received before. The contrast with the disbelief and lack of recognition which had accompanied his return from the expedition to find Livingstone is particularly striking. Telegrams and letters of congratulation poured into Zanzibar and Cairo from all over the world. When Stanley returned to Europe in May 1890 he met with a tremendous reception both in Brussels and in London. He was awarded a second gold medal by the Royal Geographical Society;

---

[1] Report of the Emin Pasha Relief Committee, 1891, M.P., pp. 100–1. See also *IDA* ii. 418.

[2] See esp. Jephson to Mackinnon, 20 Jan. 1890, M.P., 75; Parke, *Diary*, p. 369; Jameson, *Diary*, pp. 382–3.

honorary degrees at several universities including both Oxford and Cambridge; and both he and his officers were fêted everywhere. 10,000 people, including members of the royal family, attended his lecture at the Albert Hall. Jephson and the other officers were able to lecture to capacity audiences in halls up and down the country long after Stanley had finished his own exhausting lecture tour. When Stanley's book about the expedition was published in June 1890, it sold 150,000 copies in English and was at once translated into several other languages.[1]

The popular admiration for Stanley was, however, short-lived. By the autumn of 1890 the achievements of the expedition came to be eclipsed in the popular mind by its cost. Admiration gave way to criticism, and criticism to condemnation, as more and more facts about the expedition were revealed in what became the sensation of the moment.

The controversy broke out over the fate of the Rear Column. Although Mackinnon had done his best to warn Stanley against further upsetting the susceptibilities of the relatives of the dead Barttelot and Jameson, Stanley had handled the subject of the Rear Column with remarkably little tact in his book. While Mackinnon and the other European officers wrote to and visited Jameson's widow and Barttelot's father and brother in attempts to smooth things over, Stanley attacked and criticized the dead men and declared that the Rear Column had been 'wrecked by the irresolution of its officers, their neglect of their promises and their indifference to their written orders'.[2] Stanley also commenced a claim for £10,000 damages in the court at Zanzibar against Tippu Tip for alleged breach of contract. The Emin Pasha Relief Committee refused to have anything to do with this claim and after interventions by both Mackinnon and King Leopold (who wished at all costs not to alienate Tippu Tip), Stanley was persuaded to withdraw his case.[3]

The relatives of Barttelot and Jameson responded to Stanley's

---

[1] D. Stanley, ed., *The Autobiography of H. M. Stanley*, p. 422. For Stanley's popular acclaim see also F. Hird, *H. M. Stanley, the Authorised Life*, pp. 278–85.

[2] Stanley to Mackinnon, 5 Aug. 1889, printed in *The Standard*, 25 Nov. 1889.

[3] The full record of this case is to be found in the Emin Pasha Relief Committee Letter Book 2, M.P., and in the letters from Stanley to McDermott, 25 Jan. 1891, M.P., F. 1, and Mackinnon to Euan-Smith, 10 July 1890, M.P., F. 1, reporting a conversation with King Leopold. There is also a good deal of additional material on the case in M.P., F. 1. See also, Sir John Gray, 'Stanley versus Tippoo Tib', *Tanganyika Notes and Records*, no. 18 (Dec. 1944).

attacks by publishing edited versions of the diaries and letters of the two dead officers. They also wrote letters to the newspapers pointing out Stanley's share in the responsibility for the whole affair. The newspapers responded avidly. A search for the truth soon became a search for sensation as more and more people connected with the expedition were persuaded 'to tell all'. Troup was the first to take advantage of the opportunity to publish his diary—and in doing so he broke a clause of his contract with the Emin Pasha Relief Committee which had stipulated that no account of the expedition was to be published by any of the officers until six months had elapsed after the publication of Stanley's book. A case was brought against Troup for breach of contract by the Committee, but this was eventually settled out of court.[1] Meanwhile Stanley, hoping for some support for his case, had encouraged Jephson and Parke to publish their accounts, and the newspapers had persuaded Bonny, Ward, and even the inarticulate Nelson to make reports about the matter. In the search for new material statements were obtained (some of which were later retracted) from lesser authorities such as Assad Farran and one of Stanley's Zanzibaris named Saleh bin Osman. Missionaries stationed on the Congo wrote accounts about cannibal feasts initiated and attended by officers of the Rear Column; Carl Peters and the Kaiser spoke about Stanley's 'forcible abduction' of Emin from Equatoria; and Mrs. Jameson set out for Zanzibar in the belief that once there she would be able to get to the bottom of the accusations against her dead husband. Almost daily during the months of November and December 1890 the newspapers carried several columns, often whole pages, devoted to new revelations about the expedition. 'These statements', *The Times* declared, probably quite rightly 'will send a thrill of horror throughout the civilised world.'[2]

Faced with this mounting controversy, Stanley himself felt compelled to enter the lists. After hinting darkly in England that the full story about the Rear Column had not yet been told, he was persuaded in America, where he had once again gone for a lecturing tour, to tell it. There were accusations involving poisoning and cannibalism, excessive brutality, and grave dereliction of duty. Mackinnon was very distressed at the mounting controversy over

---

[1] The cost to the Emin Pasha Relief Committee of this settlement was £597 10s., Emin Pasha Relief Committee Minute Book, 10 Sept. and 11 Nov. 1890, M.P.
[2] *The Times*, 8 Nov. 1890.

what everyone had claimed, and he had been happy to acknowledge, as his expedition. 'It would have been much wiser if they had thrown a veil over all the matters which are now the subject of bitter dispute', he declared of those connected with the expedition who had written to the newspapers.[1] J. A. Grant had been unable to get Stanley enrolled as a member of the Athenaeum Club even before the Emin Pasha relief expedition, and quite despaired of doing so now.[2] The Emin Pasha Relief Committee itself participated in the controversy over the Rear Column. In its efforts to exonerate Barttelot and Jameson from Stanley's accusations, it was remarkably successful in diverting attention to Tippu Tip and getting him accepted in the popular mind as 'the principal and the . . . deliberate cause of the disasters of the rearguard and the deaths of Major Barttelot and Mr. Jameson'.[3]

The controversy soon extended from the matter of the Rear Column to the whole subject of European-led expeditions in Africa, their methods, achievements, and effects. Stanley was portrayed as a nineteenth-century *conquistador* resolutely cutting his way across Africa at the head of a slave army and leaving a wake of destruction behind him. The achievements of the expedition came to be regarded as paltry in relation to its effects and cost. The *Saturday Review* in November 1890 expressed the growing mood of disillusionment.

Many persons, not by any means belonging to the class of sentimentalists, are gravely dissatisfied with the increasing violence and disregard of human life and liberty displayed on these anomalous 'expeditions', which contrast so remarkably with the conduct and results of explorers like Livingstone, Speke, Barth, Cameron, and Thomson.[4]

The facts that were now revealed about this most publicized of all expeditions in Africa in the nineteenth century confirmed a growing popular conviction that 'exploration' had, since Livingstone, taken on a quite different character. Expeditions were now huge quasi-military affairs backed by powerful political and commercial interests, and their progress resembled that of an invading army. It was this element of the political and commercial interests behind the

[1] Mackinnon to Sanford, 10 Nov. 1890, Sanford Papers.
[2] J. A. Grant to Sir Samuel Baker, 30 Mar. 1891, Valentine Baker Papers, File 20.
[3] Report of the Emin Pasha Relief Committee, 1891, M.P., p. 99.
[4] *Saturday Review*, Nov. 1890.

expedition which Emin had found so distasteful. It was the mounting violence which now seemed to accompany African expeditions against which the Victorian public recoiled.

This change in the nature of African expeditions, and of popular attitudes to them, can be observed very clearly in the case of the Emin Pasha relief expedition. Organized and financed by parties with particular interests at stake, it had set out in 1887 amidst widespread popular support as a philanthropic 'rescue' mission. Its return amidst the very different conditions of 1889–90, though at first acclaimed, had been followed by rapid disillusionment. The four years 1886–90 have long been recognized by historians as of crucial importance both in the partition of East Africa and in the development of Lord Salisbury's African policy. During this time Equatoria came to occupy the role in the Anglo-German rivalry over the interior which Buganda occupied after 1889. The reasons for this have less to do with the events in Europe than with the changing situation in Buganda and Emin's withdrawal from Equatoria. During this period, the Emin Pasha relief expedition also aroused increasing interest in Europe and contributed to the growing Anglo-German rivalry over the East African interior. The expedition had been dispatched at a time when the Anglo-German Agreement of 1886 appeared to have stabilized the rivalry of the two powers over the area, and the position of Equatoria, astride the Nile, was not considered to be a matter of any national or strategic importance. Almost immediately, however, suspicions had arisen on the German side about the real objectives of Stanley and Mackinnon, and Emin himself had come to be regarded in Germany as a national hero. Suspicions about the expedition were entertained less in German Government circles than by Carl Peters and his associates in the *Deutsche Kolonialgesellschaft* and the German East Africa Company. A public campaign was whipped up in Germany by Peters, the object of which was to make of Emin's position in Equatoria an issue for German national and colonial assertion against the British.[1]

In England also, during the years 1887–9, there was widespread popular speculation about the objectives which might be achieved through the auspices of Stanley's expedition. Initially considered as a 'rescue' mission, the expedition came to be thought of as an opportunity for colonial aggrandisement, for staking out British claims in the East African interior. As on the German side, this

---

[1] F. F. Müller, *Deutschland—Zanzibar—Ostafrika*, pp. 466-7.

attitude reflected popular opinion rather than government policy. None the less, it was precisely during this period that Salisbury also became committed to a prolonged British occupation of Egypt and to a policy of keeping other European powers out of the Nile valley.

The Emin Pasha relief expedition not only aroused German suspicions, and rising popular expectations in England, it also focused attention on the East African interior at a time when the respective 'spheres of influence' of England and Germany in that area were only vaguely defined. By doing this, the expedition contributed to the sequence of events which was to make a second Anglo-German Agreement over East Africa necessary in 1890.

As the political interest behind European-led expeditions in Africa increased, both the character and the nature of these expeditions changed. The Emin Pasha relief expedition reflects these changes. It was large and well armed, and it encountered successive set-backs and overcame tremendous obstacles. The progress of Stanley's earlier expeditions had been accompanied by considerable violence and loss of life but the Emin Pasha relief expedition outdid all its predecessors. It was also much more widely publicized. It is rarely possible to mark, with any degree of precision, the point when images and illusions in a society cease to exist, or simply take a new form and direction. But there is a good case to be made for the suggestion that the Emin Pasha relief expedition occupies an important place in the decline and disappearance of the romantic Victorian conception of exploring expeditions led by determined Europeans through 'unknown' continents. For one thing, as King Leopold pointed out to Mackinnon, Stanley had now left few of Africa's geographical mysteries unknown.[1] For another, the intense popular feeling amidst which the Emin Pasha relief expedition had been sent was never to be repeated in pursuit of similar objectives by similar means again. Henceforth, expeditions were either organized and dispatched by governments, or their agents, with military support for openly political ends; or they were sent by geographical and scientific bodies, often amidst great popular interest, to pioneer trails across inhospitable tracts of the Arctic and Antarctic. In these latter cases, as in the more recent instance of man's arrival amidst the deserts of the moon, the popular appeal is not the same as that of a lone man or group of men battling with 'hostile tribes' on the North American

[1] Leopold to Mackinnon, 28 Nov. 1889, Palace Archives, Brussels, Dossier 82, no. 83.

or Afghan frontiers, or in the heart of Africa. The human frontier is closed and man is therefore left to contend with inanimate elements and non-human obstacles. Gone for ever is the romantic image of the aged Livingstone wandering with his Bible and his stick to bring European 'light' to the human frontier in what the Victorians liked to think of as the 'dark' continent.

APPENDIX 1

The Members of the
Emin Pasha Relief Committee

Mr. William Mackinnon (Chairman)
Colonel Sir Francis de Winton (Secretary)
Mr. H. M. Stanley
Mr. James F. Hutton
Sir John Kirk
Colonel J. A. Grant
Revd. Horace Waller
Lord Kinnaird
Hon. Guy Dawnay
General Sir Lewis Pelly
Mr. Burdett-Coutts
Mr. Alex L. Bruce
Mr. Peter Denny

Source: Minute Book of the Emin Pasha Relief Committee, M.P.
Also, Report of the Emin Pasha Relief Committee, 1891, M.P.,
p. 10.

APPENDIX 2

The Accounts of the Emin Pasha Relief Committee

The complete accounts are in M.P., F. 5. They include two statements:
1. From 1 Jan. 1887 to 31 Dec. 1888, covering the first subscription.
2. From 1 Jan. 1889 to 28 Feb. 1890, covering the second subscription up to the time when the accounts were closed.

These two statements are also given in combined form, as below.

Receipts from subscriptions:	£	s.	d.
Egyptian Government	14,000	0	0
Mr. William Mackinnon	3,000	0	0
Mr. Peter Mackinnon	1,500	0	0
Mr. Peter Denny	1,500	0	0
Mr. J. S. Jameson	1,000	0	0
Countess de Noailles	1,124	17	4
Messrs. Gray Dawes & Company	1,500	0	0
Royal Geographical Society	1,000	0	0
Mr. Duncan MacNeill	1,050	0	0
Mr. A. L. Bruce	750	0	0
Mr. H. J. Younger	500	0	0
Mr. J. Mackinnon	450	0	0
Mr. W. Burdett-Coutts	400	0	0
Mr. J. M. Hall	375	0	0
Mr. N. Macmichael	375	0	0
Sir T. Fowell Buxton	250	0	0
Mr. W. P. Alexander	250	0	0
Mr. J. F. Hutton	250	0	0
Messrs. Sampson, Low & Company	250	0	0
Baroness Burdett-Coutts	100	0	0
Mr. J. Siltzer	100	0	0
Colonel J. A. Grant	100	0	0
Lord Kinnaird	100	0	0
Sir Lewis Pelly	10	0	0
Mr. A. J. Mounteney Jephson	5	0	0
Mrs. S. Allnatt	3	3	0
Revd. J. Stevenson	2	2	0
	£29,945	2	4

Interest on Deposit a/c		£221	19	6
	B/Fwd.	£30,167	1	10

Press contributions:

The Times	550	0	0
The Daily News	500	0	0
The Standard	500	0	0
Daily Telegraph	200	0	0
Scotsman	200	0	0
Manchester Guardian	200	0	0
Indépendance Belge	50	0	0
	£2,200	0	0

	TOTAL	£32,367	1	10

Expenditure:
Total expenditure amounted to £27,709. 9s. 5d. The balance was distributed as donations to those who returned from the expedition and to the relatives/owners of the deceased Zanzibaris.

BIBLIOGRAPHY

A. PRIMARY SOURCES

I. *Official*

(a) LONDON:

Public Record Office

All the volumes in the two series F.O. 78, Turkey (Egypt) and F.O. 84, Slave Trade (Zanzibar) for the years 1885–90 were examined. Long established as a main source for any study of the partition of East Africa, they also contain the reports of the British Consuls-General in Cairo and Zanzibar on events in Emin's province during these years. The volumes in F.O. 633 (Cromer Papers) also contain some additional information concerning Sir Evelyn Baring's attitude to Equatoria.

(b) BRUSSELS

(i) *Palace Archives*

The most important collection of the private correspondence of King Leopold II. The following dossiers were consulted:

9 Correspondence with Emile Banning.

47 Correspondence with Sir Francis de Winton.

53 Correspondence with M. Fleury, the Belgian representative at Zanzibar, concerning Leopold's letters to Stanley and Emin in 1889–90. There is also material here concerning Leopold's intervention in the case brought by H. M. Stanley against Tippu Tip in 1890.

72 Correspondence with Baron Lambermont. A huge collection, only a very small part of which concerns the Emin Pasha relief expedition, Stanley's arrival at the coast in 1889, and King Leopold's suggestion that he should be appointed as a representative to the Brussels Anti-Slavery Conference in 1890.

82 The most important collection in existence of the correspondence between King Leopold and Mackinnon. It begins in Apr. 1882 and continues through to 1890. There is a gap between December 1885 and January 1888.

102 Correspondence with H. M. Stanley. Nos. 12–22 cover the period 1885–90. There are no letters from Stanley during the actual progress of the expedition. The prolific correspondence between the two men increases after 1890.

170 Relations with Great Britain: the Sudan 1886.

171 Relations with Great Britain: the I.B.E.A. Company.

181 Relations with Zanzibar: correspondence between King Leopold, Euan-Smith, and George S. Mackenzie, 1890.

(ii) *Archives du Ministère des Affaires étrangères*
Collection Afrique (AF 1/XIII). Strauch Papers (1). Part of the correspondence between King Leopold and his close adviser, General Strauch (1886–9).

Lambermont Papers. Correspondence between King Leopold and Baron Lambermont. The section covering the years 1886–90 was consulted.

Political Correspondence: Great Britain. Volume 56 (1887–9) includes correspondence about the plans of the I.B.E.A. Company to send a second expedition into the East African interior in 1888.

Political Correspondence: Egypt. Volume 6 (1886–90) includes letters enclosing newspaper cuttings from the Belgian Consul in Cairo reporting Stanley's visit in 1887.

(iii) *Archives du Musée de la Dynastie*
Strauch Papers (2). A further section of the correspondence between King Leopold and General Strauch (1886–90).

(iv) *Archives du Ministère des Colonies*
Strauch Papers (3). A further section of the correspondence between King Leopold and General Strauch (1886–90).

La Force publique, Nos. 2474/6. Memoranda on the Emin Pasha relief expedition and the campaign against the Mahdists in the Sudan.

Le Mouvement géographique. The issues and extracts for the years 1886–93 were consulted.

Dossiers Nos. 75 and 78: Affaires étrangères. These contain correspondence between King Leopold and M. Van Eetvelde (1888–9) and also with Lord Vivian, the British Ambassador in Brussels, about Tippu Tip and the Emin Pasha relief expedition. Dossier no. 78 also contains some useful press cuttings (1888) about the expedition.

Dossier No. 120. Material about Sanford's claim against the Emin Pasha Relief Committee for damages to the steamer *Henry Reed* (1887–8).

(v) *Archives du Royaume*
Van Eetvelde Papers. A large collection of the private papers of King Leopold's close adviser. The following dossiers were consulted:

25) Correspondence between King Leopold and Van Eetvelde (1886–90)
26) concerning the Becker Mission and the future employment of
27) H. M. Stanley.
63 Correspondence between King Leopold and H. M. Stanley. 1886.
112 British policy towards East Africa. Memoranda.
113 Reports on the subject of the Nile. 1889.
117 Notes and Memoranda on the I.B.E.A. Company. 1888–9.
132 Agreements with Tippu Tip. 1887–9.
135 Memoranda on the delimitation of frontiers. 1886–7.
154) Material on the ivory trade. 1885–6.
155)
168 Newspaper accounts about the Emin Pasha relief expedition. 1888.

306 BIBLIOGRAPHY

(c) KHARTOUM

Ministry of the Interior, Central Record Office. Documents in two sections of this archive were consulted.

(i) Cairo Intelligence (abbr. Cairint.).

This collection consists chiefly of memoranda and reports compiled by the Intelligence Department of the Egyptian Army under General Wingate in Cairo about events in the Sudan under the Mahdiyya. The sources were usually refugees and informers who arrived in Cairo from the Sudan. The reference numbers refer to the Class, Box, and Item in that order.

1/12/75. H. M. Stanley's Expedition. 1887. Copies of letters to and from the British Foreign Office and Sir Evelyn Baring in Cairo regarding the organization of the Emin Pasha relief expedition. Also letters from Holmwood to Baring on the same subject.

Two reports concern the contents of Stanley's letters during 1888–9. A list is present of the persons who returned with Stanley to Cairo in Jan. 1890. This is written in Stanley's own handwriting and contains comments on each head of household.

3/14/236. Report of Emin Pasha, 1 Sept. 1885 (40 pp.). In Arabic, with an English translation and a précis by General Grenfell. A long and detailed report describing events in Equatoria up to 1885.

3/14/237. Emin Pasha: various reports and documents. Extracts from some of Emin's letters to correspondents in Europe, 1883–5, in typescript. Some of these extracts may well have been assembled in 1888 after the publication of the collection of Emin's letters and articles in English in G. Schweinfurth, R. W. Felkin, *et al.*, *Emin Pasha in Central Africa* (London, 1888).

Statement by 'Uthmān Latīf ('Othman Bey Lufti'), respecting the Equatorial Province, 9 July 1890. (36 pp.). This appears to be the original statement, at an oral interview between a member of General Wingate's staff (? Na'ūm Shuqayr) and 'Uthmān Latīf after the latter's return to Cairo in Jan. 1890. It concerns events in Equatoria 1883–9.

Statement by 'Uthmān Hajj Hāmid (Qādī of Equatoria), 12 Nov. 1891 (8 pp.). This man, who had first gone to Equatoria with General Gordon, was sent by Emin on the deputation to Karam Allāh in 1885 and defected, was captured by the Mahdists and sent to Omdurman. He later escaped to Cairo. There he wrote down this statement in Arabic concerning events in Equatoria and the Bahr al-Ghazal 1884–6. A translation and explanation in English by Na'ūm Shuqayr is also present. A copy in typescript is in Cairint. 1/11/56.

1/11/56 Equatoria and Emin Pasha. Statement of Basili Boktor, 24 Apr. 1890. Basili Boktor went to Equatoria with Gordon as a clerk. He withdrew from the province with Emin and Stanley in 1889 and returned to Cairo. Here he made this statement to General Wingate's

Intelligence Department. It is an important and useful source for events in Equatoria 1877–89 and its accuracy can be attested by comparison with other sources. An edited version of this statement was published in the London edition of *The New York Herald*, 5 May 1890. A typescript of this is also in Cairint. 3/14/237.

Report of the officers, soldiers, and officials stationed in the Equatorial province. 1890. Both the Arabic original and an English translation are present. This most useful statement was made by Shukri Agha, Hawash Effendi, and others after their arrival in Cairo in Jan. 1890. It concerns events in Equatoria 1884–9.

Statement by Mohammad Bornawi, concerning the expedition, dispatched by the Mahdists under ʿUmar Sālih to Equatoria in 1888. Two copies are present: one in English, the other in French. Both are dated 17 Feb. 1889. Mohammad Bornawi himself went on this expedition and later escaped to Cairo. His oral testimony was taken down by H. G. Dunning of General Wingate's Intelligence Department.

Decree addressed to Emin Pasha by the Khedive, 1 Feb. 1887. Copy in Arabic.

Draft telegram sent to Emin Pasha by Nubar Pasha via Zanzibar, 28 Nov. 1886. A copy of the final version is in F.O. 84/1770.

Letter from Emin Pasha to the President of the Council in Cairo, 28 Aug. 1889. Copy (6 pp.). Written from Usambiro on his march to the coast, this letter announces Emin's withdrawal from Equatoria accompanied by about 70 men with their wives and children. Another copy is in F.O. 84/1972.

Miscellaneous correspondence concerning the organization of the Emin Pasha relief expedition (1887–9) and arrangements for the pay and settlement of those from Equatoria who arrived in Cairo with Stanley in January 1890.

1/35/205. Report on the arrival in Cairo of 21 Officers and Non-commissioned Officers with their families from Equatoria via Mombasa. June 1892. This most valuable account of events in Equatoria after Emin's departure was made by some of the garrison who withdrew with Lugard in 1891 and later returned to Cairo. A copy is also in the Sudan Archive, Durham, Box 253.
Selim Bey Matar and Equatorial Refugees. Miscellaneous memoranda and correspondence 1890–5.

1/13/67. Memoranda and Reports on the state of troops in the Sudan 1883–90.

1/20/112. Notes on Ibrāhīm Pasha Fawzī, Emin's predecessor as Governor of Equatoria who was relieved of his office by Gordon for actively participating in the slave-trade.

1/50/30. Lupton Bey. Miscellaneous notes and reports on conditions in the Bahr al-Ghazal and Equatoria 1883–4. Copies of Lupton's last three letters to Emin are present.

1/5/5. Relations between the Congo State and the Sudan 1894–1911. Miscellaneous reports with some useful historical material.

5/3/19. Report by Lieutenant Leverson on the possibility of an invasion of Egypt from the Upper Nile, 1884.

5/5/49. Uganda Reports 1892–6. These contain some useful information concerning the Sudanese troops taken to Uganda by Lugard in 1891.

3/10/191. Report on Emin Pasha by H. G. Dunning (of General Wingate's Intelligence Department), 17 Feb. 1889. Summarizes the conflicting information and expresses the fears in Cairo that Emin and Stanley had been captured by the Mahdists.

(ii) Mahdist Papers (Mahdiya).

Only a small fraction of this impressive collection concerns Equatoria. The following letters are of direct relevance to this thesis. All concern the expedition sent to Equatoria under 'Umar Sālih in 1888. All the letters are in Arabic, but English translations were made.

1/33/5. 'Umar Sālih to the Khalifa, Shawal 2, 1305 (13 June 1888).

1/33/6. Ibid. Shawal 15, 1305 (26 June 1888).

1/33/12. Ibid. Safar 21, 1305 (27 Oct. 1888).

1/33/19. Ibid. Safar, 1305 (Oct. 1888).

1/33/22. Ibid. n.d. (1888).

Note: Further material of a more general nature is to be found in the *Egyptian Army Intelligence Reports*, nos. 1–59 (Apr. 1892–May 1898) and in the *Mongalla Province Summary*, compiled by L. F. Nadel. Both are in the Khartoum Archives. A copy of the former is also now in Rhodes House Library, Oxford.

2. Private

(a) The Mackinnon Papers. School of African and Oriental Studies, London.

The papers of William Mackinnon were deposited in the library of the School of African and Oriental Studies by Mr. Duncan Mackinnon through the efforts of Marie de Kiewiet Hemphill in the 1950s. They form a large collection of some 20,000 items, not all of which have yet been catalogued. Mackinnon's interests and correspondents were many (few of Mackinnon's own letters have survived and he did not keep copies) but the papers cover Mackinnon's three main African ventures. Those concerning the formation of the Imperial British East Africa Company were utilized by Marie de Kiewiet herself in her London Ph.D. thesis (1955) on that subject. The papers and many letters concerning Mackinnon's interest in the Congo were used by Professor R. T. Anstey in his study of *Britain and the Congo in the 19th century* (Clarendon Press, 1962). Most of these two groups of papers have been catalogued.

It was the discovery of the third group of papers, the complete papers of the Emin Pasha Relief Committee, in a wooden packing-case, uncatalogued and, as far as I am aware, hitherto unused, which first started me on the subject of this book. It is a remarkably complete collection, but I regret that in the course of my researches I have only been able to catalogue it very roughly. Where a reference is given in the text without a number, this means that the item has not yet been catalogued. Where a reference is given a number only, this indicates that the item is amongst the section of the papers already used by Marie de Kiewiet and Professor Anstey and now catalogued. The prefix 'F' to any reference number in the Mackinnon Papers is particular to the papers of the Emin Pasha Relief Committee. I have catalogued these as follows:

F. 1. Miscellaneous letters arranged chronologically. These include letters from R. W. Felkin and letters to various newspapers. They also include material on the court case brought by the Committee against J. Rose Troup for breach of contract, and the action brought by H. M. Stanley against Tippu Tip at Zanzibar which was later dropped.

F. 2. Letters from the European officers on the expedition to the Committee (1887–9). There are over sixty items, the majority being from the officers attached to the Rear Column. Stanley's letters are not included here.

F. 3. Letters relating to the European officers on the expedition (1887–90). These letters are mostly from relatives, some of whom give useful extracts from letters they have received from the officers.

F. 4. Letters from H. M. Stanley to the Committee (Mar. 1887–Mar. 1890). They are thirteen in number and all are of substantial importance. The rest of Stanley's letters to Mackinnon are in M.P., 218.

F. 5. The accounts of the expedition and the agenda for the meetings of the Committee.

F. 6. Letters to the Committee from the Foreign Office (1887–90). This section also contains copies of the two letters written by Tippu Tip to the British Consul-General at Zanzibar.

F. 7. Map of suggested routes for the expedition. Typed extracts of letters from Emin to R. W. Felkin (1881–7). A copy of Felkin's article 'The position of Emin Bey' from *The Scottish Geographical Magazine*, Dec. 1886.

F. 8. Letters and notes concerning Sanford's claim against the Committee for damage to the steamer *Florida*.

F. 9. Accounts. Miscellaneous statements and receipts.

Letter Book 1. Copies of letters sent by the Committee (1886–9).

Letter Book 2. Ibid. (1889–92).

Letter Book 3. Ibid. (1892–3).

Minute Book. A stiff-covered black exercise book containing the minutes of and attendances at the meetings of the Emin Pasha Relief Committee (Dec. 1886–June 1892).

Blue letter book. Miscellaneous contents concerning Stanley's court action against Tippu Tip. Also present are three Parliamentary Papers about the expedition:

Africa No. 8 (1888)
Africa No. 9 (1888)
Africa No. 4 (1890)

Green File. Newspaper cuttings about the expedition (Sept. 1888–Dec. 1890).

Note: There are also two proof copies, in lilac-coloured covers, of the *Report of the Emin Pasha Relief Committee*. Written in 1891 by P. L. McDermott, this was intended for the subscribers to the Emin Pasha Relief Fund. The members of the Committee felt, however, that it raised matters which were too controversial and so it was never released.

(*b*) The Sanford Papers. General Henry Shelton Sanford Memorial Library, Sanford, Florida, U.S.A.

The paucity of Mackinnon's own letters in the Mackinnon Papers makes the 200 items from Mackinnon to Sanford in Box no. 127 of this collection particularly valuable. Taken together with Sanford's letters to Mackinnon in the Mackinnon Papers, this amounts to an almost complete corres-pondence for the period 1879–91.

Mackinnon's letters to Sanford, in the Sanford Papers, have been microfilmed and a copy is in the Tennessee State Library and Archives, Nashville, Tennessee. I am most grateful to Professor R. T. Anstey, who kindly lent me his copy of this microfilm.

(*c*) Church Missionary Society Archives, London.

Only a small section of the material in this archive has been used in connection with this work. Of particular interest is the material concerning the C.M.S. mission in Buganda, and the contact of the missionaries, especially Litchfield, Pearson, R. W. Felkin, and Mackay with Emin and Equatoria. This is filed under 'Uganda: Nyanza Mission', CA 6/o 10–15.

(*d*) The Sudan Archive, Durham.

This is the most extensive archive of material on the Sudan in Britain, but only a very small section concerns Equatoria and Emin Pasha. The most useful is the collection of documents and microfilm filed as the Jephson Papers in Box no. 14. These items were presumably obtained from the family of A. J. Mounteney-Jephson. The papers of Rudolph Slatin here also contain a few letters to Emin, filed under Box 438/651.

(*e*) Salisbury Papers, Christ Church, Oxford.

The papers of the third Marquess of Salisbury are so interesting, im-portant, and extensive that they occupy a special place, tinged with awe, in the minds of most people who have had the good fortune to work on them. For the purposes of this book they yielded one or two vital pieces of information. The letter-books for the period 1886–7 (Class C. 6 and C. 7) were particularly useful. The Foreign Office correspondence with Egypt and Zanzibar for the same years was also consulted.

(*f*) Barttelot Papers.

I am particularly grateful to Sir Brian de Barttelot, of Keepers Stopham, Pulborough, Sussex, for allowing me to raise the dust once more on the fate of his ancestor and the Rear Column through access to the remarkably full collection of material which his family assembled eighty years ago. No other aspect of the expedition has had so much written about it. No other officer on the expedition has left so full an account of his experiences on it as Edmund Musgrave Barttelot. I had the opportunity to read the full unpublished manuscript of his diary and his many letters. I also found the large file of newspaper cuttings about the expedition very useful.

(*g*) Sir Samuel Baker Papers, in the possession of Mr. Valentine Baker, 'Two Ways', Old Blandford Road, Salisbury.

This recently discovered collection has some extremely important items, including some 24 letters from General Gordon covering the period 1874–84. There are also a number of letters from Giegler and Gessi, Schweinfurth, Jephson, Chaillé-Long, and Stanley, all of which are of considerable value for the history of Equatoria in these years. In addition, there are two letters, in excellent condition, from Emin Pasha, the latter written on 1 Apr. 1890. An index of these papers is in the library of Rhodes House, Oxford.

(*h*) Anti-Slavery Society Papers, Rhodes House, Oxford.

Charles Allen, the Secretary of the Anti-Slavery Society, was writing to and receiving letters from Emin after 1883. Some of these survive. He was also in close correspondence with R. W. Felkin and acted in concert with him over the negotiations leading to the dispatch of the Emin Pasha Relief Expedition in 1886. The letter-books in the following classifications were consulted:

E 3/4 and E 3/8;
C 57/1–148; C 63/1–158; C 64/1–176; C 162/1–244.

(*i*) Scottish Geographical Society Papers, Edinburgh.

Almost nothing survives of the records of this notable Society for the period before 1914 except the full run of the issues of the *Scottish Geographical Magazine* and the Minute Book of committee meetings. The latter was of some use with regard to the role of R. W. Felkin in the discussions concerning the dispatch of an expedition to send relief to Emin Pasha, possibly under the leadership of Joseph Thomson, which was suggested by the Society in the autumn of 1886.

(*j*) Stairs Papers, State Archives, Halifax, Nova Scotia, Canada.

I am indebted to Professor George Shepperson for first informing me of the existence of the Diary of W. G. Stairs and then photocopying and transcribing certain sections of it for me.

(*k*) Royal Geographical Society Archives, London.

I am grateful to Mrs. D. Middleton for drawing my attention to the Joseph Thomson correspondence in this collection and to the original maps of Jackson and Gedge (1889–90) showing the route of their travels in East Africa and indicating their desire to extend the 'sphere' of the I.B.E.A. Company towards Wadelai.

(*l*) Jephson Papers, Mallow Castle, County Cork, Ireland.

I am even more grateful to Mrs. D. Middleton for making available to me a typescript of the full manuscript of A. J. Mounteney-Jephson's Diary which she has recently edited so excellently for the Hakluyt Society. Written by a sensitive and intelligent man, it is the most readable, as well as the most informative, of all the diaries of the European officers on this expedition.

(*m*) Emin Pasha Papers, State Archives, Hamburg.

The original manuscript of Emin's Diary, including the unpublished section for the period 1890–1892, was deposited in this archive in the 1920s by Dr. F. Stuhlmann, along with much other material about Emin. Stuhlmann himself died before he had completed work on the sixth and final volume of Emin's Diary, which was therefore never published. I have consulted much of the material on Emin in this archive. It is undoubtedly the richest source for such material in existence.

3. *Official Publications*

(*a*) DOCUMENTS AND MAPS

Documents diplomatiques français (1871–1914), 1st Ser. (Paris, 1929 f.).
Hertslet, E., *The Map of Africa by Treaty* (3rd edn. revised, London, 1909).
Provinces of the Equator: the letters and reports of Colonel Gordon (Egyptian General Staff, Cairo, 1877).

(*b*) PARLIAMENTARY PAPERS

H.C. (1886), vol. xlvii, C. 4609.
Africa No. 8 (1888) C. 5601: Correspondence respecting the Expedition for the relief of Emin Pasha, 1886–7.
Africa No. 9 (1888) C. 5602: Paper respecting the reported capture of Emin Pasha and Mr. Stanley.
Africa No. 4 (1890) C. 5906: Correspondence respecting Mr. Stanley's expedition for the relief of Emin Pasha.

(*c*) FOREIGN OFFICE CONFIDENTIAL PRINT

The volumes in the library of the Institute of Commonwealth Studies, London, and in Rhodes House Library, Oxford, were found most useful. Correspondence respecting the relief of Emin Pasha at Uganda:

Part 1. May 1887 (5433). Part 2. May 1888 (5617). Part 3. July 1890 (5978)

Correspondence respecting Zanzibar:
1888 (5673)
(5698)
(5732)
1889 (5867)
(5977)
(6025)
1890 (6051)

Charter of the I.B.E.A. Company 1888 (5668).
Précis of events on the Upper Nile and Adjacent Territories, including
Bahr al-Ghazal and Uganda, 1878–98, by Count Gleichen. 1898. (7042.)

B. SECONDARY SOURCES

1. *Newspapers and Periodicals*

Copies of *The Times* and *The Scotsman* were read selectively for the
years 1886–90. The Belgian geographical journal, *Le Mouvement géographique*, was consulted carefully for the same period. The German
counterpart, *Petermanns Mittheilungen*, has a good deal of material concerning the German interest in Emin and Equatoria during these years;
in earlier issues there are a number of articles by Emin Pasha himself. The
richest source in English for the history of Equatoria under Emin Pasha
is undoubtedly *The Uganda Journal*, where the numerous contributions
of Sir John Gray and H. B. Thomas over a period of more than thirty
years have laid the foundations on which a good part of this book rests.

2. *Theses*

The following three theses were not only of great value in the writing
of this book, but also served as models of excellence in the art of good
thesis writing:
Marie de Kiewiet, 'The History of the Imperial British East Africa Com-
pany 1876–1895' (London Ph.D. thesis, 1955).
D. A. Low, 'The British and Uganda 1862–1900' (Oxford D.Phil. thesis,
1957).
J. A. Rowe, 'Revolution in Buganda 1856–1900, Part I: The reign of
Kabaka Mukabya Mutesa 1856–1884' (Wisconsin Ph.D. thesis, 1966).
A microfilm of this thesis is now in Rhodes House Library, Oxford
(Micr. Afr. 481).

3. *Books and Articles*

This list consists only of works which have either been referred to in the
footnotes or have been of particular use in the writing of the present work.
Extensive bibliographies of the material on various aspects of this book
already exist in print. See especially:

D. H. Simpson, 'A Bibliography of Emin Pasha', *Uganda Journal*, xxiv, no. 2 (1960).

R. L. Hill, *A Bibliography of the Anglo-Egyptian Sudan from the Earliest Times to 1937* (Oxford, 1939). This was later extended by Abdel Rahman el Nasri, *A Bibliography of the Sudan, 1938–1958* (London, 1962).

P. M. Holt, 'The Source Materials of the Sudanese Mahdiya', *St. Anthony's Papers: Middle Eastern Affairs*, no. 1 (London, 1958).

T. Heyse, 'Bibliographie de H. M. Stanley 1841–1904', *Bibliographia Belgica*, no. 64 (Brussels, 1961). Also, the same author's 'Centenary Bibliography concerning H. M. Stanley', *Journal of the Royal African Society*, (Apr. 1943).

The Cambridge History of the British Empire, vol. iii (Cambridge, 1959). Also, the bibliography in W. L. Langer, *The Diplomacy of Imperialism* (New York, Second edition, 1951).

Allen, B. M., *Gordon and the Sudan* (London, 1931).

Anstey, Roger, *Britain and the Congo in the 19th Century* (Oxford, Clarendon Press, 1962).

Anstruther, Ian, *I Presume: H. M. Stanley's Triumph and Disaster* (London, 1956).

Anywar, Reuben S., 'The Life of Rwot Iburaim Awich', *Uganda Journal*, xii, no. 1 (1948).

Ascherson, Neil, *The King Incorporated* (London, 1963).

Ashe, R. P., *Chronicles of Uganda* (London, 1894).

Aumont Duc d', 'Du Caire à Gondokoro et au Mont Radjaf', *Bulletin de la Société khédiviale de géographie du Caire*, Sér. ii, no. 4 (Cairo, 1883).

Baker, Samuel White, *Albert Ny'anza, Great Basin of the Nile* (London, 1866).

—— *Ismailia* 2 vols. (London, 1874).

Banning, E., *Mémoires* (Paris–Brussels, 1927).

Barttelot, W. G. (Ed.), *The Life of Edmund Musgrave Barttelot, from his letters and diary* (London, 1890).

Beachey, R., 'The Arms Trade in East Africa in the late 19th century', *Journal of African History*, iii, no. 3 (1962).

—— 'The East African Ivory Trade in the 19th century', *Journal of African History*, viii, no. 2 (1967).

Beaton, A. C., 'A Chapter in Bari History', *Sudan Notes and Records*, (17 Feb. 1934).

Beattie, John, 'Bunyoro: an African Feudality?', *Journal of African History*, v, no. 1 (1962).

—— *Bunyoro: an African kingdom* (New York, 1960).

Becker, J., *La Vie en Afrique*, 2 vols. (Paris–Brussels, 1887).

Bellefonds, Linant de, 'Itinéraire et Notes. Voyage de service fait entre le poste militaire de Fatiko et la capitale de M'tesa, roi d'Uganda, February–June 1875', *Bulletin de la Société khédiviale de géographie du Caire* (1876–7).

Bennett, N., 'Mirambo of the Nyamwezi', in N. R. Bennett, *Studies in East African History* (Boston, 1963).

BENTLEY, W. H., *Pioneering on the Congo* (London, 1900).
BERE, R. M., 'An Outline of Acholi History', *Uganda Journal*, xi, no. 1 (1947).
—— 'Awich: a Biographical Note and a Chapter in Acholi History', *Uganda Journal*, x, no. 2 (1946).
—— 'The Exploration of the Ruwenzori', *Uganda Journal*, xix, no. 2 (1955).
BERE, R. M., and HICKS, P. H., 'Ruwenzori', *Uganda Journal*, x, no. 2 (1946).
Biographie Coloniale Belge, 3 vols. (Brussels, 1948, 1951, 1952).
BIRCH, J. P., 'Emin Pasha's fort at Dufile', *Uganda Journal*, iv, no. 2 (1936).
BONTINCK, FRANÇOIS, *Aux origines de l'État indépendant du Congo: documents tirés d'Archives américaines* (Paris–Louvain, 1966).
BRODE, H., *Tippoo Tib: the Story of His Career in Central Africa Narrated from his own Account* (London, 1907).
BUCHTA, R., *Der Sudan, unter ägyptischer Herrschaft* (Leipzig, 1888).
BURDO, A., *Les Arabes dans l'Afrique centrale* (Paris, 1885).
BUTT, AUDREY, *The Nilotes of the Anglo-Egyptian Sudan and Uganda*, ed. Daryll Forde (London, 1952).
CAMBIER, R., 'Stanley et Emin Pasha', *Zaïre*, iii, no. 5 (Brussels, 1949).
CAMPBELL, J. MACMASTER, 'Sir William Mackinnon, Bart.', *The Cambeltown Courier* (n.d.).
CASATI, GAETANO, *Ten Years in Equatoria and the Return with Emin Pasha* (London, 1891).
CECIL, LADY GWENDOLEN, *Life of Robert, Marquis of Salisbury*, 4 vols. (London, 1932).
CEULEMANS, P., 'Les Tentatives de Léopold II pour engager le colonel Charles Gordon au service de l'Association internationale africaine, 1880', *Zaïre*, xii, no. 3 (Brussels, 1958).
CEULEMANS, R. P. P., *La Question arabe et le Congo, 1883–1892* (Brussels, 1959).
CHAILLÉ-LONG, CHARLES, *My Life in Four Continents*, 2 vols. (London, 1912).
—— 'Notes sur les nègres qui habitent du Bahr el-Abiad jusqu'à l'équateur ...', *Bulletin de la Société khédiviale de géographie du Caire*, Ser. 1 (Cairo, 1876).
—— 'Stanley and Emin Pasha', *Nouvelle Revue*, 15 Mar. 1887.
CHIPPINDALL, W. H., 'Journey beyond the Cataracts of the Upper Nile towards the Albert Nyanza', *Proceedings of the Royal Geographical Society*, 1875–6, pp. 67–9.
COCHERIS, J., *Situation internationale de l'Égypte et du Soudan* (Paris, 1903).
COLLINS, R. O., *King Leopold, England and the Upper Nile, 1899–1909* (Yale, 1968).
—— 'Mahdist and Belgian leaders in the Upper Nile during the late 19th century', *Uganda Journal*, xxvii, no. 2 (1963).
—— 'Origins of the Nile Struggle', in Gifford, P. and Louis, W. R. (eds.), *Britain and Germany in Africa* (Yale, 1967).
—— *The Southern Sudan, 1883–1899: A Struggle for Control* (London and New Haven, 1962).

316   BIBLIOGRAPHY

COOSEMANS, M., 'William Grant Stairs, 1863–1892', *Biographie coloniale belge*, ii (1951).
COQUILHAT, C., *Sur le Haut-Congo* (Paris–Brussels, 1888).
COUPLAND, R., *The Exploitation of East Africa, 1856–1890* (London, 1939–reprinted 1968).
CROMER, LORD, *Modern Egypt*, 2 vols. (London, 1908).
CUYPERS, J. P., 'Alphonse Vangèle, 1848–1939', Institut royal colonial belge, *Mémoires*, Nouvelle Série, xxiv (Brussels, 1960).
DEPAGE, H., 'Note au sujet de documents inedits relatifs à deux expeditions de H. M. Stanley en Afrique, 1874–1877, 1887–1889', *Bulletin des Séances de l'Institut Royal Colonial Belge*, xxv (1954).
DOUIN, G., *Histoire du règne du khédive Ismail*, 3 vols. (Cairo, 1936–1941).
DUNBAR, A. R., 'Emin Pasha and Bunyoro–Kitara, 1877–1889', *Uganda Journal*, xxiv, no. 1, (1960).
—— *A History of Bunyoro–Kitara* (Nairobi, 1965).
EVANS-PRITCHARD, E. E., *The Nuer* (Oxford, 1940).
FARWELL, BYRON, *The Man who Presumed: a Biography of H. M. Stanley* (New York, 1957).
FELKIN, R. W., 'The Egyptian Sudan', *Scottish Geographical Magazine*, i (1885).
—— 'The Position of Dr. Emin Bey', *Scottish Geographical Magazine*, ii (1886).
FELKIN, R. W., and WILSON, C. T., *Uganda and the Egyptian Sudan*, 2 vols. (London, 1882).
FILIPPI, FILIPPO DE., *Ruwenzori: an Account of the Expedition of H.R.H. Prince Luigi Amadeo of Savoy, Duke of the Abruzzi* (London, 1909).
FISHER, REVD. A. B., 'A Note on the ss. "Khedive" ', *Uganda Journal*, xiv, no. 2 (1950).
FISHER, MRS. A. B., *Twilight Tales of the Black Baganda* (London, 1911).
FLINT, J., *Sir George Goldie and the Making of Nigeria* (London, 1960).
'La Force publique de sa naissance à 1914', Institut royal colonial belge, *Mémoires*, xxvii (Brussels, 1952).
FOX-BOURNE, H. R., *The Other Side of the Emin Pasha Relief Expedition* (London, 1891).
FURLEY, OLIVER, 'The Sudanese Troops in Uganda: from Lugard's Enlistment to the Mutiny, 1891–1897', East African Institute of Social Research (Makerere, Jan. 1959). Unpublished paper.
GESSI, R., 'The Circumnavigation of Lake Albert', *Bulletin de la Société khédiviale de géographie du Caire*, Sér. ii (June 1885).
—— *Seven Years in the Sudan* (London, 1892).
GILLARD, D. R., 'Salisbury's African Policy and the Heligoland Offer of 1890', *English Historical Review*, lxxv (1960).
—— 'Salisbury's Heligoland Offer: the Case against the Witu Thesis', *English Historical Review*, lxxx (July 1965).
GIRLING, F. K., *The Acholi of Uganda* (London, 1960).
GLEICHEN, COUNT, *The Anglo-Egyptian Sudan*, 2 vols. (London, 1905).
GORDON, C. G., *Letters from General Gordon to his Sister, M. H. Gordon* (London, 1888).

GORDON, C. G., 'Lettres sur le cours du Nil dans la region de grands lacs', *Bulletin de la Société khédiviale de géographie du Caire*, Sér. I, no. 3 (Cairo, 1876).

—— 'Notes to Accompany a Survey of the White Nile from Lardo to Nyamyungo', *Proceedings of The Royal Geographical Society* (1876).

—— 'Unpublished Letters of C. G. Gordon', *Sudan Notes and Records*, x (1927).

GRAY, SIR JOHN, 'Rwot Ochama of Payera', *Uganda Journal*, xii, no. 2 (1948).

—— 'Early Treaties in Uganda, 1881–1891, *Uganda Journal*, xii, no. 1 (1948).

—— 'The Lango Wars with Egyptian Troops, 1877–1878', *Uganda Journal*, xxi, no. 1 (1957).

—— 'The Attack on Kibiro', *Uganda Journal*, xxx, no. 2 (1966).

—— 'Mutesa of Buganda, *Uganda Journal*, i, no. 1 (1934).

—— 'The Year of the Three Kings in Buganda', *Uganda Journal*, xiv, no. 1 (1950).

—— 'Acholi History, 1860–1901, Part I', *Uganda Journal*, xv, no. 2 (1951); Part II, ibid. xvi, no. 1 (1952); Part III, ibid. xvi, no. 2 (1952).

—— 'Stanley versus Tippoo Tib', *Tanganyika Notes and Records*, xviii (Dec. 1944).

—— 'Anglo-German Relations in Uganda, 1890–1892', *Journal of African History*, i, no. 2 (1960).

—— 'Another Letter of Emin Pasha', *Uganda Journal*, xiv, no. 2 (1950).

—— 'Dr. Emin and Mutesa I: a Note', *Uganda Journal*, xxvii, no. 1 (1963).

—— 'Gordon's Fort at Mruli', *Uganda Journal*, xix, no. 1 (1955).

—— 'Ahmed bin Ibrahim: First Arab to Reach Buganda', *Uganda Journal*, xi, no. 2 (1947).

—— 'Tippu Tib and Uganda', *Uganda Journal*, xix, no. 1 (1955).

GRAY, RICHARD, *A History of the Southern Sudan, 1839–1889* (London, 1961).

DE GROOT, E., 'Great Britain and Germany in Zanzibar; Consul Holmwood's Papers 1886–1887', *Journal of Modern History*, xxv, no. 2 (June 1953).

Handbook of the Uganda Protectorate (H.M.S.O., 1921).

HASSAN, VITA, *Die Wahrheit über Emin Pascha, die ägyptische Aequatorialprovinz und den Sudan*, 2 vols. (Berlin, 1893).

HILL, G. B., *Colonel Gordon in Central Africa*, 4th edn. (London, 1885).

HILL, R. L., *A Biographical Dictionary of the Anglo-Egyptian Sudan* (Oxford, Clarendon Press, 1951), 2nd edn. (1966).

—— *Egypt in the Sudan, 1820–1881* (London, 1959).

—— 'The Gordon Literature', *Durham University Journal*, xlviii (1955).

HINDE, S. L., *The Fall of the Congo Arabs* (London, 1897).

HIRD, F., *H. M. Stanley: the Authorised Life* (London, 1935).

HOFFMANN, W., *With Stanley in Africa* (London, 1938).

HOLT, P. M., *The Mahdist State in the Sudan, 1881–1898* (Oxford, 1958).

—— *A Modern History of the Sudan* (London, 1961).

—— 'The Place in History of the Sudanese Mahdia', *Sudan Notes and Records*, xl (1959).

HOLT, P. M., 'The Sudanese Mahdia and the Outside World, 1881-1889', *Bulletin of School of African and Oriental Studies*, xxi (London, 1958).
HOPKINS, G. H. E., 'Mutesa's Letter to Gordon', *Uganda Journal*, viii, no. 1 (1940), pp. 37-8.
HORNIK, M. P., 'The Special Mission of Sir Henry Drummond Wolff to Constantinople, 1885-1887', *English Historical Review*, ly (1940), pp. 598-623.
HUNTINGFORD, G. W. B., *The Northern Nilo-Hamites*, Daryll Forde, ed. (London, 1953).
HURST, H. E., *The Nile* (London, 1952).
Imperial College Exploration Society: Report on Excavations at Wadelai and in Uganda in 1965 (London, 1966). Unpublished paper.
INGHAM, K., *A History of East Africa* (London, 1962).
JACKSON, F. J., *Early Days in East Africa* (London, 1930).
JADOT, J. M., 'Edmund Barttelot, 1859-1888', *Biographie coloniale belge*, vol. v (1958), 37-42.
—— 'Jameson, J. S. 1856-1888', *Biographie coloniale belge*, vol. iv (1955), 433-7.
JAMESON, J. S., *Story of the Rear Column* (London, 1890).
JEPHSON, A. J. MOUNTENEY, 'In Camp with Stanley', *Cosmopolitan*, xii (New York, 1892).
—— *Emin Pasha and the Rebellion at the Equator* (London, 1890).
—— 'Our March with a Starving Column and the Relief of Captain Nelson', *Scribner's Magazine*, ix (New York, 1891).
—— 'The Truth about Stanley and Emin Pasha', *Fortnightly Review* (London, 1891), pp. 14-20.
JOHNSTON, H. H., *The Kilimanjaro Expedition* (London, 1886).
—— *The Nile Quest* (London, 1903).
—— *The Story of my Life* (London, 1923).
JONES, W. O., *Manioc In Africa* (Stanford University Press, 1959).
JUNKER, W., *Travels in Africa, 1882-1886* (trans. A. H. Keane), 3 vols. (London, 1892).
KELTIE, J. SCOTT, *The Partition of Africa* (London, 1895), 2nd edn.
—— *The Story of Emin's Rescue as told in H. M. Stanley's Letters* (London, 1890).
KIRK, R., 'The Sudanese in Mexico', *Sudan Notes and Records*, xxiv (1941).
LANGER, W. L., *The Diplomacy of Imperialism* (New York, 1951), 2nd edn.
LANGLANDS, B. W., 'Concepts of the Nile', *Uganda Journal*, xxvi, no. 1 (1962).
—— 'Early Travellers in Uganda', *Uganda Journal*, xxvi, no. 1 (1962).
LICHTERVELDE, DE, *Léopold II* (Brussels, 1926).
LIEBRECHTS, C., *Souvenirs d'Afrique* (Brussels, 1909).
LIVINGSTONE, W. P., *Laws of Livingstonia* (London, 1928).
LLOYD, A. B., 'Acholi Country', *Uganda Journal*, xii, no. 1 (1948).
LOTAR, L., 'La Grande Chronique du Bomu', Institut royal colonial belge, *Mémoires*, ix (Brussels, 1940).
—— 'La Grande Chronique de l'Uele', Institut royal colonial belge, *Mémoires*, xiv (Brussels, 1946).

—— 'Souvenirs de l'Uele', *Revue Congo* (1932).

LOUIS, W. R., 'Sir Percy Anderson's Grand African Strategy, 1883–1896', *English Historical Review*, lxxxi (1966).

—— *Ruanda-Urundi, 1884–1919* (Oxford, 1963).

LUGARD, F. D., *The Rise of Our East African Empire* 2 vols. (Edinburgh, 1893).

LUKYN WILLIAMS, F., 'Blood-brotherhood in Ankole (Omukago)', *Uganda Journal*, ii, no. 1 (1934).

—— 'Early Explorers in Ankole', *Uganda Journal*, ii (1934–5).

—— 'Nuwa Mbaguta, Nganzi of Ankole', *Uganda Journal*, x, no. 2 (1946).

LUWEL, MARCEL, 'Catalogue des manuscrits exposés lors de la commémoration H. M. Stanley, Tervuren, May–June 1954', *Bulletin des Séances de l'Académie royale des sciences coloniales*, xxv (Brussels, 1955).

—— 'Considérations sur quelques livres récents ayant trait a Henry Morton Stanley', *Bulletin des Séances de l'Académie royale des sciences d'outre-mer*, viii (Brussels, 1962–4).

—— *Sir Francis de Winton Administrateur: général du Congo, 1884–1886*, Musée royal de l'Afrique centrale (Tervuren, 1964).

McDERMOTT, P. L., *British East Africa or I.B.E.A.* (London, 1895), 2nd edn.

MACDONALD, J. R. L., *Soldiering and Surveying in British East Africa* (London, 1897).

A. M. Mackay: Pioneer Missionary of the Church Missionary Society to Uganda, edited by his sister, J. W. Harrison (London, 1890).

MACKENZIE, GEORGE S., 'The I.B.E.A., and Jackson's Treaty-making', *Journal of the Royal Colonial Institute* (Dec. 1890).

MACMICHAEL, H. A., *The Anglo-Egyptian Sudan* (London, 1934).

MACRO, E., 'Frank Miller Lupton', *Sudan Notes and Records*, vol. xxviii, (1947.)

Maisha ya Hamed bin Muhammed el Murjebi yaani Tippu Tip, ed. and trans. by W. H. Whitely, with an Introduction by Alison Smith. First published as a supplement to the *East African Swahili Committee Journals*, no. 28/2 (July 1958) and no. 29/1 (Jan. 1959); reprinted by the East African Literature Bureau (Nairobi, 1966).

MANNING, O., *The Remarkable Expedition: The Story of Stanley's Rescue of Emin Pasha from Equatorial Africa* (London, 1947).

MARNO, ERNEST, *Reise in der Ägyptischen Aequatorial Provinz und im Kordofan in den Jahren 1874–1876* (Vienna, 1878).

MARSTON, E., *How Stanley Wrote* In Darkest Africa (London, 1890).

MASOIN, F., *Histoire de l'État indépendant du Congo*, 2 vols. (Namur, 1912–13).

MASON, A. M., 'Report of a Reconnaissance of Lake Albert', *Proceedings of the Royal Geographical Society*, vol. xxii (1877–8) pp. 225–9.

—— 'The River at the Southern End of Albert Nyanza', *Proceedings of the Royal Geographical Society*, New Series, vol. 12, 1890.

MAURICE, ALBERT (ed.), *H. M. Stanley: Unpublished Letters* (French: Brussels, 1955: English: Edinburgh, 1959).

MIDDLETON, MRS. D. (ed.), *The Diary of A. J. Mounteney-Jephson* (Cambridge, 1969). For the Hakluyt Society.

—— *Baker of the Nile* (London, 1949).

MOIR, F. L. M., *After Livingstone* (London, 1923).

MOOREHEAD, ALAN, *The White Nile* (London, 1960).

MORRIS, H. F., *History of Ankole*, East African Literature Bureau (Nairobi, 1962).

MOSES, M., 'A History of Wadelai', *Uganda Journal*, xvii, no. 1 (1953).

MÜLLER, F. F., *Deutschland—Zanzibar—Ostafrika, 1884–1890* (East Berlin, 1959).

MURRAY, T. D., and WHITE, A. S., *Sir Samuel Baker: a Memoir* (London, 1895).

Ntare School History Society, 'H. M. Stanley's Journey through Ankole in 1889', *Uganda Journal*, xxix, no. 2 (1965).

OBERG, K., 'The Kingdom of Ankole', in Fortes, M., and Evans-Pritchard, E. E. (eds.), *African Political Systems* (London, 1940).

OLIVER, R., *The Missionary Factor in East Africa* (London, 1965), 2nd edn.

—— 'Salisbury, Rhodes and Johnston', *Revue belge de philosophie et d'histoire*, xxxv, nos. 3, 4 (1957).

—— 'Some Factors in the British Occupation of East Africa, 1884–1894', *Uganda Journal*, xv (1951).

—— 'The Traditional Histories of Buganda, Bunyoro and Ankole', *Journal of the Royal Anthropological Institute*, lxxxv (1955).

OLIVER, R., and MATHEW, G. (eds.), *History of East Africa*, vol. i (Oxford, 1963).

PARKE, T. H., *My Personal Experiences in Equatorial Africa* (London, 1891).

PERHAM, MARGERY (ed.), *The Diaries of Lord Lugard*, vols. i and ii (East Africa) (London, 1959).

—— *Lugard. The Years of Adventure* (London, 1956).

PERIER, G. D., 'Un Artiste dans l'arrière-garde de Stanley: Herbert Ward', *La Revue belge* (Brussels, 15 Jan. 1934).

PETERS, CARL, *New Light on Dark Africa* (London 1891) (English translation of *Die Deutsche Emin Pasha Expedition* (Munich, 1891)).

—— 'Stanley's Relations with Emin Pasha', *The Contemporary Review* (Nov. 1890).

PRUEN, TRISTRAM, *The Arab and the African* (London, 1891).

RAVENSTEIN, E. G., 'Messrs. Jackson and Gedge's Journey to Uganda via Masailand', *Uganda Journal*, xii, no. 2 (1948).

ROBINSON, R. E., and GALLAGHER, J., *Africa and the Victorians: the Official Mind of Imperialism* (London, 1961).

ROWE, J. A., 'The Purge of Christians at Mwanga's Court', *Journal of African History*, v, no. 1 (1964).

ROWLEY, J. V., 'The Madi of Equatoria Province', *Sudan Notes and Records*, xxiii, Part II (1940).

SANDERSON, G. N., 'Contributions from African Sources to the History of European Competition in the Upper Valley of the Nile', *Journal of African History*, iii, no. 1 (1962).

BIBLIOGRAPHY 321

—— *England, Europe and the Upper Nile, 1882–1899* (Edinburgh University Press, 1965).
—— 'England, Italy, the Nile Valley and the European Balance, 1890–1891', *The Historical Journal*, vii, no. 1 (1964).
—— 'Leopold II and the Nile Valley', *Proceedings of the Sudan Historical Association*, vii, no. 1 (1955).
—— 'The Anglo-German Agreement of 1890 and the Upper Nile', *English Historical Review*, lxxviii (1963).
—— 'The European Powers and the Sudan in the later 19th Century', *Sudan Notes and Records*, xl, (1959).
SCHEBESTA, PAUL, 'Les Pygmées du Congo belge', Institut royal colonial belge, *Mémoires* (Brussels 1952).
SCHWEINFURTH, G., *The Heart of Africa: Three Years' Travels and Adventuring in the Unexplored Regions of Central Africa, 1868–1871*, 2 vols. (London, 1873).
SCHWEINFURTH, G., RATZEL, R., FELKIN, R. W., and HARTLAUB, G., *Emin Pasha in Central Africa: being a Collection of his Letters and Journals* (London, 1888), trans. Mrs. Felkin.
SCHWEITZER, G., *Emin Pasha: his life and work*, 2 vols. (London, 1898).
SCHYNSE, A. W., *A travers l'Afrique avec Stanley et Emin Pasha* (Paris, 1890). French edition of *'Mit Stanley und Emin Pascha durch Deutsch Ost Afrika'* (Köln, 1890).
SELIGMAN, C. G., and B. Z., *Pagan Tribes of the Nilotic Sudan* (London, 1932).
SHEPPERSON, GEORGE, 'Africa, the Victorians and Imperialism', *Revue Belge de philologie et d'histoire*, xl (Brussels 1962).
SHIBEIKA, MEKKI, *British Policy in the Sudan, 1882–1902* (London, 1952).
SHUKRY, M. F., *Equatoria under Egyptian Rule: the Unpublished Correspondence of C. G. Gordon with the Khedive Ismail, 1874–1876* (Cairo, 1953).
—— *The Khedive Ismail and Slavery in the Sudan, 1863–1879* (Cairo, 1937).
SLADE, RUTH M., *English speaking missions in the Congo Independent State, 1878–1908*, Académie royale des sciences coloniales (Brussels 1959).
—— *King Leopold's Congo* (Institute of Race Relations, Oxford University Press, 1962).
SLATIN, R., *Fire and Sword in the Sudan* (London, 1896).
SMITH, COLIN L., *The Embassy of Sir William White at Constantinople, 1886–1891* (Oxford University Press, 1957).
SOUTHALL, A., *Alur Society* (Cambridge, 1956).
—— 'Alur Tradition and its Historical Significance', *Uganda Journal*, xviii, no. 2 (1954).
—— 'The Alur Legend of Sir Samuel Baker and the Mukama Kabarega', *Uganda Journal*, xv, no. 2 (1951).
STAIRS, W. G., 'From the Albert Nyanza to the Indian Ocean', *The Nineteenth Century* (London, June 1891).
STANLEY, LADY DOROTHY (ed.), *The Autobiography of H. M. Stanley* (London, 1909).

STANLEY, H. M., *The Congo and the Founding of its Free State*, 2 vols. (London, 1885).
—— 'The Emin Relief Expedition', *Scribner's Magazine* (June 1890).
—— 'The Emin Pasha Relief Expedition', *Scottish Geographical Magazine*, vi (1890), pp. 337-53.
—— *The Rescue of Emin Pasha: Four Lectures* (London, 1890).
—— 'L'Exploration de l'Arouhouimi', *Le Mouvement géographique* (24 Jan. 1886), p. 7.
—— *How I Found Livingstone* (New York and London, 1872).
—— *Im dunkelsten Afrika*, 2 vols. (Leipzig, 1890).
—— *In Darkest Africa*, 2 vols. (London, 1890).
—— *Through the Dark Continent*, 2 vols. (London, 1878).
STANLEY, R., and NEAME, A. (eds.), *The Exploration Diaries of H. M. Stanley* (London, 1961).
STENGERS, J., 'La Place de Léopold II dans l'histoire de la colonisation', *La Nouvelle Clio* (1949-50), p. 519.
—— 'L'Impérialisme colonial de la fin du XIXe siècle: mythe ou réalite', *Journal of African History*, iii, no. 3 (1962).
—— 'Quelques observations sur la correspondance de Stanley', *Zaïre*, ix, no. 9 (1955).
—— 'Rapport sur le dossier "Correspondance Léopold-Strauch" ', *Bulletin des Séances de l'Institut royal colonial belge*, xxiv, no. 2 (1953).
—— 'Stanley, Léopold II et l'Angleterre', *Le Flambeau*, no. 4 (Brussels, 1954).
STEVENS, THOMAS, *Scouting for Stanley in East Africa* (London, 1890).
STIGAND, MAJOR C. H., *Equatoria: the Lado Enclave* (London, 1923).
STOCK, E., *History of the Church Missionary Society* vol. iii (London, 1899).
STUHLMANN, DR. FRANZ (ed.), *Die Tagebücher von Dr. Emin Pascha*, 5 vols. (Braunschweig, Berlin, Hamburg, 1917-27).
—— *Mit Emin Pascha ins Herz von Afrika* (Berlin, 1894).
SWANN, A. J., *Fighting the Slave-hunters in Central Africa* (London, 1910).
SYMONS, A. J. A., *Emin: Governor of Equatoria* (London, 1928, 1950).
TAYLOR, REVD. J. V., *The Growth of the Church in Buganda* (London, 1958).
THEOBALD, A. B., *The Mahdiya, 1881-1899* (London, 1951).
THOMAS, H. B., 'An Autograph Letter of Emin Pasha', *Uganda Journal*, xiii, no. 2 (1949).
—— 'Gordon's Furthest South in Uganda in 1876', *Uganda Journal*, v, no. 4 (1938).
—— 'The I.B.E.A. Company Medal', *Uganda Journal*, xvi, no. 1 (1952).
—— 'Jackson and von Tiedemann', *Uganda Journal*, ii, no. 2 (1934).
—— 'Muhammad Biri', *Uganda Journal*, xxiv, no. 1 (1960).
—— 'Note on the Sudanese Corps in Mexico (1863-1967) and on Fort Magungu', *Uganda Journal*, viii, no. 1 (1940).
—— 'A Relic of "S.S. Khedive" ', *Uganda Journal*, xiv, no. 1 (1950).
—— 'Ruwenzori and Elgon Footnotes', *Uganda Journal*, ii, no. 3 (1935).
—— 'A Sketch-map of Gordon's Equatorial Province', *Uganda Journal*, xxiii, no. 2, 1959).

THOMAS, H. B., and SCOTT, R., *Uganda* (London, 1935).

THOMSON, JOSEPH, *Through Masailand* (London, 1885).

THOMSON, R. S., *Fondation de l'État indépendant du Congo* (Brussels, 1933).

THRUSTON, MAJOR A. B., *African Incidents* (London, 1900).

THURIAUX-HENNEBERT, ARLETTE, *Les Zande dans l'histoire du Bahr el-Ghazal et de l'Equatoria* (Brussels, 1964).

TRIMINGHAM, J. SPENCER, *Islam in the Sudan* (Oxford, 1949).

TROUP, J. R., *With Stanley's Rear Column* (London, 1890).

TURNBULL, C. M., *The Forest People* (New York, 1961).

—— *Wayward Servants* (London, 1966).

Uganda Protectorate, a Handbook of, H.M.S.O., 1921.

VAN GELLUWE, H., *Les Bali*, ed. Daryll Forde (Brussels, 1960).

—— *Les Bira*, ed. Daryll Forde (Brussels, 1957).

—— *Mamvu-Mangutu et Balese-Mvuba*, ed. Daryll Forde (Brussels, 1957).

VAN GRIEKEN-TAVERNIERS, MADELEINE, 'Inventaire des archives des affaires étrangères de l'État indépendant du Congo et du ministère des Colonies, 1885–1914', Bulletin des Séances de l'Académie royale des sciences coloniales, *Mémoires* (Brussels, 1955).

VANSINA, JAN, *Introduction à l'ethnographie du Congo* (Brussels, 1966).

WALLER, H. (ed.), *Last Journals of David Livingstone* (London, 1874).

WARD, HERBERT, *Five Years with the Congo Cannibals* (London, 1890).

—— *My Life with Stanley's Rear Guard* (London, 1891).

WAUTERS, A. J., *Histoire politique du Congo belge* (Brussels, 1911).

—— *Stanley's Emin Pasha Relief Expedition* (London, 1890).

WAYLAND, E. J., 'Katwe', *Uganda Journal*, i, no. 1 (1934).

WERNER, J. R., 'The Camp at Yambuya', *Blackwood's Magazine* (Feb. 1889).

—— *A Visit to Stanley's Rear Guard* (London and Edinburgh, 1889).

WHITE, J. P., 'The Sanford Exploring Expedition', *Journal of African History*, viii, no. 2 (1967).

WHITE, STANHOPE, *Lost Empire on the Nile* (London, 1969).

WILLS, J. T., 'Emin Bey: Gordon's Lieutenant in Central Africa', *The Fortnightly Review* (Dec. 1887).

WINGATE, F. R., *Mahdism and the Egyptian Sudan* (London, 1891).

ZETLAND, MARQUESS OF (L. J. L. Dundas), *Lord Cromer* (London, 1932).

ZUCHINETTI, DR. P. V., 'Mes voyages au Bahr el-Gebel, Bahr el-Ghazal et Nouba', *Bulletin de la Société khédiviale de géographie du Caire*, Sér. i (Cairo, 1881).

—— *Souvenirs de mon séjour chez Emin Pasha* (Cairo, 1890).

INDEX